the radical write

BY BOBBY HAWTHORNE

SECOND EDITION

DEDICATED TO MY FAMILY,
INSIDE AND OUT OF SCHOLASTIC JOURNALISM.

© 2003 by Jostens, Inc. (Item #2000)

International Standard Book Number
0-9615570-01

Printed in the United States of America.

CONTENTS

Photo by **KARRIE MACKEY**
Northwest High School, Jackson, MI

GO AHEAD: BE RADICAL

01

I'm not talking about attempting a violent overthrow of the government. I'm talking about taking a new approach to how you report for your student publication. It begins with a love for reading and writing.

CHAPTER HIGHLIGHTS:

■ Student publications should describe, analyze and interpret.

■ Foccus on message, not outdated formulas.

■ Emphasize high-quality writing. Try to develop a voice.

■ Report. Write. Edit. Revise. Proof. Report some more. Edit.

Do you really read your high school newspaper or yearbook? Does the content make you laugh? Does it make you cry? Has a story ever moved you to write a letter to the editor? To slam your fist on your desk? Has a story ever been the subject of a big argument between you and your friends?

Probably not—unless you're one of the lucky students who receive a publication that is leading the way to good reading. Most likely, your high-school publication tells you what happened, what's happening or what will happen—safe stuff you already knew or don't care about. It doesn't grab you by the throat. It doesn't get in your face. It's not written to be read.

And that's a shame because for many, high school is the ultimate experience, the precise moment when hormones, money and freedom intersect, when teenagers get their first taste of what it is to be an adult. It's exciting and dangerous, a ripe topic for writers with imagination and verve.

But while the teenage experience is described vividly in thousands of movies and books, high-school publications too often convince us that it is nothing more than an endless series of club meetings, athletic events and popularity contests. All the life is squeezed out of the stories so they can answer who, what, when, where, why and how.

"Hi. My name is Brenda. I am a member of the pep squad, the band and the yearbook staff. My favorite food is pizza, and I love my family, school and country. I have no problems, fears or concerns."

Which isn't exactly true. Brenda's worried about getting into a good college. Her dad recently lost his job, and she fears that the family won't have money to send her to the college of her choice even if she's accepted. She has issues with her step-family. She lives in a neighborhood that isn't as safe as it used to be, attends a school that's too crowded, too big, too impersonal. Her friends are too obsessed with trivia and celebrity, wealth and fame. She worries that her life is superficial, meaningless, but she's vowed to make it not so. She's just not sure how to go about it.

But then, that really doesn't fit any of our pre-existing publications formulas. So let's just stick with the fact that Brenda is a member of the pep squad, the band and the yearbook staff, and her favorite food is pizza.

That's about as deep as a lot of student publications — newspaper or yearbooks — get. Newspapers cover events. Meetings. Activities. Contests. But they never cover the people involved in these events and never grapple with the humanity that makes students want to attend the event, participate in these activities, compete in the contests. That's getting personal, and student

❝ Watching good movies, reading great novels, seeing great plays all help you become a better writer. You just have to be open to absorb it. Observe how they do things in drama, and how they do things in good novel writing. I dog-ear all the pages of books that I read. I underline phrases that catch me.❞

— Mitch Albom of the *Detroit Free Press*

reporters don't want to get too close to their subjects.

It's a lethal mistake. It produces publications that are deathly dull.

I've judged hundreds of high school newspapers and yearbooks for at least 15 state and national press associations, and I've begged other people to judge them for me.

In fact, I was driving down the road and saw this guy holding a sign that said, "Will work for food."

When I pulled over and asked him if he'd be interested in judging a few high-school publications, he replied, "I'm not that hungry."

Then, I recognized the guy. He judged for me the year before and admitted he had to take a handful of No-Doze to finish the job.

My point is this: high-school publications should be more interested in capturing, describing, analyzing and interpreting the emotional roller-coaster ride that is high school than in telling the reader who's on the volleyball team or honor roll. Never assume that students will read either publication. They may scan it, looking for their names. But scanning isn't reading. Student reporters should make their stories so interesting, so colorful, so dramatic, so compelling that students would rather come to school sick rather than miss a single issue. I'm not kidding.

I'm not talking only of newspapers. The purpose of the yearbook is to tell the story of the year. This cannot be done by photographs alone, especially those postage stamp mug shots that are all the rage. In order to capture the real story of the year, you must write copy that explains what it all means. For example, at the end of an awards banquet I attended a few years ago, the director of the school's one-act play introduced each member of his troupe and then did a little dance and high-fived the air. Members of the troupe jumped to their feet in applause.

What was going on there? I have no idea. A good reporter will find out. So find those stories. They capture the heart and soul of the year.

Second, reporters can't do this by following all of the old rules. The old rules got us in this mess in the first place. While television, books, movies, music videos and electronic videos have exploded with graphic intensity, newspapers have satisfied themselves by running spot color or Photoshop gimmicks over boring stories. It doesn't work.

Let's do something new. It's time to take a radical look at all high school publications. I want you to forget everything that you think you know about newspapers. Forget the inverted pyramid. Forget objectivity. Forget the 5Ws and H.

Focus first and foremost on message: Which stories do I want to tell? To whom do I want to tell them? What is the best voice and tone for me to use as I tell them?

Remember that you bring a wealth of information and opinion to every story you write. That doesn't mean that you should write an editorial instead of a story. It means you should have the freedom to frame the story in terms of your own experiences.

Journalists gather information with a sense of their individual writing styles in mind and then write based on the information they've gathered. And when they return to the publications room to write, they decide whether they're going to write a straight news story, a news feature, a personality profile, a straight feature or a narrative feature. It all depends on the reporter's preferences and style and the substance of the story he or she is covering.

I am not suggesting that we toss out all the old rules and start over. Journalism will always have a place for summary and quote leads and other traditional news and feature approaches. We haven't seen the last startling statement lead.

In particular, I'm not promoting the demise of the inverted pyramid. It remains the bread-and-butter of daily reporters. But few high schools publish daily — or weekly, for that matter. So while it's important for beginners to master the inverted pyramid, it's equally important for them to know when to move beyond it. You will enjoy reporting and writing more if you imitate the network television reporters. And how do they present news? They tell the story of an event in terms of the people involved and affected. This approach allows readers to literally see how events—the economy, the West Nile Virus, hurricanes, earthquakes, famines, floods, war, globalism, whatever—change the lives of real people who aren't much different from themselves.

Telling the story of a 14-year-old sophomore

who quits school to get a minimum wage job so he can help pay his family's bills says more about dropout rates than any statistics released by a state education agency.

I am convinced students would read a story reported in these terms before they would read a story that recited mountains of numbers of facts.

Though I've heard that students today don't and won't read, I disagree. I spend much of my time in workshops reading to students, and they seem to enjoy it. I doubt it has anything to do with my mesmerizing storytelling abilities. It's the power of the stories themselves and the abilities of the reporters to tell them. And then I give them similar stories for them to read on their own, and they do because the examples I give them inform and entertain.

While I am unwilling to concede that students cannot or will not read, I'm convinced that they will not read formula stories that ignore or skim over the humanity of a story or boil it down to nothing more than the 5Ws and H.

The aim of this book is to inspire you to report thoroughly, write with passion and authority, and edit with precision. And if it radically changes your publications so that your readers treasure each issue of the newspaper and every volume of the yearbook, then so much the better.

■ WHAT IS GOOD WRITING?

That's a hard question to answer. Impossible, in fact, because what may be good to you — Thomas Hardy or Gerald Manley Hopkins or James Joyce — may bore me to tears. Your idea of great writing may be, "As a dale-gale skylark scanted in a dull cage, Man's mounting spirit in his bone-house, mean house, dwells—"

You may love that stuff. I don't. Here's my idea of great writing: "In my village," the man said, "the people stood in front of the church and cried, 'Is there a God? If there is, He would not allow these things to be.'" That was when the Germans came for the men and boys to send them away as slave labor. They took also what women they wanted; it was known that from these they would pick the girls to use in brothels on the Eastern Front. The other women would become work animals."

That comes from a piece called "Three Poles," by Martha Gellhorn, who wrote about war for almost 50 years.

Each of us has a preference, but I think it's fair to say that good writing — particularly good journalistic writing — shares certain traits. First, good writing is honest, clear and specific. It has a theme. It explores a specific person, place or event. It's not about mankind. It's about a man, in a specific situation, most likely a difficult one. It's the story of how someone overcomes or attempts to overcome a problem, and what he or she learned in doing so.

It's not the story of the attack on the World Trade Center. It's the explanation why the firefighters' radios didn't work, why they couldn't communicate, and therefore, why so many of them died in those towers that morning.

It's not about sleep deprivation. It's about a teacher who can't get to sleep and how that affects his teaching, his sanity, his life.

Secondly, good writing is full of details — sensory and otherwise. It shows. It doesn't tell. For example, "Obaidur Rahman set out to fight a holy war five years ago, at the age of 17. But as he rushed from the Taliban trenches north of Kabul, he was captured by the rebel Northern Alliance. Today, the young man from Yemen sits in a remote prison in the rugged Panjshir Valley, legs hobbled by knee-high steel manacles."

This story is about fundamentalist Muslims who say they'll continue fighting "non-believers." It's made real because Obaidur Rahman is real. He is not an abstraction. He is a young man with penetrating eyes and a scraggly beard who told an American reporter, "There were no innocent people in those skyscrapers."

Good writing is original. It doesn't intentionally sound like another writer or reporter. It doesn't mimic Rick Bragg or Dave Barry, Rick Reilly or Ernest Hemingway. It never strains to be funny or cute.

Good writing is tight, efficient. It matches the exact word to a specific situation. It gets right to the point, doesn't stammer around, chit-chatting or mumbling. Its verbs are active and precise. Its nouns are specific and colorful. It doesn't contain a lot of adjectives and adverbs, and the adjectives it contains are precise — cavernous, pouty, flimsy. They're not vague, empty. *He was a really big man.* What does that mean? *He dwarfed a side-by-side refrigerator.*

SO, YOU FANCY YOURSELF A WRITER, DO YOU?

Well, writers:

- write every day, even if for only a few minutes. Writing is a muscle that must be exercised.
- write about issues they care about deeply.
- write quickly, which doesn't mean effortlessly. But they want to get their first draft on paper as soon as possible.
- are wildly curious.
- are constantly jotting down notes and observations.
- are not intimidated by a blank screen.
- enjoy the work it takes to produce superior copy.

WRITING TIP

Why build stories around people?

■ They make abstract statements real.

■ Their quotes add color and rhythm.

■ They offer diferent points of view.

■ Their stories add drama.

■ They add credibility to reporting.

When all the pieces are working efficiently, good writing creates rhythm. Sometimes, this rhythm is slow and subtle, like cool jazz. Take, for example, this piece from H. G. Bissinger's classic book of Texas high school football, *Friday Night Lights*: *"Behind the rows of stools stood the stars of the show, the members of the 1988 Permian Panther high school football team. Dressed in their black game jerseys, they laughed and teased one another like privileged children of royalty."*

Sometimes, it rocks and rolls, like this piece from Tom French's *South of Heaven*: *"That evening, Jen and Gayle get on the phone and report the incident to the others. There are cries of anger, howls of outrage. Another challenge, that's what this is. Maybe not one specifically described in the rules of academic competitions, but definitely a challenge, issued with the impunity of ones who apparently believe themselves unbeatable. YY and Elvis and the rest of the team have their work cut out for them now. They're not just defending their title anymore; they're defending their honor. They must go to that tournament and kick these finger flickers in the teeth. They must humiliate them. Grind them into dust. Drop them, once and for all, onto the dung heap of quiz team history."*

Good writing is occasionally profound. It opens to readers a world of ideas and facts that makes them think. It inspires them, gives them hope and meaning. I can think of no better example of this than Winston Churchill's speech to the English people during World War II's Battle of Britain.

EVEN THOUGH large tracts of Europe and many old and famous States have fallen or may fall into the grip of the Gestapo and all the odious apparatus of Nazi rule, we shall not flag or fail. We shall go on to the end, we shall fight in France, we shall fight on the seas and oceans, we shall fight with growing confidence and growing strength in the air, we shall defend our Island, whatever the cost may be, we shall fight on the beaches, we shall fight on the landing grounds, we shall fight in the fields and in the streets, we shall fight in the hills; we shall never surrender, and even if, which I do not for a moment believe, this Island or a large part of it were subjugated and starving, then our Empire beyond the seas, armed and guarded by the British Fleet, would carry on the struggle, until, in God's good time, the New World, with all its power and might, steps forth to the rescue and the liberation of the old.

Such writing reverberates far beyond its moment of delivery, speaks to future generations facing their own challenges.

Good writing makes readers feel. It puts readers in another person's shoes, forces them to see the world through different eyes. It allows them to be a part of an elite Army Ranger unit, combing the mountains of eastern Afghanistan, searching for Osama bin Laden. It puts them in the shoes of a 65-year-old grandmother who's trying to make ends meet on her social security benefits and paltry salary as a waitress at a burger joint while looking after her husband, who is drifting into the late stages of Alzheimer's. Now and then, it reminds readers what it's like to be young and in love for the first time.

Just as good writing shares certain traits, successful writers share common characteristics as well. First, they read a lot. They read as much of it as possible, and if they come across a word that they don't recognize, they look it up.

So, read critically. Look for symbolism, irony, alliteration, metaphor, simile and personification. Pay attention to the subtle ways good writers turn a phrase, keep a long sentence flowing, connect opposing points of view. You'll never learn to write unless you read.

Second, good writers are aware of the world around them. A lot of this comes from reading. A lot comes from opening their eyes, seeing what others ignore. And they see the world in new and usual ways. A lot of young writers see only the obvious facts.

ACCORDING TO NATIONAL STATISTICS, many teachers and students do not get enough sleep. Some, in fact, have sleep disorders. This leads to many problems.

"I know I don't get enough sleep," senior Jeff Smith said. "Consequently, I'm tired and have a hard time concentrating."

Others see the small personal stories that give meaning to the facts.

FOR YEARS, history teacher Joe Oliver knew what was on television between 2 and 4 in the morning. Most nights, he was up, watching TV. Joe has a sleep disorder, restless legs syndrome, and without medication, he would return to old ways of dozing off around 10, waking up at 11 and spending the rest of the night, rolling around, stretching, exercising, reading, watching television, going crazy.

"It was torture," he said. "When I laid down at night, my brain continued to shoot impulses to the nerves in my legs. It felt like a thousand ants crawling up and down my legs. It was sheer hell."

Finally, his wife convinced him to visit a sleep disorder clinic in Dallas.

"She threatened to divorce me if I didn't see a doctor," he said. "The doctor diagnosed me immediately, and since then, I've been on medication and sleeping quite well. I'm not cured, but at least my problem is under control."

Mr. Oliver is typical of the many teachers and students who have trouble sleeping due to stress or a full-blown sleep disorder. Many average less than four hours of sleep per night, barely half of the required minimum. The results can be devastating: inability to concentrate, irritability, susceptibility to disease and exhaustion.

Good writers write to please themselves. They write about what they know about and care about. You can sense the joy, the pleasure they have writing. This is a long piece, but you will enjoy it — almost as much as Leigh Anne and Steve enjoyed writing it.

SHOWCASE

By **LEIGH ANNE RIVES** & **STEVE BENE**
Westlake High School, Austin, TX

IN THE COMMON, hum-drum little lives that many people are forced to lead, there is a serious lack of what the few would call "social responsibility," and what the masses would call "fun." Well, all that will change on Saturday, May 16, when Westlake holds the year's most notable fete, and the only thing that could beat a student council dance, the prom.

Unfortunately, Westlake is in an awkward position. Like other schools, Westlake has its share of horrid social gaffes at the prom every year. Unlike the other schools, however, many students know the seriousness and the disgrace of such faux pas and are accordingly offended. So rather than force those who know to swallow their tongues (and possibly their dinners) one must simply educate the masses. Now, since you and I know everything there is to know about the finer points of seating arrangements and selecting the right restaurant, please don't be offended by the following remarks. Just watch out for your neighbor. If he is reading this page too intensely he may be NOKD (Not our kind, dear).

ONE: ATTIRE

Basically, the proper look for the prom involves knowing where to experiment and where to leave well enough alone. On the whole, however, leaving well enough alone is much safer. Men, always wear a tuxedo. No suit will ever be nice enough to save you the rental fee. Don't try.

On the whole, tuxes should be black. White or gray is acceptable, colors are not. Lime green with contrasting anything will make you look like John Travolta. He is out.

Pants should be strait cut with a satin stripe down the outer seam. Follow the advice of the tux salesman and get pants that fit. Jordache does not yet make tux pants.

Coats should be traditionally cut. Experimenting with tails can be tempting. Don't. Tails are for weddings and concert pianists.

Shirts should be pleated or plain front, with a wing-tip or plain point collar. Ruffles, especially with contrast piping are to be avoided, unless you really want to look like a choir member.

A special note to choir members: Rent a tux.

Cummerbunds are optional, but increasingly popular for the simple reason that they look better than half-vests. Ties are not optional. Almost anything

STOP OFTEN FOR A REALITY CHECK

Every story has a factual reality and an emotional reality. If your story is a collection of dull data, it'll be emotionally empty — and trust me, no one will read it. Few will even bother to scan it.

Capture the emotion by writing about people, telling your major stories through the words of those affected and those in charge. Make the reader smile, laugh, frown, sigh or cry. Give them a story they'll remember, not simply a list of facts.

goes here, though metallics are to be avoided.

Black patent leather shoes with laces are the preferred shoes for men. Boots are definitely out. Please do not wear the shoes with white socks or you will be a serious candidate for the nerd farm.

Grooming should be neat and strictly conformist. Mohawks will draw laughs at first, dirty looks later. Men should be either clean-shaven or very neatly groomed. The 5 o'clock shadow should not appear until 5 a.m. If you cut yourself shaving, don't even go.

A few concluding notes: top hats can be worn, though it is generally accepted that you will only look good in one if you are Fred Astaire. Most people are not. Cufflinks and shirt studs are included for that reason. No open-to-the-navel shirts or paperclip cufflinks. A few words need to be said about velvet.

None. Anywhere. Ever.

Contrary to the whining, girls' prom groom is much easier. The only thing ladies need to remember is that your date asked you to the prom. It does not help if he cannot recognize you. Try to not drastically alter your appearance.

Choose a heel height according to date height and comfort quotient. Shoes should make you no more than a foot taller than your date. Also remember that you should never remove your shoes in public. Anyplace in the prom is "in public."

If you must wear a strapless dress, make sure it fits. Do not be caught hiking it up every 30 seconds. The "public" remark applies here too.

Before buying a dress, make sure it will fit into your date's car. Huge taffeta shirks are fine, unless your date drives a Kia. Then, try a cocktail dress.

Always tell your date what color you are wearing. This should insure the impossibility of a purple corsage with an aquamarine dress. Guys, if you don't have color sense, ask your mother what color corsage to get.

TWO: DINNER

Other than providing a list of acceptable restaurants in Austin and elsewhere, it is very difficult to tell you where to eat. Our time is better telling you where not to eat.

As a general rule, expect to spend money. Lots of money. Cafeterias and fast-food franchises are definitely out, as are Chinese restaurants, except for the really expensive places where the chef butchers and cooks the bull in front of you). Besides, you'll need your energy later.

As a rule, a good restaurant will:

a. Take you order at the table without the aid of a talking plastic clown.

b. Not have their entrees listed as registered trademarks (i.e. Filet-O-Fish, McRibs, Whopper, etc.)

c. Not have disposable napkins, china or silverware.

d. Not have visible trashcans

e. Give you lots of silverware. You will need all of it.

f. Not sponsor a million-dollar sweepstakes.

g. Have individual chairs that are not anchored to the table, the floor or each other.

THREE: PROM

Once you arrive at the prom, talking to your date is optional. Typical prom grouping will resemble an eighth-grade dance-boys on one side and girls on the other, with the band trying to get everyone to dance.

Topics of conversation during the prom have become standardized and deeply rooted in tradition. Girls, talk about how cute the waiter was, how cute everyone's dress is, how cute corsages are, how cute the food was and how much your date tipped. Guys, talk about how gross the waiter was, how much the tux cost, how much the corsage cost, how much dinner cost and what they are doing afterward.

FOUR: AFTERWARD

Right up front, to squash a trend, let us merely mention that arcades are out. Pac-man and black tie don't mix.

Some favorite and more acceptable spots are Mount Bonnell (girls, watch out for your dates), riverboat rides and private parties (being a publication of pride and dignity, swimming and socializing are the only party activities we're allowed to mention).

Going out of town after the prom holds the same

status as going out of town for spring break. Every story sounds better if it happened somewhere else.

Guys will not be able to get away with buying just one meal. You will be expected to buy breakfast. However, much to your advantage, restaurants are much more declasse (read "cheap"). In this situation, Chili's and Red Lobster immediately enter the realm of acceptable eateries. (I-HOP and Denny's will not. Ever.)

Groups are best for breakfast. Loud and obnoxious behavior is not discouraged.

FIVE: MANNERS

Possibly the grossest faux pas of all are those that involve ignorance in manners. These, however, can be avoided by using a little common sense and imported knowledge.

Overall, remember that this is a formal occasion. You may be forced to leave some of your nasty habits at home. Among to specifics are: in the restaurant, getting food on your back is generally considered bad form. Men should not throw any screaming tantrums about the check. Girls are impressed by a guy who keeps his cool in the face of great debt.

Men need only remember that they are there to show the girls a good time first, themselves second. Open doors, hold coats, pull out chairs and don't do anything your date will be teased about later.

Another invaluable rule is that you ask what you don't know. Many a tacky act can be avoided, and no one will laugh if you simply ask someone (either a friend or waiter) how to correctly order for your date.

Another way to keep yourself out of trouble is to avoid laughing at anyone else's grossity unless you are quite sure of yourself socially. Loud laughs in a restaurant tend to draw more scorn than eating with the fingers.

Despite the complexity and large scope of the preceding instructions, there is still a great deal of leeway at the prom. As a matter of fact, ingenuity is appreciated and may help save an entirely overrated evening. Those who attend prom-like activities more than once a year insist that something out of the ordinary and totally off-the-

wall takes place before they even talk about a social event. So stick to tradition, add the tiniest bit of innovation, and talk about the prom for years.

Good writers don't waste words. They crave precision and brevity. They use active verbs, concrete nouns. They aren't afraid to use contractions. They prefer short sentences to long ones but know how to use long ones without losing their readers. They use semicolons only when they want to impress English teachers.

They tend to place their nouns first, their verbs second and their objects third, and if they don't, it's for a reason. Ditto for repeating key words in a sentence. If it happens, it's no accident. For example:

"Before she had a ship, before she had any money for a ship or a nurse to go with the ship or a media representative to handle all the reporters who would want to know what she was doing with the ship, Dr. Rebecca Gomperts had an idea."

It's no accident that the reporter, Sara Corbett of *The New York Times*, repeats "ship." It's done for effect.

Good writers possess the right tools. They understand the difference between "shuffled" and "trudged." They appreciate imagery, pace and tone. They know how a gerund and a present participle differ. They know when to use a comma, when not to. They understand metaphor and simile and natural alliteration. They know when to use a news lead, when to use a feature lead, when to come up with a lead that's something in between.

Most importantly, good writers work hard.

Good writers strive to communicate a message, to express a thought. They're more concerned with their readers than they are with themselves. They appreciate that when they write something, readers —not the writer — are the all-important persons, so they write *to* them and *for* them. They don't use fancy words like "expectorate" when they mean "spit" or foggy gimmicks like "One would be wise to procure tickets to the football game as expeditiously as possible." They write, "Buy your tickets now before they're gone." They accept the fact that writing and reporting are hard work, and they're willing to track down a story to its bitter end, whatever the sacrifice, in pursuit of the concrete

JOHN LENNON ISN'T WRITING FOR YOUR PUBLICATION

So get rid of all the "Imagine you are in bungee jumper. It's easy if you try. Hard ground below you. Hit it and you die. Imagine all the people watching you go splat" leads.

Good writers and reporters show readers a real person and situation—not some figment of your imagination.

LEAD TIP

Keep your lead sentences and paragraphs short. Create pace by mixing short, medium, and long sentences. That'll also set the tone for the story. For example:

Michelle Castillo awakes on the morning before her wedding with a jolt familiar to bridges-to-be.

"It just hit me," she gasps, wringing her hands in a manner completely at odds with her characteristics calm. "Tomorrow, we're getting married."

details. It's not enough to know that the new principal attended Penn State. They want to know who his heros are, what are his likes and dislikes, who he'd invite to a fantasy dinner party. Is he a dog or a cat person? Shakespeare or Stephen King? Cheeseburger or Peking Duck?

Mostly, they want to tell a story —about trial and error, loss and restoration, overcoming adversity, coming home, love and hate, finding a place in the world. They don't want to dwell on the obvious. They want to find the invisible stories that exist below the surface. They want those stories to have a beginning, a middle and an end that bring readers full circle and provide them with a sense of satisfaction, resolution, closure.

Finally, good writing is the result of constant revision. John Lennon once said something to the effect that, "I never finished a song. We just recorded the latest version available."

Writing is the same way. Good writers rarely produce on first draft. They write, edit, revise, proof, report some more, write, edit and eventually, time runs out, and they hand in the latest version available.

In the end, good writing possesses a powerful voice, "the illusion that the writer is speaking directly to the reader," as writing guru Roy Peter Clark of the Poynter Institute for Media Studies says.

Here's a great piece of writing. It illustrates what I'm talking about:

SHOWCASE

By **KATIE KROLL**
Cypress Creek High School, Houston, TX

KEVIN DONAT loved his blue couch and his remote control. Out of the three remotes for the upstairs, Kevin was the only person allowed to touch his. He loved everything with a screen and would play his Sony Playstation, build cities and then destroy them on his computer, and watch Baywatch on his big-screen TV.

After his death, a group of his friends gathered on the blue couch and took turns holding the remote. They would not change the channel, but they passed it to each other while talking to Kevin.

Kevin was a reserved person to people he did not know; however, once he got to know someone, he was very talkative. He was always smiling.

Kevin was born on a Tuesday in 1983 and was out on the soccer field every Saturday watching his two older brothers play. He loved sports; his competitive spirit made him try his best at everything. Growing up, Kevin was very active in water polo and swimming; he still holds the record for every age group in the butterfly stroke at the Lakewood Club. During the summers, he worked as a lifeguard.

His love for football won out, though. He started playing in the seventh grade at Hamilton Junior High and continued to his sophomore year playing defensive tackle on the junior varsity team. He put his all into the game and spent hours playing outside of school. His goal was to go to Texas A&M and play college football.

Kevin loved his Toyota Camry-he washed it every night and refused to drive it in the rain. He loved to eat; his mother said he never missed a meal. Frugal with his own money, he enjoyed eating the $2.99 buffet at Cici's pizza. He had bologna sandwiches with mayonnaise every day for lunch, unless he sold it for a dollar. He especially loved to travel with his family.

In an English project, Kevin named four things most important to him: his family, his friends, his church and football.

Kevin was an "A" student in all honors classes, yet he lived his life stress free and easygoing. Though he often procrastinated, he always came through. Even the torment his brothers placed on him did not bother him, though once he wrote his brother's leaving for college was one of the happiest times of his life. He loved the idea of being an only child; he loved his space; he loved having the blue couch all to himself.

His family attends Windwood Presbyterian Church, where he was a confirmed member and very active in the youth group.

He loved Garth Brooks, and at his visitation held at Klein Funeral Home, Kevin's friends knew he would be disgusted by the generic parlor music playing in the background. They made a trip out to Kevin's Camry and replaced the trite music with the Garth Brooks Live CD. They knew he would be smiling.

COMPARE & CONTRAST

FOCUS ON THE EVENT

It's that time again. Students will go to Lakewood College to take college entrance tests, with the hopes of scoring high enough to qualify for the college of their choice.

"These tests are reliable indicators of what student know, and help colleges decide which students to accept as freshmen," Bill Jones, ACT spokesman, said.

The ACT Assessment, or "A-C-T" as it is commonly called, is a national college admission examination that consists of tests in English, Mathematics, Reading and Science Reasoning.

ACT results are accepted by virtually all U.S. colleges and universities.

The ACT includes 215 multiple-choice questions and takes approximately 3 hours and 30 minutes to complete with breaks. Actual testing time is 2 hours and 55 minutes.

In the U.S., the ACT is administered on five national test dates, in October, December, February, April, and June. In selected states, the ACT is also offered in late September.

The basic registration fee is $25 which includes score reports for up to four college choices for which a valid code is listed at time of registration.

"I'm not looking forward to taking the test, but I think I'm ready," junior Roopsha Samanta said. "I have been taking ACT prep classes at Hillside Community College."

FOCUS ON A PERSON

Every Saturday morning, junior Molly Altom rolls out of bed at 6:30, drives 45 minutes across town to Hillside Community College, and then spends the next three hours in class, studying math. She hopes this time invested will make the difference in her dream to attend Yale University.

"I know the competition for entrance is incredible, and I need to score as high on my entrance exams as possible, so I'm hoping these classes will give me that extra advantage," she said. "I think I'll do fine in the verbal section, but I've always had a rough time with math."

Altom is one of a number of students who are attending Saturday morning classes at local colleges in order to help them prepare for college entrance exams.

"I want to go to Stanford, and I don't want to have to worry about whether I'll be accepted," junior Vu Pham said. "So I'm taking a class that's helping me with the verbal section of the SAT. It's also helping with my regular classes."

School counselors say for some students the college prep classes are a good investment.

"I'm not sure they're right for everyone," counselor Evelyn Richmond said. "But the classes have been shown to help students raise their scores by as much as 15 percent, and for some students, that extra 15 percent is the difference between being accepted by Harvard or Stanford, or going to a local college."

Think you can crank out a solid story in half an hour? Think again.

Writing is a process. It begins at the idea stage. Brainstorming. Watching. Listening. Reading a magazine or book. Finding that cool story idea.

It's followed by reporting. Gathering all the facts, quotes, details.

Then, it's writing the first draft. And face it, kid, you're not good enough yet to whip out a perfect story the first time out.

So the final step is revising: editing, proofing, rewriting.

Sounds difficult? It is. But it's worth it.

Photo by **LAURISSA NOACK**
Groom High School, Groom, TX

FIND A READER

02

Student journalists have plenty to write about and a receptive audience to write for. What is needed now is the understanding that they're writing for other students, not for a teacher or another adult.

CHAPTER HIGHLIGHTS:

■ Lifeless data dominates student press.

■ Facts and news aren't the same thing.

■ Coverage must be timely, local, relavent.

■ Journalism requires reporting!

The problem with most high school publications is that they're not read.

They're scanned. Students thumb through them in search of their names or the names of friends. Being mentioned in the newspaper implies a person has achieved status within the school, regardless of the subject or the context of the story. Joe is a member of the football team. Susan was named a state champion debater. Mrs. Hunter won a teaching award. Thus, the newspaper serves as a monthly "who's who," the school's social register, and the yearbook captures for posterity the fact that the purpose of the English department was to teach language skills.

So is it any surprise that either are rarely read?

No. At a session of the Columbia Scholastic Press Association in New York City, I asked students how many of them read the *Wall Street Journal*. Out of a class of 100, one or two hands went up. Most students looked at me as though I were nuts. Why should they read it? It contains little information interesting or relevant to them.

But would you read it, I asked, if once a week your names were printed in the paper. A few more hands rose.

"You're lying," I said. "You'd scan it for your name, but you wouldn't read it."

That's what "readers" do with school publications.

And why not? Stories are not written to be read but rather to fill a space on a page, to complete an assignment, or to satisfy a source's demand for publicity—a kind of "I don't care what you say about me so long as you say something and spell my name correctly" request. The reader is the last consideration in the formulation of news, despite most staff's stated intentions to publish publications that inform and entertain. Most high school newspapers rehash old news or restate the obvious with all the clarity and style of a lawnmower manual. And they're doing better than yearbooks.

So there. Get mad. Take offense. Huff and puff. It's true.

Too many staffs treat all news questions as equals, mulching them together to conform to the traditional inverted pyramid formula so the focus of many student news or feature stories is most likely to be "who, what, when or where" even though the subject concerns an event that occurred weeks, even months, earlier.

It matters not that readers have long since forgotten or ceased to care—if indeed they ever cared—about the event. Reporters cover events because they happened, and the thrust of the news coverage is just that: they happened.

> 🔖 Is it possible to cram several hundred teenagers into a building, eight hours a day, five days a week, some weekends, and not have anything to write about? Seems doubtful."

Elections are good examples. Although the homecoming took place three weeks earlier, staffs typically report the bare-bone facts: who, what, when and where, as if no one knew that beaming Betty Jo was crowned "Homecoming Queen." Student journalists seldom explore why, how, reactions and/or ramifications. They rarely bother to answer the critical news question, "So what?"

Sports leads also provide excellent examples of the "too little, too late" coverage. Few readers need to be told or wish to be reminded the team won or lost a game played 14 days ago. They certainly don't need to be insulted with leads such as, "With the first chill of autumn air comes football season. The Fighting Vikings take to the field next Friday against Seaweed High. Members of the team are . . . "

■ DATA DOMINATES STUDENT PRESS

However, this approach to coverage and writing dominates the student press. It's fact/data oriented. The Pep Squad did this. The Debate Team did that. The Chess Club will do something else. When asked about it, the club president said, "blah, blah, blah."

Do readers care? Yes and no. Readers don't care where the Spanish Club went for its annual Cinco de Mayo lunch, but they may be interested in the Spanish Club's efforts to raise money for a fellow member who is undergoing chemotherapy. Readers may not be interested in the Academic Bowl officer election, but they may be interested in a story that captures the anxiety of the last competition. Readers may not care that the Student Council will hold a blood drive in the school cafeteria, but they may be interested in a story that reveals students' unfounded fears that they may contract SARS or AIDS by donating blood.

So it's a balancing act: These facts should be contained in the publication, albeit in sidebar lists, graphs, summaries and other reader-friendly graphic elements, but the majority of the pub should be reserved for "stories."

For some reason, though, staffs believe that if they provide details about an issue or event — write a research paper on sleep deprivation, for example, crammed full of data

GET OFF TO A GOOD START

You must hook the reader right off. The opening sentence is critical. Compare your leads to these.

SOME KIDS don't know what it's like to sit down for a Thanksgiving dinner. They've never enjoyed turkey and dressing. Never watched Macy's parade. Never cheered for the Cowboys and the Lions.

Knowing this breaks Bill Brassard's heart. That's why Brassard will again this year open his home to homeless children...

JIMMY JONES leaves school each day at noon, drives across town and spends his afternoons flushing radiators, cleaning carburetors and changing spark plugs. He wants to be an automotive mechanic after graduation. But if Gov. Frank Keatings' plans were implemented now, Jimmy would spend his afternoons on campus, studying Shakespeare and geography.

IN PARTS OF AFRICA, India and the Philippines, some children have never seen nor held a book. Former biology teacher Jeff Thorne is trying to change that. Now a director with Books for Children, an Oklahoma City charity organization, Thorne returned to Guthrie in February to talk about his experiences overseas and his efforts to help educate children in Third World countries.

THE ROOF LEAKS. Band uniforms are old, and the computers are outdated. The intercom crackles and breaks. The air conditioning in half of the high school rarely works. The restrooms at Jelsma Stadium are...well, to put it politely, a challenge to anyone daring to enter.

And there's more. Not surprisingly, school administrators say they plan to present a school bond proposal next year that will address these needs and others.

downloaded from the Internet — then somehow readers will care enough about sleep deprivation to read the article. Not true. They might scan it, but they won't read it. Fact is, if a student wants information about sleep deprivation or the latest teen heartthrob or the Super Bowl, they're not going to wait a month or a year for the high school publication to provide it. They'll log onto Yahoo and get it instantly. This begs the question, "If I can get information about a topic instantly, why do I need a high school publication?"

Answer: because Yahoo and Google don't cover your school. They don't know or care about your students. And unless you change what you cover and how you cover it, then you don't either.

You disagree? Too harsh an indictment, you argue. Fine. Conduct a readership survey at your school. Distribute the paper to a study hall. Give students 30 minutes to read it, if they choose to spend that much time with it. At the end of the half hour, give them a pop quiz on its contents. Ask data-based questions. When is the Drama Club production? Who are the leading performers? When will the ACT test be given? Where will the Speech Club compete this weekend? What is the National Honor Society planning? Who scored the third touchdown in the football team's 36-7 win?

Chances are, students won't have a clue. And why should they? They'll see the stories, give them a cursory glance for names, and then zip on through the remainder of the page.

Maybe this is too scientific a procedure for you. Try this: count the number of papers that are left in desks, in wastecans or on the floor during the same class period they're handed out.

Or ask seniors, "How many of you have read last year's yearbook?"

If you want to produce a publication that is informative and entertaining—and I think we all do—then you must rethink coverage, reporting and writing. We can begin by debunking one of the oldest myths in journalism education—that names are news.

■ THEY ARE NOT!

If names alone were news, we'd wake up each morning, smack down a bowl of Sugar Crisps and read the phone book. We don't. Why? Because nothing is less newsworthy, less interesting than a list of names, unless the story states something such as "students who'll be kicked out of school for no apparent reason today include . . . ." Perhaps then names are news. But this is rarely the case. More often, stories will state something along the lines of, "Well, it's volleyball season again, and the girls are bumping, setting and spiking their way toward a state championship. Members of the team are . . ."

It reminds me of a newspaper I found a few years back. The banner headline in the first issue, which was published on Oct. 1, screamed, "School Begins." What a shock to the students who'd been in class for four or five weeks! To make matters worse, the story stated something along the lines of:

THE LAZY DAYS of summer are now over, and students are back in class. No more lounging around the pool, sleeping late, and watching soap operas. It's time to crack the books and start studying.

Students attending school this year are…

■ IS IT NEWS TO ANYONE?

The so-called news story then listed the names of all students enrolled. Persons not listed, I assume, were free to leave. "What do you mean I don't have to be here? That's news to me!" But was it news to anyone else? No. It's data. Certainly, a focus on people is the key to readership, but we must use names to hook readers into stories of real interest. That's the key point. Three things are needed to create news:

- A message. Facts. Quotes. Information.
- An audience. Someone to say it to. High school students, for example.
- Interest. It's a fact that the water tower is 263 feet tall. It's news that it fell over. Your job is to provide the facts that are also news. Two weeks after it happened, it may not be news that it fell over. So what then? Resign yourself to the fact that you can't write about the water tower falling over because it happened two weeks ago and everyone knows about it now? Well, that's the lazy answer. A more industrious reporter might

NEWS LEADS WE WANT TO SEE

THE "WHY" LEAD

The motive or cause of an event sometimes is the most important feature. Musician Shawn Phillips said, "Whether you're 14 or 114, one always needs to question the 'why' and the 'how' because otherwise you have died inside." But he makes a lot of sense.

In an effort to teach Shakespeare to sophomores, English teacher Gina Hatley and science teacher Phil Barnes reenacted the love scene between Romeo and Juliet. "It's the only thing I thought they'd understand," Ms. Hatley said.

THE "HOW" LEAD

The method by which something is accomplished.

By flunking every course, missing 62 days of class and assaulting two teachers, Bubba Snively gravely endangered his eligibility for high school basketball.

■ CONTINUED ON 015

> **When writing a lead avoid when and where questions. They're rarely the most important news questions. Do not begin with a date, the school name or school initials. As much as possible, avoid starting with a, an, or the, and make sure the first sentence contains an active verb."**

explain why it fell over, or explore what's being done to make sure the new one doesn't fall over, or write a feature story about how the collapse of the water tower affected this or that person.

An interesting story exists. You just have to find it.

Oh, I know what you're thinking. "No, it doesn't."

Well, yes, it does. If you'll look below the surface, beyond the obvious, you'll find that public schools are full of fascinating stories. For example, it's a fact that two high school girls grew their hair long, then cut and donated it to an organization that makes wigs for children with cancer. This is a fact but it's not much of a story. A more resourceful reporter might learn that one of the girls is doing this because she's a cancer survivor herself. Now there's a story. It's a story students will read. If she were to stand in front of her class and tell her story, students would listen. They'll read it if you do a good enough job reporting and writing it.

What is it about the student publication that attracts readers? Can you identify, isolate, develop and refine reporter habits and behaviors that will produce powerful stories that that will attract, inform and entertain student readers?

Not to give away the big punch line, which I promise to reveal, bit by bit, but the answer is "YES, YES, GOOD GOLLY MISS MOLLY, YES!"

So why aren't they? Why do we have stories in high-school publications like this:

AS PART OF AN EFFORT to make philosophical principles more relevant to social concerns, the philosophy department at Concorde State College will sponsor a series of lectures and discussions entitled, "Persons, Responsibility and the Law," beginning in February and continuing until April.

The free series will feature outstanding philosophers from the United States and England addressing topics of pressing social and legal concern. Each lecture will be followed by a panel discussion involving representatives of community organizations co-sponsoring the series.

Major funds for the series were provided by the National Endowment for the Arts and the State Committee for the Humanities. All lectures will begin at 4:30 p.m. in the Gardner Lecture Center on the Concorde campus.

Among the speakers will be Herbert Charles Laughton of Kings College, Cambridge University. He will lead a panel discussion entitled, "Philosophical consequences of relativity and quantum physics."

Somehow, I just can't picture a throng of 16-year-old boys busting a gut to get into Gardner Hall so they can hear Herbert Charles discuss philosophical consequences of anything, but there it is, running front and center on the high school newspaper.

Why?

Because, students claim:

■ There's nothing to cover because nothing ever happens in our dusty little town.

■ And even if there were, it would be old news by the time the publication is published.

■ But heck, who are we kidding? Even if we did, no one would read it because our students are so dumb and lazy.

■ Unless we wrote about sex, drugs or rock 'n roll, but our cranky old administrators won't let us.

■ So as you can see, it's not our fault.

■ NO EXCUSES

Let's examine these excuses one at a time.

■ There's nothing to write about.

Is it possible to cram several hundred teenagers into a building, eight hours a day, five days a week, some weekends, and not have anything to write about? I don't think so, unless these kids are roboclones, incapable of thoughts or actions, possessing no dreams, desires, fears, anxieties, anger or joy. In addition, they neither affect nor are affected by the world outside the classroom. The Middle East explodes. They shrug. Public education crumbles around them. They yawn. They're forced-fed an endless series of standardized tests. Big deal. They are oblivious to all forces of commerce, culture, history, politics, the arts. They are mindless, faceless automatons.

These are teenagers today?

I don't think so.

Teenagers today may not know as much as adults would like them to, but they sure feel. They are hopeful, afraid, in need of love and attention, occasionally desperate. Many are children, lost and scared, even if they look grown up. And they look so grown up. They primp and posture, imitating MTV and BET heroes. They work to perfect an attitude, to create a shell. Why? Because they face problems that the Baby Boomers could never have imagined.

For the first time in our nation's history, students cannot expect to achieve a higher standard of living than their parents. They face environmental pollution, a depleting ozone layer, empty homes, the threat of cancer and AIDS, racism and intolerance, soaring divorce rates, political stagnation, a widening gap between the haves and the have nots, and, of course, the specter of world terrorism.

Given all of this, how can any publication staff suggest that it has nothing better to write about than who won homecoming queen, what the prom theme was and when graduation is scheduled.

Of course, many staffs will respond, "We had to cover these things because nothing else happened."

Sure, you need to cover prom, but it's doubtful readers care when and where prom was held, or about the theme or the fact that couples ate and danced. Tell them something new. Bright reporters would search for angles that provide a thoughtful preview of the event instead of rehashing the obvious.

And about the comment, "because nothing else happened . . . ."

What do you want? A tornado to wipe out the school so you can interview the survivors?

THE LAZY DAYS of summer are now over, and students are back in class. No more lounging around the pool, sleeping late and watching soap operas. It's time to crack the books and start studying. But wait. A tornado hit the school last week.

Students no longer attending school this year are . . .

So what are your other excuses?

■ Look, we tried to write about a big drug bust at our school, but by the time our newspaper came out, the whole thing was over.

Doesn't wash. The problem here lies not in what you're covering but in how you're covering it. Rather than concentrating on what happened, examine instead the effects of the event. What are local people saying about it? What new issues are generated? Search for reactions and response. Find a local source who can give you a fresh angle on the story. Ask more analytical questions such as "Why did it happen when it did?" and "Why was the policy changed?" Talk to administrators. Don't focus on the bust. Focus on the aftermath of the bust.

Tell readers something they don't already know. News is not static. It changes rapidly. CNN has shown us that. Updated every 30 minutes, the newscasts evolve quickly from what and when to how to why to so what in a blink of an eye.

■ Look, we know our stories are boring. We want to write about interesting stuff, but our administrators won't let us.

No doubt, prior review and restraint are problems, but they're not impenetrable barriers to superior content. Many staffs want to cover controversial issues for the sake of covering controversial issues. The best example of this I can remember was in a tiny Texas Panhandle town, where the students wanted to write about gay rights. Was it a local, timely issue? No. Why did the staff want to cover it? Because they thought it was so juicy that it would appeal to their readers' more ignoble instincts.

Student journalists have tried to cover all the controversial topics for no better reason than to say they did. The big three are substance abuse, teen sexuality and delinquent behavior.

■ *"We had a story about Satanism in our paper."*
Oh yeah. What did it say?

■ *Well, we wrote all about it, how some students are worshipping the devil and kidnapping children and doing all sorts of creepy things.*

NEWS LEADS WE WANT TO SEE

■ CONTINUED FROM 013

The following leads may be effective for briefs but are not recommended for longer news and feature stories.

THE "WHO" LEAD

If the "who" is a well-known person place or thing, it is usually the feature of the lead. The name alone attracts attention. Unless one of the other elements is particularly outstanding, the "big name" comes first. For example:

Coach Randy Fowler, who led Pine Valley to four consecutive district football championships, announced his retirement in order to sell used cars and whole-life insurance.

LEAD TIP

Get to the point. Don't waddle into the story. Don't explain. Don't summarize. Don't generalize. If the story is about a teacher who is also a rodeo cowboy, get right to the narrative.

Billy Bob Turner looked down at his right hand, callused from more bull rides than he can count.

"It don't bend like I want it to," he said.

The reason? It was almost ripped off three years ago.

Has this happened in your school or community?

■ *No.*

Are your students engaged in these activities?

■ *No, not that we know of.*

Well, if it isn't a problem here, if school and police authorities claim it isn't an issue, then why write about it, given the availability of so many local, timely and relevant issues?

■ *Well, we wrote about it because it was controversial, and we thought our students would like to read about it. And we thought the newspaper judges would be impressed that we're covering controversial issues like this.*

Where did you get your information?

■ *From Time and a couple of websites. And we talked to some students.*

What did the students say?

■ *That Satanism is pretty yucky and that they're against it.*

And that's it?

■ *Yeah. That's pretty much how it went.*

And so it goes. All coverage must be timely, relevant and local. Otherwise, it is bad journalism, pure and simple. But it is particularly offensive for staffs to cover issues simply in an attempt to appeal to prurient interests. It is not the staff's job to teach human sexuality. It's the school's job, and if the school isn't doing its job, then perhaps you have a story.

■ Okay then, if we can't write about controversial topics, then we might as well shut down because our readers are dumb and lazy anyway.

I'll grant this: readers are lazy. Not just high school readers. All readers. Give them half an excuse to quit reading and most will take it. It is possible that a few people who started reading this book quit at some point prior to here because my prose didn't fully captivate them. Chances are, they're now reading a supermarket tabloid. I can accept that.

Still, the challenge of reporting for a high school publication — newspaper or yearbook — is to engage the reader on intellectual and/or emotional levels.

The purpose of this book is to teach you how to engage the reader. Today's students may read less passionately than did their parents and grandparents, but they do read and they are still passionate.

I'm amazed at the number of high school students I saw toting J.R.R. Tolkein, even though most had seen the *Lord of the Ring* movies. Their attraction to that book suggests teenagers are capable of getting as big a jolt from the written word as they are from the latest technological wizardry.

How and what they read are not the same, and their motivations for reading are different as well. Most high-school students can and do read, if provided compelling reading material. J.K. Rowling has no problem attracting young readers.

Therein lies the trick: to write journalistically in a compelling, dynamic manner so readers will have no choice but to read. That's what this book is all about.

However, I must caution you. This method of reporting and writing is time-consuming and difficult.

Students can babble off the tops of their heads about drug abuse or rehash material already printed in a weekly news magazine about teen pregnancy. As Truman Capote said of beat writer Jack Kerouac, author of *On the Road*, "That's not writing. That's typing."

Typing is easy. Reporting—that's the difficult part. Even with desktop publishing, with its graphic bells and whistles, the heart and soul of the student publication rests in its news reporting. Without substantive information collection, you may have a student publication— but it isn't journalism.

■ THE BOTTOM LINE

In the final judgment, the student publication should be journalistic. Within that criteria, staffs have tremendous latitude in determining what to cover and how to cover it. Some will prefer a straight news approach, others will lean toward news/feature or personality profile coverage, and still others will emphasize in-depth news coverage. These decisions are based on many factors: reader needs and expectations, staff talents and interests, publication format, and the

SURVIVING IN THE WORLD OF INSTANT MEDIA

Covering the 1960 Democratic National Convention, syndicated columnist Liz Carpenter learned of the maneuvers behind the nomination of John F. Kennedy and was prepared to write a story when, to her horror, she was scooped by TV.

As I wrote my exclusive story of political intrigue . . . suddenly to my horror, I saw on the TV screen Mr. Sam (Rayburn, Speaker of the House) and his glower addressing the Texas caucus. The announcer was telling people in Austin, and as far as the cable reached, the very things I was writing for them to read the next morning. From one of those curtained panels, where I had peeked in, there had been a camera peeking in, too. My story, stolen!

Dejected, I rolled my story out of the typewriter, tossed it in the wastepaper basket, put another piece of paper in the typewriter and began again —not writing WHAT had happened but HOW and WHY.

And that was the way it was to be forever-more for newspaper reporters. Analyzing, interpreting, yes, dancing around the story with what the cameras didn't have time to show.

availability of issues and events to be covered, to name a few.

Regardless of the path chosen, the final product should be journalistically sound. In terms of news reporting and writing, this means:

- The story has news value.
- Journalistic values—clarity, accuracy, brevity, relevance, attribution, fairness, balance, identification, objectivity and truth —are observed.
- All news questions are answered in the story but not necessarily given equal prominence in the lead.
- Information is attributed to a source.
- Direct and indirect quotes provide information rather than clichés and are structured effectively.
- Stylebook rules are followed religiously.
- All news stories contain one or more news elements.
- Elements of news—timeliness, currency, proximity, consequence, prominence, oddity, conflict and human interest—are included.

■ NO ESSAYS

A lot of students enroll in journalism because they like to write. That's as good a reason as any, I suppose, but publications require more than writing. They require reporting. I've heard it from hundreds of advisers: "I don't need writers. I need reporters."

More and more staffs have allowed expressive writing — first person essays in particular — to creep into their publications. No wonder why—it's easy. Students can sit at the desk and crank this stuff out, whether they are pontificating on the latest boy band or the threat of nuclear annihilation.

These essays, posing as journalism, are labeled "features." They are not. They may be term papers, research essays or stream-of-consciousness mental tumbling exercises, but they are not journalism.

Journalism requires reporters to research, interview, observe and listen—then write because journalism always has informational value. Expressive writing requires only that the reporters have an opinion. Facts are nice but an unnecessary luxury.

The task of reporting involves the collection of facts from a wide variety of sources and then the painful realization that most of them can't and won't be used. Only the most important information, the most compelling anecdotes, the most interesting and thought-provoking quotes will be used. One of the toughest jobs a reporter faces is not determining what facts to collect but rather deciding which ones are worth using in the story.

Consider the following stories involving the

NEWS LEADS WE SEE TOO OFTEN

THE "WHAT" LEAD
Concerning an event, result, trend or policy.

A truce was declared last week between the mother of a student and the Pine Valley cheer-leaders. Mrs. Tammi Lynn Bouffant agreed to stop shooting at the cheerleaders if her daughter, Nikki Sue, is allowed to cheer with the team every other road game.

THE "WHERE" LEAD
Avoid "where" leads, except when location is signifi-cant enough to overshadow the other W's, such as in the following example:

In the living room of his mobile home, Principal Gerald Skinner stood in front of his prized velvet painting of Elvis Presley and renewed his recommendation that courses in the study of "the King" be mandatory.

> ❝ How long should the lead be? As long as it takes to hook the reader into the story, tell him or her what the story is about, and give the reader an indication of what the story will be like. But not a word longer. One of my favorite leads is six words long: She never knew she had it.❞

winter holiday season. The first represents the expressive writing mode, common to secondary language arts classes.

"SILENT NIGHT, holy night.
"All is calm, all is bright."
Is all really calm today? Or has Christmas gone from desired to dreaded? Some would think so. The peacefulness of Christmases past seems to have disintegrated in the hustle and bustle of commercialized shopping. The expenses of Christmas often discourages its sole purpose of holding a place on the calendar.

What is the purpose of Christmas? What does it really mean? Is it merely a holiday that takes place on Dec. 25 just because there is nothing else going on? Even a small child could tell you the answer—no!

Some would say that it is simply a holiday set aside to spend time with family and friends while others feel its main purpose is for the distributing of gifts. This idea would support the ever-famous myth of Ol' Saint Nick (although I think there's a little bit of love for Santa in everyone's heart). And still others believe that it is a celebration of Christ's birthday. This is certainly the most popular dogma. I, being a Christian, thoroughly support this belief.

Whatever your idea of Christmas, it is a happy time of celebration—a time of giving thanks and appreciation for all that has been given to you. These theories seemed to have disappeared over the years.

With presents to buy and no money to buy them with, people have become overly concerned with the disbursing of gifts. Where will I get the money? What will I buy family and friends? Thus, the joys of Christmas are hidden with all of the worry and fret. If Santa Claus were real, would he approve of this abuse of this custom of giving? Let's make this Christmas unforgettable and get back to the true meaning behind it all.

". . . Sleep in heavenly peace,
Sleep in heavenly peace."

A nice thought but hardly journalistic. Such stories appear in the news and feature columns as often as on the editorial pages of high school newspapers.

Here's another typical story:

CHRISTMASTIME MEANS many things to different people, but they all have one thing in common—traditions. Each family has its own traditions that it cherishes for years to come. The traditions range from putting up the tree to writing letters to Santa Claus.

The Christmas tree itself is the object of many traditions. Families go out in search of the perfect tree whether it may be in a tree lot or the woods. Some families put their trees up on the day after Thanksgiving while others put theirs up on Christmas Eve.

Traveling is also an important tradition. Families travel to visit grandparents' houses and exchange gifts among relatives. Many people attend church services on Christmas Eve. Some prefer to go to the evening service while others go to the midnight service.

Groups of people can be found shopping, caroling or enjoying Christmas parties.

For the kids, the traditions may be watching the Christmas parade, writing letters to Santa Claus or staying up as late as they can in hopes of getting a glimpse of jolly ole St. Nick eating the cookies they left for him.

Christmastime means decorating and putting up lights on the outside of the house for others to look at.

Sending Christmas cards and baking treats for others to enjoy are a few more traditions on a never-ending list.

Many individuals have traditions that bring smiles whenever they think of Christmas.

Did either of these stories tell the average reader anything new? Perhaps exchange students from Outer Bedpania may be unfamiliar with holiday traditions, but who else stands to learn much? While these articles offer sweet and safe sentiments, they are journalistic duds.

■ **REPORT FIRST, THEN WRITE**
Report! Find news. Research. Interview. Observe. Listen for dialogue. Interview some

more. Then make that news into a news story. Compare the earlier stories to this one.

SHOWCASE ■

By **ANNA HARRIS**
Irving High School, Irving, TX

THIS IS NOT YOUR average Christmas story, but all the elements are there. It includes the typical family that seems to have nothing but bad luck. Their money is tight—almost nonexistent. The father had an on-the-job accident which may cause him to lose his job. The mother was involved in a car wreck. The hospital bills pour in. Christmas doesn't look very promising.

Sound like a typical Christmas human interest story? Maybe so, but there's a difference. The family found help. Someone reached out to them.

For the second year in a row, Irving High School homerooms are "adopting" children for Christmas. The youngest child in the above mentioned family will be one of the adopted children. Her name is Cindy Jones, and she is a first grader at John R. Good Elementary School. A few weeks ago, Cindy brought home an information sheet about the Adopt-A-Child Program.

Her mother, Barbara Jones, explains how she felt: "I was embarrassed a little, at first, but Cindy doesn't understand the money situation right now. She wanted to be in the program. Then, it made me feel good."

Cindy's first reaction after receiving her parents' permission to be in the program was to make out a "wish list."

Its simple contents included a Mon Chi Chi stuffed animal and a Tippee Toes Doll. Before the adoption program, Cindy had not bothered to make out a list.

"This year, Christmas would not have been anything. Just us being together," Jones said.

Since money is not available for buying Christmas presents, the Joneses must rely on their own talents for Christmas gifts. Both Mr. and Mrs. Jones are taking a jewelry-making class. Ms. Jones also enjoys sewing clothes for her children. Besides Cindy, the Jones have two other children who both go to Austin Junior High

School. Surprisingly, Cindy's brother and sister showed no jealousy toward Cindy's being in the program. In fact, they were happy that she, at least, would have a nice Christmas.

Jones said that she and her husband have always tried to teach their children to share with each other. "All the children are extra good about sharing," she said.

Added Patty Jones, Cindy's sister: "I like the program. I think it will help her with Christmas. I was excited when I heard about it."

Cindy is looking forward to making some new friends at the Adopt-A-Child Party, scheduled for next Friday. However, she said she is a little apprehensive about talking to so many people.

To encourage Cindy, Patty said, "Cindy may be nervous at the party, but after she brings the stuff home, she'll be happy."

All of Cindy's Christmas presents will come from IHS. Since most children will receive their presents on Christmas Day, it seems likely that Cindy would be let down on Christmas morning. Cindy's mother thinks otherwise.

"It's just a part of Christmas to her," she said. "She'll just be tickled to death to get something. Time won't make much difference. Usually, she has a second-hand Christmas.

"I am very glad that Cindy will have this opportunity," Cindy's mother added. "It's something we can't give her. We need help right now, and I'm not going to turn it down. This party will be something she can remember and say that help was there when she needed it. It lets her know that she does have friends and that people do care."

This story is about a real person who is benefiting from a real program. It says far more about the meaning of Christmas than either of the former articles because it's not a pie-in-the-sky lecture or rehash of the obvious.

A key to the success of this story is that it deals with a single person rather than with a general population of needy persons. Most high school reporters make the mistake of writing about the program itself, basing the story on

MORE LEADS WE SEE TOO OFTEN

THE "WHEN" LEAD
Rarely is the time of an event the most interesting feature. However, circumstances may make it significant. For instance:

When football coaches gather to talk about the team these days, their cocktail of choice may be Maalox. As they debate how to fire up a team that hasn't won a game in three years, one outcome is virtually certain: something good better happen quickly or they'll all be looking for new jobs next year.

LEAD TIP

What makes a
good lead?

■ An anecdote

■ The description
of a scene

■ The description
of a person

■ An excellent
quote

■ A startling
statement

■ A clever play
on words

quotes from adults, supervisors or instructors rather than from the perspective of the recipient of the goodwill gesture—in this case, Cindy.

Telling the story from the child's point of view brings it to life and makes concrete the rather abstract notion of public service. The story allows Irving High School students to say, "Perhaps we couldn't help all needy persons in the season of giving, but we brought happiness to this one child. Maybe we can change the world, one 5-year-old at a time."

What more appropriate testimony to the spirit of the season? Granted, this approach requires empathetic and sensitive reporting. Recipients of charity often prefer to avoid publicity, and it would be ethically and possibly legally wrong to place under the spotlight those who would rather remain anonymous. In that case, seek alternatives.

The following article achieves the same but in a touchingly humorous way:

SHOWCASE ■

By **ERIC NICHOLSON**
Grosse Point South High School,
Grosse Point, MI

LISTENING TO YOUNG voices sing "Jingle Bells," a group of National Honor Society students stands outside a Richard kindergarten classroom.

As they enter the room, the song ends, and pairs of eyes turn to stare at those "big kids." Mrs. Marian Lamb, the kindergarten teacher, comes over and announces, "Boys and girls, these are the South students who have come to help you write letters to Santa. Now, who is ready to start writing?"

Of course, every little hand shoots up, for what 5- or 6-year-old doesn't want to tell Santa Claus what he or she wants for Christmas? Every kindergartener rushes over to one of the "big people" and places his small hand into his new friend's. They walk over to get a piece of paper and pencil and sit down at a munchkin-size table, with a munchkin-size chair to match, and begin to write what is probably a child's most important letter all year.

Part of National Honor Society's function at South is to volunteer its services and time to the

school system and the Grosse Pointe community. For several years now, NHS has helped Richard kindergarteners write their letters to Santa and then return a letter to them from "Old St. Nick himself."

The beginning journalism classes and some of the beginning keyboarding classes write replies to other young children in the school district.

As the children sit down to write their letters, the new "big" friend begins to ask them questions. Whether they begin their letters with "Dear Santa" or "Dear Santa Claus" or "Dear Santa and Mrs. Claus" doesn't matter for many of the kindergarteners wishing to rush right into their long list of "I wants."

Of course, some of the shy ones need prompting, but not many. Television commercials have helped program their little minds. Most run off a long list quite easily.

The popular toy this year must be a thing called a "Smurf," for the majority of letters included such things as "I want a Smurfette (a female Smurf?)" and "I would like a Dr. Smurf," a "super Smurf," and the "Smurf Hall." But of course, the traditional Barbie dolls, teddy bears, trucks, space ships and play dishes make the list too.

Many children's letters, however, when completed, are not filled with just "I wants." Many said, for example, "I will leave some apples for the reindeer and some cookies and milk for you, Santa."

And others wrote, "I wish Mrs. Claus a happy Christmas. And Rudolph too!"

Children, too, even at a young age, seem to have learned that Christmas is a season not just for taking, but for giving.

Five-year-old Joni Brown said, "I like when I wake up and see the lights on the tree and presents. I'm so glad when Santa eats all my cookies I gave him."

And what does he like best about Christmas?

"I like best when Santa Claus comes," Casey Collins said.

But for some kindergarteners, Santa Claus is not the first thing that comes to mind when asked what is important about Christmas. Stevie Boocher said "Jesus" is most important, but he said he didn't know why.

So classmate Elizabeth Brasseur explained, "Because he was borned on Christmas."

■ **THINK ABOUT YOUR READERS**

To summarize, student journalists have plenty to write about and a receptive audience to write for. But readers can spot quickly a story bulging with bare data, written to fulfill the requirements for a grade or to please a teacher rather than to tell an interesting story or communicate to students on their own level and in their own language.

Often, students believe they are the last considerations in any decision the school bureaucracy cranks out. Student readers don't want and don't deserve to be second-class citizens in their own publication as well. Intelligent editors and reporters will make sure that doesn't happen.

SHOWCASE ■

By **NATALIE MOORE**
Carmel High School, Carmel, IN

SETTING OUT HER UNIFORM before the big game, junior Kate Morrel grabbed the roll of first-aid tape in order to secure her shin guards. Starting on the left side of her right leg, she wound the white tape repeatedly around, grabbed the black permanent marker out of her soccer bag and took a deep breath.

She wrote "Dad" across the top.

Morrel began this ritual last May when her father unexpectedly died of a heart attack in his sleep during Memorial Day weekend. "I was in shock that night. I spent the night at the hospital. It didn't seem real. It was a weird feeling. I didn't cry at all until the next morning. I couldn't really (cry) for a month. People told me I wasn't a very emotional person, but I hadn't thought of that before. It felt like he was just on vacation, and he was going to be coming back. I didn't start missing him until three weeks later," she said.

For Morrel, he was instrumental in both soccer and basketball. "He was my biggest fan and critic. He was always on me, screaming at me to hustle. I didn't know this, but after he died, people told me he was very proud of me. He could be really supportive at times. He thought he knew everything, even though he wasn't exactly the athletic type."

LIVING WITHOUT HIM

Over winter vacation she and her mother visited Florida, just as they had done every previous year. Yet Morrel found this holiday time more difficult to handle. "Father's Day was really hard, but this was the first Christmas without him. The hardest thing for me was seeing my mom so upset. My grandma had died three weeks before he had, so we had two fewer people in Florida who were just there last year. I tried not to think about it and just ignore it."

But blocking out reality works only part of the time, she said. In other instances, confrontation can be helpful. "I usually think about him before each game. It helps me get ready and fired up. He was good at cheering. But I remember one time when he yelled from the sidelines for me to get into the game. I was so mad that yelled back at him to shut up. I got in so much trouble after the game. I was sent to my room. But I miss that."

STARTING TRADITION

When basketball season began this year, Morrel decided to wear an armband with "Dad" imprinted across. Along with the tape in soccer, she is reminded of the good times spent with him. She said these focus her on working hard and hustling.

She has learned to take on his positive qualities. "He had taught me to never give up. His whole personality was all like that. When he was younger, he almost died of rheumatic fever, so his whole life was a blessing. At times my dad acted like a kid. He was my dad, but he was more like a friend. My mom would say she was raising two kids. He was always kidding around. His death has taught me not to worry about the little things. I try to have a fun outlook on life. What's the point of being in a bad mood? People like those aren't fun to be around. He was fun."

When her dad died, Morrel said the thought of quitting either basketball or soccer never crossed her mind. "It was a release for me to play. It was time when I didn't have to think about his death. It gave me something else to concentrate on. He would have been so mad if I had quit. He would have wanted me to keep playing."

MORE LEADS WE SEE WAY TOO OFTEN

WHAT EVERYBODY ALREADY KNOWS LEAD

It's spring, and that means the arrival of golf season. Golf is a game played on a course with nine or 18 holes. The object of the game is to strike the ball with a club and get it to roll into a little cup in the ground. By the way, we have a golf team right here at our school!

Photo by **BRIAN CAHALAN**
Duncanville High School, Duncanville, TX

FOCUS ON REPORTING

While it's easy to dress up publications with squiggles and reverse type that stretches across the page, the success of the publication as a news medium and journalistic product hinges on the power of its reporting.

03

CHAPTER HIGHLIGHTS:

■ Reporting is hard but essential.

■ Stories need a theme and angle.

■ Research means interviewing, listening, watching.

■ A unified story leaves people satisfied.

When desktop publishing burst upon the scene in the mid-1980s, many student journalists embraced the personal computer in hopes that all the fancy typefaces, screens, clip art and other assorted doo-dads would save their publications. Didn't work. Even now, journalists spend too much time contemplating what the computer can do and not enough time thinking about what the reporter should do. Alas, fancy packaging can't rescue weak reporting. In other words, you can't turn a Minnie Mouse newspaper into a Marilyn Monroe simply by packing on a few more layers of eye-shadow.

A few writing teachers can't decide whether the Macintosh is a blessing or a curse. Some believe Macs encourage creativity, boost productivity and enhance the learning process. Others argue that the computer leads to both mechanical and intellectual sloppiness in composition.

Either way, desktop publishing has revolutionized student publications, at least from a production, design and graphics perspective. However, the same cannot be said for its impact on content or copy.

Undoubtedly, the computer has made revision far less painful and, therefore, more likely to happen. Students may now compose, splice and revise with unbelievable ease and then send their copy through a program that catches misspelled words.

But there's a down side. Student publications have shown a tendency to imitate microwave food. Pop them in the machine and seconds later, out comes something totally indistinguishable from everything else.

I'm not ready to place the blame squarely on the computer, but the intellectual level of student publications has slipped — some say "plunged" — in the past 20 years. However, the slippage has nothing to do with censorship or a shortage of funds or curriculum changes. It boils down to this: reporting is becoming a lost art.

Publications are full of essays, reviews, opinion columns, infographics, fiction—even poetry. Some of this writing is quite good, but good writing is not necessarily good reporting, and student newspapers are woefully short of good reporting.

Reporting is hard work. You have to get up out of your chair, interview people you might otherwise never talk to, go places you'd rather not go, spend time watching and listening to something other than the television. Reporting requires a commitment that extends beyond a hit-and-run interview.

Furthermore, reporting is a loopy process that has a before and an after, a beginning, a middle and an end—with each step in the process defining and being defined by the other steps. It requires planning, contemplation and, most importantly, footwork.

Sadly, student publications crank out lots of copy but exhibit little evidence of solid reporting. Whether the computer can be blamed for this, I can't say, other than to note that the use of screens, collages and stretched type has become something of an art form.

■ MORE THAN THE SUM OF ITS PARTS

In this day of instant gratification, students and advisers want a quick and easy critique of their writing. Are we writing about the right topics? Does the lead work? Is it long enough? Are there enough quotes?

Unfortunately, the answers are never cut and dried. Perhaps students are writing about the right topic, but what have they said? How have they approached the topic to make it meaningful and interesting to teenage readers? Why did they emphasize this news question over that one, or, more likely, why did they treat all news questions equally? Whom did they quote and why? Why did they choose to tell the story in this particular tone or voice? Have they told anyone anything not already known, and, if so, have they told it in such a way to make readers want to know more?

Students are rarely prepared to respond to such a rigorous examination of their stories. More often than not, students have taken a "path-of-least-resistance" philosophy in writing so the results are a stillborn product. Stories are approached in the same ways, time after time, with the same sources asked the same questions, resulting in interchangeable, fill-in-the-blank copy.

It need not be so. While it is dangerous to reduce reporting or writing to a series of steps, the following criteria at least force students to see each story as a living organism that is more than the mere sum of its individual parts:

- theme
- research
- angle
- focus
- order
- unity

We will look at them briefly here and in greater depth later in the book.

■ THEME

Too many stories fail because they're not about anything and rarely tell readers anything they didn't know or couldn't figure out on their own. For example: "The purpose of the Future Teachers of America is to teach students about careers in education. This year, students in FTA visited area schools. Members of the club included . . . ."

Chances are, your readers can figure out that the purpose of the Future Teachers of America is to prepare students for careers in education. So, Rule No. 1: Don't tell readers what they already know. Rule No. 2: Don't tell readers what they can figure out on their own. For example, say you're writing a story about a teacher who retires at the end of the year. It's not enough to say that "Dear Old Miss McGillicutty is off to retirement at the end of the year. She has taught English here for 85 years. She was born in Ireland at the turn of the century. She started teaching here in 1920. When asked if she'd miss her job and the kids, she said, "No."

Having read the story, readers know no more about the teacher now than they did before. So the story really isn't about a person: the teacher. It's about a thing: a retirement.

Readers aren't interested in things. They're interested in people and how things affect them. So if you're writing a story about homelessness, focus on a person. "Homelessness" is a thing. Find one teen and allow his or her story to represent a greater truth. I am not suggesting that you can't talk to several, but the story should center on one person. The reader wants to know that person, to care about him or her. Otherwise, the reader doesn't know any of the people in this story, and consequently, can't really care about any individual.

The same is true of longer, in-depth stories—the so-called controversial topics. Too often, the stories read like government research papers. Facts are piled atop facts, data on top of data, most or all of which is pulled from national magazines and Web sites rather than local sources. The result is a collection of details that leaves the reader in a fog.

For example, a staff devotes an issue of its newspaper to covering crime. How did it choose to do so? By crunching numbers. There were "X" number of crimes committed, costing taxpayers "X" amount of dollars. "X" percent were solved. "X" percent of the criminals went to jail, serving "X" amount of time. "X" percent of the offenders were female. "X" percent were males. "X" percent were teens. "X" percent of victims knew the offender. And finally, the staff tacked on safety tips to prevent being victimized and guidelines for using crimestoppers.

I'm not certain for whom the stories were written, but I'm confident they were not written for a teenage reader because no high-school student I've ever met would bother to read it.

Not only must reporters know what they're writing about, but they must also ask, "For whom am I writing?" Once determined, the reporter then asks other questions, including:

■ What does the reader expect and need?

■ How much will the reader already know about this topic, if anything?

■ How can I make certain the story remains timely?

■ How can I localize and personalize the story?

■ Who can I talk to about this?

■ Who must I talk to about this?

The answers to these questions will determine the reporter's strategy for collecting information. For seasoned reporters, the process is an unconscious one, an almost automatic assessment of their readerships. It's called "news judgment." Few

students have been on the job long enough to develop a refined sense of what is and what is not news, so it's useful to rely on news elements such as timeliness, currency, proximity, impact, prominence, oddity, conflict and human interest.

Now, let's go back to the example regarding crime. Find someone who has been the victim of a serious crime. What happened? What was going through your mind at the time? How has it changed you? Ask these questions and you'll come away with a story like this:

SHOWCASE

By **LESLIE COURTNEY**
Arlington Heights High School,
Fort Worth, TX

NATHAN SHAFFER thought about his friends, closed his eyes, and tried to imagine what it would be like to die.

Sept. 8 was just another normal day for Shaffer while he checked out customers in the express lane at Thrift Mart on Camp Bowie until two masked men with guns walked in and told everyone to get on the floor. One of the robbers told the 17-year-old Heights senior to put the money from the register in the bag. Shaffer complied. Then the robber asked, "What's under the register drawer?"

"Nothing," Shaffer said.

"Take the drawer out," the robber said.

Under the drawer, Shaffer found more money. The robber then pointed a gun a foot from Shaffer's face and said, "Now you're going to die."

"I felt like running to someone for security, but no one was there to run to. My only security was the floor."

Nothing in his life had prepared Shaffer for this experience, he said. And the trauma left emotional scars that will probably never heal.

"It makes me wonder every time I go to work whether it will happen again," Shaffer said.

One moment everything is routine—dull. Then seconds later you are fighting just to live.

"I was working in the express lane. I was checking out a customer. I didn't see the two men come in, but I heard them yell, 'Get down on the ground.' At first I thought it was some of my friends," Shaffer said.

Everyone in the store immediately got on the floor, he said. One man jumped over the counter into the office. The other one came over to Shaffer's register.

"When the robber said I was going to die, what mostly went through my head was all the time I spent with my friends," Shaffer said.

"I started to think about what it would be like to be shot. I wondered if I would just die, or if I would see the people around me slowly fade away," Shaffer said.

As suddenly as the robber decided to shoot Shaffer, he changed his mind. He grabbed the money bag and ran out the door, Shaffer said.

The first thing Shaffer did after the robbers left was run to the back of the store and throw up, he said. The trauma left him weak and shaken.

Linda Allen was working in the office when the other robber came into the office with a gun and told her to open the vault.

"This was the first time I had been in a robbery, and I was scared. I thought he was going to shoot me. I thought this was the end," Allen said.

"After the men left, I went into a state of shock. I was told I went to the hospital, but I don't remember any of it—only pieces."

Shaffer was scheduled to get off work at 9 that night, but was told to stay, clean up and keep working until 11, he said.

Mr. Bill Kiker, the manager of Thrift Mart, said he told Shaffer to continue working because one of the workers had been taken to the hospital. Kiker said there were four other workers left to continue running the store, but he felt Shaffer should stay.

He would not comment on the fact that Shaffer was the only worker left who had had a gun pointed at him moments earlier.

Shaffer said one of the most traumatic parts of the evening was having to walk home at 11 p.m.

He said the police had agreed to give him a ride but had left before he was allowed to leave work.

"It was dark and scary. I was so afraid," Shaffer said.

About two weeks later, Shaffer was called by the police to try to identify a suspect in a line up.

"I had never been to a police station until the police called me in for a line up. I was nervous," Shaffer said.

"I was behind a two-way mirror looking at the line up. When I walked in, I turned around and hid my face. It felt like the men in the line up could see right through the mirror," Shaffer said.

"I went up to the glass, and I picked out the man that held me up. When I pointed him out, he was looking right at me through the mirror. When I moved, his eyes followed me," Shaffer said.

After the line up Shaffer went back to school.

"When I got into the classroom, I couldn't concentrate. The line up kept running through my mind," Shaffer said.

Shaffer went to his vice principal and asked to be excused. Shaffer was physically ill the rest of the day, he said. Alfred Arredondo was charged with aggravated robbery after Shaffer identified him as the robber. Arredondo pleaded guilty and was sentenced to 30 years, Detective John McCaskill, with the Fort Worth Police Department, said.

A positive identification has not been made on the other suspect, McCaskill said.

"I am glad they caught a suspect so fast. I didn't really think they would catch anyone with the description I gave the police," Shaffer said. "I didn't want to be like these people who are afraid to press charges because they might be harassed."

He added, "If it ever happened to me again, I can't say what I would do.

"I'd just pray I would live through it."

■ RESEARCH

Too often, students interpret research as plagiarism. They copy information verbatim from already published sources and offer it as their own. How often have you read stories that were based on information—news facts,

TRANSITION TIP...

Use the first sentence of a direct quote as a transition, then begin the direct quote with the second sentence of the quote. For example:

In a story about how the federal government is requiring rural teachers to have as separate college degree for each subject they teach, social studies teacher Adam Dillon said: "I plan to continue teaching here.

Montana thinks I'm a certified teacher, even if the federal government doesn't agree. To tell rural teachers who barely make $25,000 a year that they have to go back to school and get a two or three more degrees is absurd. A lot of us will quit or retire, and it'll throw rural education into a huge mess."

HERE'S HOW TO HANDLE IT:

Social studies teacher Adam Dillon said he plans to continue teaching here. (Transition sentence)

"Montana thinks I'm a certified teacher, even if the federal government doesn't agree," Dillon said. "To tell rural teachers who barely make $25,000 a year that they have to go back to school and get a two or three more degrees is absurd. A lot of us will quit or retire, and it'll throw rural education into a huge mess." (Direct quote)

statistics, direct quotes—taken directly from teen or news magazines or from Web sites?

Granted, understanding the data, the background information, the context is essential. That's the ground floor of the story. Build from there. Suppose the school board announces the district will lose $6 million because voters defeated a bond package. The reporter must research beyond the minutes of the school board meeting to show the impact that such a loss of funds will have. Rather than dwelling on the results of the election or the pronouncements of the board members, the student reporter should ask, "What are the repercussions? What are people saying about it? What specifically would it mean for the school to lose $6 million?"

A lead like this would be much more compelling:

"THEY WANT US TO TEACH driver's ed, but all they give us are these Model Ts to drive," computer teacher Cheryl Ford said.

She was talking about the state of the school's computers, all of which are long outdated. Plans to purchase new computers for the computer classes are on hold now that the $6 million bond failed.

"The state's school funding situation is a mess, and no one knows what will happen there," said Bobby Reynolds, communications specialist. "Locally, we must have some relief if we are expected to do a credible job. People say they value education for their kids, but they sure don't act like it."

For example, several buildings at Andress need to be air-conditioned.

"We were supposed to be moved out of the East Wing so that air conditioning could be put in, but that's now off," history teacher Janet Elkins said. "You can't imagine how hot it gets down here some times. Students simply cannot concentrate in such an environment."

Because you are writing for a student publication, you should focus on the part of the story that will most interest and affect students. Students cannot be expected to understand the full repercussions of a loss of a bond package. But they can understand all too well what it means to sit in hot and sticky classrooms and work on computers that crash every other keystroke.

■ ANGLE

Sure, you could begin the story with a

■ Avoid separating nouns from verbs for no good reason. Don't write, "Joe, a senior who plans to join the circus after graduation, said he can't wait to clean monkey cages."

second-person question. "Do you like sitting in a hot, sticky classroom?" But then, every story could begin this way.

"Have you ever poked your eye out with a stick? Well, Bubba did." But it might get a little stale after a while. So, you want to approach each story from a fresh, original perspective.

Again, this requires reporting: interviewing, watching, listening, developing background, gathering all the pertinent facts. Once you've done this, you have to determine how you want to tell the story, in what voice, in what order, and from whose point of view. It's tough.

Imagine, for a moment, you've been assigned to write a story about the newspaper staff itself. Your tendency might be to write, "The newspaper is busy at work, putting out another issue. Students work after school to produce a publication that they hope will be popular." And so on.

MEMBERS OF THE Bobcat Blab staff are working hard to publish a newspaper that the students will appreciate. Newspaper staff members spend long, hard hours after school interviewing, writing and designing pages.

"We take our work seriously because freedom of the press is important to Americans," said Cynthia Claborn, editor. "We hope you enjoy the paper."

But then, no one would read it.

The choir is busy singing, the swim team is busy swimming, and the Key Club is busy saving the world. It's just another busy year.

Let's not do that. Instead, pinpoint a single situation that symbolizes the nuances, both the joys and the frustrations of being a member of the staff. Tell a story. For example:

THE HEADLINE WOULD not fit.

Try as she may, Eboni Johnson could not manipulate the two-line head into the too-short space. So she exercised her editorial judgment.

"Oh well, we can save this story for the next issue," she reasoned, tossing it into a folder labeled "December." Such is the stuff of high

WHERE TO PUT ALL THOSE FUNNY QUOTE MARKS?

K nowing how to use open and close quotations can be tricky. Basically, use quote marks to:

■ Surround the exact words of a speaker or writer when reported in a story:

"I am not suffering from senioritis," Sleepy said. "I'm bored all the time."

■ Capture dialogue or conversation:

"What's that in your hair?"
"Where?"
"There."
"Oh."
"Well?"
"Looks like a spider."
"Gross."
"Does that mean you don't love me anymore?"
"Yes."
"Bummer."

■ Provide a quote within a quote:

"He gazed into my eyes and asked, 'Does that little twitch bother you much?' I told him it didn't, but his cologne did."

level, journalistic decision-making on the campus newspaper staff.

"Sometimes, you have to go with what fits and what's available," Johnson said. "We'd like to include stories of every club on campus and give everyone as much publicity as they'd like, but it's impossible. So we do the best we can and hope people will enjoy what they read."

Like football players and musicians, the school's journalists spend most of their time preparing for the big game. And that is the day the bi-weekly newspaper hits the halls.

"Most people think the newspaper just pops out

of thin air," Jackson said. "They don't understand the work behind each story, every headline and every photo. Students will criticize in 30 seconds what it takes you two weeks to produce."

Why does this work? Because the reader can relate to this one incident, this anecdote. Your job as a reporter is to find those single incidents, those moments that define reality. Writing about them is not as hard as finding them. It requires that you really know and appreciate what's going on. If not, then you'll always default into cliché.

Here's another example. You're asked to write a piece about the music department for the yearbook. You could crunch some facts and toss in an obligatory quote, but then the story would sound a like this:

THE MARCHING MATADOR Band was named top band in each of the nine contests it entered this year, and the choir and orchestras also had successful years.

"We had a good year, and I'm proud of these kids," music department director Ron Nail said.

Let's go a different direction. First, the story might not be the fact that they won per se. It might be that they've never won before, and this is how they did it, or this is how they feel about having done it. Connect to the deeper emotional story lying beneath the facts. Find the incident that illustrates how pleased the director is with them. You might witness it yourself. Or you might talk to someone who witnessed it.

Here's a more interesting angle:

AS USUAL, the music hall was one of the loudest places on campus, although the noise wasn't made by trumpets or saxophones but by hammers and circular saws. For four days, carpenters worked frantically to build a new trophy case that would hold the more than 50 trophies won by music groups this year.

Standing off to the side, Ron Nail, music department director, placed his hand on drum major Ben Garcia's shoulder and said, "Who would have thought that we'd be doing this today?"

Not many.

In its second year under Nail's direction, the band surpassed all previous accomplishments. And Nail said he wanted to make certain the school's musicians understand how much he appreciates their efforts.

"I wanted to finish the project before the music banquet so we could show off our awards in the new trophy case," Nail said. "It is extraordinary what these kids have achieved this year."

Reporters' success often lies in their ability to identify, isolate and develop verbally and visually a complex situation or problem. Thomas French, a reporter for the *St. Petersburg Times* and author of *South of Heaven*, a book about students at a Central Florida High School, told Iowa student journalists, "We tell ourselves that people don't have the time or the desire to read so we hedge our bets with an archaic writing formula (the inverted pyramid) that tells the story backwards and sabotages any possible pleasures once associated with reading."

French called for a fresh, unabashed writing style that grabs readers and coaxes them to continue past the headline, and that will mean abandoning many of the old rules associated with journalistic writing.

"What kills me is that readers hate these stupid rules even more than I do," he said. "They want something different and something more. They're dying for it. And if we give it to them, they will read and read and read. All of them, even the ones who supposedly don't even know how to read."

He added, "They want to be challenged, seduced, cajoled, tickled, slapped, even bullied into picking up our paper. They are just waiting for us to wake up and make the first move."

■ FOCUS

Chances are, you will gather more information than you can or an editor will use. Get used to it. Reporters typically collect two or three times more information than they'll

MORE LEADS WE SEE WAY TOO OFTEN

WEBSTER LEADS
Avoid leading with dictionary definitions such as "Webster defines maniac as…" They are a sure sign that the writer has made no effort to use an interesting lead.

CHATTY LEADS
More often than not, these result in editorializing. For example:

"One of the fastest growing as well as friendliest clubs in school is the Young Historians Club."

It is not the job of the reporter to assign labels (good or bad) to organizations or persons. Another example:

There is a wonderful and much needed new organization here at school. It's SAVE (Students Against Violating the Earth). Just what is SAVE, you ask? Well, it's a youth organization whose purpose is to get students involved in improving the environment.

WRITING TIP

Avoid semicolons. Use periods instead. Don't write, "Jerry proposed to Sabrina; she declined."

Write, "Jerry proposed to Sabrina. She declined."

Exception: when you need to seperate phrases containing commas, statements of contrast and statements too closely related.

ever use. Even after answering who, what, when, where, why and how, you'll likely have a lot of other notes.

Thus, it becomes a matter of deciding which direct quotes, anecdotes, facts, examples, illustrations and what-not to use.

How do you choose? Ask yourself, "What is this story about?" Any information that does not advance the theme should be torpedoed. Say you're writing a personality profile on a new teacher, and you learn that he's back in the classroom for the first time in two years after surviving a bad car accident. Chances are, you'll focus the story on the accident and recovery. Therefore, it probably won't advance the theme of the story to mention that he raises hamsters and earned his associate of arts degree from a junior college in Kansas.

Or, if your story deals with the success of the senior play which survived a series of mishaps, including the destruction of its set to a freak termite attack, maintaining a clear focus means the reporter will not use the following quote from the play's director:

"I would like to thank each member of the troupe for all their hard work and Mr. Burns for letting us use his lumber and Mayor Parks for reserving the city library auditorium for our rehearsals and Mary Jo for being an absolute darling," said Dudley-Lawrence Montadale. "If I have forgotten to thank anyone, I apologize, but I think I thanked everyone who deserved to be thanked, I think. And now, farewell dear fans, I'm off to London!"

Include only the information that drives the story's theme.

■ ORDER

Doesn't really matter what order a story is told, so long as it's told in a logical order. You ever see that movie, "Titanic"? It basically started at the end, then jumped back 100 years, then jumped forward 100 years, then back, and then finally ended in heaven with Leonardo hooking back up with the old woman who turned young all over. It won a slew of Oscars, earned a boatload of money and never lost me once. Even though it

wasn't told in straight chronological order, it made sense.

Ditto for your stories. Whether you choose to start at the beginning, middle or end, tell the story in a logical order.

Consider the following approach, in which the reporter begins in the present, then works her way through the story, and concludes again in the present. Although the action takes place over a fairly long period of time, the reader never loses track of the action.

SHOWCASE

By **LISA KASBERG**
Temple HS, Temple, TX

EACH MORNING SHE looks to her sister's empty bed. Stuffed bears and other animals are piled by the headboard.

It has been two months since she's last seen Angelica, her 11-year-old sister.

Laura often walks down Houston Street where her sister was reported being last seen, and wonders about what happened there. During these times she recalls the day her family realized Angelica was missing.

Mornings are one of the worst parts of the day for senior Laura Gandara remembers all the mornings her sister Angelica was by her side preparing for school. Angelica failed to return home to her North Temple residence July 14 after visiting her grandmother.

Police believe Angelica was kidnapped.

"It was Sunday. I had gotten back from church at 4 p.m.," Gandara said. "My parents left, and I thought she was going with them because she left about the same time. Around 7, my parents came back."

"When I got home at 8, my mom was wondering where she was. By that time my mom had already called my grandmother, friends and relatives. She was hoping she would be with me.

"She made it to my grandmother's house and left around 5," she added. "She said she was going home, but she never made it home."

"We called the police, and everyone went

QUESTIONS TO ANSWER

- What is the theme of your story? Write it in a single sentence.
- Why did you choose this angle?
- Who are your primary sources?
- Why did you select them? Why should I care about them?
- Who are your secondary sources?
- Why did you select them?
- What is your nutgraph?
- Are all news questions answered?
- Does the story flow? Is information provided logically and orderly?
- Do a variety of sentence lengths provide pace?

- Have you eliminated all unnecessary words, particularly passive verbs?
- Is all information accurate?
- Are spelling, stylebook rules, grammar correct?
- Does the tone match the content?
- Have you provided description, dialogue, anecdote and/or drama?
- Does the ending provide reader satisfaction and/or resolution?
- Have you submitted information for your sidebar infographic or secondary story?
- If you hadn't written this story, would it interest you enough to read it?

MORE RULES ABOUT USING QUOTES!

- Avoid quote fragments or partial quotes. Better to use the complete quote.

- Never pull a quote out of context. Ever noticed how movie ads showcase words that may have been taken out of context? For example: "The movie is a monumental flop." The ad will herald, "Monumental!"

- Don't quote facts. Use quotes to provide opinion or explanation about the fact.

WEAK: "The meeting will be at 7 P.M.," John said. "It should be a zoo."
BETTER: The meeting will be at 7 P.M. "It will be a zoo," John said.

- The period and the comma always go within the quotation marks.

---

searching in parks, alleys and streets. We looked all night, and nobody slept," Gandara said, "We didn't sleep for the first three days. Later, some slept outside waiting for her."

The Gandara family reported to the police that Sunday, but a search was not made until Tuesday.

"I talked to Sergeant Flippo and Officer Rubik, and they apologized and said that the police force should have started right away because a child was involved," Gandara said.

Although Gandara said she realizes everything is being done by the Texas Rangers, she seeks the day when a national organization would be searching. "I wish that there were an organization, a team that would go around the U.S. searching and looking for clues. Right now they're just doing it in this area.

"One thing about the first day of school that made it real hard was that we would always be in a hurry to get ready," Laura said and paused, reflecting on past years.

"I was thinking today she would have started to Lamar," Laura said. "She was excited about starting middle school where she would be able to change classes and have different teachers. I think she would have liked it."

Gandara said her decision to return for her senior year was hard. "For a while I was thinking about whether to go back to school," she said. "I wanted to, but I didn't know how I would feel."

"I only go three periods. I stay home most of the time in case someone calls, like Missing Children, Child Find or even Angelica."

Gandara said she feels the need to remain strong for her family since both parents have great difficulty in speaking English.

"I have to be stronger because I have to talk to the news press and the police, but I don't mind because the main thing is letting people know. If they know, they'll keep interested," Gandara said.

Keeping people interested is just what Gandara intends to do. With the help of local merchants and the community, a $5,000 reward has been donated for anyone with information leading to the location of her sister.

"People have been sponsoring dances and ways to raise money," she said. "A lot of out-of-towners have come by and gotten posters to go out of state." Teenagers always wonder how they could help and believe that they can't in any way, but high school students have cars and we could give them posters. If they travel, maybe others would see and remember."

One of the biggest aids to Gandara and her family this past summer was her teachers.

"During the summer they'd call and really encourage me to not give up hope. I've received cards from some. They all said if I needed to talk, I could count on them," Gandara said.

Although teachers have been a big help, she often feels uneasy at school.

"When I go to school, I feel like people are afraid to ask anything. I don't mind if they ask questions. It seems like everyone has to be so cautious."

The Gandaras look toward their religious beliefs for strength. "I believe God is protecting her wherever she is," Gandara said. The family's Catholic faith is evident because of the many religious pictures and crosses that adorn the walls of the Gandara living room.

Laura's and Angelica's room remains the same as before. The stuffed bears and other animals piled by the headboard will be left intact in hopes of Angelica's return.

■ UNITY

Whether news or feature, an article is unified when all the individual elements—theme, angle, focus and the rest—work together to tell a concise, complete and coherent story. The lead pulls the reader into the story and introduces the major characters, setting, plot and narrative. The body of the story answers all news and reader questions. The ending brings the story full circle and leaves the reader in a state of utter bliss. At least, that's the idea.

This cool mini-feature profile is a perfect example:

SHOWCASE ■

By **LORENA MAILI**
Cypress Falls High School

NINETEEN-YEAR-OLD Ryan Fore wears a bracelet made of animal-bone skulls on his left wrist. He has holes in his pants that he's tried to sew up with plaid fabric. His tan arms show through his cutoff jean jacket decorated with silver pyramids and spikes over a black Harley-Davidson Motorcycles sleeveless tee. He likes going to concerts, ones where the punk music is raw and full of energy. He looks like the kind of kid who'd eat a spider, but in fact, he's scared of them. His favorite cartoon is the Powerpuff Girls.

"I love Cartoon Network," Fore said. "I'm not into cartoons religiously, but whenever they're on I'll sit down and watch them."

He'd like to be cartoonist himself, maybe a comic book artist. His drawings resemble the Asian-inspired Anime art that's so prevalent in comic books these days.

"I like a lot of Japanese style art, and that's the kind of comics I want to draw," Fore said.

He graduated two years ago from Tomball High, but emphasized, "I'm not a hick. All people think of when they hear Tomball is cowboys and people who like country music and wear the hats."

After graduation, Fore started working with his father at Southwestern Bell, a job he's kept since.

"Basically I dig holes," Fore said. "When people cut through their cable in their back yard, and it cuts off the electricity to all the other houses, we go out there and fix it."

Besides spiders, Fore said he's afraid of failure.

"Right now I'm not pursuing art to my fullest," Fore said. "I'm afraid that if I don't, all the talent I have will waste away."

■ IN SUMMARY

While it's easy to dress up publications with squiggles and gray squares, with reverse type that stretches or rolls across the page, the success of the publication as a news medium and an educational tool hinges on the power of its reporting. The computer can do marvelous things. But it never has been, nor will it ever be, a substitute for a reporter with a pencil, a pad and a healthy dose of skepticism and curiosity.

COMPARE & CONTRAST

FOCUS ON THE EVENT

On Sunday, Monday June 6, Americans across the nation celebrated the 60th anniversary of D-Day, the Allied invasion of France that led to the defeat of Adolf Hitler's Nazi Germany during World War II.

Hundreds of veterans of the Allied forces who defeated Nazi Germany have invaded Normandy again to gaze upon the beaches they stormed, walk the sunken roads they fought over, mourn at the military cemeteries, but most of all, celebrate their triumph.

Among those who traveled to France to pay homage in Europe was President George W. Bush and former principal Douglas Starks, who was accompanied by his wife, Helen, and their sons, David and Robert.

They arrived on June 2 in London where they met with members of the U. S. 1st Infantry Division, which was made famous by the movie "The Big Red One." Then, the Starks flew to Paris on June 4 in order to be in France for the June 6 ceremonies.

"It brought back a lot of memories," Mr. Starks said. "And it was wonderful to see so many old friends."

After the war, Starks returned to Alabama to finish his college work. He earned a degree in history and became a teacher and a football coach. He was head football coach here from 1955-1962 and principal from 1963-1976. He retired in 1976. His youngest son, David, is an assistant principal at the middle school.

FOCUS ON A PERSON

We saw the dawn before we landed. At first, everything seemed to be going pretty well: we had good smoke and fog cover."

That's how former principal Douglas Starks remembers the beginning of D-Day, the Allied invasion that led to the defeat of Nazi Germany during World War II.

It's far from how he remembers the rest of that day.

"As soon as we hit the beach, we came under heavy fire from a battle-hardened field division—the German 352nd Division," said Starks, who joined the dwindling number of of D-Day veterans traveled to Normandy for the 60th anniversary of the historic invasion.

"We were in a very bad position," said Starks, a former teacher, coach and principal here. "We were pinned down on the beach with a German division in front of us and the ocean behind us. We had nowhere to hide. There were people falling all around us. You'd go into the water, but the water was washing bodies in and out. Bodies, heads, flesh, intestines; that's what Omaha Beach was."

Starks said it was his duty and honor to return to Normandy where so many of his friends died.

"I wanted my sons to experience this so that they can tell their children about it," he said. "I didn't do this because I wanted them to think that I am a hero. I wasn't then and I'm not now. I was in the U. S. infantry, and we had a job. I was just doing my job."

QUOTE LEADS

A quote lead begins with a direct quote. It is a lazy way out.

Intersperse quotes throughout your news briefs, but make certain the quotes add substantially to the story. In too many cases, the quote either repeats other information or echoes the obvious. For example: The art teacher is planning a trip to France. Too often, the quote will read, "I'm really looking forward to it," she said.

Big deal. Avoid quotes that provide facts. The quote should state an opinion about facts. Thus, a better quote would be:

"Although they have a reputation as terrible hosts, I've always found the French to be warm, friendly and engaging. And Paris is my favorite city in the world."

Where is the REAL story?

FRENCH CLUB

The French Club recently elected their officers for this school year. They are Jennifer O'Neill, president; James Borders, vice president; Shelly Bryant, secretary; Stephanie Bonita, treasurer; and Tawanna Kemp, parliamentarian.

The club had participated in a toy drive with the speech department for the Salvation Army. Toys were collected and delivered to the Salvation Army headquarters, where they were distributed to needy families.

Take a photo of a club member handing a toy to a 4-year-old. A story that led with a scene recreation of the toy give-away and captured the emotion of the moment would have debunked the myth of the apathetic teen-ager.

FUTURE HOMEMAKERS

During the holiday season, FHA is reaching out to help local needy people by collecting food and toys. Many of the FHA students are volunteering at the Salvation Army by separating toys into groups for different ages. Others are delivering food to needy families. If you would like to contribute in any way, please contact the Salvation Army or talk to a FHA student.

Again, assign a photo of students collecting food for needy families. Talk to the students and, if possible, to the families receiving help. What are their thoughts on this? Be sure to treat them with dignity.

POLITICAL AWARENESS CLUB

The PAC would like to wish everyone a Merry Christmas. If you drink over the holidays and need a designated driver, you can call a PAC member who will arrange for two students to drive you home. For more information, talk to Mr. Johnson, who started the "Dial-A-Ride" program for high school students two years ago.

Does Mr. Johnson have a first name? Talk to him. Why did he start this program? Talk to students who performed this service last year. What were their experiences? Can you recreate a scene?

NATIONAL HONOR SOCIETY

The National Honor Society met Tuesday, Dec. 5 to discuss several topics. Tutoring assignments were given to those who volunteered. NHS members are tutoring junior-high students as part of an effort to lower the school's drop-out rate.

Also, NHS chose to produce and perform a skit for the Students Against Destructive Decisions campaign, held Dec. 11-15.

Focus the story on one student who is tutoring an at-risk junior high student. Tell their story. Describe a scene that includes dialogue. Show the special relationship between the two young men, but don't editorialize.

SPANISH CLUB

The Spanish Club met Nov. 22 and 29. At both meetings, trips and fundraisers were discussed. Nov. 21, the Spanish Club officers were on the morning show, "High School Happenings," and they talked about the club and what it has been doing this year.

The first trip that the Spanish Club has taken was to Casa Bonita on Nov. 30. Other trips for the club have not been decided and fund-raising has not been decided either, but for Christmas, Spanish Club has a few projects. They have planned to make food baskets for the families in town. They are also planning on helping the Salvation Army by ringing bells and helping sort clothes and toys for the bags given to needy families.

FUTURE BUSINESS LEADERS

Future Business Leaders of America (FBLA) have been busy this year volunteering. FBLA President Missy Jones helps handicapped children at the "A-Leg-Up" riding center. FBLA supported this organization by donating $100. FBLA also participates in "Project Ask," a foundation for the study of children with cancer and is planning a trip to the Ronald McDonald House in Memphis over the holidays.

DISTRIBUTIVE EDUCATION

Distributive Education Clubs of America (DECA) students participated in a Bowl-A-Thon on Dec. 9. The purpose of the project was to raise money for the Big Brothers/Big Sisters program. Students recruited sponsors on an individual basis to pledge money per pin. DECA raised $750 through its efforts. The funds will help support volunteer recruitment efforts to screen adult volunteers who will work with children and to provide professional staff monitor matches in the community. DECA sponsor Jim Dancey is the local chairman for Big Brothers/Big Sisters.

Because so many clubs are involved in the "High School Happenings," a feature story on the show might be appropriate. Don't dwell on what a club is not doing. Instead, concentrate on what its members are doing. For example: focus on the satisfaction of making food baskets or on the courage needed to stand outside department stores and ring door bells.

If ever a student deserved to be the subject of a feature story, Missy Jones does. What stories does she have to tell? Have her describe relationships she's formed with these children. And get a photo of Missy assisting a child.

Again, take a human interest photo of a senior Big Brother and his little brother at the bowling alley. Isolate one special relationship, and show how this project helps needy children. Dialogue and scene development are essential to the writing of a story to do justice to such a dramatic issue.

LOOK FOR THE STORY BEHIND THE FACTS.

Staffs often complain, "There's nothing going on." But when I thumb through their papers, I find one great story idea after another. The stories are out there if you know where to look for them. Here are a few tips:

■ Don't worry about the event. Find out how it happened and what are its effects.

■ Does the event or issue affect a specific group of people? If so, how and why?

■ Is the event or issue a part of a trend. If so, anticipate the next move.

■ Who is most affected by this event or issue? Find the people who are closest to the story and show how news affects them.

Photo by **DAVID SPRINGER**
Westlake High School, Austin, TX

TELL READERS A GOOD STORY

To sell anything in America, even an idea, it helps to have a human face to make it real. The problem with too many high school students is they're so busy looking for facts they cannot find a story.

Interviewed in *Rolling Stone* magazine, Don Hewitt, executive producer of CBS's "60 Minutes," said, "A producer came to me one day and said, 'Why don't we do a story about acid rain?' I said, 'Acid rain isn't a story. It's a subject. Tell me a story about somebody whose life was ruined by acid rain, or about a community trying to do something about acid rain, but don't tell me about acid rain.'"

Hewitt said the number one rule of "60 Minutes" is they don't cover issues. They cover stories. The second rule is every story must feature a captivating central character or two, and he or she must be able to speak clearly.

He added that most "60 Minutes" stories rely on the classic dramatic structure of conflict, struggle, resolution. "Little morality plays," he called them.

This is precisely the formula high school journalists must adopt to produce lively, compelling copy.

Let's begin with this premise: We're not collecting data. We want to tell stories.

How is this accomplished? By running every story idea through an obstacle course that will produce the most interesting and informative coverage. It begins when an editor or reporter asks the fundamental question, "What is this story really about?"

Every story has a theme. The theme is the essential truth of the story from which all information sprouts. Reduce it to a single sentence. This story is about what? It's about a senior football player whose father was an All-America player at the same school 25 years earlier, and the pressure he feels to achieve as much as his dad. It's about a senior cheerleader who tore up her knee during summer cheerleader camp and now has to watch from the bench. It's about a sophomore girl who wants to be a super model. It's about the anguish the debate team felt when their coach resigned in order to accept a job in private industry.

The story has to be about something *in particular*. It is not a story about football, or super models, or cheerleading or debate.

Now, get rid of anything that fails to advance the theme.

Remember: the worst four-letter word in journalism is data. We are not interested in collecting data. We want to tell a story. So let's look at the following story possibility. The school's sociology class is involved in an outreach program for elderly citizens. Your job is to write an article about this program.

QUICK TIP

Look for needless repetition. Delete the unnecessary words in the following sentence:

On Easter Sunday, the widow woman definitely decided to give a canary bird as a free gift to the pretty young debutante, her close personal friend.

The novice reporter will interview the sociology teacher and perhaps one or two students. With this data collected, he or she will write a story that sounds something like this.

A NEW PROGRAM has been started by sociology students at the school. The program is called "Telephone Buddies," and its purpose is to contact and reassure elderly citizens.

"I am proud to take part in the program because it is serving a real need in the community," senior Jeff Smith said.

While this story may satisfy all the demands of textbook journalism, it isn't going to win many readers. Given that the story ultimately deals with the fears and loneliness of elderly citizens, it is pitifully bare of heart and soul.

Compare it to the story on the following page:

ONE RING. Then another and five more after that. Finally . . . .

"Hello," answers the wheezy and somewhat perplexed voice of the 86-year-old widow, who obviously isn't accustomed to receiving many telephone calls.

"Mrs. Worsham," a young woman chirps. "It's me, Kyndra Jones. How are you doing today?"

"Well, not so good, I'm afraid . . . ."

And so the conversation begins. For the next 20 minutes, while her friends and thousands of other teenagers roam the malls, watch television or just hang out, Karen discusses arthritis, poor eyesight and, most importantly, loneliness with one of society's forgotten souls.

"It's tough," Kyndra admits. "Most of these people don't keep up with current events. All they really have to talk about is their physical pain, their families and their loneliness. I hate to admit it, but sometimes I'm bored to death."

But not bored enough to abandon her six-weeks sociology project, volunteering for Telephone Buddies, a program designed to contact and reassure elderly citizens.

▪ TELL A STORY IN HUMAN TERMS

The first story attempts only to transact data. The second attempts to tell a story in human terms. The theme of the story is "Students are trying to help lonely people," and the story places a name and a face with that loneliness.

In the next example, the reporter collects a few sketchy facts but in no way captures the essence of the event.

WOW! LOOK at the presents! Do you know what it's like to see 22 kids with a big Christmas twinkle in their eyes?

Fifty-five National Honor Society members discovered this thrill when they traveled to the Stepping Stone Daycare Center for their yearly Christmas visit. Club members furnished presents and refreshments for 3-, 4- and 5-year-olds. Santa was one of the main attractions for the kids. This year's jolly old man was portrayed by senior Randy Jones. The club left Wednesday morning for their short sojourn to Birmingham and returned that afternoon.

Everyone had a great time!

Where's the humanity? The joy? The humor? What facts, emotion, image should the reader retain after finishing the story?

In the case of the National Honor Society's Christmas visit, it is not enough to simply state what happened. To succeed, the story must use anecdotes and narrative to show the consequences of members' actions. For example:

SHY AT FIRST, the 4-year-old tottered from behind the protective shield of his teacher's khaki trousers, past the baby dolls, the record players and the musical toys to the lime-green stuffed alligator. A quick tug and flash later, again behind the khaki trousers, he was hugging his new friend.

Meanwhile, two brothers—a 4-year-old and a 3-year-old—fought over Barney. The tussle ceased when the 4-year-old ripped off Barney's head. Horrified and covered with stuffing, the younger brother began a slow wail that continued even after his older brother had, in an attempt to pacify him, tossed him the headless purple dinosaur.

And Santa—in the guise of senior Randy Jones—wasn't getting away without a few minor bruises as well. A persistent 3-year-old insisted on pulling St. Nick's beard, which though a powdered white imitation, was glued tightly to his face.

"I thought the kid was going to pull my lips off," Santa admitted.

Through it all, officials at the Stepping Stone Daycare Center called the day a rousing success, even if Santa and some 3-year-olds may beg to differ.

■ ANY STORY CAN BE INTERESTING

See the difference? Even a story as predictable as a club visit to a day care center can be made entertaining and informative. In fact, you can make any story interesting. If it involves people, you can make it interesting.

In teaching workshops, I often ask, "How many of you are interested in working conditions in meatpacking houses?"

Few raise their hands.

"How many of you think you could be interested in such a topic?"

Again, only a couple of hands appear.

Then, I read them the lead of this story by William Glaberson of *The New York Times*. Whereas business reporting is sometimes stuffy and full of jargon, this is dramatic and compelling.

SIOUX FALLS, S.D.—Mary Tvedt had learned to live with the dirt and the danger of a meatpacking house. So she did not think much of it when the huge blade jammed in the bacon slicer where she was working. She turned off the power, opened the machine and began clearing out chunks of bacon the way she had a hundred times before in her years at John Morrell & Company's plant here.

After a minute or two, a co-worker thought the cleaning was finished. From where he was standing he could not see that Mary Tvedt was still working. Morrell had not supplied the most rudimentary of safety devices, a lock to keep the power supply off. He hit the switch. The four fingers of Mary Tvedt's right hand came off in one swift turn of the big blade.

It is 81 years since Upton Sinclair's *The Jungle* described the brutal working conditions of the Chicago slaughterhouses. But here in Sioux Falls —and in places like it throughout the Midwest— history is quietly repeating itself.

Modern machinery has changed the look and the sound of a packing house. But the meatpacking industry, which employs about 100,000 people, remains today the most hazardous industry in America. Meatpackers work in extreme heat or refrigerated cold, often standing shoulder to shoulder, wielding honed knives and power saws. Grease and blood make the floors and the tools slippery. Occasionally, an overpowering stench from open bladders and stomachs fills the air.

The workers cut themselves. They cut each other. They wear out their insides doing repetitive-motion jobs. They are sliced and crushed by machines that were not even imagined when Sinclair published his book in 1906.

At one end of the plant are the yards teeming with livestock. At the other, boxed and processed meats emerge ready for market. In between, a chain carries hanging carcasses past workers who dismember the meat with a series of cuts, each person performing the same motion over and over, sometimes a thousand times an hour, tens of thousands of times a week.

A meatpacking house has always been a grisly place to work. But after years of improvements, life in the packing house has been getting worse again. Several forces have combined to make life tougher for meatpackers: weaker health and safety regulation, automation, intense competition in the industry and unions weakened by a fight for survival.

After her accident, Mary Tvedt went home, by way of the Mayo Clinic, to adapt to life with her mangled hand. The Occupational Safety and

THE DIFFERENCE BETWEEN FACTS AND TRUTH

Mary Bancroft, the famed Harvard-trained lawyer, novelist and World War II spy, said, "Facts are not the truth, but only indicate where the truth may lie."

The same is true of facts and news. Facts are not news, but may indicate where the news may be hiding.

❝ A good opener will give you momentum, a sense of confidence, and an extra incentive to make the remaining paragraphs worthy of the first. A good opener invariably has a good thesis— bold, interesting, clearly focused.❞

— John R. Trimble
Writing With Style

WHICH STORY WOULD YOU RATHER READ?

Many North Lake students are looking forward to seeing their peers at Patriot Stadium once again for the Rockfest '03, which will be held May 12.

In its ninth year, Rockfest is a service project that helps raise money for a number of clubs, including Beta Club and Key Club.

This year, 23 area bands have agreed to play, said Eileen Schmidt, Beta Club president and coordinator of the event.

"We held tryouts, and all bands were required to submit a demo tape," she said. "A lot of local bands said they would but didn't. Still, I think it's going to be the best ever."

Among the featured bands will be the Caskets, the Dirge Monkeys and North Lake's own Reckless Drivers.

The show will begin at 4 P.M. and last until midnight. Admission to Rockfest will be $4 in advance and $5 at the door. Tickets are available from any Beta Club member.

"I hope everyone comes," Schmidt said.

The rehearsals at Trey Parker's house have been long and hard. Lead singer of the Reckless Drivers, Trey said he wants to make certain the group is ready for next month's Rockfest '03.

ROCKFEST '03
May 12
4 p.m.-midnight
Patriot Stadium
Tickets: $5

"We're trying to get as much exposure as possible, and doing well here would be a big boom for us," Parker said. "We're putting in a lot of overtime. I've neglected my studies lately, but this means a lot to us."

Twenty three bands from throughout the area will perform, with proceeds benefiting school service clubs. But the reason most bands participate has less to do with charity than with promotion.

"All the musicians are young and hungry, and fans can expect one wild afternoon," Parker said. "I know we're going to put on one heck of a show."

Health Administration cited Morrell because it had not supplied a lock to keep the power off.

Sure, William Glaberson works for *The New York Times*. You don't. But you can take the same approach.

■ GETTING STARTED

Glaberson combines scene re-creation, interpretation, several literary devices and a little bit of outrage to tell a compelling story and also present a moral argument of people wronged by a negligent, greedy and cruel system.

Selecting a theme is a "chicken or egg" proposition. That's is, which comes first: do journalists report and then determine the theme? Or do they collect information to satisfy the needs of a preconceived theme?

Most likely, neither and both. In the case of the meatpackers, the reporter probably received information about the working conditions in the plant and then went

searching for a face and a story.

While it may sound insidious to say that a reporter left the office in pursuit of a story with preconceived notions about what to write, in reality this occurs almost without fail. Reporters know, in general, what happened, and they seek names and faces to show the consequences of the action.

Of course, the nature of news for a high school publication is far different than it is for a daily metropolitan. But the approach in covering the news need not be radically different. Reporters for both must balance the needs of the audience versus the constraints of their publishing realities.

When did the event occur? Who will know about it? How much do they know? How can we capture the most compelling, provocative elements of the story?

Let's face it, you're probably not investigating worker conditions in meatpacking houses. You're more likely to cover club projects, class activities, personalities, teen issues and traditional school events. Fine. But you can do better than this:

(Name) received (honor) last Monday. When asked what the honor means to him/her, he/she said, "This is an honor that I will always cherish. I was thrilled to receive this award, and I promise to uphold its honor. I'm so thrilled, I just can't stand it."

(Name) is a member of (list clubs). He/she received the (list other honors won).

This is a recipe for success if you're trying to peddle journalism like microwave popcorn. That is "hot and ready to go in 90 seconds or less. Tastes like whatever you put on it, and won't fill you up."

So if your goal is to make certain readers can skim through the paper, search for a few familiar names and faces and be finished with it in five minutes or less, then there's no need to read on.

■ USE LITERARY DEVICES

So which do you think your typical student would rather read: a Stephen King short story or a typical newspaper article? As a journalism student, you might respond, "The news article." But we're talking about the typical student. My guess: the short story. Why? Because they know enough about Stephen King to predict that he's going to give them a good ride.

Let's do that too. Give your readers a good ride. Except for briefs and late-breaking news, move away from the inverted pyramid. Stress the more human elements of the story. In addition to thinking about stories in terms of who, what, when, where, why and how, consider dramatic devices: character, setting, plot, conflict, dialogue, order, anticipation, climax and resolution.

Consider each:

■ **DRAMA**—High school is four years of high drama. Sure, some of it is melodrama. But no doubt, young people 14-18 go through amazing emotional transformations, confront all sorts of

conflicts. Encounter life and death stuggles against evil enemies every day. For example, figuring out which outfit to wear to the first day of class. And it gets worse from there.

■ **CHARACTER**—Schools are full of characters. Look around your classroom. Who are all these people? Each person has a unique character, something that makes him or her special. The school has student council elections every year. This isn't news. That someone wins the student council election isn't news. That this particular person — this character — won is news. But you have to reveal the character. Have you seen the movie *Election*? This isn't the story of an election. It's the story of a girl's unbridled ambition to achieve, and all the bodies left in her wake.

Here's another example: the school's annual blood drive. Rather than writing about a "thing" (the blood drive), frame the story in terms of a specific person for whom the success or failure of the blood drive is crucial. Perhaps you have a student in your school who is a hemophiliac. Perhaps a student was involved in a horrific automobile accident and required mass quantities of blood to survive. Perhaps a tenacious student has taken it upon herself to make this the most successful blood drive ever.

Build your story around a real person and fully develop that person's character. Give the readers a reason to cheer for or against the people embroiled in the drama.

■ **CONFLICT**—Conflict is the struggle between opposing forces. Sometimes, this conflict is internal. For example, you have a student who is struggling against drug abuse or an eating disorder. The choice is to submit to the urge or to overcome it.

Sometimes, the conflict exists between human beings and nature. For example, the baseball team has been unable to practice because of two weeks of continuous rain. How has the team coped?

The conflict may exist between man and powerful outside forces. For example, a

PEOPLE LOVE TO HATE THE MEDIA

Criticizing the media is a great American pastime. Because your publication is part of the media, it may be a target of criticism. What are your students saying about the newspaper? Is it:

■ Too soft? Does the staff avoid complex or controversial topics?

■ Too hard? Does the staff report every story as though the survival of civilization rested in the balance? Does the staff ever look for the humor and joy in life? It should.

■ Published too infrequently? It is published every major holiday?

■ Published too frequently? Some staffs lose perspective, and the deadline becomes the end-all.

teacher may want to teach curriculum that the school board or state education agency forbids. In Texas, a teacher was suspended for introducing creationism into her science class. In another state, a teacher was fired for giving too many students failing grades. The conflict in both cases was between the individual and the powers that be.

Even in an article about Quiz Bowl, the story could be framed in terms of the struggle between student and test. Each spring, I direct a current issues and events contest, and these kids are serious. They read newspapers and magazines, surf Web sites, subscribe to multiple news services and do whatever is necessary to give themselves an edge.

On top of that, they're interesting people. One group, from a tiny school in East Texas, has affiliated itself with the *World Weekly News* — so much so that the WWN (it's the tabloid newspaper that regularly features headlines such as "A Space Alien ate my Elvis clone.) ran a story on the kids. It's probably the only truthful article the paper has ever run.

■ **DIALOGUE**—Dialogue is a conversation between characters. What people say to one another is far more interesting than what they say to reporters. It is one thing to have a student tell a reporter about helping save the life of a heart attack victim. It is quite another thing to use dialogue to create the scene so that readers feel as though they are witnessing the event for themselves.

What if the reporter is not there to hear the dialogue?

If you interview the subjects in depth, if you ask the subjects "What did you say" and "What did he respond," then you can re-create the scene. Professionals do this regularly, but again, it requires saturation interviewing.

■ **ORDER**—How should you tell a story? Should you begin at the end and work your way back through? Start in the middle and then wrap back around? Or, as the White Rabbit in *Alice in Wonderland* might suggest, should you start at the beginning and go 'til you come to the end, and then stop?

A tip: before beginning to write, make an outline of the plot of the story. What are you trying to say and to whom? What was the setting? Who are the characters? What event incited the conflict? What dialogue exists? What is the climax of the story? What is the resolution?

Then ask yourself, if this were a movie, how would the director tell the story? Think of all the movies you've seen over the years. In what order were the stories told? Can you pattern your story after one of them?

Does the inverted pyramid work best? Does the story work best if you told it in straight chronological order?

Maybe a combination of the two—the diamond—would work even better. In the diamond, the writer starts in the present or immediate present, introduces the drama of the story, jumps to the distant past and moves to the recent past, and finishes with an important and specific ending.

Regardless of the story shape, the writer must have a specific plan in mind before applying pencil to paper or fingers to keys.

■ **ANTICIPATION**— This is also known as foreshadowing where the reporter plants the story's seeds and forces readers to guess what comes next. For example, "In three years as a half-miler, Jerry Hughes had never known defeat."

With just that sentence, you know that Jerry Hughes finally lost.

By writing in chronological order, you can show the unusual twists and turns in the story. One popular writing model introduces a situation and then takes the reader in chronological order through to the resolution and conclusion of the story.

One of my favorite leads of all time is, "She never knew she had it."

With these six small words, the reporter hooked readers and forced them to continue through the story, which dealt with a young woman with spinal bifida.

■ **CLIMAX**—The climax is the high point

FOCUS ON THE INDIVIDUAL, NOT THE MASSES

THEME:

The team didn't do as well as members expected.

Don't lead with "Given that three starters returned from a 16-8 team, the Lady Mavs did not do as well as expected."

Instead, determine why the season was not as successful as members had expected it to be, and then lead with an example that shows rather than tells. For example:

WHY?

- Injuries
- Bad luck
- Attitude
- Disorganization

DESCRIPTIVE EXAMPLE

With 19 seconds left against Parkview, Maverick girls basketball coach Jan Davis called time out to collect her young team and set up a possible game-winning shot.

"Melinda, you inbound the ball to Tammy out front," Davis barked. "Tammy, you wait for Molly to come across in front of the basket, then throw her the ball. Molly, you roll left and take the shot here. Ramona, you set up here and put it in if she misses. Everyone know what they're supposed to do? Okay, let's do it. Let's go!"

The referee handed the ball to Melinda King and blew his whistle. Melinda tossed the ball to Tammy Ford, who dribbled the ball, waiting for Molly Perkins to break to the basket.

"Now!" coach Davis shouted, the clock now at 7 seconds left. "Get it to her now!"

But just as Ford released the ball, Molly tripped over a teammate's shoe, and the ball sailed into the hands of a shocked Parkview guard, who raced untouched down the court for a layup that sealed the win. The Mavs fell to their knees in disgust.

"That's how it was for us all year," said Ford, a 5-6 junior guard. "Bad breaks at the worst possible time. We were really snakebit."

Despite its 12-10 mark, players and coaches alike said they didn't feel as though they had a winning season.

"We had three starters returning, and we figured we'd be in the playoffs, but it wasn't meant to be," coach Davis said. "These girls worked hard, but they didn't get a single break all season. I really felt bad for them."

The streak of bad luck began two weeks before the first game when returning all-district guard Lissa McIntyre blew out her right knee in a practice. Over the course of the year, injuries forced nine players to start at least three games.

"I don't think we had the same line-up for any two games in a row," said King, who led the team with a 21.8 points per game scoring average. "It was hard to get into a rhythm, and then it seemed like we got into an emotional funk. It was like we kept expecting something to go wrong.

"And usually, it did."

Even more frustrating, King said, was the fact that one of the teams the Mavs trounced, Ysleta (76-53) advanced to the state semifinals.

"With any luck, that could have been us," King said. "With any luck at all, this could have been our year."

YOUR STORY SHOULD READ LIKE A GOOD BOOK

DRAMA

A series of events arousing intense emotions about serious problems or humorous situations.

CHARACTER DEVELOPMENT

Unlike the fiction writer who must create and develop a character, the journalists need only develop the character. This is done by describing people physically, by examining their traits, by describing their personality and by exposing their actions.

CONFLICT

The struggle between opposing forces.

DIALOGUE

Dialogue is a conversation between or among characters.

> *"Approach your story idea as a novelist might, looking for potential elements of comedy, tragedy, irony or conflict that can be stressed in the reporting and writing. Look, particularly for tension between protagonist and antagonist, remembering that these need not be individuals."*
>
> — William E. Blundell
> The Art and Craft of
> Feature Writing

of interest or suspense, like in one of those TV shows where the husband admits that he killed his wife for the insurance money. Everyone except the defense attorney sits there gape-mouthed, and the judge tells the wrongly accused mailman he is free to go.

In the typical inverted pyramid story, the reporter begins with the climax. It's not a very effective order if you're trying to build suspense.

■ **RESOLUTION**—If you introduce a problem, readers expect you to solve it, or at least bring it as close to resolution as possible. You don't want to leave the reader hanging. If your story deals with a philosophical difference in the math department, you would want to isolate the sources of conflict, develop their characters, provide anecdotes using dialogue to make the issue real and meaningful, and finally, show how the conflict has been resolved. Perhaps the department chair has appointed a committee to propose curriculum revisions. Or perhaps the resolution is an agreement to disagree.

In this following piece, Nancy Kruh of the *Dallas Morning News* followed the Duncanville Pantherettes throughout what was to become a state championship season. Note how Nancy uses a single practice to show how dedicated each girl was to fulfilling her role on the team.

This article is an excellent example of narrative journalism. It shows how journalism can be as dramatic as the best fiction.

SHOWCASE

By **NANCY KRUH**
The Dallas Morning News

FOR THE FIRST TWO MONTHS of school, the girls' basketball practices have been only an hour. But in mid-October, the team is ready to begin longer practices six days a week. They don't end until Coach Sara Hackerott says they do. They've been known to go as long as three hours.

Coach runs the sessions with script and stopwatch, efficiently moving the girls from one activity to the next; even the water breaks are scheduled.

At the first Saturday morning practice, the girls' sweat has already turned their peppy red T-shirts the color of crimson when Coach tells them to divide up among the gym's six baskets. They are to attempt 10 free throws, she instructs, keep track of the number they make, then go to one end of the court.

The girls obey quickly; among the traits they all share is what's known in competitive sports as "coachability." They don't have to be told twice, and they don't ask why.

Once they're finished with their free throws, Coach asks if anyone has sunk all 10. No? Then run, Coach says.

Running is the part of practice the girls dread the most. Not only does it sap the energy they'd rather expend practicing the game, but also the simple truth is, it sears the lungs, it squeezes the muscles. Running hurts.

But when Coach says, "Go!" they do, full out, galloping down the length of the court and back again.

They're still trying to catch their breath when Coach asks if anyone sunk nine baskets. No? Then "Go!" The girls run again, up and back.

Eight? Jalie Mitchell, one of the team's starters, raises a hand. "Get a drink," Coach says, and Jalie heads to the water cooler. The others must run. Up and back again.

Seven baskets? A couple more girls raise their hands, and they have earned their water. The rest run. Up and back.

And so it goes — six, five, four — until only one sweaty, panting girl remains: Portia Lowe. She's a senior, a small and quiet guard, and this is only her first year on the varsity. On any other high school team, she probably would have started last year. Not here. Here she's just hoping to earn some game time.

Now, she's alone, segregated from her teammates, who are gathered around the cooler, taking great, satisfying gulps of water.

Then, as Portia awaits Coach's order to run, something happens: One of the starters, senior

Andrea Bentley, puts down her cup. She trots over to Portia, and without a word, takes a place beside her. And when Coach says, "Go!" the two girls run together. And then they walk to the water cooler, together. Nothing is spoken, but everything is said.

With these practices, the opportunity for such defining moments – of leadership, of teamwork, even of heroism – comes often. Less than an hour later, another one arrives.

The girls are all on the baseline, and Coach is going over the new "running" rules: She will pick one player to attempt two free throws. The fate of the whole team now will be up to her. If she misses her first shot, everyone must run up and down the court - twice. If she misses the second, everyone runs up and back once. But if she sinks both shots, nobody has to run.

Jalie – the one who earlier had sunk eight of 10 shots – is called. She takes aim and muffs the first shot.

Time to run. Up and back, and up and back again. They're sucking air by the time Coach picks Portia to shoot next.

"Take your time!" Kenya Larkin exhorts breathlessly, in what she probably intends as encouragement, but it comes out sounding more like a plea for an extra minute before she surely has to run again.

Calmly, Portia takes aim, then releases the ball. The ball arcs toward the basket, and . . . swoosh. Nothing but net.

The relief on the sidelines is momentary – there's still another shot. Portia hefts the ball in her hands. She aims. She fires. This time the ball bounces off the rim. Thunk, thunk. And then it decides to drop . . . through . . . the . . . net.

Not a word is said, nor is there a need. Portia Lowe, second-string Pantherette, is the hero of the hour.

■ IN SUMMARY

Write about specific people and their situations. Do not write research papers about general topics. For example: don't write about phobias. Write about the 6-foot, 4-inch, 265-pound senior football player who's scared to death of spiders.

SHOWCASE ■

By **KYLA PERRY**
Devine Texas High School

IT'S A POOL PARTY. All around the pool, inside and outside the house, are attractive young men and women—the girls in short skirts, the guys in edgy button-downs and khakis. Rock music floats through the doors of the house to the outside. There's dancing, swimming, flirting and laughing. It looks like the place to be.

Everyone's beautiful. Everyone's happy. And everyone's drinking.

But these people aren't drinking beer, oh, no. No wine for them either. It seems that all anyone at this party wants comes in a tall blue bottle with the word Skyy printed on the side. Yes, Skyy Blue is the drink of choice here.

Welcome to the world of malt liquor.

True, to most people alcohol ads on television are no stranger. Rarely a day goes by without a Budweiser ad flashing on the screen, and for special events like the Superbowl the public might as well give up hoping for "family friendly" advertising. But since the initiation of some restrictions, alcohol companies like Jack Daniels and Smirnoff have had to relegate their ads to the pages of adult-audience magazines and the realm of billboards.

But that was before "alcopops," the name being used to describe the brightly packaged, easily accessible spiked fruit drinks that are the new age of malt liquor.

Since the release of Zima a few years ago, these "alcopops" have risen in popularity, mainly due to their sweet flavor, which disguises the taste of the 7% alcoholic content.

"The commercials advertise them as

YOUR STORY SHOULD READ LIKE A GOOD BOOK

ORGANIZATION
The order in which a story is told.

ANTICIPATION
Keeping readers hooked by making them guess what comes next.

CLIMAX
The turning point, which involves decisiveness or suspense.

RESOLUTION
The point in which the central conflict ends. In some cases, it follows the climax. In others, it is the climax. You cannot have resolution unless all news questions are answered.

SETTING
Specific details about the place where the action takes place.

tasting better than beer," junior Jacob Martinez said. "They flavor them like lemonade and stuff like that. I guess people would drink it who don't like how beer tastes."

Martinez isn't the only one who thinks so. According to a poll conducted for the Center for Science in the Public Interest (CSPI), more than half of all teens polled said that the "sweetness that disguised the taste of alcohol is a major reason teenagers choose 'alcopops' over beer, wine, or cocktails."

And apparently, teens aren't the only ones who realize this. Because of this preference, major liquor labels like Bacardi, Smirnoff, Jack Daniels and Captain Morgan's have unleashed their own versions of the drinks onto the market.

So what's the problem? According to many critics, it's in the ads.

Because of their malt content, "alcopops" don't suffer the same banishment as hard liquor advertisements—which means they can be advertised on television and made available in convenience and grocery stores.

And it seems the liquor companies know it. According to Advertising Age, alcohol companies spent nearly $77 million marketing alcopops in 2001. And while the liquor industry's voluntary guidelines allow alcopop advertising only in the evening, statistics show that the ads are still reaching teens.

In fact, 77% of teens watch TV after that time, and 73% have seen ads for alcoholic beverages, with Bacardi Silver, Smirnoff Ice, and Mike's Hard Lemonade receiving the highest recognition.

But it is the content of the ads that provokes the most controversy.

"I've seen commercials for Michelob Ultra and Bacardi Silver on TV," sophomore Tabitha Hymer said. "And it's like it's telling you or encouraging you to live young and party hard at a young age because the media has put adults and teens together in the same age group. So it appeals to all viewers, including teens. It's like they're telling us we're old enough, too."

Junior Amos Edgett agrees with her. "The commercials are cool. There's pretty girls in them, and they're funny," he said. "The commercials seem kind of tempting. I bet most of the people who have tried it wouldn't have tried it if they hadn't seen the commercials."

He may be right. Statistics show that 17- and 18- year-olds are more than twice as likely as adults are to try the drinks. Possibly it's because of ads for drinks like Stolichnaya Citrona, which uses the catchy "Should I Stay or Should I Go" tune originally by The Clash and popular among teens. Perhaps it's because of ads for drinks like Mike's Hard Lemonade, Rick's Lemonade, or Doc Otis' Lemonade, which some critics say use men's names to make them more familiar sounding to teens. Either way, 41% of teens have already tried one.

Some experts say that's the whole point, calling them "gateway drugs that ease young people into drinking and pave the way to more traditional alcoholic beverages," while others feel that the drinks are aimed at an even more specific audience.

"I think more girls will drink them now," senior Jeremy West said, "because most girls don't like the flavor of beer."

Despite allegations regarding the target audience, the commercials keep coming, with few signs of letup. With companies expected to spend $450 million in 2002 on advertising alone, teens may soon be caught in the middle of the alcopop ad campaign.

Still, some teens feel that the alcopop may soon go the way of the wine cooler as another fad that will give way to something different.

"I don't think that they'll necessarily be the greatest drink ever," senior Stevie Monreal said. "I would like to think that eventually all the hype will go away and everyone will move on."

But until then, some like CSPI Director of Alcohol Policies George Hacker still feel that teens are being targeted unfairly.

"Kids think they're being turned on to liquor, and not just malt beverages," Hacker said. "That must be music to the liquor industry's ears."

COMPARE & CONTRAST

THE TYPICAL STORY

February is Black History Month, and the school will again participate in a wide variety of activities commemorating the many contributions blacks have made to the United States and to the world.

Activities already scheduled include guest speakers, assemblies, film strips, videotapes and a gala.

The chairman of Black History Month is history teacher and coach Dennis Sims.

"The main theme of Black History Month is to celebrate the past and define the future," Sims said. "This year, we will have a number of student projects, but we also plan to have a gala in which citizens are invited to experience firsthand the African-American culture."

The African-American gala will be Friday, Feb. 7. The gala will include poetry recitals, films, guest speakers and fashion displays of various ethnic clothing and jewelry. Booths serving African-American foods will also be set up.

Sims said students are currently involved in planning an ethnic awareness assembly.

"The purpose of the assembly is to look at the contributions to science, business, education and other fields made by African-Americans," Sims said.

"Many people fail to understand the many contributions that blacks have made here in the United States," he added. "We want to educate them on these many achievements."

THE CREATIVE ANGLE

History teacher Dennis Sims remembers his high school days all too well, and the memories aren't particularly good ones.

"Although I lived only a mile from school, I was forced to travel 10 miles out in the country to attend an all-black school," he said. "We weren't allowed to mingle with the white kids even though I'd played with many of them all my life."

He said he remembers how members of his family were denied basic rights such as voting and recalls the night a band of thugs lynched a young black man for talking to a white girl.

"I grew up in a segregated community that treated us harshly," he said. "Thank God that's all changed."

As evidence, the school will again participate in February's Black History Month, and Sims will be in charge of the annual event.

"I don't want this to be something kids feel like they have to do or is forced on them," Sims said. "I want all students to be excited about learning about African-Americans in our society because we must come to understand and appreciate each other in order to live in peace together."

Sims said ethnic wars around the world confirm his belief in the importance of Black History Month.

"We must begin to appreciate the things that make us unique," he said, "and those things that are common to us all if we are to survive."

A GOOD LEAD CAN CREATE SUSPENSE

You want to hook readers with a provocative lead that will pull them into the story. One of my favorite leaders: Minutes before the meeting began, Bill Farney got the bad news.

Another good one: She never knew she had it.

Photo by **AMANDA CRABBS**
Nickerson High School, Nickerson, KS

FIND AN ANGLE

05

American high schools are more similar than different. Not surprisingly, student publications look and read alike, whether the school is in Connecticutt or California. It isn't anything to brag about.

CHAPTER HIGHLIGHTS:

■ Story angle must be timely, accurate and original.

■ Find the most interesting part of the story.

■ Tell the reader something new.

■ Avoid generalities, abstractions, composites.

Finding an interesting angle begins with a promise not to default into cliché. Here's my all-time least favorite lead: "Imagine you are stuck on a desert island with seven or eight other people who are trying to beat you to a million dollars. Well, that's exactly what happened to blah blah blah."

Do not do this.

Imagine you are writing an original lead, something that's a natural extension of the story, something that isn't forced by nature of habit. Oh, I can hear a kid saying, "But I begin all of my stories with a second person question." That explains the "Have you ever been hit by a train? Well, Bubba was" lead.

Explains, but doesn't excuse.

Some confuse the angle with the lead. It isn't. The lead introduces the angle but ends fairly quickly while the angle weaves its way through the entire story. Okay, the theme of the story is "the debate team agonizes over the loss of its teacher and coach, who resigned to take a job in private industry." A reporter who's none too interested in angle might write, "While most students are not in agony, members of the debate team are because their coach and teacher dumped them."

That hardly captures the heart of the story. So say you're covering this story. You might talk to the teacher, to veteran members of the team, to beginning members of the team. The angle might involve the guilt the teacher feels for leaving the classroom for a special opportunity in private industry. The angle might involve the severed relationship between one or two students and the teacher. The angle might deal with the difficulty of being the new teacher who's replacing a beloved coach. You might be able to think of a half-dozen other plausible angles.

How do you select one? Report. Interview. Watch. Listen. The best information will float to the surface. Pay attention and be patient. Be willing to expend enough time and effort to allow the story to surface. Once it does, then develop it.

During the reporting process, you notice that the students are having a hard time getting accustomed to the new coach's techniques and personality. There's the story. It's not an editorial or an essay. It's a descriptive piece that will show how the debate team is recreating itself under this new leadership.

■ INTERESTING AND ACCURATE

The lead pulls the reader into the story. One solution: begin every story with the following word: SEX.

> **❝** Finding the right angle is sometimes a process of elimination, shuffling through the possibilities until you come up with the most compelling story.❞

It's not a good solution, but I guess it would grab readers' attention, at least once. Better still, write a lead that is factually accurate, whose tone and context are correct. This lead might be factually correct, but its tone and context are entirely wrong: "He's rolling around the aisles but it's not because of his sense of humor. Freshman Joey Jones has spinal bifida, and he says, 'I don't mind because that's just the way I am.'"

What a hoot that is.

Here's another winner: "Sophomore Cindy Smith did something that affected the rest of her life. She killed herself."

No.

The lead must be accurate. It must be honest. It must be interesting. It must pique the reader's curiosity enough to compel them to keep reading. One of my favorite leads: "Minutes before the meeting began, Bill Farley got the bad news."

Chances are, the reader will be curious enough to read the next paragraph. What bad news? And if the reporter (and in this case, it was a "he") did his job properly, then he'd plant enough facts in the following paragraphs to continue to hook and pull the reader through the story.

■ GETTING BACK TO ANGLE

The angle is more complicated. It is a multi-layered process that begins when you ask yourself, "Who is the most interesting subject in this series of events? Through whose eyes should I tell this story? Which stories are most compelling? Who will the readers want to know about? What will they want to know? How can I capture the spirit of this story, not simply the facts?"

Reporters take a fairly roundabout way of finding the angle. It's not as simple as "First, here's my theme. Now, here's my angle. Okay, now here's my lead. Now, here's the rest of my story. And finally, here's my ending. Done!"

Instead, it twists and folds back on itself. In developing the angle, you may realize the theme has changed. Then, in developing the body of the story, you may decide to change the angle. It can get a fairly confusing and frustrating,

particularly for beginners. Be patient. Koby Bryant didn't always wear a size 20 shoe.

Let's take the story of a teacher's retirement. Retirement stories provide rare opportunities for great features if students will take the time to do something with them. Often, reporters stack a few irrelevant facts on top of one another, toss in a predictable "I'm going to miss everyone . . ." quote and call that a feature. It isn't. It's a collection of data—cold, heartless and empty.

Instead, a reporter should be trying to reveal the character of the retiring teacher, to give meaning to the event, to capture the humanity of the moment. The following story, by John Bryant of the *Austin American-Statesman*, tells something more than how long the person taught and where.

EVEN WITH 50 YEARS of classroom experience, retiring Crockett High School home economics teacher Minta Palmer couldn't get Debra Favors to bite into a slice of mango.

"What does it taste like?" asked Favors, one of 24 second-year food students who had just prepared a glazed-ham dinner.

"It tastes like peaches," said Mrs. Palmer. "It's my gift to you."

"Well, I hate peaches," Debra complained.

Mrs. Palmer, who is being honored today with a breakfast in the school library, likes to urge students to try new foods and use good manners to eat them.

"They will be better adjusted to life," said Mrs. Palmer. "And good manners will take them places that money never will."

Mrs. Palmer, who was 71 in April, started teaching in 1938 in the North Texas German-American oilfield community of Goree in Knox County. She stayed for two years and was paid $100 a month. She taught in Shamrock and George West in Texas and 20 years in Raton, N.M. before she married Charles L. Palmer and moved into the Austin school district in 1964.

She was at Johnston High School for four years, then was one of Crockett's original teachers when the South Austin school opened in 1968.

That adds up to being the school district's only retiring teacher this year with 50 years of experience and lots of good memories.

Mrs. Palmer has two bulletin boards that compare what students learned in 1940 and in the 1980s. On the 1940s board, she noted that "a teacher became addicted to teaching."

In 1988, Mrs. Palmer said, "I'm still addicted."

Wednesday, her second-year students created a meal that attested to Mrs. Palmer's teaching abilities. The dinner they prepared and served to invited Crockett faculty and staff members featured an orange-pear salad, glazed ham, rice au gratin, green bean-bacon bundles, sour dough bread, cheese soufflé and chocolate cheese cake.

The semester's biggest cooking project was an unqualified success.

"I'm not hard to please, but this would be good anywhere," said satisfied eater Jim Houston, a Crockett guidance counselor for 14 years.

The third-period students took time from their meal to share plenty of the credit with Mrs. Palmer.

"She's real nice, and she helps everybody," said sophomore Deanna Ybarra. "Now I know how to set a table at home, and I can help my mom with the cooking."

Raymond Foster, a sophomore who plans to attend a cooking school and become a pastry chef, said, "She's a wonderful teacher. She's the neatest person I ever met."

Later in the morning, when the first-year food students started eating their pastry assignments, Mrs. Palmer raved about senior James Jones' lemon meringue pie.

Mrs. Palmer said having boys in her home economics classes is not new. She had male students in her classes at Shamrock High School back in 1940, she said.

Mrs. Palmer said home economics curricula in the 1980s have put an emphasis on family living and relationships instead of cooking and sewing skills.

But she still likes plenty of lab work in her classes. "Unless students are making something, they are not as happy," she said.

In her retirement, Mrs. Palmer said she and her husband will raise cattle, dogs and "lots of hell."

■ PROCESS OF ELIMINATION

Finding the right angle is sometimes a process of elimination, shuffling through the possibilities until you come up with the most compelling story.

One summer, a student I taught at the University of Oklahoma summer workshop wanted to know how such an approach would work with hard news. His school had recently changed its graduation requirements. "How do you find an interesting angle for a story like that?" he asked.

My response: Find a kid who will be affected. See if his or her situation is similar to that of others. If so, how? If not, why not?

The late NBC news commentator John Chancellor defined news as the "chronicle of conflict and change."

Find the conflict in the new graduation requirements. Explain to the reader in human terms what change means.

Here's your assignment. You're a student at a school that has won three consecutive girls' state basketball championships. I want you to write a story about the coming season in which the girls are aiming for their fifth consecutive crown.

How would you do it? I'd begin by researching the story immediately after the school had won its fourth championship. Here's what I learn: seniors had dominated that team, which means there will be a lot of new faces this year. That might make an interesting angle. Use a sophomore as the focal point for the story. Tell how she has attended games since she was old enough to walk, watched her two older sisters play for championship teams, has dreamed of playing for the Lady Whatevers and is now ready to step into the limelight.

Now that you have an idea of how to begin the story, spend some time with the girls. Go to practices. Look for that right scene, anecdote or incident to pull the reader into the story.

WE FROWN ON STORIES LIKE THESE

Sophomore Casey Hall is not your average student. He looks normal enough, but on the inside he is a character to behold. His off-the-wall sense of humor makes him impossible not to like.

"He's the funniest, most bizarre person I've ever met," junior Dana Smith said.

Everyone seems to think that Casey is very funny.

"He is a very clever person," junior David Gutierrez said.

So what's wrong with this? The reporter says Casey is funny but gives us no proof. Don't tell us. Show us. Describe a scene. Do something. But don't simply tell us.

> ❝ It has been said that we should write as we speak. This is absurd. What is meant by the advice to write as we speak is to write as we might speak if we spoke extremely well. This means that good writing should not sound stuffy, pompous, highfalutin, totally unlike ourselves, but rather, well— "simple and direct."
>
> — Jacques Barzun
> Simple & Direct: A Rhetoric for Writers

Capture the drama, the character, the conflict of the season. There will be a lot of decisions to make: Who to interview? What questions to ask? Which information to use? In what order? What kind of lead? What kind of tone? Working with editors and adviser, the reporter makes all of these decisions and more. It's hard work.

But then, that's also the fun of it.

■ COMMON PROBLEMS

Whether in California, Texas, New York or Hawaii, high schools are more similar than dissimilar. They have clubs and activities. They have classes of students engaged in pretty much the same academic endeavors. They are run by adults who share a common vision, and they are supported by parents who think they pay too many taxes for what they're getting in return, unless it's a winning football season. That's the big picture.

Not to belabor the point, but high school publications often look and read alike. High school journalists cover the same stories and events in pretty much the same way as they did the year before and pretty much the same way other student journalists do. Many stories are interchangeable. Fill in the year, the name of the school and two or three names, and the story could apply to any school, any year. Oh, to have a dollar for every time I've read these leads:

■ While other students slept late, swam and watched television, the (fill in name of club) attended summer camp.

■ The purpose of Student Council is to serve as a bridge between students and administrators.

■ Biff and Spike are members of a rock band, the Lost Causes, and they're working hard so they'll be big stars one day.

■ It's (choose one: football, basketball, baseball, etc.) season again.

■ (Fill in name of person) was crowned homecoming queen before a packed stadium. "I was so excited when my name was called I could just die. This is an honor I'll cherish for as long as I can remember," she said.

■ Students took college entrance exams, specifically the SAT test. The purpose of the tests is to prepare . . .

■ (Teacher's name) announced her retirement last week. She has been teaching here for 30 years. She is a graduate of Arizona State University and has a master's degree from Pepperdine University. Her first teaching job was in Seaweed where she taught for five years before moving here. She is married and has three children. When asked what she plans to do in retirement, she said, "Read, travel and work in the garden." She added that she will "miss the students, too."

■ On Nov. 30, the Future Farmers of America traveled to Tulsa for a national convention. While they were there, several competed in various competitions. Students who won include . . .

■ Blood. What does it mean to you? To millions in need of blood, it means the difference between life and death. Blood donations are important for those who need transfusions. Transfusions have saved hundreds of thousands of people suffering from severe bleeding, shock and blood-destroying diseases. The Student Council will conduct its annual blood drive next Tuesday. Students who want to donate should . . . .

■ BEING CORRECT ISN'T ENOUGH

You get the idea. Although the stories may fulfill the requirements of textbook journalism, they aren't likely to attract many readers.

What follows are stories that typically appear in high school publications. I've tried to show that there are no boring subjects—only lazy and careless reporters.

■ FANS AND FANATICS

Schools have sports teams. Teams have fans. Some of the fans go a little overboard. Hey, maybe there's a story here. Maybe not. The first example begins with a statement of the obvious and goes downhill from there.

THE WEATHER WILL soon turn cooler, and the leaves will start to fall—and that means the arrival of football season. Fans are important to the success of the team because they cheer for the players and support them even when they lose. Coach Jimmy Duncan said the fans are an important part of the team.

"Speaking for the players and coaches, we appreciate the support of our loyal fans and hope everyone will come to the game and cheer us on to victory," he said.

Leading the fans are the cheerleaders.

"It's so important for our team that everyone come to the pep rallies and the games and scream real loud and participate in our cheers so that the players will know we're behind them win or tie," head cheerleader Penny Purcell said.

When asked, students said they enjoyed going to games and cheering for the team.

"It is fun to go to the games and watch the boys play," said freshman Becky Powell. "Even though I have no idea what is taking place on the field, I scream real loud a lot at the games."

"I feel it is my duty as a loyal athletic supporter to go to all of the games," sophomore Stuart Goldsmith said. "The best part is looking at the cheerleaders."

■ TELL THE READER SOMTHING NEW

The following story, on the other hand, focuses on a football fan—not fans. It's interesting and fun. It develops the subject's character and personality and, most importantly, tells the reader something new.

THE FIRST GAME he attended, the players wore leather helmets and played the game in an old cow pasture. Sixty-three years and almost a thousand games later, Wallace Simpson is planning for another football season.

"I ain't missed but one game since 1938, and that's hard for some people to imagine, but I've been healthy and in town, so I never saw a reason not to go," said Simpson, a retired engineer whose three sons played for the Bulldogs back in the 1960s. His youngest son, Heath, quarterbacked the 1968 Bulldogs to their only state football championship in the school's history.

"I saw my first game—a 35-0 win over Cleardale—in 1938 when I was 14 years old, and from that moment on, Bulldog football was my passion," Simpson said. "I played for four years here—four of the worst teams in the school's history, I might add—and then went to school over at Commerce so that I'd be close enough to home to go to all the games."

Every game except one, that is.

"My senior year in college, I was married, and my wife was expecting our first child," he said. "She was getting real close to delivering, so I decided it would be best if I stayed home rather than going to the game. Good thing too. My son was born at 2:30 that morning, and we lost the game anyway. I'm just glad that the one game I missed was a loss rather than a win. I'd hate to think that I missed a game that we won."

Simpson served 16 years on the school board and was president of the Football Booster Club for eight years. "I don't miss all of that a bit," he said. "But when I get tired of going to games is when they'll need to plant me six feet under. I may be just another old fool, but I love them Bulldogs."

■ FOREIGN EXCHANGE STUDENTS

All too often, stories about Foreign Exchange Students rehash clichés by focusing on food, hobbies, how schools differ and similar silliness. Do we really need another story that says, "I like being in (fill in the name of your school and community) because the people are so friendly, but I miss my family and friends"? I don't think so. Here's one of my all-time favorite losers:

IN CASE YOU HAVEN'T noticed, Huckleberry High School has two new special additions, and they are Michelle and Claudia Shafi. Michelle is 16 and a senior while Claudia, who is 13, is a freshman.

When asked how she likes HHS, Michelle replied, "Very much." Some of her hobbies are needlepoint, playing basketball, belly dancing, swimming and sewing. She also likes Ben Affleck and saw "Pearl Harbor" four times in Beirut.

Claudia's hobbies include sewing, belly dancing

ONE CAN FIND A BETTER WAY TO WRITE IF ONE TRIES

Makes you wonder, "one what?" Rather than the stodgy "one may find . . . ." lead, it is better to refer directly to the subjects.

For example, rather than "On Friday night, one might find members of the Film Appreciation Club at the local theatre . . . .," here's a better approach:

If it's the opening night of a much-anticipated film, they're there, sometimes dressed in tuxes and long gowns, sometimes in cheap T-shirts they found at a thrift shop downtown.

"They" are the members of Oscars Anonymous, a bunch of cinema lovers who look forward to the night of the Academy Awards as eagerly as others anticipate Christmas morning.

and creating art. Singing is also a favorite hobby of hers, having sung in the Greek Orthodox Church Choir in Beirut.

When asked what Claudia and Michelle did in Beirut, they described the beaches and said they had picnics, went to movies and went to school, which they started when they were only three years old. Michelle also likes to do homework, which is a change from what you will find here (Ha, ha).

Now that these two girls have been introduced to HHS and the student body, you might want to talk to them and ask them about their country. It will help if you know French, for their English is not yet up to standards although it appears to be better than some students at HHS (Ha Ha).

■ LACK OF EMPATHY

Pretty sad. Here, you have two girls from war-torn Lebanon, and all the reporter can find to ask them about is their favorite food.

I came across another story many years ago about a young girl who, with her family, had escaped the Killing Fields of Southeast Asia. Rather than capturing what certainly was a harrowing tale, the reporter asked every dumb question imaginable.

What is your favorite color?

What is your favorite food?

Are schools harder in this country?

What is your favorite extracurricular activity?

Such a lack of empathy is appalling. Who cares what her favorite food is? Who doesn't know that foreign schools are harder? Doesn't it seem reasonable that her favorite extracurricular activity may be staying alive? With minimal effort and imagination, the reporter might have captured the heart of the situation.

MICHELLE SHAFTI remembers the first time the jets flew over Beirut, her hometown.

"We thought it was some kind of demonstration," the senior said.

Suddenly, an explosion threw her to the floor, and she lay there, listening to the screaming American-made F-17s as they pounded the city with 2,000-pound bombs. The invasion of Lebanon had begun.

"People here now think of Beirut as a war-torn city," Michelle said. "But it wasn't always so. A few years ago, it was considered the Paris of the Middle East, and it was a wonderful place to grow up."

That was until the civil war began.

"The Christians were fighting the Moslems, the Syrians were everywhere, the PLO had come into the city, and it was just a mess, a horrible, dangerous mess," Claudia said. "We heard gunfire every day, every night. We saw dead bodies on the streets. Our beautiful city was reduced to ruins."

That's when her father decided to take his family to the United States. In September, Michelle's father, mother and younger sister, Claudia, arrived here. Claudia is a freshman.

"It is so different. I'm trying to get used to the language, the food, the culture," Michelle said. "One thing I have grown used to is the silence. No jets. No bombs. No death."

■ CONSIDER CURRENT EVENTS

In writing these stories about foreign exchange students, consider the current events of their country. How can you use those events as an news peg? For example, in the days after the Sept. 11 attacks on the World Trade Center and Pentagon, several student publications ran stories about Muslim students who feared retribution and alienation. Others ran stories about students and teachers who lost or almost lost friends and family in the 9/11 attacks.

They found a way to localize and update an international story. They brought new meaning and understanding to an event that happened weeks, even months, earlier. After George Harrison's death, a young reporter wrote a lovely piece explaining the significance of his passing, especially to the Baby Boomer teachers and parents. But I saw far more mini-Harrison bios, stuff I find on the Internet in a heartbeat. He was the quiet Beatle. He played lead guitar.

But I saw only one article that localized the big story. This story focused on a teacher who grew up with the Beatles, whose classroom was (probably still is) papered with Beatle posters,

HOW TO FIND YOUR LEAD

B ased on Donald Murray's "30 Questions to Produce Leads" these questions will launch you toward your perfect lead.

■ What's your single most interesting or important piece of information?
■ When you were researching the story, what interested you the most?
■ Did someone tell you an interesting story that symbolizes the issue or person?
■ Do you remember a dominant emotion or image?
■ What is the central event in the story?
■ Do you remember a dominant sensory detail: smell, feel, taste, sound or image?
■ Tension: what's the problem?
■ Conflict: Can you boil the issue down to one-on-one conflict?
■ Ask yourself: so what? Then, explain it to your reader.
■ Is the setting important? If so, why?
■ What caused this situation?
■ What's the story's tone: kind, obnoxious, quizzical, satirical, skeptical, etc.?
■ Do you have a single quote that captures the essence of the story?
■ What's the most important: who, what, when, where, why or how?
■ What's the best way to tell the story chronologically?
■ Can you and if so, have you given the story a human face?
■ Have you told the story through the most interesting character's eyes?
■ What are the problems in the story? Have they been solved?
■ What can the reader leave from these people's experiences?
■ When will the story run?
■ How much space do you have?

who saw the Beatles at Shea Stadium in 1965, who must now because of George's death come to grips with her own mortality.

That's a story I wanted to read.

So, look beyond the obvious. Let's go back to the stories about foreign exchange students. Do we really need to be told that education here is not as hard as it is there? Do we need more stories about how America differs from their countries, and about how students are getting accustomed to hamburgers, shopping malls and driving on the right side of the road?

I don't think so. We can do better. Case in point:

FOR 18-YEAR-OLD Kari Hati of Finland, North Mesquite High School is not as academically challenging as the small school he attended in his native country last year. That's why he doesn't spend much time on homework here.

Jose Antonio Perez of Barcelona, Spain, a high school student at Greenhill School in Dallas, finds that American schools place more emphasis on factual knowledge than on creativity.

Maria Kim Helena Lidbeck of Sweden doesn't understand why American schools have so many rules. Such practices as going to detention hall, wearing identification badges and not being allowed to walk through the halls during lunch hour are unheard of in her native land. But at Skyline High School in Dallas, where she is a junior, they are a vital part of everyday life.

For these exchange students and many others, attending school in Dallas is dramatically different from attending school abroad.

In interviews with six exchange students from Finland, Sweden, Denmark, Ecuador and Spain— each of whom attends a different public or private school in the area—no real consensus emerged as to how American schools stack up against foreign school systems.

But they all agreed that the language barrier makes learning harder—regardless of the subject matter.

"The language—it's horrible," says Christian Pederson, a Danish student and currently a 10th

WELL, THAT'S A DUMB QUESTION!

Coaches are notorious for answering questions without saying anything. But sometimes, they are responding as best they can to meaningless questions.

For example, what kinds of questions could have prompted these responses?

■ We are looking forward to the season. If it all falls our way, we could win a few games.
■ The ground game was successful because of our offensive line and backs.
■ I think they ran to the best of their ability but not potential.
■ They got their heads bashed in, but they're better people for it.
■ If you don't look at the losses, we had a pretty successful season.

> " Another paradox of the writing process is that a narrow topic provides the writer with more opportunities to collect information efficiently. Most students believe they can write more about "pollution in Florida" than "why it smells in Bayboro Harbor." Information on the harbor is easier to acquire and organize. It is likely to be more specific, descriptive, concrete and anecdotal."
>
> — Roy Peter Clark
> Free to Write

grader at St. Mark's School of Texas. "Some days, when I come home from school, I have to look up 20 different words to see what they mean. I learned English, not American English, before I came here. There's a difference."

Saane Norgard, another exchange student from Denmark who is a junior at the Episcopal School of Dallas, faces a similar challenge. "I spend more time studying here, partly due to the language and curriculum," she says. "School is harder because I have to take it in English. I don't know if it would be harder if it was in Danish."

Most exchange students already speak English when they arrive here, according to Nancy Bryant, area coordinator for the International Education Forum, a California-based, non-profit organization that matches American host families with foreign students. Still, the most difficult task facing exchange students, she says, is learning to think in English.

"All our students speak fluent English and are screened vigorously for their English language skills, academic skills, health records and their ability to get along with other people," she says. "Initially, they have a hard time because they're thinking in their native languages. The breakthrough comes when they think in English."

Ms. Bryant believes that the quality of American education depends on how much each student is willing to put into it. "All my students are eager to come here, and I'm sure it's not because they think it will be easy. Yet, in spite of the language problems, they tend to do well."

Now, let's look at the cliché articles and try to determine how they could have been approached.

■ CLICHÉ—SUMMER CAMP

While other students slept late, swam and watched television, the (fill in name of club) attended summer camp at Florida State University. Attending the camp were (fill in names of students).

"It was a lot of fun, and it broke up the monotony of the summer," club member (fill in name of club member) said. "It gave us a head start on the year."

★ CREATIVE —SUMMER CAMP

SUNBURNED AND EXHAUSTED, her throat parched and her feet swollen, junior cheerleader Linda Moreno rolled out of her dormitory bed—a flimsy rock-hard mattress, resting on a set of springs that screeched at every motion—at a quarter past 6 in the morning.

"Get rolling girls," a dorm resident boomed. "We don't have all day. Breakfast served in 10 minutes."

Twenty-five minutes later, Linda and the other members of the varsity cheerleader squad marched out onto the Florida State University football field to begin another day of drills under the blistering sun.

"Anyone who thinks cheerleading is just hopping around and squealing needs to come here for a few days," Moreno said. "This is the Marine boot camp of workshops. There's nothing very glamorous about it."

The purpose of the workshop is to forge a tight-knit unit than can fire up even the most jaded of fans. It isn't for the meek or the weak.

"Cheerleading has gotten a really bad rap," senior Christi Zulani said. "Too many students think it's just a popularity contest. If any of us are popular, then surviving this camp has meant that we earned that popularity."

■ CLICHÉ—AFFIRMATIVE ACTION

The issue of affirmative action and college entrance is a major topic these days. "I believe in affirmative action," senior Mario Peña said. "For many years, minorities were discriminated against. It's only fair to give them a little help now."

Others disagree. "Race should play no part in determining who gets into college," senior Bijah Patel said. "Each person should qualify on the basis of grades and other accomplishments."

★ CREATIVE —AFFIRMATIVE ACTION

Tabrina Tijerina is the first in her family to go to college. A solid A-B student, she wants to go to Duke, but she's waiting to hear whether she's been accepted. Meanwhile, Mick Anderson, a solid A-B student, has already been accepted to Duke, just as his father and grandfather had been. He's a 'legacy,' and they're given preferential treatment by college admissions officers.

The issue of legacies is among the factors that make affirmative action so complicated and controversial. Warren Burnett, counselor, said he's not sure which way the courts will rule on race-based college admissions but added that "fairness will always be in the eyes of the beholder.

"Some young people have advantages over others," Burnett said. "They come from families with a long tradition of higher education."

Anderson said he's visited Duke "countless" times.

"It's like a second home to me," he said. "I can't wait to get there."

But first-generation college applicants face a huge uphill struggle.

"I'm the first in my family to go to college. My parents have worked all their lives," senior Tabrina Tijerina said. "Neither graduated from high school. I feel a huge disadvantage, compared to the kids whose parents have been there, done that. I don't expect to be enrolled just because my skin is brown, but I hope colleges appreciate how far I've come and how hard I'm willing to work."

■ CLICHÈ—SPORTS SEASON STARTS

It's (choose one: football, basketball, wrestling, track, baseball, etc.) season again. Members of the team include . . . .

✪ CREATIVE — SPORTS SEASON STARTS

COACH BILL JACKSON pushed his cap back on his head and rubbed his hands across his face, obviously tired and frustrated by his junior quarterback.

"I told you, when the end comes across the line of scrimmage, you flip the ball to the tailback," he told Brad Simmons while jabbing his finger in his chest. "Now, try it again."

For Jackson's Lions, the season has been a series of "try it agains." The loss of 16 starters off last year's 9-2 team, plus the decision to go with a new one-back offense has the team scrambling to prepare for the opening game.

"We found out last year that we were getting most of our big plays out of the one-back set," Jackson said. "So we've switched from the Houston Veer because I think the one-back set will be the offense of the '90s."

The offense features more formations and puts more pressure on the quarterback and ends to read defensive alignments.

"We hope we can spread out the defense, which has to respect the possibility of the pass," Jackson said. "We're a little ways from having it all down, but we're getting there."

The success of the offense will rest largely on the shoulders of Simmons, who played sparingly as a sophomore.

"Brad has tremendous ability," Jackson said. "He's a smart kid, a good runner and a very strong passer. Once he becomes comfortable with the system, he could be unstoppable."

Simmons will be joined in the backfield by senior Randy Glover, a second-year starter who ran for 852 yards last year while gaining second-team all-district honors. However, the offensive line was decimated by graduation—only guard Alan Moore returns. Both wide receivers —key elements in a one-back offense—have only junior varsity experience.

Defensively, the Lions return four starters: tackle Jeff McNair, end John Maher and outside linebackers Christian Ramos and Lavon Gannon.

"We're going to be green for a few games, but I think we'll put it together quickly," Ramos said. "Everyone is excited about this team. We think we can make up in hustle what we lack in experience."

The Lions open the season Sept. 6 at home against Port Wheeler.

■ CLICHÉ—HOMECOMING QUEEN

(Fill in name of person) was crowned homecoming queen last Friday night before a packed stadium. "I was so excited when my name was called I could just die. This is an honor I'll cherish for as long as I can remember . . . ."

✪ CREATIVE —HOMECOMING QUEEN

FOR KAREN MAYS, the joy of being named

WELL, THAT'S A DUMB QUESTION!

"It is not the answer that enlightens but the question," said dramatist Eugene Ionesco. Given the dimness of the answers below, imagine what the questions must have been like.

■ I took art because I like to draw.

■ I took Algebra II and Geometry because I want to take Trig, and you have to take Algebra II and Geometry in order to take Trig.

■ Being in a club is important because it makes you feel like you're a member of an organization.

■ (On using the library): It's the best place I know to find a book.

homecoming queen last week was tempered by the concern she felt for Larry Buckner, a 6-year-old at Matthews Elementary School who was undergoing surgery in Memphis for a tumor in his leg.

"It was truly thrilling to win, but I spent all day thinking about Larry," Karen said. "I couldn't take my mind off the fear that he and his family must have had. I wore a ribbon with his name on it."

Larry was taken to St. Jude's Children's Hospital in Memphis for the surgery. Karen met Larry at the Ronald McDonald House, where she is a volunteer.

"When Larry was 5, doctors found a tumor in his leg," Karen said. "The tumor was removed, and he went through chemotherapy to remove any final traces of the cancer. This second surgery was to determine whether the chemotherapy worked."

Doctors found no new signs of the tumor.

"Winning homecoming queen was great," Karen said, "but nothing like the feeling of joy that I had when Larry's parents told me the good news."

■ CLICHÉ—TEACHER RETIREMENT

(Fill in name of teacher) announced her retirement last week. She has been teaching here for 30 years. She is a graduate of the University of Kansas and has a master's degree from the University of Missouri. Her first teaching job was in Plainville, where she taught for five years before moving here.

She is married and has three children. When asked what she plans to do in retirement, she said, "Read, travel and work in the garden." She added that she will "miss the students, too."

☆ CREATIVE —TEACHER RETIREMENT

LUCY SWANSON ran her hand across the desk and inhaled deeply. In three weeks, her 30-year tenure as a mathematics teacher will end, and she is feeling the mixture of nostalgia and exuberance that comes with retirement.

"My husband and I own a little place in New Mexico, and we want to spend as much time there as possible," she said. "There's nothing quite like sitting on your patio, looking out across the desert toward Santa Fe as the sun sets behind the mountains."

But Swanson admits that many of her thoughts on those Indian summer days to come will probably take her back to her long career as a math teacher.

"I never wanted to be anything other than a teacher," she said. "I've had an opportunity to touch so many lives, to really be a part of the world as it changes and not just be a spectator. "

When Swanson arrived here in 1962, she was one of the thousands of college students, imbued with the enthusiasm of the new Kennedy Administration.

"We were out to change the world, and I suppose to a degree, we did," she said. "I think it is interesting that I came to to the classroom just after the Berlin Wall was built and am retiring in the year that it was torn down."

Teaching all those years had its challenges.

"Once, a boy put a snake in my desk drawer. I almost had a heart attack. The boy is now a school teacher himself," Swanson said. "Many years ago, some boys put my Volkswagen Bug on the guard rail. But I was lucky. I was never the object of meanness but rather playful pranks."

Looking back, she's seen a lot of changes in students.

"Kids today are so much more worldly than they were 10 or 20 years ago," she said. "The kids in the '60s weren't nearly as radical as people think. The schools have changed as society has changed, but it's odd that the kids pretty much remain kids, and that's what I'm going to miss most of all."

■ CLICHÉ—THE CLUB TRIP

On Nov. 30, the Future Farmers of America traveled to Tulsa for a national convention. While they were there, several competed in various competitions. Students who won include . . . .

☆ CREATIVE —THE CLUB TRIP

EACH MORNING, Saturdays and Sundays included, Susan Clark rises at 5:30 a.m., tosses some cold water on her face and walks 400 yards to the barn on her father's dairy farm. There she spends the next two hours petting, grooming and cleaning

AVOID SEVERAL GENERALITIES

Avoid words such as 'many, several, some, most, a few,' and other words that don't really tell the reader much. Students often write in generalities.

- Many students did this.
- Most of them enjoyed it.
- Some did not.
- A few did other things.
- Several just slept in.
- And then, we had teachers.

Don't do this. Or this:

MOST TEACHERS do a good job, but few of them receive awards. However, last week, science teacher Dan Garcia was named the 'Teacher of the Year' by the Hispanic Association of Colleges and Universities. The HSCU is an organization whose purpose is to blah blah blah. "I am proud and honored to have received this award," Garcia said. "I know that many teachers didn't win it, and I'm tickled pink that I did."

Instead, find out what it is about Garcia that earned him the award. Don't focus on the award. Students don't care about the award per se. They want to read about the person — their teacher — who won the award. For example:

CHALLENGE YOURSELF. Lay it all on the line. Go for broke. Just do it.

That's the challenge Dan Garcia has given his students. But he isn't a football or basketball coach. He's not preparing his students for a competition, unless you consider "life" a contest. In that case, Dan Garcia would agree.

"Life is a contest, and there will be winners and losers." said Garcia, science department chairman. "Kids are now putting their marbles where it counts. They want to be challenged to higher concepts of thinking. The kids who can think, who can solve problems, who can work in teams, they'll be the winners. The rest? Well, I worry a little about them. I'm not sure where they'll end up."

Clearly, he's gotten his point across. More than half of the school's 2,200 students are enrolled in science classes. New physics classes have been added to meet the demand, and 100 students recently were turned away from chemistry classes because every seat was filled.

There are various reasons for this surge in the sciences, but administrators say all indications lead to Garcia, the school's popular, do-everything science teacher. Last week, Garcia was named the "Teacher of the Year" by the Hispanic Association of Colleges and Universities.

Garcia said the sciences are a way to raise the expectations of Hispanic students. His classes are explanations of new concepts, that Garcia hopes will push his students toward fields in medicine, engineering and high technology.

Garcia has a personal stake in how his students do because he is deeply embedded in the community around the predominantly Hispanic high school, where he has taught for 15 years. He is a Hillview product. He grew up in a neighborhood near the school and today lives only a mile from Hillview.

He said he believes a large part of his teaching responsibilities are tied to his involvement in the community. A teacher who is not a part of his community loses a key ingredient in identifying with his students.

"How can you solve the problems of a community by isolating yourself in another part of town?" he asked. "You won't solve any problems by being aloof.

"People have to see you in action. You have to go to the football games, the *quinceañeras*, all kinds of extracurricular events — academic, music, fine arts — and just show the kids that you care."

Garcia is an unabashed booster of his students. He believes they are as capable and talented as students anywhere else in the city. They only need a boost to believe any subject is within their reach.

"Knowledge gives you confidence," Garcia said. "It's that will, that desire, that takes you as far as you want to go. I try to get them started."

WE FROWN ON LEADS LIKE THIS

What does the word "recession" mean? If you said, "a temporary slowdown in economic activities," you are absolutely right. We're having a recession here. And it has some students worried.

"I want to find a job, but right now it's not looking too good," said Tom Jones, senior.

"People need to work, and right now, there just aren't many jobs around," added Mary Brown. "But I'm confident it will turn around soon."

Don't tell us what a recession is. Tell the reader how the recession affects specific people in your community.

her prize steer, Rusty, and occasionally sneaking him junk food.

"He really likes barbeque potato chips," Susan said. "Don't ask me why."

This ritual—rain or shine, temperature be damned—has been going on for 18 months, and Susan hopes the big pay-off is near.

"The State Fair is in two weeks, and I think I've got a good shot at winning Best of Show," she said. "That's what all this work has been for. I want that blue ribbon."

For students in Future Farmers of America, such is the stuff of great dreams. FFA students know they're stereotyped as ropers and hicks but figure the occasional jabs are a small price to pay. For example, the "Best of Show" steer at the State Fair often sells for as much as $20,000.

"If I win, my college education is paid for," Susan said.

If not?

"Well, I've loved taking care of Rusty, and I've made a lot of friends in FFA," she said. "No matter what happens, I think I've come out ahead."

■ CLICHÉ—BLOOD DRIVE

Blood. What does it mean to you? To millions in need of blood, it means the difference between life and death. Blood donations are important for those who need transfusions. Transfusions have saved hundreds of thousands of people suffering from severe bleeding, shock and blood-destroying diseases. The Student Council will conduct its annual blood drive next Tuesday. Students who want to donate should . . . .

★ CREATIVE —BLOOD DRIVE

JOHN SPIVEY KNEW it was bad, but he wasn't prepared for this. His 17-year-old daughter, Hillary, bruised and swollen, connected to half a dozen monitors, lay in critical condition at County Memorial Hospital.

Thirty minutes earlier, doctors were frantically working to save her life after a drunk driver had slammed, head-on, into her Volkswagen Passat. Although she was wearing a seatbelt, she suffered serious head injuries, a fractured leg and numerous cuts and bruises. The driver of the other car was killed immediately.

"She lost a lot of blood," Spivey said of his daughter, who is now a junior at Temple University. "If there had been a shortage, she might have died. You never think about how important it is to have a good supply of blood available until something like this happens to you or someone you love."

This is why Spivey, a senior history teacher, is again chairing the annual blood drive next Tuesday.

■ CLICHÉ—THE CLASS ACTIVITY

The speech class is currently participating in mock trials. The purpose of the mock trials is to duplicate the action in a courtroom and to teach students about the judicial process.

"Being in mock trials is very interesting," junior Sam Smith said. "I want to be a lawyer some day, and this is good training."

★ CREATIVE —THE CLASS ACTIVITY

TERRY JAMESON'S lawyers did everything they could to convince jurors that a plastic bag of "crank," a methamphetamine, was confiscated from his school locker without his consent, violating his right of privacy.

They argued that Jameson should be found not guilty of possessing the drug.

Six teenage jurors disagreed.

Jameson, a fictional character, had the best mock trial team in the state. The "attorneys" were students from Bigtown High School. Although their defense did not succeed in a practice classroom trial Thursday, they have fared better in competition.

The Bigtown team, which has won competitions at the district, regional and state levels, will match courtroom wits with 23 teams from other states in a national mock trial meet Friday and Saturday at the Dallas County Courthouse, said Alice Oppenheim, a lawyer who has helped prepare the students.

"These students are an exceptional combination of talent and energy," Oppenheim said. "Austin and the state of Texas should be proud of them. I've enjoyed working with them. If anybody is cynical about young people today, these students would change their minds."

Bigtown's mock trial program has come a long way, said Jack Woods, a teacher for 35 years, who started the program four years ago when he began working at Bigtown.

"The first year it was too new, and we did not have a successful program," Woods said. "The team fell apart when we got to division competition."

Students were involved in other activities and were not committed to the program, he said.

"The commitment has gotten stronger each year," he said. "I think that is the reason we won the regional and state competitions."

The team of seven senior students went to district competition after placing first among 16 Bigtown teams, Woods said. Members of the top team are Kristen Silverberg, Bryan Taylor, Jennifer Bradley, Karen Kocks, Trudi Donaldson, Tiffany Gurkin and Alexander Renwick.

Silverberg, who plans to go to law school and then go into politics, said the mock trial experience has given her skills to use in everyday life.

"I guess I really enjoy the practices," Silverberg said. "It has taught us all so much. One thing that is extremely important in mock trials is the ability to be flexible.

"You have to be able to respond to any charges by the other team," she said. "That means you have to be clear on the facts. It helps you in real life to understand your own position and to be able to defend it to others."

■ CLICHÉ—STUDENTS IN A BAND

Rock 'n' roll is here to stay, as witnessed by juniors Biff Willows and Spike LeMond, who are members of a rock band, the Lost Causes.

"We started playing a few years ago over at Spike's house," Biff said. "Pretty soon, we picked up a few gigs at parties and stuff. We really want to make it big, to play in the huge arenas and have a lot of groupies and stuff. I mean, my personal goal is to be on "Beavis and Butthead" some day. That would be cool."

Spike said the band has a wide range of influences.

"We like the harder stuff: Metallica and Scorpions, for example. The whole point is to make a lot of money and meet girls."

SHOWCASE ■

By **CHRIS BARTON**
Sulphur Springs High School,
Sulphur Springs, TX

★ CREATIVE —STUDENTS IN A BAND

"THIS IS A FARCE of an interview, I have to tell you," concedes Jim Smith.

And it's true. It's often impossible to get Smith or his younger brother Rick to comment on their family's Dixieland jazz band with anything but offbeat asides or twisted one-liners.

Relating his early musical career, Jim recalls an eclectic folk trio he formed with his parents. "That was pretty irrelevant to what we're doing now, but it was my start in show biz. We usually played the community center circuit."

"All the way from Sulphur Bluff to Hagansport," Rick helps out.

Later, when Jim describes their two performance ventures to New Orleans as "war," Rick offers a cheerier view:

"It was like springtime flowers tossed to and fro."

If Jim and Rick, a senior and a junior, seem to play well off each other, it's because they've had lots of practice. Along with their brother Jeff, a 1987 graduate, each has played a musical instrument since third grade and for the past eight years has been a member of the Sulphur River Jazz Band.

"Our dad had bought the instruments each of us would play before we could even talk," says Jim, the band's trumpet player.

After Rick had learned the trombone, the band began to form. Along with Jeff on clarinet and their father Hank on banjo and vocals, Jim and Rick were joined by Loren Seely on bass.

In 1984, Mark Chapman became the permanent drummer. Once the band jelled, their

WE FROWN ON STORIES LIKE THIS

To most people, Aug. 18 was just another ordinary day. Some people may have been shopping, water skiing or playing softball, but on that particular Saturday, senior Natalie Smith was being crowned Miss Junior Neat-o Mosquito.

"I was so thrilled to be named Miss Junior Neat-o Mosquito," Natalie gushed. "It's been my life's ambition to receive a big award named after a blood sucking insect."

Natalie is president of the Beta Club, vice president of the Chess Club and a member of the cross country team.

If Natalie wins an award of any consequence, then concentrate on how she won it. Don't stack a dopey quote on top of a mini-bio.

performances included spots at church socials, service clubs and the Fall Festival—the gig Jim calls "that great nurturer of the arts."

"And who could forget Tots on Parade?" Rick asks.

"Our first really big gig," admits Jim.

Of all the concerts the Sulphur River Jazz Band has given in its eight years, at least two are particularly memorable to the Smith brothers. The first, a performance at the Country Club, was "the one where everybody got drunk and left," Rick recalls.

"Not the band," clarifies Jim. "The audience. We got paid $300 for playing pool in the back."

Another memorable gig sticks out, not because of the audience of the band itself but because of the exotic behavior of the other performers on stage.

"We were playing for a bunch of Catholic luminaries, and we shared the stage with some people from the South Sea islands," Jim says. "They weren't wearing shirts, and they were carrying spears. They kept playing with Mark's drums, and when one kid climbed on top of the drums, his father knocked him off with a spear."

As unstructured as their performances often are, the Sulphur River Jazz Band's rehearsals are even more so.

If the bassist is late or no one is available to replace Jeff, the band simply does without. Rick sits slumped back in a couch and shifts his eyes from ceiling to floor while Jim plays, and during Rick's solos Jim wanders around the room, empties his spit valve, grabs a mute off a shelf and returns to his straight-backed chair in time to pick up on his cue.

"Our rehearsals are not very structured at all," Rick says. "We just learn the music and play it."

"Not necessarily in that order," Jim adds. "The freedom of Dixieland is what appeals to me. You can just play what you want to, within limits."

That freedom includes improvisation—one of the integral features of Dixieland jazz. On "St. Louis

Blues," a band favorite, "a lot of times we'll just keep taking solos indefinitely," Rick says.

"We once stretched it into 15 minutes at a gig," says Jim, who also gravels the song's vocals in an impression of jazz great Louis Armstrong. "It just depends. Jazz is such a flexible form. But since you're making stuff up, you have to listen to what everyone else is doing or you'll clash."

Rick and Jim agree that part of their band's tightness and improvisational skills arise from the family element, particularly when Jeff is home to join in.

"Rick and I and Jeff can tell what each other will play," Jim says. "It's like we're on the same wavelength. We can predict each other's musical response."

"Sometimes we'll even pick up our horns and play the exact same note," adds Rick.

Being without Jeff, both as a brother and as a clarinetist, has altered how the Sulphur River Jazz Band sounds as well as how Jim and Rick fit into the band's musical scheme. Sometimes, they have to go as far as to play the clarinet parts on trumpet or trombone.

"I have to adapt my style a little bit and play a few more runs and licks," Rick says. "It doesn't sound as good with no clarinet. That takes away from the music."

Jim, however, finds a few advantages to Jeff's absence. "There's less going on, and it's not as cluttered," he says. "We have more freedom because the instrumentation is not as full."

Besides, Jim adds, "We get a larger cut of the paycheck."

■ CLICHÉ—THE STUDENT WITH A DISEASE

■ Junior Benny Lupino is in Boston, where he is undergoing chemotherapy for leukemia. The cancer was discovered over the summer. Because of the disease, Benny has been forced to quit the high school football team. However, his mom said he is working hard to keep up his studies. "He wants to graduate with his class," Mrs. Etta Lupino said.

Benny is also a member of the National Honor

Society, the Latin Club, the Jazz Band and the yearbook staff.

"We are all praying for a speedy recovery," NHS sponsor Beverly Richmond said. "He's a wonderful young man, and if anyone can beat this, Benny can."

★ CREATIVE —STUDENT WITH A DISEASE

JOHN FILBECK WAS more afraid of never playing football again than he was of cancer. A 13-year-old has his own priorities. In the fall of 1998, increasing pain in his legs forced him out of the Pop Warner league in West Pittsburg, CA. The doctors found a rare and fast spreading tumor—neurofibrosarcoma—near his spine. As John lay in the hospital after surgery, his teammates paraded his jersey around the field.

In early 1999, John's father took him to Dr. Jordan Wilbur at the Children's Cancer Research Institute in San Francisco. The boy's first question was, "Will I die?" and the second, on hearing that he could but might not, was "Can I play football again?"

"Not this year," said Wilbur. "Maybe next."

John chose to hear, "Next year for sure," and that prospect sustained him through the next 18 months of treatment.

Wilbur prescribed a nasty brew of four drugs and radiation therapy. Each time John entered the hospital for another round, he tried to psyche himself like an athlete. He shaved his head to preempt the effects of the chemotherapy. He led the cheers for other sick kids on the floor. He reminded himself, as his stomach heaved again and again, what a coach always said: "Pain is mental, John." And: "If you're not hurting, you're not helping."

The strain aged his face, put lines of character on an already expressive brow. But the round-eyed fear showing in the picture above is still that of a little boy. The doctor is telling him that although his tumor has shrunk dramatically, he still might not be fit to play.

In August, John finished his treatment. He was in the clear—for now, perhaps forever. Eight times in three days, he telephoned Wilbur with the same question. When the doctor at last consented, John returned to the hospital to have the permission slip signed.

Tan and cocky, he strutted down the hall. He was wearing shoulder pads. When he got down on the shiny floor to demonstrate his four-point stance—a 96-pound defensive tackle—the wan children around him gaped in delight, and the nurses rubbed his head as if it were a magic lamp.

■ IN SUMMARY

Don't tell readers what they already know. Look for a fresh angle or point of view. Then report: interview, observe, listen for dialogue, interpret. Pay attention to those small details that allow you to tell the story of the event or issue. Reveal the real drama of real people, real places and real events. For example:

SHOWCASE ■

By **BRENT STINSKI**
City High School, Iowa City, IA

HER HAZEL EYES have given up crying about it. Now they just gaze back with cool acceptance, like they were looking at a scar, a bitter memory. She remembers that destroying thing that stole a piece of her life years ago. Incest.

It's taken her five years to look at it like this. Today she doesn't cry. Today she doesn't hate, use drugs, or live in depression like she did for so long. No, now Dede* realistically sees what happened between her and her brother and has moved on. She's a lucky one.

At City High there's a lot like her—teens who have dealt, or are dealing, with incest. Some are recovering. Others have been abused and keep it a secret. Maybe some will be abused tonight.

Chances are, you either unknowingly know an incest victim—he or she could be one of your friends —or you are one. Considered to be the best recent report on incest, *The Secret Trauma: Incest and the Lives of Girls and*

The Battle of Little Big Horn

As reported by an untrained high school journalist

MISTAKES TO AVOID

Second person, question lead

Definition from Webster

Editorial comment

Quote that provides no meaningful information

Anonymous quote for no good reason

List of names

Quote cliché

Obvious information asked

Editorial comment

H ave you ever been shot by an arrow and scalped? Well, General George Custer was. Custer and a lot of his men got together and went on a field trip to Little Big Horn. While they were there, they were attacked by Sioux Indians and killed in a massacre.

Webster defines massacre as "the act or an instance of killing a number of usually helpless or unresisting human beings under circumstances of atrocity and cruelty."

Well, you can bet General Custer wasn't helpless, but that didn't seem to matter because he's dead just the same. And the whole thing has really upset some people.

"This is very upsetting," commented President U.S. Grant. "Custer was a good soldier and was loved by all. We are going to miss him."

An unnamed soldier remarked, "I hate to hear about soldiers getting killed because I know it could happen to me."

Members of the Seventh Calvary who were killed included . . . .

When asked if he was pleased with the tribe's performance, Chief Sitting Bull was quoted as having expressed, "And how. Heap big victory."

Asked if he would comment on future battles, Chief Bull proclaimed, "We are not looking ahead. We fight them 'um, one battle at a time."

The Seventh Calvary didn't look so good this time out, but you can bet they'll get their act together and come on strong in battles to come.

Women, by Diana E. H. Russell, states that incest is of an alarming frequency. One in every six girls and one in every 10 boys is an incest victim before the age of 18. If that holds true, then there are about 160 incest victims at City.

"Incest basically is sexual behavior with a family member," says Ronnye Wieland, a therapist at Iowa City's Mental Health Center. She says incest can be any type of sexual contact, even just fondling, and that only about one-third of all incest actually involves intercourse.

"It can be touching in inappropriate places by any family member," Wieland says. Any relative can cause the scarring effects of incest. Lifelong effects like depression, intense stress, difficulty in establishing relationships, and flashbacks, the same kind experienced by war veterans.

Susan was five years old when her uncle started sexually abusing her. He was stopped nine years later.

"I sleep with a red stick," she says. "It's like a baseball bat, but only smaller. I'm scared he'll come and try to hurt me.

"You see, he carries a knife with him. And every time he sees me he puts a hand on that knife, and he just stares me down. I get cold chills. I start shaking and just run.

"That's why I sleep with that red stick."

That kind of fear has been with Susan for five years—ever since her uncle was reported to the police and forced to stop the abuse. But Susan, like many incest victims, finds she still loves him. Many incest victims find that even though they want to hate the abuse, they can't.

"My family's very important to me," Susan says. "I hate my uncle, but I love him because he's my uncle. I hate what kind of person he is, but I cannot hate him. He's my uncle."

Dede says she might have once loved her brother. Once, that is, when incest wasn't a part of their lives. But Dede remembers how she used to look up to him: the way any 11-year-old would to their older brother of four years.

"He was in high school, and I was in junior high," she recalls. "I was a little kid. I had a little mind. It was kind of neat at first because my older brother was finally paying attention to me.

"He was the only male in my life whom I looked up to," she says. "He was my older brother. He was supposed to protect me and take care of me. And then he does this. When you are a little kid, you trust everybody. When I was still a little kid, my trust in the world was totally shattered."

The betrayal of trust, therapists believe, is one of the most damaging aspects of incest.

"If a child cannot trust a relative, then they lose the ability to trust anyone," says Mary Ellen Lester, Susan's therapist. "The child is confused about what to believe. She is often told, 'This won't hurt; you'll like it,' and yet she knows inside she doesn't like it at all. Soon, she thinks that she can't trust her own feelings."

The victim can't even trust that her own emotions are valid. She's too insecure to be mad, too scared to be happy. To escape this insecurity and pain, "victims often self-medicate with illegal drugs," Lester said. "They don't want to face the pain of the recovery process."

At 15, Dede began abusing drugs. Now, she says, she's sure she did it to escape the effects of her brother's incest.

"If I couldn't leave or make it stop, then I'd check out of my head and go to a safe place until whatever was happening was over. That's how I dealt with it."

She pauses. "Or not dealt with it. Whichever."

Her self-abuse evolved into self-hate and self-blame. "It was easier to hate myself than to hate my older brother," she says. "I felt like: Why didn't I stop this sooner? Why did I let this happen in the first place? I felt like it was my fault. I hated myself; I hated him; I hated everybody."

COVERING CONTROVERSIAL ISSUES

So, you went to the national journalism convention and heard some guy from New York say, "Why are you covering prom when you should be covering real news?"

And from that, you interpret, "controversial topics: race, gender, politics, religion, teen sexuality, deviant and bizarre behaviors."

Before you dive in over your head, ask yourself:

■ Is this an issue at our school or in our community? If your school doesn't have a problem with gangs, don't cover gangs.

■ Do you have a conflict of interest?

■ Are you approaching a story with an open mind? Or are you hell-bent on finding a problem, no matter what?

GRAMMAR TIP

Know the difference between which and that as relative pro-nouns.

"Which" is non-restrictive. For example: The lawnmower, which is broken, is in the shed.

Here, "which" provides information about one specific lawnmower. We're not talking about multiple lawnmowers. We're talking about one lawnmower.

"That" is restrictive. For example: The lawn mower that is broken is in the shed.

Here, "that" identifies which lawnmower is broken. There are several lawnmowers. The one that is broken is in the shed.

Lester says self-blame is "something characteristic of almost every incest victim."

"Children don't understand that feeling bad doesn't make them bad," she says. "They think it's their fault, and they carry this assumption into adulthood. Recovery means realizing they are good people who had something bad happen to them."

After three years of abuse, Missy broke her secret about her stepfather. Police arrested him, and he spent three weeks in jail. Missy suffered for three years. He got three weeks.

"It seemed like I was getting the punishment and not him," she says. "I was ordered by the court to do all these things, like go to a counseling group. He was ordered to go to the groups too, but he never went."

He should have. Going to counseling was a godsend for Missy.

"Recovery is hard, but it's worth it," Missy said. "There are times when you go into depression, and you don't want to work at it, but there are also times when you feel good about yourself. When you make it through a group sessions, you just feel really good."

Wieland leads an incest group at the Mental Health Center.

"It's really mostly educational," she said. "We talk about taking care of ourselves, learning how to be assertive, and learning that our feelings are okay."

THE KEY TO RECOVERY? Find help. Immediately.

"It's the only way you can get on with your life and put your past in your past," Susan said. "You have no future if you can't deal with your past."

Susan said she's not going to let her uncle rob of the rest of her life.

"I will not let him have that," she said. "He's taken too much from me already. That bastard's not going to get any more."

Susan began therapy one year ago. But, she says, she feels she is only one-fourth of the way to full recovery.

Dede said she's given up the anger, the resentment and the drugs that came in the wake of the abuse at the hands of her brother.

"They brought my brother there to the treatment center, and we talked about it," she said. "He told me that he wasn't trying to hurt me, that he wasn't really thinking about what he was doing. The reason, he told me, was because I was somebody he trusted, that he couldn't do that to somebody he didn't trust.

"That doesn't make it all okay, but in that meeting I kind of let it go. It wasn't any big flash of lightning or revelation," she said. "It just kind of happened. I realized: Okay, this happened. Okay, it sucked. And I'm holding this big resentment against him, and I have for five years. Where is it getting me? Nowhere. I have to let it go now. I don't need to hurt about this anymore. I've hurt enough."

Dede knows she will never forget her past. The scars will always be too painful for her to do that. But at least now she accepts her life, herself. And those hazel eyes that used to cry are now looking to the future.

COMPARE & CONTRAST

FOCUS ON A SUBJECT

In a teenager's life, one thing is always true: the need for money is the same. Some teens can get money by working in stores, or by doing odd jobs, but perhaps the most popular way to earn fast money is through baby-sitting.

Baby-sitting at first glance seems to be the ideal job. You can sit and watch television and eat other people's food. At the same time, just keep an eye on their kids, and soon you've got a small fortune in your pocket. However, baby-sitting does have its share of problems.

For one thing, children don't always do what you tell them to do.

"Once, I had a boy lock himself in his room and begin tearing his shelves down," sophomore Clyde Zeigler said. "Another time, an 8-year-old let the family's dogs out of the back yard. It took me an hour to round them up."

Most students who baby-sit say they are paid at least $8 per hour and work from 7 p.m. until midnight. In addition, the kids usually go to bed at 9 p.m., leaving them three hours to talk on the phone or watch TV.

"Baby-sitting is boring, but it's easy," said Christy Dayton. "I usually talk to my boyfriend on the phone, or sometimes he comes over, and we watch movies together."

Most students said that they baby-sit once a week.

"Generally, I go out one night on the weekend and baby-sit the other," Christy said. The money she earns will be used to pay for gas and food, she added.

FOCUS ON AN INCIDENT

It only took a second.

Sophomore Clyde Zeigler turned his back on Josh long enough for the mischievous 8-year-old to open the backyard gates, allowing the three black Labradors to escape into the neighborhood.

"I really panicked," Clyde said. "The last thing Mr. Nelson, Josh's father, told me was to make certain the dogs didn't get out of the yard, and just like that, they were gone. I chased them down for an hour."

Welcome to the wonderful world of baby-sitting, where anything goes.

"On good nights, it's the best job in the world," junior Katie Dayton said. "But when things go bad, they go really bad."

For example, one night, a 5-year-old Katie was baby-sitting locked herself in a closet.

"I didn't have a key, and the light in the closet was off. She was screaming bloody murder, and I thought the neighbors were thinking that I was torturing her," Katie said. "Eventually, I had to get a screwdriver and remove the door knob. Boy, was that ever a nightmare."

The problem with baby-sitting, students say, is that little children rarely appreciate the gravity of their deeds.

"Once, when I was baby-sitting, this little boy put his cat and her four kittens in the dryer and turned it on," Lisa Gray said. "By the time I found them, three of the kittens had died, and the mother was totally freaked out. I had a hard time explaining what happened. Even now, I can hear that poor cat screaming."

■ Are your sources credible? Remember: one complaint doesn't necessarily constitute a problem.
■ Are your facts air-tight?
■ Have you double-checked all allegations?
■ Have you overstated facts?
■ Have you taken facts out of context?
■ Have you interviewed all sides?
■ If you promised anonymity to a source, have you made sure the source is protected?
■ Have you answered all obvious questions?
■ Is the tone of the story balanced and fair?
■ Is the story as close to the truth as possible?
■ If the story is potentially libelous, have you run it by an attorney?
■ Are you seeking controversy for controversy's sake?

Photo by **ADAM HOGG**
Bryant High School, Bryant, AR

SHOW ME, DON'T TELL ME

06

Describe it and be specific. Show the reader what it looks like, what it feels like, what it sounds like. Sure, descriptive reporting takes a lot of time and work, but the pay-off is well worth it.

CHAPTER HIGHLIGHTS:

■ Transport the reader to some place new.

■ Appeal to the senses and emotions.

■ Keep facts connected to the theme.

■ Connect with both the subject and the reader.

I like leads that take me somewhere, that transport me to another place and time. I want to be there, and I want stories to take me. I don't want to read a lead that says: *The city's homeless rate reached record high levels, a spokesman for the mayor's office announced.*

I want the lead to show me. What do these numbers mean in human terms?

RAY TUGGED the plastic garbage bag that served as a raincoat in a mostly unsuccessful attempt to stay dry, drew a few last puffs from a cigarette stub he found on the floor of a 7-11 store and joined the back of a line of down-and-out men, waiting for a warm bunk in the warehouse that serves as a shelter for the homeless on nights like this one.

"It must be 15 degrees out here," said Ray, who refused to give his last name. "It seems like every time the weather turns bad, this damn line gets longer and longer."

Ray is right.

A city official announced yesterday that the homeless rate has reached record high levels.

The strength of any descriptive piece lies in its use of details to appeal both to human emotions and to physical senses: sight, smell, hearing, taste and touch.

In an article about a man who suffered near-fatal brain damage in a bicycle accident, a reporter said the brain "resembles nothing more than a large, soft, very wrinkled walnut. It weighs almost three pounds. Of that, about 2 1/4 pounds is water and the rest tissue. The combination explains why the brain is often described as looking like Jell-O, but the better comparison would be mayonnaise. Push your finger into this gray blob of protoplasm, and it will adhere."

Now that's descriptive. And it only appealed to two of the five senses. Each of the next three leads use selective details to create an image that carries with it an emotional response. Not only do readers see something, but they also feel something as well, even if that something is a queasy feeling in the pit of their stomach.

■ DESCRIPTION OF A PLACE

NINE RED LEATHER chairs rest behind the mahogany table in the properly paneled and softly carpeted auditorium in the central administrative building on West Cabell Street.

All of the chairs are equal—but one is more equal than the others. It is the fifth chair, the one in the middle of the table. The back of the chair is slightly taller than the rest. This one is reserved for

Dr. Marvin Layne, who for the past 11 years has served as school board president. From this post, Dr. Layne has guided the district through several of its most turbulent years.

Flanked to the left by blue-tinted photographs of school board presidents dating back to 1911 and to the right by U. S. and Illinois flags, the 64-year-old college marine science professor has used this seat to cajole, intimidate and hammer through policies and procedures that he says have saved the district from disaster.

■ DESCRIPTION OF A MOMENT

IN THE BACK of ambulance 703, paramedic Hank Harky battles to keep a 17-year-old breathing, but the young man's airways are rapidly contracting. The teenager is suffering a heart attack from a drug overdose.

With sirens blaring and emergency lights flashing, the ambulance races along R. L. Thornton Freeway at 72 mph shortly before 10 p.m. Thursday, bearing down toward the Veterans Administration Medical Center.

"How far, Ben?" paramedic Harky shouts through a small window to his partner, driver Ben Bryan, who is working hard just to keep the shaking ambulance in one lane.

"Twelve minutes. We can still make the cut over to Parkland," the driver yells above the din.

The pain and excitement are exacting a toll on the patient, and his heart starts to beat erratically. Despite the intravenous medication he is receiving in his left arm, he starts grabbing at his chest and screams painfully between each laborious breath.

"Do it," paramedic Harky shouts to his partner, who revises the ambulance's destination to Parkland Memorial Hospital because it is closer.

This is a typical run on "box" 703, Dallas' busiest ambulance and the 11th busiest in the country, according to a national survey.

■ DESCRIPTION OF A PERSON

WALKING INTO A SMALL coffee and pizza shop, South grad Lisa Spindler cannot help but steal the attention of those inside. One by one, everyone in the room takes quick glances at the woman who searches for a vacant table. Dressed in a long trench coat, overlaying a white shirt, with a peach sweater wrapped around her dark jeans and a black hat that surrounds her porcelain-like face untouched by make-up, Spindler could be one of the models who have helped create her growing fame.

Spindler, who graduated from South 14 years ago, has made a career out of her love of photography that began in high school. Her career began primarily with fashion photography, but her current project tells the story of a homeless man through nude photographs.

"When I was younger, I used to look at many magazines, especially European publications," she said. "I always wanted to be a photographer after looking at these very powerful images."

After thanking the waitress who brings her tea, Spindler resumes her train of thought.

"I decided to borrow a camera and take Jack Summers' class. I took photography for two years at South, and it wasn't until the second year that the pictures started clicking, and I started to get a feel for the camera. That was the first year that I won awards for my work. I cannot remember how many. I think eight, but I won more awards than anyone else in southeast Michigan."

As Spindler speaks, she absent-mindedly drags the tea bag around the bottom of the cup by the string. She pauses only for a short moment to take a sip of tea.

■ APPEAL TO THE SENSES

Successful description does more than describe. It appeals to the senses and emotions. It generates empathy between the reader and the subject by forcing readers to judge the action in terms of their own experiences.

Identifying the theme and determining the angle will assist you greatly in collecting detail. For example, the reporter in the story on page 71 has decided to tell the story of PALS, a peer drug counseling program, by examining its positive influences on a specific student, Joey Eberhart. So the theme of the story is "For Joey Eberhart and students like him, PALS has not only saved his life but allowed him to save others."

Now, the reporter has to decide on an angle, how to approach the story. She attends several sessions in which Joey counsels younger students. She interviews Joey, his counselors and the students he counsels. But she decides to angle the story on the relationship between Joey and a younger student, Brian Kennedy.

Finally, she opts to begin the story by describing one specific, though typical, counseling session. Notice how the theme, the angle and the description work together to pull the reader into the story by evoking images and emotions.

IT IS HARD TO TELL whether he is more tired or bored or ashamed as Brian Kennedy rubs his hands through his greasy, coal-black hair and then down across his chin that has yet to grow anything more than peach fuzz. He stares down at the table or darts his eyes across the room. He refuses to look forward.

For sitting across from him is Joey Eberhart. And Joey is mad.

"Damn it man, I can't believe you did this to me," Joey says. "I can't believe you did it to yourself."

Brian, a freshman, knows he has let Joey down. He closes his eyes and speaks slowly.

"You don't know what it's like out there. I just couldn't turn it down. I really didn't want to get drunk. Getting drunk isn't that much fun anymore. But I got stuck with the wrong people."

Joey understands. Three years ago, he was a ninth-grade drunk himself. Today, the senior is a member of PALS—teenagers who licked their own abusive habits and now help younger kids beat their own. Still rail-thin, like he was when he was popping pills and boozing, Joey's skin is a translucent orange-yellow, the result, he says, of a vegetarian diet.

■ DESCRIPTION MAKES A POINT

We learn a lot about Brian and Joey in these five paragraphs, and what we learn is relevant. The description isn't a random collection of details. It makes a point. Some writers overwhelm the reader with details that fail to add anything substantial to the story. (For example: Joey's favorite band is Smashing Pumpkins. His favorite food is meatless spaghetti. The person he'd most like to meet is Robin Williams.)

Unless you're being paid by the word, there's no excuse to ramble on and on. Compare the story above to this flat, one-note article:

A GROWING NATIONAL concern about the prevention of alcohol and substance abuse has led to the development of the Peer Advisory program in Pine Valley schools.

PALS began three years ago in the Brookland district by an initial grant from the federal government. Students who are part of the PALS program voluntarily take part in an initial 16- to 20-hour training program and monthly two-hour training sessions throughout the school year.

Senior class president Cindy Greene, member of PALS, said, "Peer Advisory is a worthwhile organization because students have fellow students who can understand the problems they may be facing in their day-to-day lives."

PALS volunteers visit ninth grade homerooms every Tuesday and offer Lunch Bunch every Thursday. Lunch Bunch is held during all lunches and openly discusses a different topic each week.

Every word of your story should advance action. The following leads contain information that serves no function other than decoration.

■ EXAMPLE A

Sitting in a room filled with broken radiators and jumbled desks, valedictorian hopeful Joanna Brown looks across the brim of her wire-rim glasses and expresses her feelings about life, how she divides her time between social and academic activities and how she still maintains the highest GPA in a class of 271.

■ EXAMPLE B

In England, soccer fans are as likely to get bashed in the head and then crushed into a steel fence. Last year, six people were killed at a soccer

WE FROWN ON LEADS LIKE THESE

THE "HAS ANYONE TRIED THIS BEFORE" QUESTION LEAD

Avoid question leads like "Have you ever . . . ." or "Do you know . . . ."

Why? They create an artificial connection between the subject and the reader. If the story is about an astronaut, the reporter should focus on that the astronaut, not the reader.

Have you ever flown in a space ship around the moon and back?

Well, Bucky Jones has. He is an astronaut, and he said he loves flying around in space at a billion miles per hour.

> **"** If your story meets all the criteria, it will, in the language of editors, "work." That means it will consist of a real person who is confronted with a significant problem, who struggles diligently to solve that problem, and who ultimately succeeds—and in doing so becomes a different character."

— Jon Franklin
Writing for Story

APPEAL TO THE SENSES

WHAT DID IT LOOK LIKE?
Coach Miles stepped out of the field house into the blinding lights of the television cameras. The bags under his glassy eyes hung like leather pouches on a white horse. He'd been crying.

WHAT DID IT SMELL LIKE?
I remember that my grandmother's house smelled like old perfume and cat boxes.

WHAT DID IT TASTE LIKE?
On their first date, Jerry kissed Sue, perhaps more passionately than she had expected or wanted. She tasted like Wintergreen Altoids. He tasted like Frito pie.

WHAT DID IT FEEL LIKE?
The steak was as chewy as rubber vomit.

WHAT DID IT SOUND LIKE?
He plays for a rock and roll band whose music sounds like a lawn mower at full throttle falling through a plate-glass roof into a pile of aluminum pots and pans.

match in Liverpool. Pine Valley High School also has a soccer team, but it's more laid back.

■ EXAMPLE C
The Spanish Club started off this year with the breaking of a piñata. Club members also learn, little by little, the culture of Spanish speaking countries and how to learn Spanish, too. The Spanish Club will hold its next meeting next Tuesday.

■ IS IT SIGNIFICANT?
In example A, what is the significance of the broken radiators and jumbled desks? Why mention her wire-rim glasses?

In example B, the story concerns the high school's soccer team. Focus on it. That soccer is popular in England is irrelevant.

In example C, who cares how the Spanish Club began the year? Provide the specific

incidents and details that show the process by which students come to appreciate a different culture. Breaking a piñata isn't one of them.

Consider these next two stories. The first involves romantic obsession, a provocative topic rarely covered by high school publications but certainly a reality among American teenagers. Rather than taking a wide-angle view of it, the reporter chooses to focus on a specific girl and her experience with an obsessive young man.

SHE THOUGHT HE WAS going to kill her. He had been angry before, even punched his hand through a window once, but he had never threatened her, never scared her like this.

Now he was out of control. He pushed her into a corner and then shoved her back down when she tried to escape. "All I could think was 'I have to get out of here." I just started crying."

That was a month ago. Today, Julie (not her real name) has ended her relationship with Jim (not his real name), but he didn't give up without a fight.

"He'd circle my house, leave me little notes, stare at me in class," Julie said. "He kind of lost it."

Other high school students have similar stories. Obsessive love is all too real for many teenagers . . .

■ CREATE THE DESIRED IMAGE
This is far more effective than "Webster defines obsession as. . . . Many students are involved in obsessive relationships." Even though we haven't described Jim or Julie, we have described the situation sufficiently to create the desired image.

The next example involves long distance relationships, and, again, note that it focuses on a specific couple and uses their experience as the universal experience.

NANCY AND BILL WERE the darlings of last year's senior class. They dated all through high school and even into the first year of college. But there was a problem. Nancy attended the University of Maryland, Bill the University of Virginia.

"We'd see each other on weekends and talk to each other on the phone a lot," Nancy said. "But

I began to feel that I was missing out on my college life, and so I started thinking about breaking up."

Bill had gone one step farther.

"I was still technically going with Nancy, but I started dating a few women at UVA," he said. "And I started seeing my relationship with Nancy as a drag."

During the Thanksgiving weekend, Nancy and Bill agreed to break up.

"I still loved Nancy, but the long distance relationship wasn't working out," Bill said.

Too often, it doesn't.

Counselor Mike Barry said . . . .

Now, pick up with whatever statistics and other general information needed to fully develop the story. Make certain to return to the narrative about Nancy and Bill.

■ STRIP STORIES TO A SINGLE THEME

Here's a trick I picked up along the way: strip subjects to a single sentence and then rebuild them around stories. For example, use a review of a book about teenagers and their jobs to find story ideas. Look for a local and timely angle and place at the heart of the story a teenager—a student at your school—rather than the book or the author. Do this, and the article will have personal impact. The following example shows the kind of shoddy efforts we see too often.

EDUCATORS ARE concerned that part-time jobs are robbing teenagers from receiving a full high-school education, according to Cameron Barton, education professor at the University of South Carolina and author of *Teenagers and Their Work.*

■ **PREDICTABLE LEAD.** While this isn't plagiarism, it makes no attempt to localize the information.

FOR MANY STUDENTS, putting in a full day's work means more than sitting in class from 8 to 3. More and more, students are working four-, five-, even eight-hour shifts daily at minimum-wage jobs.

However, part-time jobs are an increasing concern to educators, who worry that students lose more than they receive in their pursuit of a weekly paycheck.

According to *Teenagers and Their Work* by Cameron Barton, education professor at the University of South Carolina, "We are challenging the myth that part-time work is good for teenagers. In fact, our findings suggest the opposite."

★ **UNIQUE ANGLE.** This lead localizes the situation to the school in a descriptive, appealing manner.

AT TWO each afternoon, while most of the students at Reagan High School are bent over their books, struggling against afternoon torpor, trying to hang in there for two more hours, senior Ricky Moreno is headed out to the parking lot.

He has an hour to dash home, change clothes, grab a bite, then drive to Tom Thumb where, for the next eight hours, he'll handle customers' questions and complaints, issue refunds, send cashiers on their breaks and in general keep things running smoothly at the front of the store.

Ricky is the customer service manager. It's an unusually important job for a teenager, and he is proud of it.

"It's teaching me responsibility," he says, "how to deal with my own money and how companies work inside and outside."

But many educators, sociologists, labor leaders and parents would disagree. Increasingly, they're critical of such after-school work.

In Florida, Hawaii, Nebraska, New York, North Carolina and Ohio, state legislators are debating laws that would limit the number of hours teenagers can work. Tennessee already has passed such a law.

■ **PREDICTABLE LEAD**

LAST WEEK, Mrs. Joyce Cripe's senior government classes participated in the Citizen Bee contest. According to Mrs. Cripe, the purpose of Citizen Bee is to help students understand world issues and events.

"We learned a lot about what's going on

WE FROWN ON LEADS LIKE THESE

THE "I'M NO JOURNALIST BUT MY CREATIVE WRITING TEACHER LOVES ME" LEAD

Ominously, anxious eyes visible and invisible gazed up from the Cypress-filled banks of the Palm River, its bone-chilling waters running gently over oval, white stones, to the visage of a young woman as she inched to the rim of the bridge. Would she do it? Would she take the plunge? The spectators sat transfixed, frozen both by the frigid waters and the anticipation of the next jump.

In a flash, Sue Bob answered their questions by diving like a swan into the voluminous gulch. As the elastic rope snapped her back from the jaws of death, she realized she should have brought with her another pair of underwear.

Get to your nutgraf quickly? The nutgraf explains what the story is about. For example:

Nikki Spivey's lunch today consisted of one apple, eight onces of non-fat peach yogurt and a rice cake. She skipped breakfast and says she'll probably skip dinner too.

Nikki is on a diet. Has been for two months. She's trying to lose 20 pounds—down to 110.

"Lower if possible," she says. "I can't go out in a swimsuit looking like this."

Like thousands of other teenage girls, Nikki is starving herself in order to fit into society's cookie-cutter image of what an attractive woman look like.

around the globe and how events in one part of the world affect us here," junior Lance Brinson said.

★
UNIQUE ANGLE
JENNIFER BRIGGS couldn't believe the question: Who was the mayor of Berlin at the time the wall was built?

"Who cares?" she thought. Seconds earlier, her opponent had received what she thought was an easy question: Who was Ronald Reagan's vice president?

"Why didn't I get that one?" she asked herself, hoping all the while that the correct answer to her question would pop into her head.

It didn't. And so another student advanced in the Academic Club competition.

"I guess the most frustrating thing is that you never know what they're going to ask, and there's so much history that you can't learn everything," Jennifer said. But that hasn't stopped her from competing in the meets.

"I'm a big Jeopardy fan, and this is my way of playing Jeopardy," Samantha Haney said. "It's nerve-wracking, but I love it."

Now, try a few of your own with these sentences:

1. The Student Council had a busy year.
2. She was a popular and excellent teacher.
3. The National Honor Society participated in many charitable activities this year.
4. Computers made a big difference in the school this year.
5. Soap operas remained popular with students.
6. The death of a popular sophomore after a long bout with cancer had a tremendous impact on students.
7. A spirit of volunteerism swept through the school.

■ **WRITE THE WAY YOU THINK**
Go to the thesaurus when you know there is a better word but can't think of it. Never use it in the futile attempt to prove to everyone what a great vocabulary you have.

Readers won't be impressed.

So if you're writing about video games, say, "Red-eyed, pale as a ballerina, Zippo slouched over Mortal Kombat, his latest video addiction, and continued slamming buttons and blurting, 'Die, Mother.' "

Don't write: "Imbued with a veritable plethora of vexation augmented by his physical dissipation, Zippo engaged the computerized entertainment facility, thus terminating his video adversaries."

■ **MAKE IT COUNT**
As stated earlier, make certain the description contributes to the development of the story's theme. Don't describe for the sake of describing. For example:

PRINCIPAL MADGE O'BRIEN said it is an honor to be nominated as Administrator of the Year but added she really doesn't expect to win.

"I'm pleased that the faculty thinks enough of me to nominate me for this award," O'Brien said wistfully, her pretty blue eyes looking up over her half-moon glasses. "It's like an Academy Award. I'm thrilled to be nominated, but I don't expect to win."

Wearing a white silk blouse and blue skirt that looked more like a first-grade teacher than a principal of a tough high school, O'Brien said softly that she appreciates the support she has received from students and teachers alike.

The description here has little impact on her nomination, and the story really goes nowhere. What she wears, the color of her eyes and how she speaks are not irrelevant to the theme of the story. With another angle—an anecdote that shows why she was nominated—they could be. For example:

MADGE O'BRIEN stared over the top of her rimless, half-moon glasses, straight into the junior's eyes and said, "One more mistake, mister, and you're out of here."

The junior nodded, not daring to meet her cool-blue glare. He didn't confuse the soft voice for a lack of authority. He knew she'd do it.

TRAIN REPORTERS TO SEE THE ACTION

This exercise, created by H.L. Hall, former adviser at Kirkwood High School (Kirkwood, MO) asks students to rewrite each paragraph, making it as descriptive as possible. Students are free to use their imaginations to create scenes as they think they may have existed. The purpose of the exercise is to spur students to think descriptively.

- Jeff Wagner, senior, ran more than 500 miles during the summer to practice for the cross country season. The temperature was over 100 for nine consecutive days. The high temperatures caused other runners to get sick to their stomachs.

- Up and down country lanes, heat waves rose from the sweltering pavement, the result of nine consecutive 100-plus days. In the distance, a pack of young men—sunburned and drenched in sweat—slogged forth, battling the record temperatures in preparation for the fall cross country season.

  Leading the pack, Jeff Wagner pushed on, rolling up more than 500 miles this summer, hanging tough at times when others dropped to the sides of the road, sick to their stomachs and gasping for breath.

- Four students spent the summer lifeguarding at city pool. Whistling down children for running and breaking other pool rules occupied much of their time. They also operated the concession stand and battled throbbing headaches and sunburn. The best part, they said, was watching other teenagers.

- The lifeguards' life isn't as glamorous as it's made out to be. Sure, they get a killer tan and a plenty of time to check out members of the other sex. But they also must sell hot dogs, soft drinks and candy while keeping tabs on hordes of elementary and junior high kids whose primary interests almost always include running on wet pavement. A typical day is

likely to conclude with a hammering headache and a sunburn.

- Students stood in line for hours to buy tickets to a Rolling Stones concert. One student got in line 84 hours before tickets went on sale. Traffic jams the night of the concert delayed the start of the concert by one hour. There was standing room only, and the crowd went wild.

- The line started to form days before tickets went on sale. One student waited in line for 84 hours to snatch front row seats. For what? The Rolling Stones, one of rock 'n' roll's most celebrated bands, a group that survived the '60s intact and whose appeal stretches from 50-year-old former hippies turned investment brokers to 15-year-old skateboarders.

  As usual, the band didn't disappoint. The standing-room-only crowd went wild when Mick Jagger and group stormed onto the stage, despite an hour delay due to a traffic snarl created by the throngs of fans coming to see the show.

- Four students participated in the Moonlight Ramble, a 20-mile bike ride at night. Jon Byrd, sophomore, attempted to ride under a rope barrier at the start of the course. The rope caught on the seat of his bike and threw him to the ground. He still won first place.

- Sophomore Jon Byrd overcame a rough tumble at the beginning of the Moonlight Ramble—his bike seat snagged on a rope barrier, tossing him to the ground—to win the 20-mile night rally over three other students.

WE FROWN ON LEADS LIKE THESE

THE 'BUT WAIT!' MAYBE NOT LEAD.

Armed with a sword and shield, the man charges into battle. His opponent blocks every swing of his mighty blade. Exhausted, the man lets his defense down, giving his enemy an opportunity to attack.

With one slice of a sword to the leg, the man is on the ground, screaming and clutching his mutilated leg. Soon, the opponent has killed the disabled man—a mighty slash that splits the man's head—and the battle is over.

But wait! There is no blood. The corpse hops up and is shaking his enemy's hand. No longer enemies, these two are now friends! They are participants in the annual Round Top Shakespearean Festival.

> ❝ Good journalism thrives on good quotations. The right quotes, carefully selected and presented, enliven and humanize a story and help make it clear, credible, immediate and dramatic.❞
>
> — Paula LaRocque
> Championship Writing

O'Brien is all-business even though she looks more petite than potent. In fact, faculty members are so impressed that they nominated her for state Administrator of the Year.

"Women administrators are a relatively new phenomenon," O'Brien said. "The stereotypical administrator is a male and often a former coach, so women have had to fight to enter the higher echelons of administration and then fight even more for respect once they arrived."

Respect is not a commodity in short supply when it comes to O'Brien.

"I've taught here for 25 years and have seen six or seven principals here in that time, and Mrs. O'Brien is as good as any of them and better than most," science teacher Edwin Holt said. "She comes from the classroom and is sensitive to the needs of classroom teachers. She's tough, but she's fair. That's what has impressed me the most about her."

Even students say O'Brien is a cut above.

"She's open and honest, and she treats us like equals," Student council president Liz Collier said. "She doesn't patronize us, and she's made the Council a partner in some decisions affecting students. She's great."

The purpose of description is not merely to decorate but to help the reader understand why the visual details are important. Specific details allow the readers to see not only what you've seen but also to appreciate why the subject is interesting and important.

■ DESCRIPTION OF NEWS

Nor is description confined to features and other non-timely content. The lead of a next-day news article can be as descriptive as the reporter wishes to make it.

As the city editor of a weekly newspaper in California, I was forced to cover school board meetings. I don't wish this on my worst enemy. School board meetings are deadly tedious unless the subject of sex education comes up. And then everyone turns into jihad warriors.

Fact is, sex isn't discussed much at school board meetings, at least not during the public

YOU SAID IT , friend!

Use the verb "said." Avoid synonyms, such as:

- believes
- feels
- evoked
- states
- expressed
- commented
- according to
- remarked

"Explained" may be used occasionally but only if the quote presents an obvious interpretation or clarification. You may believe an idea or feel an emotion, but you cannot believe or feel a direct quote. You may use synonyms for "said" if the synonym implies an emotional tone or action, such as whimpered, screamed, complained, whispered, charged or argued. Synonyms are usually reserved for dialogue—not quoted material. For example:

"I told you to quit hitting golf balls in the journalism room," Miss Offset snapped.

"Oh golly gee, I'm just trying to have a little fun," senior Billy Ingrate whined.

session. Budgets are. So are outcome-based education and higher order thinking skills and performance assessment models and all kinds of eduspeak, which explains why most people would rather clean chicken coops than attend a school board meeting.

Still, school boards make decisions that have a direct impact on students. When this happens, you'll be expected to report them. If your school board is accommodating, it will meet a day or two before deadline so that your stories will be fresh and timely. Don't bank on it though. To wit: Meetings often end late on Monday nights, forcing parents to choose among their children's education, Monday night football and a good night's rest.

Consequently, you are responsible for reporting news about an event that students wouldn't attend, even if it opened with Eminem. Still, it's your job to make students want to read about it, to know what happened and why, to understand what the decision means to the average Nick and Nora in the halls.

■ IT CAN BE DONE.

Let's assume that the school board votes 4-3 to shut down a school. Citing declining enrollment in the district, the board votes to close Kennedy High School and divide its students among the three other schools in the district. It's not a popular decision.

How do you cover this?

Remember that your job is to answer not only all news questions—who, what, when, where, why and how—but also all reader questions like, "How much?" and "so what?"

Answering all the applicable questions does not enslave you to the summary lead. In fact, you may even use the inverted pyramid form so long as you begin the story with the most important idea or angle. In developing this idea or angle, you may use a straight news lead, and there's nothing that says a straight news lead cannot be descriptive.

You will choose the approach based on your determination that one approach more effectively communicates the content of the story. So you'll use an anecdotal lead because you believe it best tells the story. Or you'll use a news lead that emphasizes "why" because you believe it best tells the story.

The point is this: you will have options available to you, and you will choose the option that best fits the tone, style, readership expectations and content of the story. You will not use the inverted pyramid merely because "that's what we've always done."

Let's return to the matter at hand. The school board has voted to close Kennedy High School. To adequately report this story, you must begin by collecting information: Who voted in favor of the plan? Why? Who voted against? Why? How many students will be affected? Where will they go? When will this go into effect? How much will it cost? How much

will it save? What will happen to the faculty, staff and administration at Kennedy? What was the percentage of enrollment decline that prompted the board's decision?

Finding answers to the questions will mean you'll have to interview a number of people, perhaps two or three times.

Let's assume now that you've collected this information. Are you through? No. You need now to find an angle that will give a human face to this news event. So you ask yourself, "How does this news event, this school board action affect students? Which students are most affected? How so?

So now, you're off to interview students. You could wander up and down the halls, asking the people you bump into, "What do you think about the board's decision?"

I can predict their answers: It stinks. Let's go for a more unusual, provocative lead. If the school has been around for any length of time, it's probable that two or three generations of family members are graduates of the school. That being the case, interview Grandpa, Pa and Junior.

Perhaps you have a young woman who was to be the last of nine children to graduate from the school. What are her thoughts? Perhaps a teacher would have retired next year after having taught her entire career at the school. What are her plans?

Sit down with three or four members of your staff and brainstorm. How many other angles could you find for this story? It's almost unlimited. Your major restraints will be time and space. You don't have an infinite amount of time to devote to the article. And the publication does not have an infinite amount of space. So you must pursue the story from what you think will be the most lucrative direction, select and organize your data, determine the key news element to the story and then choose an angle that best presents that news element.

THE PORTRAITS OF sophomore Laura Hall's eight brothers and sisters are scattered around the school. Her oldest brother, Rick, was an all-state basketball player in 1997. His photo hangs in the

WE FROWN ON LEADS LIKE THESE

THE "WHAT EVERYONE ELSE IS REPORTING" LEAD

Last month, Time magazine reported bungee jumping is growing in popularity throughout the United States. Bungee jumping, Time stated, is the act of leaping off bridges and having an elastic cord spring you back up, right before you smack the ground.

According to Bungee Illustrated, more people are into bungee jumping these days than sumo wrestling.

"It's the nation's fasting growing sport, involving 150-feet rubber bands," David Marks, a bungee jumper from West Virginia, stated in the magazine.

Develop a scene that puts the reader in the middle of the action or moment. For example:

When news broke about the mayhem and killing at Santana High School, Charles Williams frantically dashed to the school to make sure his 15-year-old son wasn't hurt. As he searched the chaotic tableau of sobbing teens and panicked parents, Williams asked a girl, "Do you know where Andy is?" Her quiet reply, "With the cops."

boys' gym. Her sisters, Teresa and Rebecca, were both chosen "Most Likely to Succeed" several years ago. Their photos are in the oak trophy case in the senior hall.

Laura had hoped her senior picture might one day join them, collecting dust next to the plaques and trophies that the school has accumulated over the past 40 years. It won't happen. Not because Laura isn't an honor student. She is.

But next year—Laura's senior year—the school won't exist. By a 4-3 vote Tuesday, the school board voted to close the school and divide its students, faculty and administrators among the district's three other high schools.

For Laura and hundreds of others, the decision was devastating.

"Every day I walk these halls, I am conscious that my days here are numbered," she said. "Since my freshman year, I've looked forward to being a senior, going to the football games, homecoming, the prom. I remember watching my sisters and brothers and knowing that one day, my time would come. And now, it's all gone."

School board president Donald Sweatt was among the four members who voted in favor of the plan to close the school. He was joined by Richard Moreland, Kathy Mayeux and Mary Richter. Voting "no" were Doug Abel, Adam Cavazos and Wilma McCormick.

"It has been an unpopular move, but sometimes you have to do what you know is right, whether it's popular or not," said Sweatt, a retired Army officer. "I graduated from Kennedy. I know what these kids are going through, and I feel for them. Believe me, I do. But we could not endanger the entire district to save this high school."

The board cited declining enrollment as the primary reason for its decision. Since 1996, enrollment at the school has dropped 25 percent—from 1300 to just over 950 this year. District officials say they expect another decrease next year.

"The economy here is flat," superintendent Lois Sexton said. "We have no new businesses moving in, and we're losing population each year. Until the

THE RIGHT WORD

You'll read this in every book about writing, but it needs to be repeated: Concentrate on action verbs and specific nouns. If you have a choice among words, select the one with the narrowest meaning.

Choose specifics rather than generalities:

STRONG	WEAK
Air Jordans	shoes
Toyota Camry	car
trudged	walked
jabbered	talked
Stetson	hat
stroked	touched

You get the idea.

economy picks up, I don't see how we can expect enrollment to stabilize."

Dr. Sexton said the district will save $2.1 million by closing Kennedy. She added that at this point, school officials are more concerned with reassuring Kennedy students that they are committed to as easy a transition as possible.

"Under the best of circumstances, moving to a new school is difficult," counselor Bob Murphy said. "We will be working especially hard to see that this move is as painless as we can make it."

For Laura Hall, that isn't good enough.

"No matter how hard they try, we're still going to be the new kids at school," she said. "We won't hold the offices. We won't edit the yearbook or be homecoming queen. We'll be at school, but we won't be at our school."

■ SPORTS DESCRIPTION

Look for the theme of the story, and then find a way to illustrate the theme. Describe a scene. Capture a moment. Tell a story. For example, the volleyball team is in the midst of its best season in history. The typical story will say something like this:

THE VOLLEYBALL team has compiled a 27-3-2 record, its best in school history. Leading the state's fourth-ranked team are Tara Fumerton, Sara Kurth and Markisha Drayton.

Head coach Greg Vraspier said, "The team has been playing real well so far, and we think we can go a long way once we get in the playoffs. If we maintain our focus and intensity, we could challenge for the state crown."

Members of the team include . . . .

Unless readers are already volleyball fans, they are not likely to read this story. If they're interested, they probably go to games or follow the team in some other way. Thus, this story tells them nothing they don't already know. How can sports provide meaningful and compelling information for both the fan and the non-fan? By concentrating on the psychological or emotional elements of the game: fears, disappointments, frustrations and dreams.

The following lead puts readers in the middle of a quiet locker room seconds before the start of a big game so that they can be a part of the dynamic tension of the moment. The reporter uses interpretation to place the season into a historical context. It's the winningest season in history. The team won its first victory over its big rival in five years. Success is the result of an intensive off-season regiment.

SHOWCASE ■

By **STEVE DOOLITTLE**
City High School, Iowa City , IA

INSIDE THE GIRLS' locker room, the volleyball team waits. The players are nervous with anticipation. Clustered together, the players display emotions in different ways. Some yell, scream or laugh. Others are quiet, searching for inward motivation. Silently to themselves, they all wonder: will we win the match?

But winning is not the only thing on their minds. They hear the crowd assembling in the gymnasium outside, producing a noise sounding like the slow, steady beat of a drummer. To the players, the fans are a distant rumbling but a reality they will soon face. They know that tonight the bleachers will be filled. Their ability, skill, team unity and emotion will be displayed to all their fans.

And the fans come for all types of reasons. They come because they know a player on the team, because they expect to cheer on the team that represents their school and because they want to have fun. But most of all they come because this year, the Central High School volleyball team is a team that can make things happen. A team that has been opening the eyes of people throughout the state.

A HISTORY LESSON

"We're number one," senior Tara Fumerton yelled while running across the court after beating Cedar Rapids Washington in four games 17-15, 10-15, 15-12 and 15-7. Even if, according to Division 4A ranking, they were number five, after the emotional victory, CHS felt as though they were number one.

This year, with a 27-3-2 record, the volleyball team is having its best season in school history. They've already set the CHS record for most wins in a season and have a chance to win more at district and state. The impressive season began earlier this year when they beat West High for the first time in five years.

The secret to the team's success seems to be its stamina.

"We've been outlasting most of our opponents," head volleyball coach Greg Vraspier said. "In the final games of our matches, our opponents have been slowing down and reacting poorly. But we've been ready on our feet and jumping to play until the very end."

For the moment, the volleyball players are basking in the glory of their success. Their satisfaction is well deserved after the intensive

WE FROWN ON LEADS LIKE THESE

THE WACKY COMPARISON LEAD

Most people think that jumping off a bridge is crazy, but not Judy. Judy loves it! She doesn't use a parachute either. Is this wacky or what?

THE "I'M TOO DUMB OR LAZY TO COME UP WITH A FEATURE LEAD SO I'LL JUST LAY OUT THE FACTS AS I SEE THEM" LEAD

Senior Judy Smith is a bungee-jumper. Bungee jumping is a sport in which persons are attached to a long, elastic cord, much like a huge rubber band, and then jump off bridges or other high suspension structures.

Asked why she does it, Judy said, "Because it's fun."

training they have been through over the summer.

"We were determined to improve during the off-season," Fumerton said. "So we went to the weight room three times a week and conditioned by running stairs at Hawkeye Arena. Our strength is what makes us better than other teams."

Vraspier agrees that the players' increased strength has been key to their success.

"They hit the ball so much harder and with so much more force," he said. "They never fade at the end of games."

THE FUTURE

With the MVC tournament and a match against Linn-Mar coming up before districts, the volleyball team just has to work on the tiny details. Although careless errors are hard to eliminate, CHS wants to keep them to a minimum.

"The careless errors are the only things that slow us down," Vraspier said.

CHS is being recognized as a contender throughout the state.

"We're in that situation where all the other teams are gunning for us. We're a team to beat, and we'll continue to be a team to beat," he added.

Vraspier said he is optimistic about the team's chances at districts.

"When we enter districts, we'll be going for revenge against Davenport North. They've beaten us twice. Now we're going to beat them. After we win, we should be on our way to state. I hope we win state, but this is the first year in a long time where CHS actually has a fair chance.

"Whenever I'm asked, 'Just how good is your team?' I remember an experience I had earlier this season," Vraspier said. "I was sitting in the stands when some players from a varsity team that I had previously coached came up to me and asked if it would be possible for them to play on our varsity team. I said 'no' and thought to myself, 'maybe the freshman team.' "

Here's another exceptional sports lead. Note how Patrick combines story-telling and scene development to capture more than the score. Note also how the interesting and informative direct quotes build drama.

SHOWCASE ■

By **PATRICK HEALY**
Grosse Point South HS, Grosse Point , MI

THEY STAGGERED OFF the court after five minutes of play, sweating and red-faced like students taking the world's worst final exam.

"If I live through the second half I'll be OK," wheezed social studies teacher Tom Briske, one of 11 South teachers who took on their Grosse Pointe North counterparts in the first North/South teachers' basketball game Tuesday, Feb. 23. The lead bounced between the sides for the first of two 25-minute halves, but South's teachers rebounded late in the game and won 57-44.

"Winning was a pleasant surprise," said social studies teacher James Cooper. "We just wanted not to make fools out of ourselves."

South's team only squeezed in one half-hour practice before the game while the North teachers had been practicing for weeks. This made the victory especially sweet, Cooper said.

Scorekeeper and North science teacher Art Weinle didn't know what to think when he walked into the gym. He saw 49-year-olds taking (and missing) practice jump shots and their 5-year-old children crawling all over the team bench. Compared to high school games, this was chaos.

"How are we going to keep track of personal fouls? Is someone going to keep an official score?" he asked two Student Association (SA) representatives who helped organize the game. "Somebody's got to decide these things. Are we having a regulation game or not."

The students stared at Weinle like he was speaking Russian. He shrugged and flipped his North hat on backwards.

Like most basketball games, this one started with the national anthem. Only someone forgot to rewind the tape.

When announcer Mike Kaselitz '99 pressed

BE LIKE REALLY, TOTALLY INTOLERANT OF ADVERBS

In other words, dump as many adverbs as possible. They're clumsy crutches for weak or underdeveloped verbs. For example:

- Joe walked slowly down the lane.
- Joe trudged down the lane.

- Rosemarie quickly drank her bottle of Gatorade.
- Rosemarie guzzled her bottle of Gatorade.

- Upon hearing the news that the administration had banned low rise pants and tube tops during the school day, freshman Katie Melton wept pitifully.
- Upon hearing the news that the administration had banned low rise pants and tube tops during the school day, freshman Katie Melton blubbered like a baby.

"play," the song began near the end. The crowd laughed as Kaselitz rewound the tape, but the teachers were too impatient. They blared out a version of the "Star Spangled Banner" that could have shattered the gym's fluorescent lights.

Then they took the court. The game started off friendly enough. It picked up when North teachers in the stands chanted, "Go North! Beat South!" Then it got serious.

"Work it now, work it now! Push it, push it," science teacher Ranae Ikerd hollered as she waited to jump into the game. "There's a lot of hacking out there, but I'm worried about just making it up and down the court."

Going by the numbers, North football coach Frank Sumbera was the meanest. He racked up four personal fouls as he lumbered back and forth across the court.

"We tried to keep it (the game) under control, but it didn't happen," referee and SA President John Bershback '99 said.

During the second half, science teacher Werner Schienke led a cheer with the South fans. Normally a forward, Schienke showed up to the game with crutches and a severed Achilles tendon, an injury that happened during the team's lone practice. His jersey said it all. Unlucky number 13.

South's team broke away with a 20 point lead in the second half. But by the buzzer, North's teachers narrowed it to 13 points.

The victorious teachers slapped high fives and wiped the sweat off their bodies. They shook hands with their opponents and headed out, some to celebrate and some to bed.

North Principal Caryn Wells watched them go.

"They played an awesome game," she said, "but look out for next year. The mighty Norsemen will be ready."

In the next example, Laura Matthews describes a moment that captures the feelings of a group of young women whose season ended weeks earlier than they had hoped. This lead serves as a smooth and effective transition into the body of the story. It is not a stack of statistics but a discussion by the players of when and where the wheels came off.

SHOWCASE ■

By **LAURA MATHEWS**
Westlake High School, Austin, TX

ALL WAS SILENT except for the sounds of the gravel grinding beneath the bus tires, and the air was suffocatingly heavy with disappointment. Faces started blankly out of the half-opened windows, lost in their own thoughts, as an artificially bright voice cut through the gloom.

"Hey guys, remember that spike in the Georgetown game? We really took 'em by surprise with that one . . . ."

There was lack of success stories for the varsity volleyball team to recall after its playoff loss to Taylor. But even with a season record of 21-8 and a three-way tie for first place in the South Zone, the

WE FROWN ON LEADS LIKE THESE

THE "FALSE ALARM" LEAD.

On a hot Saturday afternoon, a blood-curdling scream echoed through the Snake River canyon. Was someone falling to his death? Was it a heinous murder?

No, Todd jumped off the 150-foot bridge on purpose. He is a bungee jumper! And he said it is a lot of fun.

volleyball team members, who expected their season to end weeks later than it did, were less than satisfied.

"It's really hard to read about the state playoffs now because I keep thinking we could have been there," coach Jane Patterson said.

"It's real tough to be on top and have people gunning for you. It's a really mental game at that point," she added. "The other teams have everything to gain and nothing to lose, and you're just the opposite. It was like we were the only game of the season for a lot of the other teams."

Leander, Georgetown and Taylor psyched themselves up enough to beat Westlake in the last three games of the season, putting Westlake in a three-way tie for first place with Leander and Taylor.

"After Leander, it was like 'what happened, what went wrong?' so we all worked on our mental preparation and all the other things we thought we had done wrong," Patterson said. "We really got ourselves primed for the Georgetown game, and then we lost that, too."

■ THE CLASSROOM SPEECH

A much-overlooked source of powerful content is the typical classroom speaker. These people spend their time and effort to talk to high school students because they believe they have something to say. The messages they bring can and should be made into educational experiences for the entire school. This certainly is the case in the story below:

SHOWCASE ■

By **LORI LESSNER**
Eastlake North High School, Eastlake, OH

JOE MUHARSKY knows what it's like to hear the agonizing screams of an American soldier tied to a tree while being skinned alive and to have gasoline and salt water poured all over his raw body.

Muharsky knows what it's like to hold a friend and watch him bleed to death in the jungles of Cambodia while President Nixon makes his 1 1/2-hour speech denying allegations that American troops were in Cambodia in 1969.

As a member of the U.S. Navy Black Berets, Muharsky has been to hell and back. He spent 22 months of his life in combat along the Mekong Delta during the Vietnam War.

Muharsky, a graduate of North in 1965, is an annual speaker for Mr. Ray Smith's senior democracy classes as well as for Mr. Bob Beutel's senior government classes. He returned to North once again on Nov. 12 and 13.

Muharsky told students simple yet incredible facts about the horrors of the war, which he witnessed first-hand. He also discussed his opinions based upon his knowledge and experience in the Vietnam War.

"I'm not saying you have to agree with me. They are my opinions, but I want to leave you with questions to make you think. I certainly don't have all the answers.

"I think the Vietnam War is the most tragic mistake this country ever made. World War II, Korea, Vietnam—all wars are the most horrible things. If you think they are glamorous, think again," Muharsky said.

In patrol boats that lacked armor, Muharsky would go on raids in canals located in Vietnam and Cambodia. He used guerilla warfare in the jungles against the Viet Cong (whom the Americans referred to as "Charlie") as well as against the second enemy, the North Vietnamese Army.

"You have one-tenth of a second to feel sorry for the buddy of yours who was blown away with an M-16. The .223 caliber bullet travels 4,000 feet per second to kill a human being. You know you are next unless you keep fighting. I became something over there that really bothers me," Muharsky said.

Muharsky contrasted World War II with the Vietnam War. In 'Nam, there was no such thing as a front line. Instead, people fought as individuals. Success was determined by which side had the lowest body count after a battle.

Muharsky recited facts that are etched in his

memory forever. He said that out of 3 million Americans who served in Vietnam, 175,000 became disabled. Thirty percent of the men in his platoon died by friendly fire. They never even saw the enemy. Fifty-five thousand veterans committed suicide upon their return home because the American public badly rejected them. There were also few jobs available for them because of their limited education.

"Why did so many veterans kill themselves?" Muharsky said. "Well, psychiatrists believe that who you are going to be and your development occurs between the ages of 18-25. The boys coming home fell into that category and only knew how to kill. The war determined that. They had nowhere to turn."

Muharsky also stated that he thinks there are Prisoners of War (POWs) still in 'Nam.

"I believe there is good evidence towards the allegation that many captured servicemen were left behind in Southeast Asia. I would not go back to rescue them unless I knew for sure they were alive and in a specific location we could find by helicopter."

"I think Muharsky is very dedicated to the veterans. I see him as a strong-willed person," Smith said. "He has an interesting story to tell."

Muharsky can tell of the flashbacks he experiences daily. The smell of cat food makes him smell the rotten flesh in a jungle once again.

Muharsky can tell why all the American troops carried not one but two dog tags around their necks for identification.

"If you are about to be blown up, you put one tag under your tongue. This way, because rigor mortis sets in, you can still be identified and sent home for a proper burial," said Muharsky.

Vietnam veteran Muharsky remembers what those 22 months on the Mekong Delta felt like every single day that passes.

Muharsky knows. He was there.

This story is so much better than, "Joe Muharsky spoke to Mr. Ray Smith's senior Democracy classes about his experiences in

Vietnam. Muharsky said the war was 'the most tragic mistake this country ever made.' "

What makes this such a special story is the empathy the writer feels for the speaker and the extremes to which she goes to capture the power of his message without sensationalizing or sermonizing. Instead, she provides an unflinching and unglamorous look at what it must have been like in the midst of a firefight and what it has meant to the men who were there.

■ **RECREATE THE SCENE**

Perhaps you're saying: "We don't have time to attend all of these activities that you want us to write about. We are high school students, and we're expected to attend class and satisfy all the hoop-jumping which that entails. A few of us also participate in other programs, and band directors aren't always so understanding when we tell them we need to skip rehearsals to watch the homeless stand in the rain.

"So how are we going to describe events that we haven't witnessed?"

First, failure to witness an event is often an error of staff management and planning. Know what's happening and when, and be there. Or assign someone else to cover the story.

Second, open your eyes. Learn to see, hear, taste and feel the world around you. Be aware of your environment so that you can recreate it when the situation demands.

And in those times when you can't witness an event first hand, then interview the people who were there to a degree that you can re-create the moment anyway. Professional reporters do this when it's the only alternative. It's never the best option, but sometimes, it's the only option. For example, a story in a Miami newspaper dealt with police raids on alleged crack houses. The reporter described how police kicked in the door, chased a suspect into a bedroom, threw him onto a bed, stuck a gun in his ear and said, "You blink, and your brains will be splattered all over this mattress."

The reporter wasn't sitting on the officer's

WE FROWN ON LEADS LIKE THESE

THE "I NEVER MET-A-PHOR I DIDN'T LIKE OR A CLICHÉ EITHER, FOR THAT MATTER" LEAD.

■ The divers were fueled with the excitement of the jump...
■ Spectators on the ground were full of anticipation...
■ The air was thick with suspense...

THE "I CAN BUTCHER LINCOLN OR SHAKESPEARE" LITERARY ALLUSIONS LEAD . . . .

■ Four score and seven years ago, our fathers brought forth on this continent, a new nation, conceived in liberty and dedicated to the proposition that all men should go bungee diving!
■ King Richard II may have traded his kingdom for a horse, but we'd give just about anything for a win against Pike High.

shoulder during all of this. In fact, he wasn't there at all. But he interviewed the officers in such depth that he was able to re-create the scene. He had them describe the apartment. Were there dirty dishes in the sink? Were the beds made up? Were the ashtrays bulging with cigarette butts? He had police officers tell him what the apartment smelled like. He asked them if they could remember what was playing on the radio when they kicked the door in.

This technique is difficult and time-consuming, but the payoff is substantial. For example, the lead of the next story is one of the most powerful I've ever read in a student publication. The image of the young mother, who is rocking her baby and crying, is unforgettable.

SHOWCASE

By **CLARE BUNDY**
Duncanville High School, Duncanville, TX

A GROUP OF candystripers stand around the nursery, holding incubator babies. It's "loving time." Another young girl steps in with her mother and picks up a baby, too. She is not in a uniform, but in a hospital gown, for the baby she holds is her own—and it's her "loving time."

It's also time to say goodbye.

"I sat in a rocker and held him and rocked him, and I cried and cried and cried," Amber, a senior, said. "I wanted that moment to last forever so I could always hold him and always be there for him.

"But I knew I couldn't. That's what hurt."

Amber was 16 years old when she gave up her child for adoption. The factors: "a meaningful relationship turned sour, failure of contraception, and little-to-no parental support," she said. "I was also only a sophomore in high school, and I had a desire—a need, really—for higher education."

Whatever the reasons or reasoning involved, they didn't lessen the hurt of losing her child. She

remembers the day: June 19, 1985, and she vividly recalls the rest of the memory.

"When the time came to let him go, to set him down in the crib, I was still crying and I walked away," Amber said.

"But as soon as I reached the door, he started to cry. And I knew that if I turned back to get him, I'd never be able to leave the room.

"So I just walked out."

This traumatic situation was also an ironic one for Amber, who at 8 years of age decided she wasn't going to have any children.

"Coming from a big family, I knew how much time and energy it took to raise children," she said, "and I thought as an adult I'd be too selfish to devote all of that time and energy to one person."

Yet when she found out about her pregnancy, she said, she changed her mind. She didn't want to give up her child.

"But my parents forced the decision of adoption on me," Amber said. "I didn't have any choice in the matter. No alternatives were given."

The adoption was closed through Catholic charities, and though she said she felt "99.7 percent good" about her child's new parents, she reserved the other 3 percent for herself.

"I think I would have made a good mother," Amber said. "I have a good sense of judgment and three little sisters as experience.

"I know what it takes to make a family," she said, "but I also know it wouldn't have been complete without a father. That helped with their decision."

For it was all "their" decision in the end. Amber said that by the time her son was born, she "just wanted to hold him, just feel his presence," she said. "I wanted to feel his tiny body resting on my chest."

And she did get to hold him—for five days Amber mothered her child before leaving the hospital. The time she had with him was helpful as well as painful.

"It helped in that the experience was good. I

felt good about it," Amber said. "Everything from breast feeding to changing diapers was a new, yet old, experience.

"It hurt because I knew that what I was holding and experiencing would never be mine."

When her son turns 21, however, he will be free to contact his mother. But Amber said she is not sure if she'll ever be emotionally prepared for their meeting.

"But I would still die to see him," she said.

And what would she say?

"I'd tell him that I love him and always will, no matter who or what he becomes," Amber said. "And I'll tell him the truth about what happened between his father and me. And what's happened to me because of it. There's no reason to lie to your children."

Yes, there is still a "strong maternal bond," and Amber said there always will be. This experience has left its mark on her now more than ever.

"During the pregnancy, I was loving the child, but I was apathetic to the situation," she said. "Now I either speak cynically about it, or I cry. I never used to cry."

This was evident as she stated the one word that described the whole ordeal:

"Pain," she said, tears streaming down her cheeks and falling onto her pale blue sweater.

"True pain."

SHOWCASE

By **PATRICK HEALY**
Grosse Point South High School,
Grosse Point, MI

HERE ARE ONLY A FEW wisps of hair on the girl's soft head but they are the color of autumn leaves, just like her mother's. Her hands are still too weak and too tiny to grasp her daddy's finger, and she can only stay awake for a half-hour at a time. Her parents don't mind, though.

Psychology teacher DeEtte Horan and her husband Patrick gently bathe their daughter Shannon Lydia, change her diapers and sing to her while she's awake. And when the baby girl yawns and her crisp blue eyes shut, they hold her 3-pound body and gaze at her wrinkled and red face.

"She's perfect, I think she's perfect," Horan said, with more pride than a smile can hold.

On Jan. 4, Horan gave birth through cesarean section to a 2-pound, 6-ounce baby girl after Horan's blood pressure skyrocketed to deadly levels.

Shannon wasn't due until March 20 and arrived at 29 weeks, making her 11 weeks early. At that age about 20 percent of newborns never make it out of the hospital, said Dr. Ali Rabbani, the director of St. John Hospital's Neo-Natal Intensive Care Unit (NICU).

Their doctors call the babies preemies, and some weigh as little as 1-pound, 3-ounces when they are born. The babies smaller than that, not even a miracle can save, Rabbani said. The ones who do survive initially rely on machines to eat, breathe, fight off infection and control their body temperatures.

"You have to be on your toes because the babies crash and everything falls apart," Rabbini said, and smacked his hands for emphasis. "Just like that. Every minute, you never know."

Horan's family knew this and prayed for Shannon, asking God to save her tiny life.

Her walnut-sized heart kept beating during the first critical weeks. Her parents nicknamed the feisty lightweight "Scrapper" and now joke that Shannon's red hair gave her fiery strength. Now, after more than a month of tests and doctor's the parent's hold their daughter up like a tiny trophy for pictures and grin into the camera.

The smiles didn't come so easy when Horan checked into the hospital on Dec. 30.

Horan's blood pressure had always been high and she knew she risked developing pre-eclampsia when she became pregnant. For

WE FROWN ON LEADS LIKE THESE

It has been a year of ups and downs for Mr. Pinchon. He taught at York and was recently married. Those are definitely ups.

More recently, however, he was diagnosed with leukemia, a form of cancer.

That's a definite down!

No commentary required.

women with this condition, if something goes wrong during labor or if the mother's blood pressure shoots up too quickly, the placenta can sever, causing the baby to lose its oxygen supply and die. The mothers risk kidney failure, seizure or stroke.

But Horan said she monitored her blood pressure during the first six months of her pregnancy and visited her doctor regularly. She left South for Winter Break on Dec. 22, not knowing that she wouldn't be back for months. Five days after Christmas, Horan's blood pressure began climbing. The doctors started worrying and admitted her to the hospital and gave her drugs to lower her blood pressure.

They tried Hydralazine. No luck. A Beta-blocker cocktail. Nothing.

As Horan's blood pressure jumped past 200/100, her doctors decided to deliver the baby through emergency C-section. Shannon wasn't due for 11 weeks but the doctors knew delivering was the only way to save the baby and the mother.

Her voice drops off to a murmur when she thinks about it. "Scary and surprising," she said. "It was just scary and surprising."

Horan stayed awake for the operation. As the doctors cut her stomach open to deliver the baby she slipped her hand into Patrick's. She barely remembers anything about the operation, not even saying "I love you" to Patrick, only a feeling of constant tugging below her navel.

Shannon cried when the doctors pulled her out, and so did her parents. Her tiny lungs only let out a squeak, but Horan thanked God for the sound. It meant the baby was breathing, that she had a chance.

The next day felt like a constant battle to wake up from a deep sleep. The painkillers fogged Horan's mind until she was too groggy and weak to leave her bed. Patrick visited Shannon in NICU that day and snapped a few proud Polaroids. Horan got her first good look of her baby from the eye of an instant camera.

"She has everything: two eyes, a nose, hands,

feet, all her fingers and all her toes," Horan said. "Everything is just so small."

She also has a feeding tube in her nose and tiny electrodes stuck to her chest. As she sleeps, glowing green and white lines trace the little girl's heart and breathing rates across a monitor above her incubator. The doctors and nurses chart her progress as the baby slowly gains weight and strength.

Two days after Shannon was born Horan climbed into a wheelchair and took the elevator to the hospital's fifth floor NICU where Shannon and 34 other babies lie in their plastic wombs.

From a distance it looks like they are nothing but wires and computers, as nurses in fruit salad-colored scrubs track the babies' progress on machines and monitors that hiss and beep throughout the day. Teddy bears and Beanie Babies sit in the corner of the incubators and watch over the babies when their parents are at work or asleep.

There is a glimmer of hope beneath the muffled yellow lights in the NICU as nervous parents learn how to bathe and hold their tiny children. Most hesitate at first, treating their babies as if a breath could topple them like a house of cards. As Horan stretched out her arms to hold Shannon for the first time, she said she felt that same twinge.

"I was nervous at first, worried that I'd hurt her," Horan said. "But you get used to them being so small."

Horan stayed in the hospital for the next week. She does not plan to return to South until next fall and she spends the bulk of her afternoons and evenings at the hospital. Horan and Patrick said they hope to bring Shannon home by March 20, her original due date.

The new parents wait for the day when they can give Shannon a bottle and tuck her into her crib for the night. But the pink-walled nursery is still empty. For now, they simply drape a pink patchwork quilt over the girl's hospital incubator, say "I love you" and drive back home.

SHOWCASE ■

By **STEPHANE MCCOLLUM**
Central High School, San Angelo, TX

AS THE TEACHER wrote notes on the blackboard for the class to copy, a student readjusted the bundle she was cradling in her arms.

"She's burping," explained Michele Acevedo, junior and proud mother of April Marie, a bouncing 5-pound flour baby. Darlene Hoggett, home and family living teacher, continued to scribble notes on the board.

Hoggett reminded the class that their baby books were due the following Monday.

"If you've been carrying 'it' all week," she said, "go ahead and give 'it' a name."

"What if you don't know how to spell the name you gave the kid?" asked an unidentified "father."

The home and family living teachers, including Hoggett and Gay Young, designed the unit on parenting to answer questions students may or may not have about parenting, according to Mrs. Young. She stressed that she wanted the students to realize the responsibilities involved in parenthood.

For one week, the students carried sons or daughters made out of 5-pound sacks of flour and stuffed pantyhose. The flour babies replaced the traditional hard-boiled egg last year after Young heard about the flour babies from a friend. Mrs. Young said that the idea of using eggs had become outdated after seven years. She decided that the flour babies are more life-sized and therefore got the point across to her students. She added that cases of "egg-napping" had caused some students' failing grades.

"I love it when they make comments like, 'This isn't any fun,'" Young said, adding that she did not object to students having fun at school, but "I have a very serious motive behind it."

As part of her effort to stress the responsibility of childhood, her home and family living classes take up units "in sequence."

Teenage pregnancy is taught first, followed by marriage and parenting.

Young stressed that the unit was not all ruffles and pink lace—it includes serious topics including abortion, child abuse and how to handle incest. One speaker planned for the classes is a mother of a handicapped child who talks about her experiences.

Along with getting a preview of parenthood, Young said that the students seemed to enjoy the project. She said that a group of students who were eating lunch off-campus received strange looks from curious adults. Junior Tracy Ballard even received a warning from a Department of Human Resources worker not to mistreat her child. Not to worry—the doting mother had made a trip to Angelo Community Hospital, along with junior Gigi Kassay, to seek bottles and birth certificates for her child.

The class project also created financial opportunities for senior Sheila Hopkins, who began work on her flour baby at the beginning of the semester. Hopkins sold disposable Cabbage Patch diapers to her classmates at 25 cents each. Young reported that most of the "children" in her fifth period class are bedecked in the latest in babywear.

Hoggett's class geared up for the "prettiest baby" contest. The proud parents introduced their children. The babies' attire ranged from footy-pajamas to sunshades and drew many snickers from the class, despite Hoggett's warnings to the contrary. "Don't ever tell a mother, 'Your baby looks just like a little monkey,'" the teacher admonished.

"He's gonna be a basketball player cause he's got long legs," junior Vanalyn Ocker boasted. Such displays of pride were evident among the "fathers" when they dressed their sons in clothing they wore as infants.

The votes were in. The class voted "Spanky," the son of junior Gene Hernandez, as winner. The "father" admitted feeling "good" about his son's accomplishment. Hernandez added that his child was very quiet, and "he didn't wet his pants either."

DON'T WADDLE INTO THE STORY

Sibling rivalry is as old as time itself. Who sits in the front seat of the car? Who gets the last piece of pie? Who gets the new clothes? Who has to help with the dishes?

This may explain why Bill beat up his younger brother, Don. Of course, it may not as well. At any rate, he did.

Times have changed since the horse-and-buggy days. Today, if people need to go someplace, they have a variety of options: airplanes, buses, trains and, of course, cars.

Many students here have cars.

"I have a Honda Civic," senior Ashley Brewster said. "I love it."

But finding a place to park the car is a problem, especially since administrators decided to ban on-campus student parking.

Photo by **KARIZZA LASO**
Salida Middle School, Salida, CA

TALK TO THE RIGHT PEOPLE

07

Face it, the perfect source is not going to walk up to you in the hall and say, "Hi, I hear you're writing a story. I'm the guy to talk to."
You have to go out there, find and talk to the right person.

CHAPTER HIGHLIGHTS:

■ Find and cultivate sources.

■ Listen, watch and respond.

■ How to handle direct and indirect quotes.

■ How to conduct a successful interview.

Ask a group of publications students why they enrolled in journalism, and chances are they'll answer, "Because I like to write."

I've always hoped a few would answer, "Because I like to talk to people." That's because powerful writing begins with keen, insightful reporting, which means interviewing. Good reporting is about 80 percent interviewing, and good interviewing is more than the hit-and-run encounter where the reporter asks a quick "What do you think about . . . ." to the first person he or she bumps into. Or interviews his or her two best friends — for every story.

Shortly after the attacks on the World Trade Center, I spoke at a state press association convention on "How Student Journalists Have Covered the War on Terrorism." Consistently, the stories were dated, vague and bland, primarily because reporters asked dumb questions such as "What do you think about American involvement in Afghanistan?" to anyone they encountered on campus. Consequently, the stories consisted of large quantities of jingoistic, ill-informed and sometimes downright dopey comments.

"I think we ought to nuke them back into the Stone Ages," many students said. Other comments were neither so perceptive nor informed.

Fortunately, a few reporters knew how to cover such a story. They knew that the theme of the story was fear and a sense of loss. And so they interviewed the people most likely to possess these emotions—the families of soldiers who were sent to fight in the mountains of Afghanistan.

These stories packed a punch. One reporter wrote of one family's first Christmas without Dad, who was a staff sergeant. The story was accompanied by a photograph of the family decorating the Christmas tree—the first tree, by the way, that Dad had not been home to pick out himself. It was a moving and powerful story because it touched on the emotions that each of us would feel had we been in that situation.

The key to successful reporting is finding and cultivating the right source. For example, if you're writing a story about teen runaways, talk to teen runways or members of their families. Don't build the story around adult counselors and social workers. Quote them, yes. But focus the story on runaways. Again, it is best to select one or two persons to stand as universal examples. You want to show how this person or these two persons represent a larger truth about all runaways. Someone once said, "Don't write about man. Write about a man."

Trick is, you have to find the right man (or woman), the person who represents the closest thing to "truth" or "reality" you can find. This is no small task, especially in light of the fact that few agree on what constitutes "true" and "real." But, hey, no one said this was going to be easy. Trust your training and your inclinations. Look hard. Ask around. Be willing to follow unlikely leads. The perfect source exists, but you can't expect to find that person at your doorstep prepared to hand you written comments.

"Hi, my name's Dave. I heard you are doing a story on teen runaways. Well, I'm your man. Ran away two years ago. Live in a trash dumpster. I've taken the liberty to type out a few comments. Feel free to use them as either direct or indirect quotes. If you need more information, you can reach me through my answering service. Or check out my website: www.dumpsterdave.com. Thanks and have a good day."

If this is what you're expecting, reconsider journalism.

And, except in rare circumstances, do not rely on e-mail or telephone interviews. Hiding behind a computer screen restricts your ability to use the interview process as a means of gathering more and better information. Sure, faceless, cyberworld journalism is easy. Just dial up or Instant Message a source and toss out a couple of questions. But you'll get a far richer story if you sit down with a source, get to know him or her, pay attention to body language, note whether they look you in the eye during the interview and have a really good conversation.

In short, walk your beat. The right sources are out there. It might be the superintendent. It might be the janitor. Might be both. Find them and earn their trust. You might not have noticed, but journalists are neither universally beloved nor trusted, and unless you've cultivated a relationship with your sources, they won't tell you much. Except on daytime talk shows, people tend not to bare their souls to complete strangers, especially people with cameras and tape recorders.

You need the ability to talk to people and convince them that you'll treat them fairly and accurately. If you can't do this, all your quotes, if you get any at all, will be guarded, superficial and artificial.

◼ LISTEN, WATCH, RESPOND

Good interviewers get as much out of their sources as possible. They know how to listen critically, analyze statements, watch for shifts in logic or argument and then respond.

In order to do this, you have to be prepared for the interview and poised. You prepare by finding out as much about the subject as possible prior to the interview so that the subject is giving you opinion, analysis or interpretation of facts you already know. For example, if you're interviewing the new superintendent, you should go into the interview knowing where she grew up, where she was educated, where and what she's taught, how long she's been in administration. You need to know if she's married and has three children, one of whom is dyslexic. Thus, your task is to ask questions like, "How did growing up on an Indian reservation prepare you for a career in education?" Or "what did you learn in your 20-year career as an English teacher that's helped you most as an administrator?"

You should go into the interview knowing that the new superintendent faces a financial crisis. Your question should be, "What will be your guiding philosophy as you work to to solve the financial crisis?"

Do your homework before the interview. As much as anything else, that will help you be more poised during the interview. First off, it'll impress the heck out of the person you're interviewing.

And second, it'll help you feel in command. You do not want to walk into the new superintendent's office and announce, "I'm supposed to interview you but I don't have any idea about what."

It's won't go well. But we're getting a little ahead of ourselves. Let's go back to square one. Say you're preparing to interview the new superintendent. Find out whom you should talk to first. The old superintendent would be a good choice. The district personnel director. Someone from the new superintendent's old district. Don't be embarrassed to contact people. People like to be interviewed. It's ego-inflating. No one wants to walk into the office at 8 a.m. Monday and find the crew from "60 Minutes" or CNN waiting with microphones drawn, cameras buzzing and some strange person who points a finger at you and

THAT'S MISTER TO YOU, BUDDY...

Each staff should either develop its own style manual or keep a copy of a style manual close at hand and refer to it often. Common style errors often involve the use of titles. Here are a few basic rules.

■ Use of courtesy titles *Mr., Mrs., Ms.,* and *Miss* are optional. Be consistent.

■ Capitalizatize formal titles used directly before a person's name. Use only the first name of the student on second reference. With adults, use the last name.

■ A formal title is one that denotes a scope of authority, professional activity or academic accomplishment so specific that the designation becomes almost as much a part of an individual's identity as a proper name itself. For example: *President Bush, Gov. Frankenfurter, Lt. Col. North, Pope John Paul, the Rev. Billy Tilton.*

■ Most school personnel need not have their titles capitalized. Exception: *Superintendent* John Woolridge, *Principal* Mary Roberts.

■ Most school titles serve primarily as occupational descriptions. Example: *head football coach* Bill Smith; *band director* Richard Murray; *assistant principal* Rhonda Hayes.

Do not capitalize identifying titles or occupational descriptions unless they are the first word in a sentence. *Coach Smith gave assistant principal Murray a hug.*

■ Avoid double titles such as *Mr. John Woolridge, superintendent.* Instead, on first reference, identify him as *Superintendent John Woolridge.*

Titles not used with an individual's name should be written in lower case. For example: The *superintendent* issued a statement.

■ On initial reference, place complicated occupational titles after the person's name. Also, place the verb *said* before the source.

WEAK: "Heads will roll," *assistant superintendent for instruction* Richard Bates *said.*
BETTER: "Heads will roll," *said* Richard Bates, *assistant superintendent for instruction.*

■ When using pronoun clauses, place the verb *said* before the source.

WEAK: "Heads will roll," Richard Bates, assistant superintendent for instruction, who witnessed the food fight, *said.*
BETTER: "Heads will roll," *said* assistant superintendent for instruction Richard Bates, who witnessed the food fight.

For more info, refer to the AP Stylebook.

NO, YOU CAN'T JUST INTERVIEW YOUR FRIENDS

Most stories need a minimum of two quotes. Quotes give stories credibility, timeliness and interest.

■ Quotes must be firsthand. Don't lift them from other publications. If readers want to read quotes from Newsweek, they will read Newsweek.
■ Quotes must be real. Don't interview your friends or friends of your friends. Many students are turned off by their school newspapers and yearbooks because they consist of the same quotes from the same people, page after page.

---

says, "That's him. He's the one who did it!"

But short of that, most folks find being interviewed a pleasant experience and will grant you a few moments of their time. Some of this background interviewing can be done over the telephone. Some can be done via e-mail.

Now, once you've gathered enough information to conduct an intelligent interview, contact the new superintendent. Make an appointment if possible. Clearly define the purpose of the interview. Explain what you're trying to accomplish with your story and why you

need to interview her.

Give her an idea of what you plan to discuss so that she can prepare as well. Use your common sense about this. Don't say, "I need to interview you because my teacher told me to." Use a little charm. Also:

■ Arrange for privacy. Don't be interrupted by telephone calls, secretaries, bells, go-fers or others who are likely to stroll in and out of the person's office.

■ Never attempt to see someone under false pretenses — tell the band director you're there to

How do I use a direct quote?

■ Use them early. Don't bury quotes deep in your story. Showcase them early: second or third graph at the latest. Anything written within the quote must be exact word for word.

■ Open the sentence with the quote. Then identify the source. For example:

WRONG: "I was so surprised when my name was announced. I'll cherish this honor for as long as I can remember because not just anyone can be a Homecoming Queen. It helps if your daddy is president of the School Board, and your first name ends in an 'i'," said Suzi.

RIGHT: "I was so surprised when my name was announced," Suzi said. "I'll cherish this honor for as long as I can remember because not just anyone can be a Homecoming Queen. It helps if your daddy is president of the School Board, and your first name ends in an 'i'."

■ Avoid unnatural breaks in a simple-sentence quote. Place the attribution at a natural pause or thought break in the sentence.

WRONG: "I did not," principal Leroy Jones said, "have an improper," he continued, "relationship with my secretary," he added.

RIGHT: "I had an improper relationship with the English teacher," principal Leroy Jones said.

■ If the subject matter of the direct quote changes, then open a new paragraph. *For example:*

"Pep rallies were like so much fun," head cheerleader Lizza Van Hamptonshire said. "I know they got me all excited before the games.

"Of course, there are those dweebs who don't think that school spirit is that important, like it doesn't even matter if we lose the football game," she added. "Like, where do they get off?"

■ Don't bury the attribution in a multi-sentence quote. Identify the source early and then complete the sentence.

WRONG: "I am real proud of this team. We played a whole bunch of tough teams, and the boys were right there, scrapping and biting and clawing to the bitter end. We improved as the season progressed, and we learned to depend on each other right up there to the last few games when everything went straight to Helsinki, and we got the snot beat out of us, " Coach Bubba said.

■ Never use the qualifier "when asked." If the source provides the statement, then the reader will assume that the source was asked the question. It is incorrect to bring yourself into the story, which is what happens when the "when asked" phrase is used.

WRONG: When (I) asked (her) about the new tardy policy, assistant principal Madge McCormick said, "If you're late twice, we'll hang you by your thumbs."

RIGHT: "If you're late twice, we'll hang you by your thumbs," assistant principal Madge McCormick said,

■ Generally, open a new paragraph with each new quote. For example:

"I quit," Mrs. Jones said. "This place is a zoo, an absolute zoo. And you're the most incompetent administrator I've worked with in 40 years of education."

"Well boo-hoo," principal Jones replied. "Don't let the door hit you in the backside on the way out."

"You, sir, are a brute and a nincompoot," she snapped and stormed out.

■ When a source changes thoughts in a direct quote, it is sometimes best to close the direct quote after the first thought is expressed, then paraphrase the second thought as a transition device into the remainder of the statement.

"Even though they're kind of old now, NSync is still the greatest group of all time," Heather said. "And the best looking and the all-round hunky-cuddliest!"

For now, anyway.

"I have to admit, the boys in O-Town and Dream Street are so cute and talented," she added. "Are we like living in the best musical era of all time or what?"

■ Use the verb "said" — not stated, remarked, commented, expressed, opined, recited, related, replied, according to. Synonyms for "said" may be used only if the synonym adds information about the nature of the quote or the conditions in which the statement was made. These are generally used in dialogue attribution.

WEAK: "The Student Council will meet next Monday to discuss prom," Lisa purred.

BETTER: "Why don't you come over to my place after the Student Council meeting," Lisa purred.

■ You may use the verb "says" in attributions that have a timeless or lasting value versus a short-term declaration. But it's a judgment call.

WEAK: "Student alcohol use could result in suspension," Martin says.

BETTER: "I once had a problem with alcohol, and it almost destroyed my life ," Martin says.

■ Use meaty quotes from knowledgeable sources, not snippets or quick quotes from random students. Don't string together two one-line quotes and think you've written a story.

■ Place interesting opinion or reaction in the quote, not fact. Note also that commas go inside the quotation marks.

WEAK: "The meeting will start at 2 p.m.," Johnson said.

BETTER: The meeting will start at 2 p.m. "Heads will roll," Johnson said.

■ Identify on first reference all students class and teachers by subject taught unless a more formal title is required. Attribution is generally title/name/said unless the title is unusually long. In that case, lead the attribution with the verb "said" followed by name and title. For example:

"For the better part, the senior year in high school is wasted," said Dr. Herb Collins, president of Bard College and chairman of the National Commission on the High School Senior Year.

QUOTES MUST HAVE AUTHORITY

Quotes must be valid. The sources must have knowledge about or experience with the subject. Compared to freshmen, juniors and seniors are experts. So are adults in charge of groups or decisions.

The insight conveyed in the quote should be precise, relevant, timely and packed with a newsworthy viewpoint.

Insist on anecdotes, although the subject may seem more comfortable spinning generalities. If he says, "I owe my 40 years of marriage to absolute understanding and compatibility," ask him, "What do you mean by understanding and compatibility? Can you give me some examples?"

— John Brady
The Craft of
Interviewing

talk about the weekend's marching contest and then, in the final question, ask, "And what do you have to say about the rumors around school that you're embezzling music department funds?"

■ Be there on time.

■ Dress appropriately—not too far above or below the subject. Neutral.

■ Show up prepared. Bring pencils, pens, pad, tape recorder if possible.

■ Prepare a list of questions, but be ready to deviate from it.

What do you ask? David Knight of South Carolina suggests to students that they consider the kinds of information that people tend to want to know about: Family, gender, politics, music, work, aging, religion and recreation.

He then suggests that they apply these to the news questions (who, what, when, where, why and how) as well as to the elements of news: timeliness, currency, prominence, oddity, impact, human interest, proximity and conflict.

■ Frame your questions so that they will elicit anecdotes. Get your source to tell you stories.

■ Anticipate your interviewee's mood. For example, what tone might you have to take if your job is to interview the coach whose team lost by one run for the third consecutive year and to the same team in the state championship baseball finals?

■ Ask your questions in a logical order. Let the subject do most of the talking. Ask follow-up questions if necessary, and in most likelhood, it will be.

■ Act interested. You won't get anywhere if you take on an attitude that suggests, "Let's get this over with because I gotta go to my girlfriend's house."

■ Be polite and appreciative. Make your interviewee feel special, as though he or she is part of something special. Don't put your feet up on anyone's desk unless you call them "Mom" or "Dad" on a regular basis.

■ TYPES OF QUESTIONS

Begin with questions the source can answer quickly. This will provide the source a sense of control. Who? What? When? Where? Questions that begin with "do, are, can, will . . ." tend to yield "yes/no" answers. What is the last good book you read? Who are your heroes? What are your hobbies? How do you spend your leisure time? Ask these relatively simple questions early on, and the subject is apt to think, "This is easy. I can handle this."

While you may begin the interview with simple questions, use them only as long as it takes you to develop a rapport with the source. If you walk into the person's office and notice that she has a photograph of her children on her desk, it is better to ask, "Tell me about your children" than "How old are they?"

Note how the following questions call for a one-word answer:

■ Do you plan to run for re-election?

■ Are you happy with the team's play?

■ Can the team overcome this loss?

■ Will the board approve the bond proposal?

As soon as possible, make the subtle transition into memory questions. What was your childhood like? What were your childhood ambitions? Who were your childhood heroes? What annoys you? What pleases you? What do you say are your worst weaknesses? Strengths?

These answers may provide clues to the subject's personality, character and philosophy. Ask relevant questions—questions that will elicit as much information as possible. The best question is the one that brings the highest return with the smallest investment in words.

Rather than asking the football coach, "Are you satisfied with the team's play?" ask, "What do you think about the team's play?" Or better yet, "The team rushed for only 95 yards against Deerfield. What happened?"

But make certain your question is properly worded. The late John McKay, former head coach of the Tampa Bay Buccaneers in the National Football League—a team that set an NFL record for consecutive losses — was asked, "What do you think of your team's execution." He responded, "Sounds like a good idea to me."

So ask your question precisely.

It's okay to ask the source to analyze or interpret. "How" and "why" questions force the source to think, to connect the dots, to infer and deduce. You want this. Ask the source to respond to hypothetical situations. What if this? What if that? These questions are especially good for personality profiles. However, make certain the hypothetical situation is relevant. Avoid the "if you were on a desert island, what kind of cold cuts would you most want to take along?"

■ CONDUCTING THE INTERVIEW

Talk casually. Ask brief, concise questions. Good interviewers do about 20 percent of the talking. You won't learn much if you're doing all the talking. While the interview should assume a conversational tone, the opinions should be dominated by the source, not the interviewer.

Empathize with the subject. Try to understand that person's point of view. Get inside his or her head a little bit. You may be interviewing the lowest form of humanity possible, but don't roll your eyes, pretend to throw up with each of the subject's answers. Don't argue with the subject. Don't pump your fist in the air and shout, "You da' Man!" each time the subject says something you like or agree with.

Don't use the interview as a forum to expound your own views either. If you reveal your feelings about a subject, it may prompt the source to tone down his or her answers or tailor them to be in line with yours. Students sometimes ask questions that all but scream how they feel about a particular issue. Avoid these so-called "frame up" questions. For example, avoid asking a question in the following manner: "The Supreme Court's decision in the Hazelwood case was a disaster. What is your opinion?

BETTER: The Supreme Court's decision in the Hazelwood case elicited strong opinions on both sides. What is your opinion about the decision?

Simply listen in a non-judgmental way. You'll elicit more spontaneity by responding "Yes," or "I understand," or "That's interesting," or by providing non-verbal clues such as nodding, smiling, etc. But they must be genuine. Don't just sit there like a dog waiting on a whistle. You expect your source to think. You need to think too.

■ INTERVIEW WITH YOUR EYES

Pay close attention to gestures, inflections, voice tone and regional accents if they are meaningful for the story. Observe body language. Does the source twitch uncontrollably? Sweat profusely? Does the source try to stare you down?

Does he or she avoid looking you in the eye?

I once worked with a man who attempted to intimidate reporters by getting in their faces. Like former President Lyndon Johnson, he pressed the flesh, and his technique more often than not worked, in part because he kept a wad of tobacco in his left cheek. Reporters would recoil in shock and remain on the defensive from that point on.

Don't be intimidated. Remember, you are offering the subject an opportunity to explain or clarify. Ask your questions, then give the source an opportunity to respond. If he or she doesn't or can't, perhaps that says as much about the situation as any direct quote would.

Pay close attention to the person's environment: What art if any is hanging on the walls? What would it say about the new principal if he had a large photograph of Marilyn Manson hanging on his wall?

What does his or her desk look like? Fastidiously clean? A disaster?

What kind of clothes does the source wear? How does he or she wear them? In some cases, you can judge a book by its cover.

Sometimes not. Your primary goal is to glean from the source the best information possible. Always look for the dynamic comment, the dazzling quote that establishes the theme of the story. Polished politicians know that reporters are searching for "sound-bite" quotes, and they are adept at giving them more than a few. Find those quotes that are a window to the soul, that may say more about the subject than the words themselves individually may denote.

Of course, make certain you record specific data such as dates, names, spellings, ages, etc. Your memory can be relied upon for concepts and anecdotes, but specific figures are elusive. Write them down. If you have any questions about a fact, double-check. A 25-inch personality profile can be sunk due to a simple fact error in the lead.

Don't be afraid to ask the source to repeat or clarify a statement. It is your job to control the interview. Sometimes the interview might wander off in directions you did not anticipate. If this new direction offers story potential, go with it. If not, wrangle the interview back on track.

WHY WOULD A SOURCE WANT TO TALK TO YOU?

People like to talk, especially about themselves. Beyond being ego-inflating and unusual, it's...

- an opportunity to be recognized for their work.
- a chance to tell their side of the story.
- a chance to be an "educator" of the public as well as a figure of authority.
- a chance to clarify positions or eliminate rumors.
- a chance to influence or impress others.
- a touch of immortality because their words may be frozen in print.

❝ Good writers often talk of finding an angle. They do not mean some gimmick or trick by which to dupe their readers into trying what cannot be interesting or useful to them. They mean a line of direction which will intersect writer, subject and audience on the way to a point, an intersection of valuable meaning.❞

— Ken Macrorie
Writing to be Read

■ CONCLUDING THE INTERVIEW

Don't expect the source to read your mind. Don't ask, "Is there anything I haven't asked?" or "Did I forget anything?" Ask instead, "Is there anything you'd like to add?"

Conclude the interview on time. If you promised the source that the interview would take 15 minutes, be prepared to leave in 15 minutes. If the source agrees to extend the interview, so be it. But don't keep the source guessing when you'll be finished. And never, ever force the source to call an end to the interview. The perceptive reporter will know when the interview should conclude. Again, be aware of body language.

Close on a positive note. Tell all sources how much you appreciate their time, their hospitality and their honesty.

Request permission to contact the source at a later time and date should additional information or clarification be required. Chances are, you won't be able to read all of your notes. So get a number and best time to call, just in case.

■ THE E-MAIL INTERVIEW

Now and then, students ask, "Why can't I just e-mail my questions to the source?"

You can. Like telephone interviews, e-mail interviews are a great way to get quick quotes and information. For example, if you need a quick quote from the Art Club president about the big art show next weekend, it's really not that crucial that you conduct a face-to-face interview. So what that his eyes dart and he has a weird facial tic while saying, "We plan to have works from more than 50 local artists, and we're serving punch and pie to the first 100 people who show up."

And with e-mail, you never worry about misquoting someone. For beginners who are simply looking for data from hard-to-reach sources, they're as handy as a cell phone.

But you'll rarely get a great story out of one. E-mail interviews consistently sound wooden, pre-packaged because they are. The source has ample time to ponder their answers and provide you with the absolutely most bland, guaranteed-not-to-offend anyone response possible.

A great personality profile about the Art Club president, who plans to study in France after graduation, can only come from a face-to-face interview, from the rapport between journalist and source, from the give and take of a spirited conversation. Great stories come from being able to read your subjects' faces, watch their mannerisms, those darting eyes, that facial tic, and make them respond to the unexpected follow-up question.

"France, huh. You couldn't find a country that's a little more pro-American or are you one of those liberal artists who hate freedom?" young Bill O'Reilly asks.

"What? Well, er..., ugh...Paris is the center of the art world," he stammers while his facial tic acts up, eyes dart, beads of sweat pop across the brow.

"No, you're wrong. New York is the center of the art world." O'Reilly replies. "And New York is in the U.S.A., so spare me any more of your ridiculous spin."

Great stories capture a mood, an attitude, a personality, an environment. E-mail interviews are great at saving time, avoiding phone tag, reaching sources who live on the other side of the planet. But e-mail doesn't capture the source's voice, how it rises and falls, quickens and slows. Electronic mail doesn't show how the source cracked his knuckles during the interview or tapped his fingers on the desk when you asked the unexpected follow-up question. It may generate a useable quote or two, but it'll rarely produce a revealing interview.

■ CONDUCTING E-MAIL INTERVIEWS

■ Double-check to make sure you have contacted the right source. Don't fall victim to a hoax or fraud.

■ Identify yourself as a reporter. Make certain the source understands that you're working on a story that will be published.

■ Craft your questions carefully. You may not have an opportunity to ask a follow-up question.

■ WORDS OF WISDOM

You may think you've just made the best friend you ever had. Good sources have a way of making you feel special. Perhaps you are. But never sacrifice your own integrity or the integrity of your publication by suggesting to the source that he or she can dictate when the story will run, on what page it will run or how much of the interview will be used.

Rarely if ever promise the source that he or she can read and edit the story prior to publication. In writing certain stories about highly technical matters, I have allowed sources to read portions of stories to check accuracy, but I have never allowed a source to change a quote or determine the angle or tone of the story.

Be very careful with "off-the-record" comments. I once knew a man who would make outrageous comments in public meetings and then blurt out, "That's off the record." It took only a few times before he learned his lesson: if you say it to a reporter, expect it to show up in print.

Some sources will attempt to bully you by providing ghastly, even slanderous quotes, and then quip, "of course, that's off the record." If you ever accept off-the-record information, then you have compromised *all* the information you receive from the source.

Deep background information is fine. Sources often provide background information with the understanding that they won't be quoted. The information guides the reporter to sources or helps the reporter understand a situation so that they can better discuss it with their on-the-record sources.

Again, this is perfectly permissible. But be wary of "off-the-record."

Time after time, reporters have been burned by sources who claimed certain information was "off the record" merely because a portion of an entire interview, they thought, was closed. Your philosophy should be, "If you don't want to see it in print, don't say it."

■ SUMMON YOUR COURAGE

Many young reporters are too shy—or think they are—to properly conduct an interview. They think, "I'm just a reporter for the student publication. Why should the superintendent want to talk to me?"

They fail to appreciate their importance to the staff, the students and the community. You are entrusted with an opportunity to meet with persons who may be unavailable to the average student. You carry the responsibility to act as the eyes and ears of all potential readers.

This is no small obligation. Despite the stereotype of reporters as obnoxious jerks, the majority of reporters I have known are quiet, introspective and serious. However, their placid natures never stand in the way of an important story. Nor do they confuse a reclining nature with passivity. They are relentless in their pursuit of the facts, even though they don't make a lot of noise during the chase.

So, rise to the occasion. Many photojournalists admit to a certain shyness but claim they overcome it when they raise the camera to the eye. Looking through the lens creates an invisible barrier behind which they can hide. In other words, students personally are not taking the pictures. Instead, students are an extension of the camera.

You may need similar tricks to overcome your shyness as well. If so, then visualize yourself as an extension of the readers. I do not mean to suggest that you wrap yourself in artificial pomposity. But pursue the story as you think a daily newspaper reporter would. If you see yourself in this role long enough, it will become apparent to you what others have long since realized: that you are in fact a reporter for a worthwhile publication. You become a journalist as well as a student. You might one day come away with a story as powerful as this one:

SHOWCASE

By **FRANCES JOHNSON**
Dow High School, Midland, MI

IT'S A LOVELY HOUSE in a well-to-do neighborhood, a little way out of town. Two small, brick pillars welcome you into the twisting driveway. Blinds cover most of the windows, but a light upstairs shines through. People walk down the street and pass the house which is normal and comfortable in appearance. But someone is missing form that house. Someone will never come home to it again.

When Jason Begue's mother, Vickie, opened the door, she immediately welcomed me into her home. She and her husband ushered me into the neat living room. I wondered where to begin.

GET BOTH SIDES OF THE STORY

A student comes to you and says, "The coach wouldn't start me because he didn't like my long hair, and eventually, they kicked me off the team."

This could be a story. But it might not be.

Sure, get the student's story. But then, talk to other players. Was he kicked off the team or did he quit?

Do other players have long hair? If so, is their hair length an issue?

Talk to the coaches. What do they have to say about it? Chances are, you'll get a "no comment."

Ask yourself: does this issue deserve coverage? Given that space in our publication is valuable, is this a topic that deserves our time and attention? Or is this simply a kid with an axe to grind?

"Our hearts are broken," she told me very quietly, her hand on her chest.

"I understand," was all I could think of to say.

"I loved Jason," she told me, "but I liked him, too. Every age he was at, I enjoyed being with him. I will miss his companionship," she whispered. Her husband, Denny, continued. Even though they had different interests, he enjoyed his son's company.

"I really thought of Jason as a good friend," he said. "He never gave me a reason to not like what he did. He was a great son to have." There is another pause. I can see them reflecting on the life of their only child, on the person he was.

"He expected a lot from us," Vickie said. Her husband broke in with a laugh.

"All of a sudden I was getting lectured. All of a sudden, I couldn't drive worth a damn," he said with a chuckle. As they laugh together, they reach out to each other across the coffee table. Qualities of their only son continue to emerge.

He was very private, Vickie said. "And I respected that privacy. If he wanted to talk about something, great. If not, I didn't push it." She said sometimes he would follow her around the house, "talking her ear off," as her husband put it. He would tell her about an essay he had written, a movie he had just seen or a new computer game.

"And apparently I'm not a very good driver either," she said with a smile.

As quickly as the chatter came, it would go. "Even two hours later he would be up alone and silent in his room and you would think, 'What just happened here?'" his father said, his arms spread to encompass his house.

Following in his pattern of privacy, he kept his friends and his family separate. Many of them had never even met his parents. But his parents know that he had friends. His dad said theirs was never a house where the phone was ringing every 20 minutes with "chicks and buddies" making plans on the other line. His mother said despite this he often performed small acts of kindness that surprised even them.

They told of a small boy for whom Jason had done a favor. He had gotten a game for the boy off the computer. "The boy asked his mother to take him to the funeral. He came up to us and told us he was there because Jason had done something nice for him," his father said quietly. Both his parents pause and look down at their laps. Mention of the funeral reminds them that the boy of whom they speak is no longer with them.

It also reminds them of a bedroom full of untouched memories. He loved to collect things, and he could never let anything go. "He got that from me," Vickie said. But all of his relics were organized. "Everything had its place." Those things still remain in their place. "There's a lot of stuff upstairs," his mom said, motioning with her hands.

That "stuff" includes momentos from receiving the rank of Eagle Scout, a goal which he had had since elementary school. When an adult friend told Jason that he had been just short of getting his Eagle and had never made it to the end, Jason promised he would get his Eagle, for him.

"He was what? Nine? Nine then?" his father asked. "When he did get his Eagle he gave one of the pins to him (that man)." His father is running his fingers through his hair, tears are filling his eyes. He stops. His mother is nodding. Tears streak her cheeks.

"It's so hard to pick just one thing," she said. "He was our whole life."

But one thing does stick out. The infamous Halloween costume.

When Jason told his dad how much it would cost to rent a Joker costume, his dad told him he could pay for it himself.

"He said, 'ok Dad, ok' I've got it all figured out."

He got the costume and wore it to school, complete with a white painted face and green hair. "We sprayed his hair I don't know how many times," Vickie said.

But the costume didn't end there. That night Jason stationed himself on the front porch with the soundtrack to Tim Burton's *Nightmare Before Christmas* blaring from his boom box. He greeted trick-or-treaters with an eerie smile and silently

WHY DID YOUR INTERVIEW FAIL?

■ You had no idea why you interviewed this person.

■ You didn't prepare for the interview. Instead, you walked in, interrupted the source and asked, "So what can you tell me?"

■ You didn't bring a pencil, pen or pad. You brought a tape recorder but forgot to bring a tape, which wouldn't have helped anyway because the batteries in the tape recorder were dead.

■ You had no idea when the story would appear in print. "I just write 'em and hand 'em in," you told the source.

■ When they weren't stupid ("What is your favorite food?"), your questions were vague, soliciting comments that restate the obvious ("What is the purpose of the Future Teachers of America?")

■ Even when the source provided interesting information, you didn't follow up or probe questions that needed to be clarified. "Yeah sure, you know who really killed JFK. Now, just once more, tell me the purpose of the Future Teachers of America? See you in the funny pages."

■ You wore blue jeans that are too sizes too small and one of those T-shirts that doesn't cover your belly-button to interview the school board president, who is also a Baptist preacher.

■ You went into the interview with a preconceived notion rather than listening to what the source said and meant. In fact, you told the source, "I know you're a crook, and I'm here to prove it."

■ You didn't listen to the answers. Instead, you drummed your fingers on the table as though you couldn't wait to end the interview. You yawned every two or three minutes.

■ You talked too much. Rather than asking the question and waiting for the source to respond, you answered for him or her.

■ You allowed the interview to wander off track or to interrogate you about your opinions.

■ You were insensitive to the source. You referred to the source's children as "rug rats." You asked if he buys his ties at Discount World.

■ You overstayed your welcome. To make matters worse, you barged back in 10 minutes after the interview ended and said, "I forgot to ask, 'What did you say your name was?' "

■ On the way out of the office, you take the last peppermint from the candy tray and say, "See you in the papers!"

DON'T ALWAYS TRUST YOUR SOURCES

President Ronald Reagan was proud of saying, "Trust, but verify."

The same advice goes for interviews. Any story that makes your source or sources look perfect should set off a few alarms. Sources speak in words that serve their own purposes and interests. They puff themselves and try to bluff you.

When a school board member says, "The new policy will be good for everyone," the reporter should hit the halls, looking for opinions from a wide range of people.

Bottom line: if a subject in a story seems too good to be true, he or she probably isn't.

---

placed candy in their bags.

"We do that a lot these days," she tells me. "Our minds have been a bit muddled."

They are taking it one day at a time. It's the routine things that they concentrate on now.

"I get up in the morning and I remind myself that he's not here. I would have made his breakfast, he would have said 'bye, Mom,' and then left for school. I would have been here when he got home. He doesn't come home anymore." His mother is crying, her hand resting on her chest.

As I get up to leave, they turn on the outside lights and usher me to the door.

"You didn't wear a coat?" his mother asks incredulously. "You came all this way without a coat?" I nod sheepishly as I step out the door.

I steal another glance at the house before I drive away. He lived in that house. Maybe that window on the right is his room. He ran down this driveway every day to catch the bus. He walked up it after a long day at school. I cry when it hits me.

He won't come home again.

Photo by **KIRSTEN ZASTROW**
Amherst High School, Amherst, WI

ORGANIZE YOUR FACTS

08

Now that you've collected all that information, you must do something with it. Begin by asking, "What part of this story will most interest my readers?" If you've done your reporting, something will rise to the top.

CHAPTER HIGHLIGHTS:

■ Tell the story in a logical order.

■ Use transition sentences to hold the story together.

■ Attribute facts to a source.

■ Keep the story tight and on track.

I came across an article in a Houston newspaper that said that some of the nation's top students are weak, disorganized writers. One reason, educators theorized, is that students spend so little time writing in schools.

Experienced writers always use order, transition and attribution to develop fluent copy. It's second nature. I once interviewed a basketball coach who toured Africa with a group of students. The coach literally wrote the story for me. All I had to do was string his quotes together, never giving a thought to order, transition or attribution.

For a beginning writer, it's rarely that easy. Part of the problem with organizing a story is a failure to collect enough information to compile a story. A random collection of unrelated facts isn't fodder for even minimal storytelling, no matter in what order it's placed.

But even with students who have gathered sufficient information, marshalling that information into a logical and coherent order remains a formidable obstacle, so students decide to tell every story in straight chronological order, no matter what.

For example:

HOMECOMING WAS held last week.

The day began with a parade during which the homecoming princesses rode down the middle of town on a fire engine. Then, a pep rally was held during which students voted for homecoming queen.

That night, the Lions played the Clearview Panthers to a 21-21 halftime tie. At halftime of the game, Linda Elkins was named homecoming queen. In the second half of the game, Ron Stone scored from two-yards out with six seconds left to lift the Lions to a stunning 28-21 win over the top-ranked, undefeated Panthers.

Head coach Roland Grewe was so shocked by the win—the team's first in four years—he had a heart attack on the sidelines. He didn't die, but he's in no shape to coach again, that's for darn sure. So the search for a new coach continues next week when the school board interviews Jon Gruden, who stunned everyone by quitting the Tampa Bay Buccaneers and applying for the position, saying, "It's the only job I ever really wanted."

Typically, you want to present the big news early in the story, especially if you're using the inverted pyramid, which shoehorns the 5Ws and 1H into the first or second paragraphs.

Longer, more complicated news and

> ❝ Flies take off backwards. So in order to swat one, you must strike slightly behind him. An interesting detail, and certainly one a writer would be able to pick up on. Other people see flies; a writer sees how they move.
>
> — William Ruehlmann
> Stalking the
> Feature Story

feature articles require a more sophisticated approach, more thought, more feeling, more sensitivity, more empathy. You can't just write a news lead, tack on two or three obligatory quotes and call it a day. Nor can you write a feature lead, stack three quotes on top of each other, tack on an editorial summary and close, either.

Consider the following scenario: Three students from your school, located in an upper middle-income suburb, join 16 other students who volunteer to repair homes in an inner-city neighborhood. The inner-city neighborhood—with its rows of run-down homes—is a bit of a shock to the students, who are more accustomed to well-manicured lawns and clean, tidy streets.

You're writing their story. Here are three possible approaches, two of which are bad. The third is passable.

■ THE NO-QUOTE APPROACH

THREE STUDENTS helped repair homes in an inner city neighborhood this summer. The students—Ralph Smith, Jim Jones and Ruth Ortiz—were part of a project sponsored by the First United Methodist Church. The project combines two existing programs—the United Service Project, in which kids from suburban areas repair homes in the city, and Servants at Work, in which members of the church repair homes of people physically unable to do so themselves.

The three students worked on the home of Tony Lema of 2120 Lennox Avenue. The house needed a new roof. Students said they enjoyed the work and were happy to be part of the project.

■ THE DUMB QUOTES APPROACH

THREE STUDENTS helped repair homes in an inner-city neighborhood this summer. The students—Ralph Smith, Jim Jones and Ruth Ortiz—were part of a project sponsored by the First United Methodist Church. The project combines two existing programs, the United Service Project, in which kids from suburban areas

repair homes in the city, and Servants at Work, in which members of the church repair homes of people physically unable to do so themselves.

"We worked on the home of Tony Lema of 2120 Lennox Avenue," Smith said. "The house needed a new roof ."

Jones said they enjoyed the work.

"We were happy to be part of the project," he added.

■ THE STACKS OF QUOTES APPROACH

THREE STUDENTS helped repair homes in an inner-city neighborhood this summer. The students—Ralph Smith, Jim Jones and Ruth Ortiz—were part of a project sponsored by the First United Methodist Church. The project combines two existing programs—the United Service Project, in which kids from suburban areas repair homes in the city, and Servants at Work, in which members of the church repair homes of people physically unable to do so themselves.

"We worked on the home of Tony Lema of 2120 Lennox Avenue," Smith said. "The house needed a new roof. Lema is unable to do the repairs because he has heart trouble."

"We were told the neighborhood was pretty violent, but the people I met were friendly and really nice," Ortiz said. "Every day, Tony cooked us a different Mexican dish. One day, he cooked us some corn tortillas with beef and beans. The homemade tortillas were a lot better than the fast-food kind that we get in our neighborhood."

"We saw a lot of homeless people," Smith said. "That was really sad. If you live in our neighborhood, you don't even know that homeless people exist. You hear about it on TV, but you never see them."

"We really enjoyed the work," Jones said. "We were happy to be part of the project."

■ MAKE IT MEANINGFUL

Now, let's take the "stacks of quotes" story and turn it into something entertaining and meaningful. It'll require a bit more reporting. Begin by writing a more compelling lead.

WHEN RALPH SMITH volunteered to come to the inner city for one week this summer, he was warned what to expect.

"We were told the neighborhood was pretty violent," the 13-year-old said, "but the people I met were friendly and really nice."

Smith and two friends, Jim Jones and Ruth Ortiz, were among 18 students from suburban communities who took part in the City Service Project, in which they spend part of the summer fixing up homes in the mostly Hispanic neighborhood. The project combines two existing programs—the United Service Project, in which kids from suburban areas repair homes in the city, and Servants at Work, in which members of the church repair homes of people physically unable to do so themselves.

The students were part of a crew that repaired the roof of Tony Lema's home at 2120 Lennox Avenue. Lema is unable to do the repairs because he has heart trouble.

The student volunteers, though, experienced culture shock. For one thing, the rows of run-down homes with small yards were a strange sight for teens used to wide-open spaces and well-manicured lawns.

The change in scenery led to an unexpected bonus.

"Every day Tony cooked us a different Mexican dish," Ortiz said. "One day he cooked us some corn tortillas with beef and beans. The homemade tortillas were a lot better than the fast-food kind that we get in our neighborhood."

But food wasn't the only difference the students found.

"We saw a lot of homeless people," Smith said. "That was really sad. If you live in our neighborhood, you don't even know that homeless people exist. You hear about it on TV, but you never see them."

That aside, students said they learned much from the project.

"It wakes you up to reality," Jones said. "A lot of my friends spend all of their time in their cozy little homes and have no idea what is going on in the rest of the world. A lot of people out there need help, and it was very gratifying to be there for them. As much as anything, they need to know that people care."

Notice that the last quote is new and required additional reporting. I hate those "It was fun" and "I was proud to take part" quotes. If you are patient and persistent, you can get people to communicate this message in a fresh, compelling way. However, you must ask better questions than, "Are you glad you participated?"

Instead, try something like, "How did the week change your view of social problems?"

News isn't the only area of the student publication to suffer from the organizational pitfall of the chronological order. Quite a number of sports stories and entertainment reviews do so as well.

■ **SPORTS EMPHASIS**

Don't cover sports in chronological order. No one waits weeks to learn whether the team won or lost. It serves no purpose to rehash the play-by-play of each game. Instead, build the story around the common elements in each game. Did the weather play a role in the score? Were there key injuries? Last second losses? Bad luck?

Or, as in the case below, the team—depending on three returning starters from a 16-8 squad the year before—in game after game snatched victory from the jaws of defeat.

Compare the following story to the sidebar example on page 043.

THE LADY MAVS lost two out of their last three basketball games to finish the season with a 12-10 record and in fourth place in district.

The Mavs beat Ysleta, 76-53 on Jan. 7. Serena King led all scorers with 31 points, followed by Tammy Ford, who scored 17. The

■ CONTINUED ON 105

DON'T BEGIN AT THE BEGINNING

Chronological order may work for some stories, but it rarely works for sports game summaries, concert reviews or record reviews. For example:

SPORTS

The game began when we kicked off to the Buzzards, and then they scored on a 23-yard pass. Then we scored but missed the extra point, and then it was halftime. The bands then marched. Then, they kicked off, but we didn't score again. But they did in the fourth quarter, and the game ended. They won.

CONCERTS

The Hangnails' concert was awesome. The dudes stormed on stage and ripped into their number one hit, "Lizard Gizzard." They played "Snake Bake," and then they played "Frog in my Egg Nog." Also, they played some other songs, and then we all went home half-deaf.

Mavs led at the end of the first quarter, 24-10, and at the half, 51-30. Leading 66-39 going into the fourth quarter, the starters were pulled out of the game.

Three days later, the Mavs fell to Parkview, 59-56, even though they held the ball trailing 57-56 with 19 seconds left. King again led all scorers with 22.

In the last game of the year, the Mavs fell to Aurora, 63-49. Molly Perkins led all scorers with 18 points.

"These girls worked hard, but they didn't get a break all season," said coach Jan Davis. "I really felt bad for them."

King was chosen first-team all-district, and Ford and Perkins were selected honorable mention all-district. King led all scorers with a 21.8 points per game average. Other leading scorers were Ford (11.1), Perkins (10.2) and Ramona Griffin (7.6).

This story fails because it dwells on the facts. The common elements that made the season so disappointing for the players are ignored. The heart and soul of the story—that these girls who fully expected to compete for a state championship didn't qualify for the playoffs—isn't addressed. Instead, the story bogs down in a quagmire of statistics and play-by-play rehash.

Find these common elements and use direct quotes to explain them. Just know that no one—not even the players themselves—will read a story that recaps the season, game by game, play by play. They may scan it for their names. But they won't read it.

■ **PACK A WALLOP**

The following story is one of the best examples of story-telling that I've read. The article deals with the struggle of a mother to overcome her daughter's suicide.

The story packs a wallop. Its use of descriptive scene re-creation and narrative, coupled with its clear, logical organization and superb use of transitions makes it one of the most powerful stories ever published in a student publication. Pay attention to the use of direct quotes and transition sentences.

SHOWCASE ■

By **STEVE DOBBINS**
Duncanville High School, Duncanville, TX

"DON'T BE MAD. I took some pills," Karen Keaton cried as she stooped over the toilet.

A few hours later, the 14-year-old freshman died after a series of coronary arrests.

Only that morning Karen had sat among her friends in the crowded church pew listening intently to the pastor's sermon.

And that very same day, she had eaten a big Sunday lunch with her parents and her two little sisters.

And that afternoon, she had applied at Burger King for her very first job.

And only hours earlier, she had giggled and gossiped with her best friends while experimenting with a new hairstyle.

And that spring day had been happy, relaxing and pleasant for the Keaton household.

But sometime about 10 that night, after the rest of the family had gone to bed, Karen went into the bathroom, closed the door and opened the medicine cabinet. One by one, she swallowed each of the 250 heart pills taken from her mother's recently refilled bottle.

For Karen, the pain was short-lived. For those she left behind, the pain will never completely cease.

Though it has been almost six months since her daughter's death, Mrs. Linda Keaton still feels Karen's presence in their home daily.

"We often find ourselves waiting for the front door to open and Karen to pop in just like she always did," she said.

Even after realizing how many pills Karen had swallowed, Mrs. Keaton believed her daughter would survive the ordeal.

"She walked herself into the emergency

room," she said. "I thought she'd just get her stomach pumped, and then we'd go home and everything would be OK."

Four hours and six coronary arrests after Karen had been admitted into the hospital, the doctors told Mrs. Keaton that Karen's brain was dead, and if she lived, she would be a vegetable.

Two hours later Karen died.

"Those few hours seemed like an eternity," Mrs. Keaton said.

She describes the first few weeks after Karen's suicide as a period of shock.

"I just felt numb," she said. "I couldn't feel anything. It didn't really start hurting for a couple of weeks."

The initial shock eventually began to wear off.

"After the shock, you start to feel angry," she said. "You want revenge for your child's death. You want someone to blame it on. Then you start to feel guilty. You begin to think 'If only I had done this or that differently.' Even now I find myself constantly tracing back to see if there was something I could have done or something I could have noticed."

Karen did not show the usual signs of depression before she committed suicide.

"She didn't seem depressed at all," Mrs. Keaton said. "But it was always so hard to tell with Karen when she was unhappy. She was so energetic. She could hide her feelings from everyone."

Mrs. Keaton said she believes Karen's suicide was not premeditated.

"I don't think she realized the finality of suicide," she said. "On television, people are always attempting suicide. But they really don't die; they just get attention and sympathy. We'll never know why she did it. We can speculate, but we'll never really know for sure."

Mrs. Keaton attributes Karen's suicide to peer pressure.

"A few months earlier she and her friends started experimenting with alcohol," she said. "It worried me, but I really couldn't stop it. All

YOUR LAST WORDS SHOULD NOT BE "SHE SAID"

If you end the story with a direct quote, make certain the last words are those of the source, not the writer.

For example, this three-sentence quote was used to conclude a story about an important game.

"We have a chance to make history here," coach Jones said. "This school has never won a state championship. We plan to be the first."

This ending would not have been nearly as effective if it had been:

"We have a chance to make history here. This school has never won a state championship. We plan to be the first," coach Jones said.

If the story ends with a one-sentence quote, it is better to place the attribution before the quote or break the sentence at an appropriate thought pause than to end with the attribution.

of the kids were drinking. Maybe Karen just couldn't cope with the pressures of keeping up with everyone else," she added. "What she wanted to do and what everyone else wanted her to do went against each other. She couldn't deal with that."

Still, suicide was against the image Karen put forth.

"Several of her friends had talked to her about suicide, and it had been she who had talked them out of it," her mother said.

If she had ever thought about suicide before, she never made her thoughts verbal.

"She never told anyone," Mrs. Keaton said. "Not even her closest friends. She had lots of friends, but she only had a few close friends. And even those were kept at a distance."

DON'T BEGIN AT THE BEGINNING

■ CONTINUED FROM 103

RECORD REVIEWS

The Hangnails' third album, "Lizard Gizzard," is totally awesome. The first song, "Snake Bake," is about this reptile who's in love with this girl, but she thinks he's gross. It's awesome. The second song, "Frog in my Egg Nog," is about this guy who has a really awesome girlfriend. It's awesome. The third song is—you guessed it—awesome.

Karen's suicide had a devastating effect on many of her friends.

"Some of them took it harder than the family did," Mrs. Keaton said. "For a month we had them here every night. They were trying to cling to her. They wouldn't let her go."

The friends reacted in many different ways.

"Some of her friends who were drinking sobered up; others turned to drugs," Mrs. Keaton said. "One of the girls was a camp counselor this summer. Another one still dreams of Karen every night. It's had a diverse effect on everyone."

Karen's suicide was a traumatic experience for her two younger sisters, Michelle and April. Michelle, an eighth-grader, still finds it difficult to talk about Karen.

"For a long time, Michelle wouldn't go down the hall where Karen's room was unless someone was with her," Mrs. Keaton said. "She kept telling us Karen was just playing one of her jokes, and she would pop out of the bedroom door and laugh. It's easier now that we've made the room into the baby's room."

Michelle still doesn't talk much about her sister's suicide.

"It took her a while to learn to deal with it. I'm sure she thinks about all of it a lot, but she is getting better," Mrs. Keaton said.

Two-year-old April was sent to stay with friends during the days after Karen's death. No one ever told April that Karen was gone, "but somehow she knew," Mrs. Keaton said.

Before Karen's death, April would knock on her oldest sister's door and call out her name. Karen would let her in and play with her.

"April worshipped Karen," Mrs. Keaton said. "But since Karen's death, April has not once said Karen's name. For a while she kissed Karen's picture every night before she went to bed, but to this day she has not spoken Karen's name."

A few weeks after the funeral, the family took April to the cemetery.

"We explained to April that this was where Karen was," Mrs. Keaton said. "We tried to get her to say Karen's name, but she wouldn't. As we were walking off, April suddenly stopped and looked back. Softly she said, 'Bye bye.' Somehow she understood Karen was gone."

Mrs. Keaton has adjusted slowly to her daughter's death.

"At first I didn't want to see any teenagers," she said. "Her birthday and my first trip back to the high school were especially painful. The next really tough time is going to be Christmas. It's going to be hard."

Some days it is really difficult for the family to cope with their loss.

"But we have rules," Mrs. Keaton said. "One is we never not mention her name. Karen is a part of all of us. We don't want to forget her, but we have accepted her death. Also, we haven't been afraid to say suicide. It isn't a disease."

Mrs. Keaton has found that she must go on with her life. Much of her time has been devoted to the High on Life program here at the high school. Also, she has been researching the causes and effects of teenage suicide as well as helping to organize a local chapter of Students Against Drunk Driving (SADD).

"At first I kept saying, 'Why Karen?' Now I'm starting to think maybe her death can help save 3,000 other lives," she said. "That's what I'm working for. I want suicide to stop. Kids who commit suicide don't realize the finality of the act. Life has its peaks and valleys. When you're in the valleys, you have to look forward to the mountains. They're there, but so many kids can't see them."

Mrs. Keaton is quick to point out that suicide can happen in any family, regardless of their economic background or culture.

"Parents need to take seriously anything their kids say," she said. "Take the time to listen to them. Take an interest in their lives."

Since the death of her oldest daughter, the Keatons have found themselves becoming more protective.

"I find myself watching for things," Mrs.

WHO SAID THAT?

Attribution tells the reader who is talking. Unless you attribute information to a source, readers will assume that the publication stands behind the information printed. If the information is wrong, the reader will blame you—not your source. So it's a good idea to attribute information to a source. Here are a few tips to help:

■ What is said is more important than who said it so place the attribution after the quote and start a new paragraph immediately after the attribution. For example:

WEAK: Principal Bo Simmons said, "I am going to run over you in my truck if you don't get out of my way."
BETTER: "I am going to run over you in my truck if you don't get out of my way," Principal Bo Simmons said.

■ But sometimes, "who" is more important than what if the "who" is an important person. For example:

WEAK: "I quit. I've had it up to here. My bags are packed, and I'm rolling out in the morning," Superintendent Anita Change said.
BETTER: Superintendent Anita Change said, "I quit. I've had it up to here. My bags are packed, and I'm rolling out in the morning."

■ Place "said" after the name because the name is more important and because the person-said order is easier to read.

WEAK: "You can't leave me with this mess," said principal Bo Simmons.
BETTER: "You can't leave me with this mess," principal Bo Simmons said.

■ Don't bury the attribution. Identify the source after the first sentence of a multi-sentence quote. This method focuses on the story itself without using extra words. It also promotes easier reading and allows for a shift of emphasis.

WEAK: Superintendent Anita Change said, "I am going to run over you in my truck if you don't get out of my way. I told you once, and I ain't going to tell you again. This here's your last warning. Move it or lose it!"
WEAK: "I am going to run over you in my truck if you don't get out of my way. I told you once, and I ain't going to tell you again. This here's your last warning. Move it or lose it!" Superintendent Anita Change said.
BETTER: "I am going to run over you in my truck if you don't get out of my way," Superintendent Anita Change said. "I told you once, and I ain't going to tell you again. This here's your last warning. Move it or lose it!"

■ Use indirect quotations for factual information when the source's exact words are not necessary or when the direct quote is unclear.

WEAK: "Approximately 200 persons attended the dance," chairman Ron Dukes said.
BETTER: Approximately 200 persons attended the dance, according to chairman Ron Dukes.

■ Use "explain" only when someone is indeed explaining something.

WEAK: "We are pleased that the SAT scores have improved," assistant superintendent Bob Francis explained.
BETTER: "Our new strategies that focused on math, reading and writing skills were responsible for the improved SAT scores," assistant superintendent Bob Francis explained.

■ Every time you introduce a new direct quote, begin a new paragraph.

"AVOID SYNONYMS FOR SAID," HE STATED.

■ Use said unless the person definitely yelled, whispered, blurted, etc. Be careful with loaded words such as "admitted, explained, charged, accused, demanded" or any other verb that comes close to editorializing. Note how the word admitted implies some sort of wrongdoing.

WEAK: Principal Bertha Newhouse admitted she needed help to lead the school.
BETTER: Principal Bertha Newhouse said she needed help to lead the school.

■ Avoid synonyms such as declared, remarked, commented or expressed.
■ Avoid qualifiers such as "when asked . . . ."

Can you ever use second person? Yes!

Have you ever been hit by a truck? Well, Irene has. She was on the way to school, stepped off the curb and was smacked right between the eyes by a Ford pickup. When asked how she felt about it, she said, "Not so great."

Boy, do I hate those question leads so I urge students to avoid second person. However, second person works quite well when the reporter is writing about the reader. The story above is Irene getting hit by the truck. It's not about the reader. Does the reporter actually expect the reader to answer, "Why yes, I do know what it's like to be hit by a truck!"

Of course not. But reporters often write about subjects or events that are real to the readers. Use second person when the reader is personally involved in the action.

EXAMPLE 1

Your car engine is knocking, your wool sweaters are dirty, and you need a haircut. Taking care of all of these chores may cost a tiny fortune, you lament as you thumb through the Yellow Pages.

Not necessarily.

All this can be done, at a fraction of the regular cost, by students. In public schools, colleges and private trade schools, students are studying every sort of trade and profession—horticulture, dentistry, small-engine repair, cosmetology, dry cleaning. And they need something—or someone—to practice on.

Because they are still learning, these students charge much less than professionals. But, of course, there are strings attached.

First, your needs must mesh with those of the students. For instance, the auto repair students at the high school won't fix your car's transmission if they are studying brakes when you call . . . .

EXAMPLE 2

Your coffee maker doesn't keep coffee hot, and your electric blanket doesn't keep you warm. And both appliances broke after the warranty expired.

If you're like many people, you toss out the broken appliance or donate it to Goodwill, the Salvation Army or another charity, and hope it will find new life in someone else's hands. You figure the appliance isn't worth the cost of returning it to the factory and paying for repairs.

Well, you may be mistaken. A number of fix-it shops and factory-authorized or factory-owned service centers are located in the western suburbs. You may be able to get your appliance repaired with a minimum of inconvenience.

EXAMPLE 3

Ripped apart. Torn at the seams. After dating him for a year, you realize it's over. You still like him. It's not something he did. It's just that, well, your time has run out. The time on that little meter in your heart has expired, and you're out of pocket change.

"I'll tell him tomorrow, after school," you tell yourself. But you know it won't be any easier tomorrow. Besides, if you tell him now, he'll have time to find someone else to take out Saturday night.

So you draw a deep breath, stand back a foot or so and tell him it's time that he hit the road. Jack.

Keaton said. "I'm not sure for what. I'm just watching."

■ ORGANIZATION STRATEGY

Several points to be made about the story:
■ The lead opens with a scene that pulls the reader directly into the story and then uses a parallel sentence structure (and that morning/ and that afternoon/ and that evening...) in the next four paragraphs to take readers from the time before Karen's suicide to the days just after the funeral, an approach that sets the scene for Mrs. Keaton to enter the picture.

■ The writer allows Mrs. Keaton to tell her own story—and it is a story so forceful that it requires little intervention by the reporter.

■ The story displays a lot of common sense. The writer understands that the best narrative is usually told in chronological order. Mrs. Keaton describes the scene at the hospital, her reaction following Karen's death and funeral, her attempts to understand Karen's motivation, the impact on Michelle and April, and finally her resolve to give meaning to Karen's death.

■ So often, long stories bog down into a series of dull, data-driven paragraphs. Not so here. The writer uses the anecdote about April at the cemetery in the middle of the story to propel the reader through to the end.

■ The story closes with a powerful quote that gives it a sense of resolution and even momentum. We are left with a powerful image of Mrs. Keaton, watching. Just watching.

The writer, Steve Dobbins, said he interviewed Mrs. Keaton four or five times, each time thinking he had enough information to finish the story only to find he needed more. Fortunately, she was willing to accommodate him.

She probably recognized as we do that this young man was on something of a mission himself.

■ I CAN'T WRITE THAT WELL?

Why not? Steve's an excellent writer, but the strengh of this story is the reporting, the interviewing, observing and listening. Once he collects the information, he lays it out and tells the story naturally — just as if you were telling it to a friend.

If you find yourself blocked, talk it through with your adviser, editor or friend. Most people are natural storytellers. They just haven't figured out how to translate that into writing. Veteran reporters write their stories as they go. As they collect information, they unconsciously catalog it. "This quote will work well here. I'll use this information to develop the lead. I can end with that quote."

The more you report and write, the better at this you'll become. But that doesn't get you out of the hole now, does it? So, where to begin?

First, ask yourself, "What is this story about?" Then, discard information that does not advance the theme of the story. Don't feel territorial about the information you've collected. If you've done an adequate job of reporting, you'll have far more data than you can or will want to use.

Second, ask yourself, "What part of this story will be most interesting to the readers? What will be something my readers don't know? What part of the story most interests you? If it interested you, it'll probably interest your readers.

Consider the story in Chapter 2 about Nathan Shaffer, the kid who was robbed at the convenience store. The author, Leslie Courtney, did not conduct a flash interview with Shaffer and then whip out the story. In fact, Donya Witherspoon, Leslie's adviser, said the first draft was a dull, quoteless story.

"Nathan Shaffer was a student of mine, so I interviewed him again in front of the journalism class to demonstrate how to interview someone and get good quotes," Witherspoon said. "Then when the reporter went to confirm some of the information with the police, they told her the defendant had taken a plea. So I helped her rewrite the story into its present state."

So what did the adviser and reporter think would most interest readers? A descriptive anecdote that ends with "Now

THE STATE OF USING 'STATE,' ACCORDING TO...

Use state when a source reads from a prepared text. For example, if the principal reads a statement at a press conference, then use stated.

Use "according to" when the source is a written report or letter that announces conclusions. Avoid "according to" as a synonym for "said."

WEAK: The number of poor school-age children became increasingly concentrated in the West and Southwest during the 1990s, the U. S. General Accounting Office stated.

BETTER: The number of poor school-age children became increasingly concentrated in the West and Southwest during the 1980s, according to a report by the U. S. General Accounting Office.

you're going to die."

It's an emotionally-charged, powerful lead that takes the reader through the frightening experience. The lead works well because it appeals to the human desire to read stories about things we want to happen to us, such as winning the lottery, and about things we pray never happen to us, such as having a stranger in a ski mask stick a gun in our faces.

■ **KEEP READERS ON TRACK**

A compelling lead doesn't insure that the entire story will be read. You can't put 95 percent of their effort into the lead and skate through the rest of the story. Keep the story focused and moving forward. If necessary, outline your story. If the lead begins with an especially dramatic moment, decide how to build back to that moment and then resolve the dilemma. In other words, a young man has a gun stuck in his face. How did he get there? How does he get out?

At this stage, it makes sense to go with chronological order. Description and dialogue of the events would be balanced with direct quotes that explain what was going through the student's mind during the robbery. The success of the story will be determined largely by the writer's ability to dovetail description with analysis and/or interpretation. What happened? Describe it. What was the source thinking while it was happening? What happened next?

Keeping the reader on track is difficult but essential. If readers become confused or cannot figure out where they are in the story chronology, they'll give up.

A tip: use the computer to help organize the story. Type up all quotes and information. Copy and paste all related information into what you think will make the best order. Search for the dramatic statements that will make the most powerful opening or concluding direct quotes.

The process will also help you determine where additional interviewing or reporting is needed. If you want to use an anecdotal lead, it will help if you've collected a few interesting stories.

DEFINITIVE ANSWERS...

SIDEBAR STORY: a minor story that accompanies a major news story. It provides a new angle or perspective.

INFOGRAPHICS: Combination of photography, computer art and text that provides visual and verbal messages to give readers information they want without having to read long passages of type.

SURVEY SIDEBARS: Results of a survey are used to supplement a major news story.

INDEX: a directory or summary of information. These guide readers quickly to the information that interests them.

READ-IN: also called a nutgraf, this is a quick synopsis of a story. It gives the reader an overview of the news without having to read the entire story.

MARGINAL: Sidebar information that runs down the side of a story or the page. We use them on odd-numbered pages of this book.

FACT BOXES: Sometimes called "factoids," these boxes provide details that readers find interesting and useful such as where to find additional information on a topic.

PULLED QUOTES: Used to lure readers into the text, they provide interesting details. They should never be used merely to fill space.

BULLETS: little dots (•) used to organize and summarize information.
• easily digested by the reader
• visually pleasing
• fun to use

BRIEFS: Short news articles, generally two to five paragraphs at the most.

However, do not use the computer merely to transcribe your notes and stack quotes. Work with the direct quotes. Weave them together. You're not so much building a block fort as you are weaving a Persian rug. Which information should be quoted? Which part of this direct quote should be used within quote marks? Which part in the transition? Can you use partial quotes? If so, how? Most importantly, how do you combine direct quotes, indirect quotes, transition sentences, transition paragraphs and description into a tight, focused package?

Consider the following story:

SHOWCASE

By **AARON BROWN**
City High School, Iowa City, IA

"I REMEMBER going up for air once. And I remember taking a big gulp of water. And then it was black," junior Phil Fort said. But that wasn't all. Fort experienced more than blackness while submerged, and dead for a minute and a half, in the waters of the Coralville Reservoir.

"At first I saw a red thing, I don't know what it was, and then I saw this white light and I saw my family and my friends. It was like a dream," Fort said. "I saw my family in front and all my friends that I have ever met and talked to were right behind my family."

Fort had been working at GS Marine that Sunday. He noticed earlier, while filling boats with gas, that the pump was giving off shocks. Not strong shocks, just enough to give "a numb feeling." Later, the shock was much worse.

"At about 1:30 a boat caught on fire because of it. The end of the nozzle caught on fire, and the tube going down to the gas tank caught on fire. I put that out.

"I was putting gas into a boat, and I felt a tingling so I grabbed the hose with both hands [to avoid another fire] and grounded myself. It blew me about three or four feet in the air and about 10 feet back. I landed in the water." The shock contracted Fort's muscles, and he couldn't let go of the hose.

"I was scared when I was awake. I was really scared. I know I was saying, 'Help, get this thing off me.' I remember seeing all of that. And then I just remember taking a big gulp of water. That was it," Fort said.

"They said I was down about 10 feet. The only thing that saved my life was the fact that my muscles hung on to the hose, and that's how they pulled me out. Otherwise, I'd be lying on the bottom of the lake.

"It seemed like it took forever," he said. "It felt really good when I was in that dream. It was the best thing I've ever had. Ever. I had no more worries. No more problems.

"I think that if I'd decided, I would have stayed there." But he didn't decide. Two men pulled the hose up, and Fort's hands were still locked onto it. The men began CPR immediately.

"When I woke up, I was scared. And I didn't know where the hell I was," Fort said. "There was a guy on my legs and a guy on my face. I kicked them both off." Fort was hot while lying on the dock, but he wasn't allowed to move. The ambulance had gotten lost and took four and a half minutes to arrive.

The paramedics gave Fort oxygen; too much. He had a seizure in the ambulance and lost consciousness again.

"All I heard the nurse say was 'We're losing him.'" He regained consciousness before the 20-minute trip to Mercy Hospital was over.

"When I got to the hospital, they pushed me in a wheelchair to the emergency room. The doctor came in and looked at me and said 'You shouldn't even be alive.' "

Fort has learned from his experience. "I realize now how close I am to my family and friends."

Forget the inherent power of the story itself. Let's look at how Aaron Brown chose to relate the information and how he connected each paragraph to the next.

HOW DO I GET THERE FROM HERE?

Moving from one paragraph to another is called transition. Two common forms of transition are the "key word" and "key phrase." This phrase can be a repeat of specific words or a repeat of synonyms of those words. Example:

A former Seaweed High student was named "SuperModel of the Week" by DimBulb magazine.

A 1999 graduate, Nikki Lee has been modeling in New York and London for the past two years.

"I love New York, but modeling is the hardest job in the world," she said. "All that blow-drying and posing. It gives me a headache."

Transition words: former student/graduate; modeling/modeling.

> The best conclusion is a natural extension of the story. It flows as smoothly and effortlessly as the ending of a song."

First, he used a quote lead. Quote leads are not recommended unless the statement is exceptionally powerful. This one is.

The second graph continues the direct quote. In it, he relates a near-death experience, the center of the story around which all other information evolves.

The third graph takes the reader back to the beginning. From that point, Brown allows Fort to tell his own story. Brown's job here is to keep the narrative moving and focused, which he does through the eighth paragraph. Note the delicate use of transition sentences. At this point, no one can tell the story with more power than Fort, so Brown relies heavily on direct quotes.

The ninth paragraph is a transition from the accident to the rescue and resuscitation. The 12th and 13th paragraphs describe what Fort heard and said while paramedics worked frantically to save him.

The final paragraph brings the story a logical conclusion—that is, what he has learned from this experience: "I realize now how close I am to my family and friends."

It is a gratifying resolution.

■ HOW TO END THE STORY?

"How long should my story be?" Journalism advisers have heard this question a million times. And what does your teacher reply? "Write until you've answered all the news questions."

Or "Write until you've told the whole story."

This is the journalistic equivalent to "go ask your mother." You think it doesn't answer your question, but it does.

Tell the story. Put in all the essential information. Leave out everything else. When you've done that, quit. Actually, students aren't really interested in the length of the story. Conditioned by years of writing-by-rote assignments, they're really seeking permission to quit writing.

"Well, my teacher told me it had to be 500 words in length. When I hit 501, I stopped."

Right in the middle of a sentence fragment, no less. So the question arises:

WHERE'S THE TRANSITION?

"I'd say our chances of winning are about as good as the Berlin Wall coming down," coach Ray Danson said. "No one thought it was possible, but it happened.

"We know how good they are, but we're not intimidated. We think we're a pretty good team too."

The absence of closed quote marks after the first graph tells the reader that the source is continuing to talk in the next graph. Had the quote been closed after "happened," then the reader knows that the second graph is a direct quote from a new source. Of course, you want to avoid stacking quotes on top of one another. In this case, a transition sentence would make the passage clearer and more readable.

---

when to stop?

If writing the lead is the hardest part of any story, then finding a way to end it is the second hardest. Of course, the inverted pyramid offers a fairly quick and simple way to end the story: push the least important information to the end of the story. This works as long as the students are able to identify the least important information. This isn't always the case. For example:

THE TURNIP TRUCK ISD School Board met Tuesday night in the school cafeteria. School Board President E. M. Bezzle called for the reading of the minutes of the last meeting and then led everyone in the pledge of allegiance. He then asked Mrs. Elvira Doyle to introduce the members of the Future Farmers of America, who won third place in last week's potato peeling contest. "We congratulate each and every one of you," Mrs. Doyle said.

Then, the Board awarded a $150,000 contract to replace the light bulbs in the band hall to Buck Tooth, Mr. Bezzle's brother-in-law, prompting a fist-fight between Mr. Tooth and Mayor Rob

Emblind, who complained that he bribed Mr. Bezzle first and should have been awarded the contract instead. The meeting was adjourned due to an explosion that resulted when an Air Force C-130 cargo plane crashed into the building.

If you plan to take the inverted pyramid approach, make sure you're able to figure out what's the most important and the least important fact in the story. End with the least important.

For everything beyond the inverted pyramid, there are countless ways to finish a story. Textbooks are filled with chapters on "how to end the feature story." Most of these are hideous.

One of my least favorites is the "leave them with some good advice" ending. For example:

"SNORTING BATTERY ACID is really not very good for your health," Dr. Casket said. "In fact, putting anything up your nose except a Kleenex is pretty stupid."

So, the next time you think about popping the top off a DieHard, just say no!

I don't care what the textbooks say, don't preach to your readers.

Don't be a wise-guys either. A lot of young writers, particularly beginning sports writers, try to slip a clever comment onto the end of every article even though the comment has nothing to do with the story. I once worked with a reporter who tried to end every story with a snickering quip. In a story about an outstanding freshman golfer, he could have closed with the following quote: "It's strange beating these older guys, but it's something I'm getting used to."

Instead, he tacked on a gratuitous and dopey, "So watch out, Tiger Woods. You could be next!"

Gag me.

My advice: end a feature story with a strong direct quote that brings the story to a logical conclusion and leaves the reader with the feeling that the dilemma has been brought to a satisfactory resolution.

Finding this quote isn't easy, especially if you're working on a 35-inch story that contains quotes from six or seven sources. Sometimes, I'll finish the first draft and realize that I placed the quote that I should use to end the story in the fifth or sixth paragraph. No problem. Cut quote here, paste it there, cover up the scars.

I generally outline my story to determine which quotes I'll use and in what order. I always look first for the zinger quote, the powerful quote for the second or third paragraph that pulls the reader into the story. Sometimes that quote comes from an interview. Sometimes, it's a piece of dialogue. Regardless, I want that powerful quote to give the story immediacy, credibility and vibrancy.

Of course, it requires that I collect a few powerful quotes. If the best quote at my disposal is "If you don't look at the losses, we had a pretty successful season," then it'll be a real toss up whether to use it as the zinger or ending quote.

Even with a couple of hot quotes in hand, too many young writers bury them rather than showcase them. If you have a powerful quote, use it as early as possible and let the narrative flow to a logical conclusion. Don't tell the readers what happened. Let your sources tell their own stories. Your job is to string together the direct quotes in an orderly, logical and unobtrusive manner while maintaining the drama of the story through to a strong conclusion.

The best conclusion is a natural extension of the story. It flows from the story as smoothly and effortlessly as the ending of a good song. The Beatles' "Eleanor Rigby" for example.

Or so it seems. In reality, finishing a story is often as hard as beginning it. The best advice I can offer is to let the last words the reader hears come from the characters themselves. If the story is good enough, the reader will hear the voices of the people speaking rather than simply reading the quotes.

HOW DO I GET THERE FROM HERE?

Transition words and phrases are like garlic. A little bit goes a long way. Avoid "heretofore" and "henceforth." And try not to begin every paragraph with "therefore."

- After all,
- And
- Also
- Although
- As a result
- At least
- Besides
- But
- Consequently
- Finally
- For example
- Furthermore
- However
- In addition
- In conclusion
- Incidentally
- Lately
- Later
- Likewise
- Meanwhile
- Moreover
- Naturally
- Nevertheless
- On the contrary
- Or
- Otherwise
- Then

Photo by **NICK KREEGER**
Kearney High School, Kearney, MO

LOOK BEYOND THE FACTS

Perfect objectivity is impossible to achieve because decisions must be made by imperfect human beings. Therefore, it's necessary for the reporter to analyze and interpret facts. But that's not a license to editorialize.

09

CHAPTER HIGHLIGHTS:

■ The reporting process is hardly objective.

■ Truth is often a matter of perspective.

■ Interpre-ation gives meaning to cold hard facts.

■ Strive to be as fair, balanced and objective as possible.

In theory, it works like this: the reporter writes a straight news story without first-person references (I, we, our) or personal opinion, presents both sides of a controversial issue and refuses to participate in any news event or take a stand on a news issue.

The idea is that each story is a mirror, a reflection of the day's events. For example:

THE MARCHING BAND placed second to rival Clearwater at the district marching band competition Saturday. In his second year as director, Sandra Dodd said she was pleased with the judges' decision.

"I thought we marched well enough to win, but that is not my decision to make," Dodd said. "We have a few kinks to work out before regionals."

That's a fairly dry approach. It leaches out all the emotion, the disappointment of finishing second to the arch rival. On the other end of the spectrum is the reporter as fanatic commentator.

OUR SCHOOL BAND placed second at the district marching competition Saturday. They should have won and would have had it not been one particularly crooked, blind judge who somehow apparently was reading the newspaper while Clearwater marched because their performance absolutely stank. Band director Sandy Dodd refused to admit it, but everyone in the stands agreed that our band was light years better than pathetic Clearwater outfit.

Thanks to Mr. Moron Judge, we got the shaft. Thanks for nothing, creep.

We'll see Clearwater at region, where the judges don't stuff their pockets with Clearwater dollars. And then we'll see who's laughing. HA HA HA HA HAAAAA....

■ CONVEYING A JUDGMENT

Colorful but not very journalistic. You need to reach a balance between dry dictation and foaming at the mouth ranting. Achieving absolute objectivity is impossible because decisions must be made by humans. Even when these decisions are made according to established news procedures and values, the process is hardly objective. Certainly, once they've decided what to cover and how, reporters should approach the subject with an open mind and sense of fair play.

However, reporters have great latitude in selecting sources and then deciding which information gleaned from those sources to

> ❝ Don't editorialize. Don't say the new chemistry teacher i s handsome and charming. say he's 6-foot-3, with eyes the color of milk chocolate, a square jaw and wavy black hair. When he speaks, grown women giggle and swoon and turn into little girls.

use and in what order. Simply by picking out one element to emphasize in the first sentence of a news story, reporters convey a judgment about what is important and what is not. Whenever reporters decide that one part of a statement should go as a direct quote and another part as an indirect quote, they're making a subjective decision. Another reporter might do it exactly the opposite, and yet both are correct.

Objectivity is easier to attain in event-oriented stories: Four persons were killed in a three-alarm fire at a downtown apartment building yesterday. Reporters talk to the fire chief, the apartment building manager, witnesses at the scene. They go to the hospital to interview doctors or nurses. They attend the press conferences conducted by the appropriate city or medical officials, then go back to the office to pound out a story.

They do not attempt to assign blame. They don't hypothesize beyond the facts in evidence. They don't mourn the dead, curse the guilty. Whatever information they generate comes from authoritative sources.

All of this, one might think, would demand that reporters produce nothing more than a simple, condensed presentation of facts. Not so. Consider the following story, written by Colin Nickerson and Allan R. Andrews of the *Boston Globe*.

JEAN NICKERSON sat stunned in the Salvation Army office, unable to accept the dreadful news. "No," she kept saying, shaking her head as her husband, Leslie, sobbed beside her. "No."

A block away, clearly visible through the window of the makeshift emergency headquarters in the Salvation Army office were the still-smoldering remains of a three-story rooming house where 14 people were killed in one of the deadliest fires in Massachusetts history.

Nickerson had just been told that her two sons—Richard, 21, and Ralph, 9—as well as her 73-year-old mother, Hattie M. Whary, were among the victims who died when flames ripped through the shabby structure early Wednesday morning.

The older son lived with his grandmother, Whary, who managed the rooming house. The younger boy was there for a summer visit from the family home in Auburn, Maine. Their bodies were among the first found when firefighters entered the burned-out second floor.

Five of the dead were found in the vicinity of a second-floor fire escape. Many of the residents of the building were former mental patients.

Some of the bodies were not found until midday and had to be dug from the sodden debris. One by one, they were removed from the building in clear plastic body bags, loaded into waiting hearses and taken to funeral homes in Beverly.

The fire, which broke out at about 2 a.m., raced through the 80-year-old wood structure in a matter of minutes, gutting the second and third floors but leaving a ground-floor pharmacy and other stores relatively intact.

Firefighters said the blaze appeared to have started in a front stairwell and spread quickly through the building. Though firemen arrived within minutes of the alarm, flames could be seen at every window of the upper floors.

This approach captures the tragedy of the event in human terms without pointing fingers or relying on hearsay evidence. It recognizes that the drama of the story arises from the event itself, not artificial attempts by the reporters to create it.

■ **TRUTH IN CONTEXT**

Interpretive reporting has challenged the entire notion of objectivity. Many journalists today believe the reader needs to have a given event placed in its proper context if truth is really to be served. Otherwise, journalism becomes a rather banal exercise in interviewing people who are telling the truth and then interviewing the liars.

Like politicians, journalists today face a more cynical and suspicious populace. "Don't believe what you read in the newspaper" is no longer merely a sly warning to the wise. It has become a universal sentiment. Newspapers are seen as either lackeys of the military-industrial state or as organs of the liberal intellectual elite.

Distrust of the mainstream media has contributed to the rise of alternative journalism. While circulation of daily newspapers has continued to plummet during the past two decades, circulation and advertising revenues for alternative newspapers—those which are written from a distinct perspective—have soared. Consider the successes of the *Village Voice*, the *San Francisco Bay Guardian* and the *Dallas Observer*.

In my hometown, I often have more confidence in the *Austin Chronicle*—a weekly alternative newspaper with a distinctly left-of-center point of view and sardonic edge—than I do in the *Austin American-Statesman*, our local daily whose former publisher was once the president of the Austin Chamber of Commerce, a group that has promoted development in sensitive areas of our environmentally-conscious community.

■ PRACTICAL OR PRINCIPLE?

The principles of fairness, balance, accuracy and objectivity don't always prevail. As a young reporter for an East Texas newspaper, I covered a city hall meeting at which the town council refused to issue a license to operate an ambulance service to a black-owned funeral home.

As I sat through the meetings, I became more convinced that the council would deny the request and that their rationale for doing so didn't make a lot of sense.

Those seeking the permit asked for nothing from the city except to operate a service in a part of town that was being inadequately served by the established medical communities. Response time in the minority neighborhood was something like four times greater than it was in the white neighborhoods.

From where I sat, it looked like a case of racism, pure and simple. Of course, I could never write that, but I thought I could at least

report the story from the black perspective. I wanted to take one case involving a late response and show the consequences of the city's negligence. Reporting a group's request to operate an ambulance service is a fairly dry story. Reporting that a young man died unnecessarily because the ambulance arrived 10 minutes late could be a powerful feature.

My editors thought the story was a great idea. Someone higher up the chain of command didn't. "Not on your life," I was told. Report what happened at the council meeting. As I expected, the council cited some bureaucratic reasons for denying the permit and moved on to the next issue, a zoning change request. My story the next day stated,

AFTER MORE THAN an hour of discussion which included some heated exchanges between members, the city council voted today to deny to Pierce-Moss Funeral Home an application to operate its ambulance service on city streets.

■ PERCEPTON DICTATES OBJECTIVITY

The remainder of the story included some of the "heated exchanges" and listed the reasons cited by the council for its decision. I ended the story by reporting that the council also approved a request to change the zoning of a local warehouse from industrial to commercial. Someone wanted to open a restaurant and bar.

Now, was this an objective story? Well, it depends on your point of view. To a casual reader of the newspaper, it had all the outward appearances of being objective. But if you were a black person who had lived in the North Tyler community and had seen friends and neighbors die because of slow or negligent services, then it was blatantly subjective in favor of powerful, well-connected interests.

How objective would my story about someone's death have been? Wasn't I approaching this story with a large dose of unwarranted cynicism that may not have had any connection to this particular decision by the city council? Who is to say that the one

THINK PAST THE FACTS

Often, a conclusion is more newsworthy than the mere reporting of fact.

WEAK:

The School Board appointed Bill Jones to a blue-ribbon committee studying the school district boundaries. Johnson owns Continental Pumps.

"I am pleased to have been appointed," he said.

BETTER:

Supporters of the forced busing plan appear to have lost control of a blue-ribbon committee, appointed by the School Board to study the school district's boundaries.

Over the objections of the busing proponents, the panel voted 10-3 to approve a plan that would end busing in all but two junior high schools.

"Bill Jones has consistently opposed any plan to equalize education," said Ron Hicks, chairman of Equal Education for All, a group that opposes the end to cross-town busing.

example I might have chosen to showcase would have accurately portrayed a universal truth? Wouldn't some have found this story to be blatantly subjective, merely another case of a bleeding-heart liberal preaching to society?

It all depends on where you stand.

Consider, for example, the following story, by Steve Lize of Glenbard East High School in Lombard, Illinois. This feature story has a decidedly anti-military perspective.

"HELLO, BIFF? THIS IS SGT. Bob from the Marines. Now that you're a senior in high school, I understand that you have plans for college at College of DuPage or DeVry. Did you know that the Marine Corps can help you with your education and prepare you for life in the real world?" Sgt. Bob said.

As his voice reverberated through Biff's head, it conjured images of an officer from a "Ren and Stimpy" cartoon. Biff thought the Marines were honorable, but he wasn't into the discipline and physical exertion required for the status.

"Uh, I'm really not interested right now," Biff said.

"We think that the Marines would benefit from an individual with your capabilities," the sergeant said.

"But, I'm not interested so . . . ."

"If you join the Marines, we will pay for you to go to college, give you and your friends free posters and even throw in a pair of socks! It is to your benefit that you join the Marines, Biff," Sgt. Bob pleaded.

"Just leave me alone!" Biff commanded, slamming the receiver down. A sudden air of superiority passed over him as he realized that he told a military officer off. Little did he know that this wasn't the end of the government's pestering.

The recruiters are at it again, feeding upon the nation's youth, specifically high school teens. They hunt for able-bodied individuals who want to "be all they can be" through methods that are considered invasion of one's privacy.

Harold Miller, parent of a Glenbard East senior, objects to the military's method of recruitment. He was angered after a phone call from the Marines. "I don't like invasion of family privacy without being invited," he said.

Because his number is unlisted, Miller wanted to know how the Marines got his family's phone number. He tried, without succeeding, to find out how the number was obtained.

"I never got a straight answer out of the guy," Miller said.

One Marine Corps recruiting station claimed they gather phone numbers by talking to people on the street and through referrals. They also claimed to get numbers from "interest" cards students may have filled out as far back as sixth grade when they had no idea what they wanted to do with their future.

The recruiters, Miller thinks, solicit and take advantage of minors.

"It's impertinent to ask to talk to underage individuals who haven't much experience dealing with things in life," Miller said.

Students throughout school receive flyers from the government that glamorize the Armed Forces. By the time they're seniors, students feel pressured by flyers, pamphlets and phone calls.

"I was hoping to go through all four years of high school without being pestered by a recruiter. Besides, if a guy can't handle going through training, how can I?" senior Chrissy Erickson said.

Angered students disapprove of the recruiters' phone calls.

"I don't appreciate the military knowing my phone number," Erickson said.

"If they call me, I'll tell the Army to shove it," senior Drew Ludwig said.

"The Marines always call me. Like I want to join the Marines. I can't even jog a block," senior Phil Brow said.

In their effort to find young adults, the military invades students' and their families' privacy.

"Joining the Armed Forces should be a family decision," Miller said, "not a military sergeant's who is trying to fill a quota."

Keep in mind that it's less risky to convey a viewpoint in a feature story than in a news story. Lize's story appeared on a page titled, "Reactions." This page was a new concept by the staff to connect news with opinions.

■ IT'S ACCURATE, BUT IS IT TRUE?

Sometimes, reporters pass along bad information in an unwarranted attempt to be objective. Lazy reporters get their stories by going back to the same sources, time after time. Or worse, failing to give the story a sense of context by seeking out the opposing point of view.

I can be accused of this myself. As a young reporter, I was sent to report on a speech, given by the president of a power and light company. The speech was mostly gloom and doom, slamming then President Jimmy Carter, Congress, the Environmental Protection Agency, environmentalists, Ralph Nader and just about anyone else who didn't agree that big oil companies were more philanthropic than capitalistic.

My lead was, "The nation's energy situation is at an all-time low. And with a little help from the government, it's probably going to get worse. That was the message brought Thursday by so and so, who spoke to more than 100 members of the Downtown Rotary Club."

The rest of the story was pretty much free public relations on the part of a company that at that moment had requested a $58.2 million rate increase—an increase that was later approved. Even though the speaker sent a letter to the newspaper's publisher congratulating me "for the accuracy of his article," I think the only thing accurate about it were the quotes. I reported what he said.

But did I report the truth? I somehow doubt that I did. In the final scene of the movie "Absence of Malice," a reporter is questioning Sally Fields about her relationship with Paul Newman. Upon hearing Ms. Fields' answer, the reporter asks, "Is that true?"

"No. But it's accurate," Ms. Fields replies. Objectivity demands that we be more than merely accurate. We must attempt to report the truth. Whether novices or beginners, journalists must learn to detect the biases, both subtle and blatant, of all sources. If we can't always eliminate them, we should at least learn to recognize them.

I'm seeing more and more of this in the daily media. For example, note this portion of a story by Christopher Lee of the *Dallas Morning News* about how Texas Republicans were distancing themselves from the state's GOP party platform:

Gov. Rick Perry, making a stop Tuesday in Dallas, declined to discuss his opinion of the platform, saying he had not had time to study "the voluminous document." It is 24 pages.

Adding those four words — It is 24 pages — changes the truth of the story.

Here's another example: *U.S. Sen. Tim Hutchinson came to Arkansas on Monday with President Bush as the president was touting his welfare-to-work reform plan.*

Whether it will help re-elect Mr. Hutchinson, the conservative, family-values candidate of 1996 who divorced his wife and married a former staff member, is open to question.

A more easily duped or more politically-motivated reporter would have skimmed right over the small fact that he divorced his wife and married a member of his staff. It is a fact that casts Hutchinson in an different light than from the conservative, family-values candidate he claims to be.

The following story, I believe, beautifully handles a sensitive topic: problem teenagers. It does so without condescending to either parent or child, without sensationalizing the subject, without appealing to maudlin emotions and without belittling the importance of the program by thinking that the reporter's own appeal for help or support would carry more significance than simply reporting the actions of the Tough Love parents themselves and letting those actions stand on their own.

READ A GOOD NEWSPAPER EVERY DAY

On any given day, a bad newspaper is a better classroom tool than a good journalism textbook. Not that I think student journalists should be deprived of textbooks.

Still, journalism students can learn more by reading a newspaper every day. Familiarity with a daily newspaper will teach the subtle differences between news, news-features, features, personal opinion and staff opinion.

In every journalism classroom, students should have access to the most important local or regional daily newspaper. Examine it every day. What stories is it covering? And how is it covering them?

If possible, subscribe to the most influential newspaper in the state. This will be a metropolitan daily. Compare and contrast its coverage with the local newspaper.

SHOWCASE ■

By **SHERRYL MORANG**
Utica High School, Utica, MI

IT IS 7:30 THURSDAY night, and the Presbyterian Church of Utica is deserted except for its well-lit cafeteria.

Slowly they straggle in, individually or in pairs. They are a friendly yet haggard group, bearing the signs of a long emotional struggle.

They are the parents of problem teenagers. There are no straight A honor roll students here, no football captains or cheerleaders—only drug addicts, alcoholics and runaways.

This is the weekly meeting of Tough Love, the parent support group that has recently been started in Utica. According to Agnes Stevens, one of the driving forces behind this program, Tough Love is a disciplinary method that involves setting limits for children and making them responsible for their own actions.

"Soft Love," Agnes explains "is what most parents use. It's where you can more or less trust your kids and set easy limits. Tough Love is when you have to set harder limits. What we try to do is enforce these limits and make our kids aware that they are responsible for their lives."

The meeting begins with Don Stevens reading a blurb about problem children and the Tough Love method. The 40 or so parents are seated in metal folding chairs, smoking, drinking coffee and leaning over to exchange greetings now and again.

The Stevens are amiable hosts, quickly putting newcomers at ease. "Hey, did I tell ya' about the three young punks they had up at the police station the other night?" Don asks. "Yeah, they'd been hauled in for smoking pot and were hanging around feeling pretty loose."

"Feeling good, man," Agnes cuts in, grinning and dragging on an imaginary joint.

Don continues. "So they take the stuff down to the lab to have it analyzed. In a little bit the police officer comes back and says, 'Well guys, how do you feel?' "

"We feel g-o-o-d!" Agnes counters, "That was good stuff, man."

"And the officer says, 'That's good because we just found out that you've been smoking horse crap.'" The laughter is uproarious, and there is a smattering of applause.

"Now," Don says, "Let's see about our bottom-lines. Does anybody have one from last week?"

Bottom-lines are another facet of the Tough Love method. At each meeting, members will hash out their problems and try to pinpoint one thing that particularly irritates them. This they try to eliminate by drawing a "bottom-line."

There is silence. Then one woman tentatively raises her hand. "My son is 25 years old," she says, "and I told him I was finished picking up after him."

The Stevens grin and call for applause. The hesitation is gone, and people are literally falling over one another to share their bottom-lines.

"What we try to do," Don explains later, "is establish a controlled crisis situation. See, most of the people who come here really have problems with their kids, and it's very difficult for them to maintain a sense of control.

"We try to pick on something that really irritates them—it could be something as simple as a messy room, but it's something that the parents feel they can control."

Agnes adds that most problems begin with a poor attitude and that once you make one change, no matter how small, others will follow.

Making changes and enforcing discipline are the focus of Tough Love. This group is part of a national organization known as the Communications Service Foundation. The CSF was founded by Phyllis and David York, a Sellersville, PA. couple. The Yorks have published a pamphlet explaining the Tough Love method and have information available for anyone who would like to start a group.

There are currently 10 or 12 Tough Love groups in Michigan—five of which are in the greater Detroit area—with approximately 500 families involved.

The Shelby-Utica group, which has been in existence for about five weeks, has almost 50 members. According to Pat Hante, group supervisor, the membership has been increasing steadily. Pat and another woman, Marilyn Kalvin, plan to take over leadership of the group when the Stevens leave.

Tough Love has not gotten the outright public support it wants, but there has been no opposition. They have the full cooperation of the police department, schools, counselors and therapists.

At meetings, parents are encouraged to send their children to therapists only when necessary. The Stevens maintain that most problems are better solved at home. However, there is no hesitation to contact proper authorities if a critical situation does arise.

The parents are divided into small discussion groups. The talk goes from evicting children, to threatening them, to alcohol, parent and drug abuse, to picking up clothes. "Just keep reacting differently," she says. "Shock 'em constantly."

Someone else describes the DRUGS sign that she keeps on the refrigerator door, and there is a suggestion that everyone rotate kids on a monthly basis. The group laughs at this, and there is almost the air of a Tuesday night bridge game, rather than a meeting.

But this is misleading. These people do have serious problems. Most have children who drink, use drugs, abuse them or periodically run away.

"When people first come to the meetings," Agnes says, "they are usually very depressed. They feel like failures as parents.

"Parents suffer a lot for what their kids do, and they always try to rescue them. But teenagers are perfectly capable of making choices, and if we don't let them experience the consequences, then they won't realize if their choices are the right ones."

So parents turn to Tough Love for support. Here they can discuss problems without feeling guilty. They share experiences, offer advice, laugh, cry, comfort each other.

"We all need support, and the Tough Love groups give this," Agnes says. "There are a lot of pressures in parenting nowadays, and it always helps to have someone there who knows how you're feeling and can say, 'Yeah, I've felt that way too.' "

She stops, searching for words. Then her voice breaks, "We really love our kids, or we wouldn't be doing this."

■ CHANGING ROLE OF THE PRESS

The notion of objectivity is a fairly recent one for American journalism. In colonial times, each political party had its own newspaper. Balance and accuracy were the last of their intentions.

When the Associated Press came along in the 1880s, newspapers of all political stripe began carrying the same stories, so these wire service stories had to be objective. Today, newspapers continue to operate under the assumption the content will be consumed by a mass audience and thus has to satisfy a widely diverse readership. Given that virtually no one likes the press, it is a matter of great debate whether this is being accomplished. Liberals and conservatives alike defile it as a lackey of the other, and journalists are consistently ranked barely ahead of politicians and right behind used-car salesmen on the "most trusted" lists.

On the high school level, we should strive to see that our news stories are as fair and objective as possible, but that should not stop us from taking an interpretive or analysis approach when it is appropriate. In non-daily publications, a straight news story may achieve little more than rehashing the obvious.

However, the analysis or interpretive piece may bring the readers as close to the truth as they are likely to get. It's worthwhile

THEY'RE THE BIGGEST FOR A GOOD REASON

Occasionally you will want to read one of the nation's most important newspapers. They include:

- The New York Times
- Washington Post
- Wall Street Journal
- Los Angeles Times

Access to these papers is restricted by circulation area, and daily subscriptions are costly. So let's not be media snobs. The nation is blessed with outstanding papers. These come to mind:

- Boston Globe
- Philadelphia Inquirer
- Kansas City Star
- The Dallas Morning News
- Miami Herald
- Minneapolis Tribune
- Detroit Free Press
- Detroit News
- Portland Oregonian
- Chicago Tribune
- St. Petersburg Times

Many of these have free on-line editions.

> ❝ Good writing is clear. Clarity depends on the use of everyday, simple-to-understand words and on the meticulous attention to transitions, so sentences and paragraphs are linked together in a logical order.❞

to consider the words of the late Martha Gellhorn, a brilliant writer and war correspondent. She wrote in the introduction to her book, *The Face of War*, "It took nine years, and a great depression, and two wars ending in defeat, and one surrender without war, to break my faith in the benign power of the press. Gradually I came to realize that people will more readily swallow lies than truth, as if the taste of lies was honey, appetizing: a habit."

Don't make it your habit.

■ INTERPRETIVE REPORTING

It is difficult to teach interpretive reporting to beginners who have yet to grasp the basics of objectivity, who believe in their hearts and souls that it's their duty to end every sports story with, "Congratulations, team! You guys rock!"

If your paper contains a lot of cutie-pie comments such as "The Pep Squad at our school outdid itself last week . . . ." or "Our most excellent principal received another honor last week . . . .," then it may be a good idea to read the chapter on objectivity again.

At the same time, we should remind ourselves that the most objective newswriting always involves a degree of interpretation. By deciding who to interview, which quotes to use and which facts to include in the story, the reporter judges what is important and what is not important.

As mentioned in Chapter 8, absolute objectivity is a myth.

Responsible interpretive reporting is not. It is the attempt to provide sufficient facts to help readers understand complex events. Rather than telling readers what to think or do, interpretive reporting provides unbiased background information that allows readers to form their own opinions or to take specific action based on perspective and knowledge.

Here's an example:

OBJECTIVE REPORTING—Louisiana televangelist Billy Lee Braggard called for an end of sin and a return to traditional family values yesterday.

INTERPRETIVE REPORTING — Louisiana televangelist Billy Lee Braggard, who twice in the past year has been convicted of mail fraud, called for an end of sin and a return to traditional family values yesterday.

OPINION—Louisiana televangelist Billy Lee Braggard called for an end of sin and a return to traditional family values here yesterday, a hypocritical move for a man who has twice been convicted in the last year of mail fraud.

It's obvious how the insertion of a small bit of information can have a profound impact on how readers interpret the news.

In the race for the Texas Attorney General's office in the mid-1980s, one candidate called the other a liberal, anti-gun crusader who would force sportsmen to "jump mounds of paperwork" to purchase handguns and assault rifles. The other candidate responded by saying he had unanimous support of law enforcement officers.

The newspaper story about these charges and counter-charges included the results of a survey, taken earlier that week, showing that more than eight out of 10 Texans supported such restrictions on the sale of certain weapons.

Reporting the results of the survey provides the context against which the day-to-day political sparring is cast, giving the story greater meaning than it might otherwise possess.

Here's a scenario student reporters are more likely to encounter: A high school, faced with the difficult choice between raising taxes or cutting costs, chooses to scale back various programs to keep expenses under control. Over the course of several months, the school board votes to eliminate academic and fine arts trips, freeze teacher salaries, fire art and music teachers and cut by 25 percent the library budget. However, the board does not reduce its administrative staff, nor does it reduce the athletic department budget.

A student reporter can cover each school board action, but the true story emerges only when each action is reported in context with the others.

So how might the story have been reported?

STUDENTS CAN FORGET about that educational trip to New York or about enrollment in a music class. Librarians are going to have to try to do as best they can with the outdated books that pock-mark the shelves. And teachers are being forced to stretch their paychecks.

When it comes to the current financial crisis, school trustees have allowed academic and fine arts programs to take the big blows while administrators and athletic departments go untouched.

In the past three months, the board has voted to scale back academic field trips, freeze teacher salaries, fire special area teachers and cut the library budget. The decisions have prompted teachers to wonder whether the board has lost sight of the purpose of the school.

"It strikes me as odd that academics have taken the brunt of these cutbacks," said trustee Scott Gentry, who voted against each. "Our job is to educate students, and these actions are making it harder, almost impossible, to accomplish this mission."

Teachers say they also fear the board will raise student-teacher ratios and/or slash faculty rolls. The Parent Teacher Association protested the board's decision to fire art and music teachers, and the local chapter of the American Federation of Teachers has discussed filing a lawsuit against the school district to save jobs.

School board members are reluctant to cut athletic budgets, given the success of the school's athletic teams and the strength of athletic boosters, teachers claim. Two members of the board are former officers of the Football Booster Club.

If additional budget cuts are needed, the school board will almost be forced to take a close look at the administrative and athletic budgets, teachers say. Educational funds have been cut to the bone. What frightens some is that the school board may look to the minor sports—particularly girls' athletics—for cuts while leaving the sacred cows, football in particular, untouched.

"While many schools have moved forward in developing a girls' softball program to complement the boys' baseball program, I don't anticipate any such movement here soon," said Karen Lyle, who monitors school board actions. "At this point, I'm willing to suggest that all of the minor sports—boys and girls—are in jeopardy."

But classroom teachers say they wish they had it so good.

"The athletic coaches are complaining that they may be hit next, but we're the ones who have taken all the cuts so far, " chemistry teacher Lanell Raborn said. "I've been told that plans to build a new chemistry lab are postponed indefinitely. I don't want this to turn into an academic versus athletic problem, but it sure looks like the school board plans to cut us to the bone before considering any cuts to sports programs."

■ **WHAT ARE THE IMPLICATIONS?**

This story does not editorialize. It does, however, analyze a series of actions, comes to a conclusion and anticipates future action based on past performances.

Remember the kid who divorced his parents? What are the implications of his success in court? Mitchell Landsberg of the Associated Press analyzed the situation like this:

IF HEATHER HATES her homework, can she sue? The correct answer is that the question is absurd. But that was the sort of outlandish scenario being suggested last week after a 12-year-old Florida boy went to court to "divorce" his parents.

More sober critics warned that American families might be threatened by less frivolous lawsuits filed by angry children who consider their parents abusive. But that appears to be a minority view.

Although legal experts mostly agree that young Gregory Kingsley's case established an

DRAWING A REASONABLE CONCLUSION

In *The Professional Journalist*, John Hohenberg wrote, "Interpretation adds the factor of judgment to what is called straight news—the unvarnished recital of fact and poll taking which may or may not represent the truth. The difference between interpreting and editorializing, broadly, is that the interpreter applies the rule of reason to the news but stops short of recommending what should be done about it. The province of the editorial writer is to urge a course of action upon the reader or viewer."

STYLE TIP

Use an apostrophe with omitted figures. Examples:

■ The class of '71 will meet hold its reunion next fall.

■ Mr. Lucia's class will discuss the Roaring '20s.

important legal precedent, few expect it to have much practical effect.

"It isn't that big a deal," said Sanford Katz, a Boston College law professor who specializes in children's issues.

The remainder of the news analysis reinforced this point.

■ WHAT DOES IT MEAN?

More than anything else, readers need to know the meaning of the news. I once worked for a newspaper whose editor dictated that any time the Dow Jones Stock Market jumped or fell 10 points or more, the story automatically went on the front page even though few people understand the importance of the stock market rising or falling 10 points or 100 points.

The "Week in Review" section in the Sunday edition of *The New York Times* is a superb source for good examples of interpretive and analytical reporting. Rather than simply describing what happened, reporters explain why it happened, what effect it has had and how much impact it is likely to have. The writing in this section illustrates how a reporter may draw conclusions based on personal observations without recommending what should be done. That task is left to the writers of editorials and columns.

High school reporters can and should attempt interpretive reporting in the appropriate situations as well. These pieces may be labeled "analysis" although it is not always essential. They should carry a byline.

■ DIFFERING APPROACHES

Consider these two ways to report the same story. In June 1993, the United States Supreme Court ruled that it is constitutional for a public school district to send a sign language interpreter into a religious school to help a deaf student learn. Reporters localizing this story may take a traditional straight news approach or a more challenging interpretive approach.

■ STRAIGHT NEWS APPROACH

LAST JUNE, THE UNITED States Supreme Court ruled it is constitutional for a public school district to send a sign language interpreter into a religious school to help a deaf student learn. The ruling marks the first time the court authorized a public employee to participate in religious education and the third time in a month the justices issued a decision favorable to religion.

Superintendent Robert Eudy said he does not expect the decision to affect the district.

"I attended a seminar this summer in which this decision and others were discussed, and I do not believe it breaks any new ground to extend public aid to parochial schools," he said. "I don't anticipate this district sending employees into private or parochial schools for any reason. While our officials will need to study the ruling before deciding what, if any, action needs to be taken, I can tell you that providing such services for students in private schools would be costly."

For example, providing an interpreter for a deaf child could cost between $12,000 and $25,000 per child, depending on the interpreter's experience level and how much time daily he or she spends with a student, Eudy said.

Eudy said some feared the Court was paving the way for vouchers or other forms of public funds for private aid, but added, "With the seating of Justice (Ruth) Ginsburg, who appears to be a separationist, I do not anticipate this happening."

The Rev. William Perry of the First Baptist Church said he welcomed the decision but added he did not anticipate the private school asking for or receiving assistance.

"We believe in the separation of church and state, but we believe the line has been drawn unfairly," Perry said. "We welcome this ruling as a victory for handicapped students to have freedom of choice of schools and to get the services they're entitled to."

Let's not kid ourselves. This would be an excellent story for the high school newspaper. However, it simply states the facts and then allows two sources to respond to the facts. It does not attempt to explain or interpret the facts in a future context.

The next one does.

▪ INTERPRETIVE NEWS APPROACH

SENIOR JERRY HAMMERS is hard-of-hearing, which is not to say that he can't hear anything, only that his hearing is so bad he's categorized as legally deaf.

The school district, required by federal law to provide education for all handicapped students, pays for an interpreter to work with Jerry at a cost of more than $10,000 per year.

Jerry also attends services at the First Baptist Church and once considered enrolling in its high school.

"I might have, but my parents couldn't afford an interpreter, so I stayed in the public schools," he said.

Early in the summer, the Supreme Court rendered a decision that would have helped Jerry's family, had he decided to attend First Baptist High. The court ruled it is constitutional for a public school district to send a sign language interpreter into a religious school to help a deaf student learn.

"I think it's an excellent decision, not because I want to go to private school, but because my family pays taxes just like everyone else's, and we deserve access to the same services," Jerry said.

But don't expect the school district to begin picking up the tab for impaired students at local private or parochial schools. And don't think this is just the first step toward government vouchers for private or parochial education, as some have suggested. Even though the Supreme Court gave religious groups equal access to public schools used as after-hour community centers and upheld a religious group's right to sacrifice animals during worship services, few believe the court will swing so far as to approve vouchers.

For one thing, the court is likely to shift with the retirement of Justice Byron White, who joined the majority in the ruling. His replacement, Ruth Bader Ginsburg, is believed to strongly support strict separation between church and state.

How this ruling may affect the school district will not be determined until a handicapped student attending a private or parochial school seeks district funding for a taxpayer-paid tutor.

"I don't anticipate this district sending employees into private or parochial schools for any reason," superintendent Robert Eudy said. "While our officials will need to study the ruling before deciding what, if any, action needs to be taken, I can tell you that providing such services for students in private schools would be costly."

For example, providing an interpreter for a deaf child could cost between $10,000 and $25,000, depending on the interpreter's experience level and how much time daily he or she spends with a student, Eudy said.

Religious leaders argue that the government should offer a neutral service as part of a general program that is not tilted toward religion.

The Rev. William Perry of the First Baptist Church said he welcomed the decision but added he did not anticipate the private school asking for or receiving assistance.

"We believe in the separation of church and state, but we believe the line has been drawn unfairly," Perry said. "We welcome this ruling as a victory for handicapped students to have freedom of choice of schools and to get the services they're entitled to."

Although both stories use essentially the

WHEN THE FACTS LEAD YOU TO A CONCLUSION

In many cases, the reporter examines the evidence and draws a conclusion. For example:

A request by seniors to travel to Miami Beach may be dead in the water, school officials said. An administrator who asked not to be named said school officials would not approve of a plan to allow seniors to take the three-day trip.

> **The differences between interpretation and editorialization, broadly, is that the interpreter applies the rule of reason to the news but stops short of recommending what should be done about it."**
>
> — John Hohenberg
> The Professional Journalist

same information, this angle better explains the decision in a local context.

■ **WHAT DID THE ELECTION MEAN?**

One of the great opportunities students had for interpretive reporting came during the 2000 Presidential election. Almost all schools conduct a mock election, and the high school newspapers dutifully report the results. However, this reporting rarely if ever goes beyond a rehashing of numbers, supported by one or two statements of the obvious. Here's the typical story:

GEORGE W. BUSH defeated Al Gore in a mock election held here, and he didn't need the help of the Supreme Court this time. Mr. Bush out-gained Vice President Gore 248-162 while television commentator Patrick Buchanan finished third with 24 votes. (57 percent to 37 percent to 6 percent)

Students had varied ideas about which candidate would do the best job as president.

"I am glad Bush won the election because he put forth the most effort," senior Mickey Mathis said. "I think he will be an excellent President and return dignity to the office."

However, others disagreed.

"Bush is just like his father. He'll give tax breaks to his rich friends and run the U.S. into the ground," junior Harry Copeland said. "Gore was robbed."

While this story reports the fact that Bush won both the general and the mock elections, it provides little real news. Taking an interpretive approach provides an opportunity to use the mock election in context to the national vote to explain "why." For example:

IN 1996, COUNTY RESIDENTS voted overwhelmingly for Bill Clinton. But that was four years ago, before Monica Lewinsky and the rest of the current administration's scandals. Not surprisingly, students in a mock election last month predicted a Bush/Cheney victory, favoring the Republican team over Vice President Gore

and Sen. Joe Lieberman, 57-37 percent. Television commentator Patrick Buchanan picked up the final 6 percent of the votes.

"It's time to clean house," senior Becky Frans said. "It's been eight years of one scandal after another, and while most of them involved Clinton, I think it's fair to say that birds of a feather flock together. So I'm voting for Bush."

Despite the strong economy, other seniors who support Bush/Cheney say they hope to return integrity to the White House while reducing the role of the federal government.

"Gore is a typical tax and spend liberal," senior Wayne Moorehead said. "Sure, the economy has improved in the past eight years, but I see no reason to believe that it won't get even better under Bush, especially if Congress passes his tax proposals."

Even a few Democrats voted for the Texas governor.

"Normally, I vote for the Democratic candidate, but I took Bush on his word about being a compassionate conservative," senior Wendy Tsai said. "On the whole, he seemed like the lesser of two evils."

This story focuses on the news question "why" rather than restating the obvious. Instead of dishing out all the campaign rhetoric, it seeks informative direct quotes to give a sense of meaning to the election results.

Interpretive stories can also appear as sidebars to major news stories. The news story presents the latest decisions, and the sidebar places the latest event into a historical context.

■ **INTERPRETIVE FEATURES**

Interpretive angles are not confined to the news sections. One of my favorite leads comes from a story about midnight bowling by Steve Levine of the *Dallas Morning News.* I've placed the interpretation in italics.

THE APPEAL IS NOT immediately apparent when you walk past the Camaros and vans in the parking lot and reach the front door where teenage boys smoke cigarettes *and try to impress the girls.*

Inside, it's not the too-bright fluorescent lights blinding you to young love at the shoe counter, not the dull chorus of balls rumbling down the lanes and the resulting explosion of pins. It's not even the great expanse of carpet, Formica and multicolored shoes with numbers on the back. Everything is just as it should be until you glance at a clock and see that it's past midnight.

And then glance at the lanes and see that they're all full. And glance at the shoe counter and see that all the size 9s are gone. Don't glance at your favorite video game. It probably has a waiting line.

Welcome to midnight bowling: haven for insomniac bowlers, home for lonely singles searching for a different kind of score and hangout for people just looking. Midnight bowling, where you can dress up silly, act foolish and be considered normal. Where the guys slug their beer like it's the last one of this lifetime. Where foreigners test their English on teenage girls and harried waitresses. Where gambling — bowling for dollars— is part of lane life. It is, says one alley aficionado, "very, very different."

At least five area bowling alleys regularly offer after-midnight bowling . . . .

■ INTERPRETIVE STATEMENTS

Do you think Steve walked up to the guys at the front door and said, "I see you boys are smoking cigarettes. Why?"

"Cough, hack, gag. We are trying to impress the girls, sir," one pimply-faced sophomore said. "But I don't think it's working."

Probably not.

Nor did he approach a particularly lonely soul and ask, "Might you be searching for a different kind of score?"

These comments are interpretive statements that provide a context for the rest of the story. Reporters see an event, but rather than simply describing what they see, they attempt to explain what the event means. Consider the story on page 105 about a young man with cancer.

■ SENSE OF TIME AND PLACE

The beauty of this story lies in its fresh and original angle, its capture of detail and its sense of time and place.

A reporter rang the doorbell, hoping no one would answer. . . .

A reluctant photographer. . . sat beside her, nervously readjusting his focus . . . .

These small but hardly minor touches separate the truly gifted journalists from the formula writers. In the midnight bowling story, note the graceful use of parallel sentences beginning with "where."

■ DON'T STATE THE OBVIOUS

The next two stories show how interpretation by the reporter can turn what might otherwise be a bland, predictable story into something unique and interesting.

The first story gives us little new information. The quotes are predictable. The plot is poorly defined. There's no context for the action. Given that most persons can figure out for themselves the nature of a mock trial, it is important that the reporter attempt to explain a bit more than what we have here:

FROM MARCH 25 through March 28, Jim Bronson's senior Government classes performed a mock trial.

According to Bronson, the purpose of the trial was to help the students understand how a court of law worked.

"He made the witnesses 'swear in' just like in a real court," senior Steve Griffin said.

Class members said that every student was involved in the trial either as a witness, judge, defense attorney, prosecuting attorney or jury member.

The case being decided that week centered on involuntary manslaughter by automobile. The defendant was charged with hitting an older lady

NOT SURE YOU CAN GET AWAY WITH THAT STORY

Before you write that story that says your principal is a member of the American Nazi Party when he's not having his fun smoking crack and microwaving kittens and has a particularly virulent case of body lice, consider that the following material is not protected free speech:

■ obscenity
■ libel
■ invasion of privacy
■ advertising of illegal products or services
■ content that creates a clear and present danger and substantial disruption of the school.

> Interpretive reporting is one of the few times when a reporter is allowed to draw conclusions based on his personal observations without actually recommending what should be done."

on a winter night after attending a party and having two or three drinks.

Chad Pitre, who played the judge, said it was hard to decide because neither side truly proved the driver guilty or innocent.

"I had a difficult time reaching a decision," he said.

Bronson said that making tough decisions was part of the lesson.

"I wanted this to be a learning experience for my classes. This was a fun and easy way to teach this particular lesson," Bronson said.

What did we really learn here? Not much. The story states the obvious: if a class is putting on a mock trial, it stands to reason that students will portray judges and lawyers. Tell us something new, something we don't already know, something we can't figure out for ourselves.

Given that a specific story can take many twists and turns in the weeks between issues, it would seem that more staffs would attempt interpretive reporting. The following lead, written by Jonathan Eig of *The Dallas Morning News*, gives a deft little twist that truly captured the essence of a high-school mock trial:

THE LAWYERS DIDN'T care about money, and the journalists were all objective, so it had to be a mock trial.

But if not for those nagging details, the legal drama Saturday at the Earle Cabell Federal Building might well have been the real thing. Or better.

Should Jesse Goodall, a fictional college student, go to jail for leading an environmental protest that turned into a riot? Or was Sidney Chernobyl, the nuclear-waste company official, responsible for the mayhem? And could journalistic accounts of the incident really be trusted? (The answer: Of course they could.)

More than 100 high school students grappled with these issues at the Texas High School Mock Trial Competition. Entering

evidence, grilling witnesses and swaying jurors, the attorneys did everything that real lawyers do—except bill their clients.

When U. S. Judge Jerry Buchmeyer announced the verdict in a crowded courtroom Saturday afternoon, Richard King High School came away the state champions, earning a trip to the national competition in New Orleans.

But even the students who failed to reach the final round of the tournament said the outcome pleased them.

"It gives you a chance to express yourself," said Christopher Jones, a senior at Booker T. Washington High School for the Performing and Visual Arts in Dallas. "You learn to get up and think on your feet."

In the pressure-packed finals before Judge Buchmeyer, "attorneys" Lara Hammerick and Daniel Nelson of Richard King High teamed up to defend Jesse Goodall against the prosecutors from Berkner High School in Richardson.

Anusha Chagan and Lisa Wong of Berkner tried to prove that Jesse Goodall frightened a crowd of protesters by displaying barrels full of bright green, bubbling liquids. In the ensuing panic, one woman in the fictional riot fainted and suffered a miscarriage.

But Lara and Daniel said the liquid was only anti-freeze mixed with dry ice. They said Sidney Chernobyl incited the melee by screaming and charging toward Jesse.

The same arguments were presented over and over as teams competed, but with every case came a different strategy. Sometimes, as the teams called witnesses and filed objections, the courtroom scene seemed real. Dallas-area lawyers and judges served as jurors, grading the students based on their courtroom conduct more than on the facts of the case.

To prepare, the students spend months researching the same fictional court case and rehearsing their courtroom demeanor. Most of the schools get coaching from a teacher and a local lawyer.

Dallas County Criminal Court Judge Marshall Gandy, who heard one of the preliminary cases Saturday, said the students showed more poise than a lot of real lawyers.

"They're incredible for high school students. It doesn't even show," he said. "I wouldn't mind seeing any of them in my courtroom. They may even pass themselves off as attorneys."

"The lawyers didn't care about money, and the journalists were all objective, so it had to be a mock trail."

Both a clever lead and an engaging interpretive statement that plays to its audience. The success of this story is that it explains the essence of the mock trial rather than merely keeping score and listing names.

Adrian Jones of James Bowie High School in Austin, Texas, captures the magic of Disney World in the beginning of a story about a student who was employed there the previous summer:

THERE COMES A TIME when the tender innocence of childhood begins to melt away. All those nursery rhymes and storybook characters give way to "real" life. The sweet memories of warm laps to cuddle in and homemade sandboxes to play in give way to conflict resolution discussions and environmentally balanced gardens.

It doesn't have to be that way. There is an escape, a place where Mickey, Donald and all the other friends come back to life.

It's a place where 100-degree afternoons and long lines are unimportant. It's a park with unusual and exciting shows, extraordinary rides and some of the most warm and fuzzy characters around.

It's Disney World, the most popular theme park in the world, and it can make even Oscar the Grouch smile.

"Smile," John-Paul Beltran said. "Always smile. When so many people around you are smiling, you just can't help but smile along with them."

Beltran's summer was filled with smiles.

It started with an offer to audition to work as a Disney character at Disney World in Orlando.

"Everything really starts with my brother Ricky," Paul Beltran, John-Paul's father, said. "All of my side of the family, and all of my wife's side of the family, have been working at Disney World since 1975. My brother Ricky was the first one to work as a character. My other brother Freddy is in charge of the MGM stage over there."

Fred Beltran feels it is ironic so many members of his family worked at Disney World.

"When Ricky worked as a character, I used to come and see him," Fred said. "A few years later, I was a character. So it's like passing down the torch because now I'm in management."

■ INTERPRETIVE SPORTS STORIES

Sports can also be the subject of interesting interpretive pieces. This lead analyzes the effects of a defeat rather than merely reporting the fact that the team lost the game:

THE JAGUARS ARE OUT of the district race, at least for the time being. And unless Anderson or Reagan unexpectedly stumble, their hopes for a football playoff berth are practically nil.

The Jaguars dropped a 21-17 loss last week to then-winless Bowie, shattering their dim hopes of securing a runners-up playoff berth.

"We shot ourselves in the foot," head coach Cecil Plummer said. "We never got focused, and by the time we got our heads on straight, it was too late. I'm really sick about this loss."

Unfortunately, sports reporters are prone to sneak in an opinion or two. The following piece might have been an interesting interpretive feature on off-season workouts, but the writer attacks the subject with such a bias that the content of the story is obliterated.

FOOTBALL PLAYERS DON'T just vanish after a football season. Flashing their flamboyant letter jackets in the faces of other students is a

LEARN AS MUCH AS POSSIBLE ABOUT THE LAW

This book is about writing. It's not about student press law. For that, you absolutely must read "Law of the Student Press," by the Student Press Law Center. You can reach the SPLC via the Web at http://www.splc.org/.

In particular, you should know about the following cases:

■ Tinker v. Des Moines Independent Community School District
■ Hazelwood v. Kuhlmeier
■ Bethel School District No. 403 v. Fraser

common practice of the football jocks.

These jocks also appear to be buffoons by their actions and apparel resulting from the "class" which is an after-effect of football: off-season workouts.

The shabby garments worn by these beastly jocks tell the story of their animal-like personalities: sailors' caps, bandanas, florescent shorts over sweats, baby bonnets and half shirts ripped to shreds offering the sight of their hairy navels to anyone who might be watching.

An astonished passerby viewing this untamed pack of cutthroats may be tempted to turn and flee.

These ornery bandits often release their endless energy along with their obscene body odor as they charge up and down the gym floor. A different native call is shouted each time the pack tears down the floor.

An innocent mother on her way down to pick up her toddlers may catch a horrifying glimpse of this wild bunch of students tripping on their tongues as they struggle up the "hill." This infamous "hill" prompts a hot line from each agonizing muscle as it screams "Death."

"Gut check," shouts the merciless chief known to the delinquents as "Coach." The mere sound of these horrendous words send the love handles of each jock into relentless spasms as they fear the grueling day.

And so on. This article is designed not to analyze or interpret but rather to attack. For a better example of the sports interpretive article, look at page 131.

Again, don't editorialize

Personality profiles in magazines such as *Vanity Fair*, *Esquire* and *Rolling Stone* often contain generous portions of interpretation, but they avoid blatant editorializing. Likewise, high school reporters should avoid stories that look more like come-ons than serious journalism. As evidence, I cite the following story in a high-school newspaper:

AFTER LISTENING TO A FEW witty and varied comments on "some new England dude" who recently arrived at our school, my curiosity overcame me and I felt stirred to follow it. By that, I mean I felt the spark of challenge that most of us reporters often feel as an excuse to stick their noses into something foreign and unknown thus far.

I then commenced to meet this interesting and slightly mysterious foreigner.

The new student is a junior whose name is Brian, a quiet-mannered, 17-year-old who hails from Nottingham, the middle of England.

When I first approached him, the nervous tension that had been building up inside me was quickly dispelled as he mentally took notice of my uneasiness, smiled pleasantly and smoothly accepted giving the interview.

Brian has a relaxing presence, very much at ease with himself and those around him; surprising since it seems anyone would be easily overwhelmed and unnerved by all the attention and stares which he takes in stride.

Asked how the school courses he took back in England compared to the ones he is taking here, Brian said the classes in England are much harder with less variation for the students' pleasure. Also, the attitudes of the students there aren't quite as casual, and they are more serious-minded.

When I tried probing into him about how he sees American girls and the dating scene here, he gave a big grin and replied it was all the same to him.

Subtle, huh? Kind of an "I'll write a story about you if you'll go out with me" approach.

The entire notion of objectivity always comes under scrutiny, but staffs on the cutting edge still want to take a shot at interpretive reporting. However, be warned: The line between editorializing and interpreting is so thin that only the best reporters, working with veteran editors and advisers, should attempt to tackle it.

COMPARE & CONTRAST

AN INTERPRETIVE APPROACH

Laura Orr never set out to be the All-American girl. It just turned out that way. She plays volleyball because it clears her mind, she said. She's not sure why she's so good at it. "I enjoy it, so I work at it a little harder, I guess," she said.

Her parents have always stressed academics, so it's no surprise that she's an honor roll student. "They've never really pushed me, but I understand their expectations," she said.

Orr never ran for class officer to prove anything except that she wants to serve. Whether she set out to be a teacher's dream without being a teacher's pet is unlikely.

Still, there's no denying that Laura is something special. Last week, she was named most valuable player on the team's state championship volleyball team, and next week she will travel to Washington, D.C. as part of the school's academic decathlon team.

"I wish I could say that I've had to overcome great obstacles to attain whatever success I've had in school, but that isn't true," Orr said. "High school has been easy and fun for me. I owe a lot to my parents, who prepared me for school, and I've been fortunate to have had some great teachers."

She said she expects college to be a bit rougher. She's already been accepted to Ohio State on a volleyball scholarship, and she said she may try her hand at tennis as well.

"I plan to major in biology," she said. "I want to be a pediatrician, and since I come from a family of doctors, I know how much work is involved. Plus, sports at Ohio state is very competitive."

Not that she is intimidated.

"I enjoy a challenge," she said. "I'm ready to move on to the next big one."

UNRELATED STACK OF DATA

Laura Orr has been named Student of the Month. Laura is a senior and last week was named most valuable player on the state championship volleyball team.

Her favorite activities include water skiing, tennis, reading and watching movies.

"I really like old films, especially The Godfather and Apocalypse Now," she said. "But I also enjoy some of the current films, like The Royal Tenenbaums."

She is a senior class vice president and a member of the academic decathlon team, which will go to Washington, D.C. next week to compete in the national finals.

"I enjoy the academic decathlon quite a bit," she said. "It forces you to look at the world and understand what's going on around you."

Laura is a member of the honor roll and is a National Merit Semifinalist. She plans to major in biology at Ohio State University in Columbus, Ohio in hopes of becoming a pediatrician.

"I've always wanted to work with children," she said.

As to advice that she would give to incoming freshmen?

"Study hard, but try to have a good time in high school because the four years will pass by quickly," she said.

Photo by **CARAMARIE GOW**
Northwest Community Christian School, Phoenix, AZ

LOCALIZE THE STORY

10

Cover your school. Sure, it's tempting to write about glamours events that take place half a world away, but you serve no purpose parroting what's been covered ad nauseum elsewhere. Localizing news is essential.

CHAPTER HIGHLIGHTS:

■ Cover your school and its students.

■ Focus the story on local sources.

■ Concentrate on local implications, effects.

■ Know limitations of computer-assisted reporting.

I'm a big fan of *Education Week*, "American Education's Newspaper of Record." It covers any and everything education-related, and I've stumbled upon dozens of story ideas by wandering through its pages. Here's one: "Philadelphia Students Turning Up the Heat on Energy Wasters." The story deals with a school district that employs students to raise awareness of energy use and energy-related issues. Students learn, and the school district saves money. Not a bad deal.

Now, how could you turn this into a story for your high school publication? Well, start by asking a few questions:

What are the school's monthly energy bills? Which department spends the most? The least?

Does the district have an energy conservation plan? If so, what is it? How successful has it been? Who's in charge? How much has it saved?

What are its current goals? Any plans to install solar panels or skylights? Low-watt light bulbs? More efficient air and heating systems?

If not, why not? Is energy economy on the agenda at all?

This much alone is likely to produce an interesting, local story. Don't rehash what's going on in Philadelphia. Localize this story — all stories — to your school, your student body,

your community. Here's how:

1. Interview at least six people and use no fewer than four quotes from different sources in the story.

2. Do not interview friends or other students in class.

3. Write a feature story, not a news article. The story should have a descriptive lead. Use anecdotes to illustrate your points.

4. Write in third person.

5. Keep your opinions to yourself.

5. Think.

For example, another school district approves a no-tolerance rule on profanity in school. You want to localize this issue to your school. What's the situation at your school? Is profanity an issue? If not, why not? Look at the issue from different points of view: student to student; student to teacher; teacher to teacher; student to administrator; administrator to teacher, etc. Look at the issue from the differing perspectives of the classroom teacher and the athletic coach.

■ LOCALIZE

Do not tell readers what they already know. It serves no purpose to publish a Super Bowl game summary three weeks after the fact. No one waits a month to find out who won the

> Rather than writing a research paper on sleep deprivation (based largely on data downloaded from a Web site or lifted verbatim from a brochure provided by a sleep disorder physician), talk to someone at your school who has a sleep disorder."

World Series, the NBA championship or the presidential election. Update and localize.

For example: According to a recent federal report, teen drug use increased by 4.2 percent in the past three years. To localize this story, you'd want to interview students, teachers, counselors, administrators, substance abuse counselors, workers at the local drug hotline and law enforcement officers.

National rates are increasing. Are they increasing here?

How do you know? Can you cite specific cases?

Why do you believe teen drug use is increasing?

Is the school doing everything possible to combat this?

In what ways if any has the school failed in attempting to get its "don't use drugs" message across?

What do students say about reports of increased teen drug use? How do they explain it? Talk to intelligent students who can provide informed responses. Don't talk to morons. You know who they are.

■ **POSSIBLE STORY:**

ON A RECENT SATURDAY NIGHT, Police Chief John Spivey and two of his officers waited patiently outside a local home where he suspected a group of under-age youths were drinking.

"The parents were out of town," Spivey said. "We figured it was one of those typical kids and light beer deals. But when we finally moved in, we were shocked to find that many of these kids — and some of them were as young as 13 — were stoned. Someone showed up with a bag of marijuana, and it seemed like they all smoked some of it."

Nineteen youths were arrested.

Spivey said drug use by teens here is on the rise, which makes Seaweed a typical American community. According to a recent federal report, teen drug use is at its highest in three years.

"We have a problem and unless we get a grip on it soon, it's going to get worse," Spivey said. "Somehow, we need to get out the message that

drugs and alcohol are one-way tickets nowhere."

But students say they don't see it that way.

"First, almost all of the parents drink," junior Bill Coleman said. "It seems a little hypocritical to hear all this anti-alcohol stuff at school and then go home and watch all of the parents drink. A beer now and then isn't going to kill anyone. And then, I guess students figure that if the school will lie about alcohol, it will lie about drug use too."

Several school officials said current anti-alcohol and drug programs may have backfired.

"Schools tried the 'just say no' method and it didn't work — at least, not in the long run," health teacher Maxine Blanchard said. "We need to provide honest information without all of the hysteria. I don't think you can scare teens into anything. Driver's education has proven that. But I think they'll respond if we're more open and honest with them about alcohol and drug use."

Some students aren't sure.

"Teenagers experiment with all sorts of things," senior Amy Logan said. "They know the risks but take them. That's what being a teen is all about."

■ **DIG DEEPER**

You saw the story about teenagers and sleep? Basically, researchers told us what anyone who has ever been a teen knows: they don't get enough sleep. But rather than writing a research paper on sleep deprivation (based largely on data downloaded from a Web site or lifted verbatim from a brochure provided by a sleep disorder physician), talk to someone at your school who has a sleep disorder. Tell his or her story. Insomnia is a common problem among school teachers and students. It should not be difficult to tell powerful stories here.

FOR YEARS, history teacher Joe Oliver knew what's on television between 2 and 4 in the morning. Most nights, he was up, watching it. Joe has a sleep disorder, restless legs syndrome, and without medication, he would return to old ways of dozing off around 10, waking up at 11 and spending the rest of the night rolling around, stretching, exercising, reading, watching television, going nuts.

"It was torture," he said. "Sheer hell."

Finally, his wife convinced him to visit a sleep disorder clinic in Dallas.

"The doctor diagnosed me immediately, and since then, I've been on medication and sleeping quite well," he said.

Mr. Oliver is like many teachers and students with sleep problems...

Tell his story, along with the stories of a couple of other people who have sleep disorders. You can tack on a sidebar list of "Signs you have a sleep disorder" and "How to get a good night's sleep" if you like, but the primary thrust of the coverage should be first person, local sources.

■ EMPHASIZE NEW INFORMATION

In every story, ask, "What do our readers NOT know?" Then, lead with that information. Say, for example, the community has recently approved a school-finance proposal. What is it about this proposal that our readers don't understand or appreciate? Perhaps that with the new funds, the crowded lunch room situation will be resolved. Or that students will have a new Media Center and six individual classrooms.

Therefore, your lead could go something like this:

FRENCH TEACHER JOHN Baker is accustomed to bouncing around from classroom to classroom, but that doesn't mean he likes it.

"I never had my own room and I couldn't do the things in class I want to do," he said. "I couldn't put up posters or assignment sheets. I was always operating on someone else's turf."

That's about to change. Within the next year, Mr. Baker is expected to occupy one of the six new rooms that will be built as part of the bond election improvement plan.

"With my own classroom, I can do more interesting activities that require props," he said. "I could never do that before."

Among the improvements scheduled are...

Say the school failed to pass the bond proposal. You would need to examine how this proposal would affect students. Talk to teachers and tell their specific stories. Okay, John Baker, taxpayers said you don't need your own classroom. So what do you say to that? How will this affect the education you offer your students?

Another example: the governor of your state wants the state legislature to pass a bill raising the student-teacher ratio. How would you localize that story?

First, what's the current ratio? Does the state even have one? If not, why not?

What's the impact on teachers? Keep in mind that the impact on an English teacher, who is expected to grade term papers, will be much different than on a math teacher, whose tests are multiple choice and Scantron-graded. Show the differences.

JANICE KNIGHT TEACHES four AP English classes per day. Each class contains at least 25 students. On any given night, she spends two or three hours grading essays or writing assignments.

"You can't Scantron writing," she said. "You have to read it and comment on every line. It takes a lot of time."

A proposal in the State House to eliminate jobs in an effort to save money angers her, she said, because "if they cut jobs, my class size will increase, and that means I either burn out quicker or cut back the quality of instruction I can offer my students. Either way, kids lose."

This is a common reaction among teachers to Governor Frank Ketchum's plan to increase the student-teacher ratio in an effort to save money.

■ OPEN YOUR EYES

Let's get back to *Education Week*. In perusing the Aug. 7, 2002, issue, I stumbled upon this short news article:

CIVIC DISENGAGEMENT

The voter turnout rate for Americans ages 18 to 24 has dropped by a third over the past three decades, a recent report has found. Moreover, young Hispanic citizens are less likely to vote than

IS THIS SOMETHING WE CAN LOCALIZE?

The U.S. Department of Agriculture announces that it has lifted its ban on irradiated ground beef in the National School Lunch Program.

How to localize? Ask yourself:

■ Is this a story our readers need to know about?

■ Is this a story our readers should care about?

■ Is this a story that affects our readers?

■ Can our readers get this information faster and easier elsewhere?

■ Can our local sources provide authoritative information?

■ Can we provide a timely angle on an otherwise dated story?

■ Will our coverage serve as an advocate for students?

WRITING TIP

Avoid "to be" verbs.

Don't write "Senior Joe Hernendez will be competing in the National Spelling Bee." Write, "Senior Joe Hernandez will compete in the National Spelling Bee."

other young adults, with only 30 percent of eligible Hispanics in that age range voting in the 2000 elections, compared with 42 percent of non-Hispanic whites and African-Americans.

Localize this. Explain it in terms of your school, your community, your students. If you school is located in South San Antonio, it's going to be a much different story than if it's located in Shawnee Mission, Kansas.

You're surrounded by great story possibilities. Cover them.

■ COMPUTER-ASSISTED PLAGIARISM

When I was a student reporter and wanted to plagiarize something, I had to go to the school library and look up the topic—for the sake of argument, let's say "teen smoking"— in a big green book called the *Reader's Guide to Periodical Literature*, which listed every article published on the topic by 125 or so magazines, most of which my school didn't subscribe to because the librarian was afraid they may contain photos of women in bathing suits. Then, I'd have to find the magazine and article — no small task either — before I could begin copying information, word for word, into my story or report.

Kids today have it so easy. When you need to find information about a story, you don't have to lug around six or seven volumes of the Reader's Guide. You just hop onto the World Wide Web, which means if you're writing a story on teen smoking, you go to Google or Yahoo, type "teen smoking" and up pops a couple hundred sites. In my case, I found, for starters, a White House press release on pending tobacco legislation, several *Washington Post* stories on tobacco-related topics and a Web page called Nicotine Free Kids, which has been voted the No. 1 teen tobacco site. By whom, it doesn't say.

I have enough material here to plagiarize a 26-part series. But then, who would read it? No one, other than the health teachers and a few coaches. So what am I going to do? First, I'm going to plow through several of the more credible Web sites, looking for information I might use. I'll probably avoid the Tobacco

Institute's "Smoking Makes You Look Like a Real Man" site.

I'll look for relevant and interesting facts, some of which will go into the main story, the rest into secondary packages.

For example, here's a Web site called "Quit4Life" (http://www.quit4life.com/html/splash.html).

It's sponsored by several Canadian health care groups and features three really hip young people, Tony, Natalie and Zoe, and another kid, Matthew, who must be the son of the president of Health Canada, if you catch my drift.

At any rate, I click onto "Natalie" and learn that she has great clothes and a great boyfriend, Andy. But something has come between them. Andy has started smoking, and cigarette smoke is made up mainly of tar, nicotine and carbon monoxide. It also contains poisons — cyanide, formaldehyde and ammonia. Tobacco is as addictive as heroin, I'm told.

What's more, young people who smoke or who use chewing tobacco are at immediate risk for health problems including nicotine addiction, increased heart rate and blood pressure, reduced oxygen supply to the brain, increased coughing, reduced lung function, fatigue, early tooth decay and gum disease.

For young women who take birth control pills, smoking increases their chances for serious heart disease, stroke and high blood pressure. On the plus side, they won't need the birth control pills because smoking will turn their skin to Naugahyde and your fingers and teeth the color of cheap whiskey.

Besides that, tobacco use causes cancer in many people — especially of the lung, mouth, throat, pancreas, bladder, kidney and cervix — as well as respiratory and heart diseases. Smoking can have a bad effect on babies, both before and after they are born.

And that's just the start of it. This Web site has more information about smoking than you can shake a stick at. You don't even want to know Tony's story. At any rate, this Web site is chock full of facts. I'll use a bunch of them, and I'll identify the sources. Readers need to know where I got this information and they need to trust that this source is credible,

BEWARE THE SEDUCTION OF THE WWW

Before you lift information from a Web site, ask yourself:

■ Who is responsible for the Web site? What is their agenda? Quotes on the "over-stated dangers of smoking" offered on the tobacco.com website might not be as accurate and balanced as you might expect.

■ Is this propaganda, misinformation, disinformation or credible information? Much of the World Wide Web consists of advertisement and political advocacy. If you're researching a story on global warming, would you trust a political organization to provide it? If you're researching a story on Hillary Clinton, would you trust the Rush Limbaugh Web site you provide fair and balanced information?

■ Is the Web site sponsored by an organization that is recognized in the field that you're studying? Or is it the vitriol of a weird fringe or hate group?

■ Does the document include a bibliography or links to other reputable sites?

■ Who wrote this stuff and why? What are the author's credentials? What's his or her point of view and biases? Who is he or she working for, and what's their agenda? Never quote an author whom you don't know, whose name or affiliation isn't well-known or well-regarded. The Web site should provide full biographical documentation and additional links to reputable sites.

■ Can I verify the information from another reputable source?

■ How old is the information? Does the site include the dates in which information was gathered and updated?

■ If I found it through a search engine like Google or Yahoo, doesn't that make it a credible source? No. It's your job to determine whether the site can be used as a credible source.

The World Wide Web is a bottomless pit of unfiltered, biased information, much of it of questionable origin and value. Excellent resources float among the most dubious. The bottom line: Never use information that you can't verify.

Garbage in. Garbage out.

which means using a White House press release may pose a problem.

Just kidding.

Anyway, computer-assisted reporting is just that—assisted. The real reporting comes later, in the old-fashioned way: interviewing, observing, listening. Your story needs to be more than:

DO YOU SMOKE? Are you thinking of starting to smoke because you think it looks cool or glamorous? Well, think again! Smoking is for losers! L - O - S - E - R - S!

Statistics from the White House indicate that 3,000 children every day start smoking and 1,000 of those children will die early as a result.

Cigarette smoke is made up mainly of tar (which builds up in your lungs), nicotine and carbon monoxide. It also contains poisons — cyanide, formaldehyde and ammonia. Tobacco is as addictive as heroin.

Young people who smoke or who use chewing tobacco are at immediate risk for health problems including nicotine addiction, increased heart rate and blood pressure, reduced oxygen supply to the brain, increased coughing, reduced lung function (shortness of breath), fatigue, and early tooth decay and gum disease.

If you are a young woman who smokes, taking birth control pills will increase your chances for serious heart disease, stroke and high blood pressure. Smoking can also make you look old before your time, stains the fingers and teeth and

HIGH SCHOOL JOURNALISM ON THE INTERNET

Thanks to the Internet, journalism has never been easier or more accessible than it is today. Anyone who has a computer and an Internet connection can publish a Web site or stream video or audio. Just about anyone can become an information provider and spread facts (or rumors). But even on the Internet, not everyone can be a journalist.

The Internet's history has a Wild West feel to it—almost anything goes. Journalists on the Internet, however, still must adhere to the core values that underline traditional journalism, whether television, radio or print media. Your writing and reporting must be fair, accurate, ethical, objective, legal and truthful.

— Lisa Habib
PLUGGED IN: Using the Internet for High School (And Professional) Journalism

> ❝ Obtaining stories that enable readers to participate in areas where their involvement can make a difference requires intelligent and energetic local reporting. It is easier—and cheaper—to download stories from the computer than to provide competent local coverage. But if serving readers is a priority, there is no choice.❞
>
> — Walter Fox
> *Writing the News*

makes you shake.

Tobacco use causes cancer in many people — especially of the lung, mouth, throat, pancreas, bladder, kidney and cervix — as well as respiratory and heart diseases. Smoking can have a bad effect on babies, both before and after they are born.

President George W. Bush is attempting to curb teen smoking.

"We're going to stick with the children and their future...and keep working to get a bill that will increase the price of cigarettes enough to deter smoking, that will have strong advertising restrictions, that will have strong access restrictions, that will invest in public health and do something honorable for tobacco farmers," President Bush said on Jan. 19, 2003.

Piece of cake. I compiled this story in less than 10 minutes, and the average teenager could probably do it in five. But the result isn't journalism. It's computer-assisted plagiarism. To qualify as journalism, the story needs a local angle, local sources, a news peg, a reason to exist.

Here's a news peg. The Texas Department of Health (TDH) recently found that 43 percent of high school students and nearly a third of middle schoolers—including about a fourth of all sixth graders—chewed tobacco or smoked it through a cigarette, cigar or pipe on at least one day during the previous month. Thirteen percent of high school students and four percent of middle schoolers said they smoked or chewed tobacco on 20 of the past 30 days.

The TDH billed the survey as the most comprehensive look at youth tobacco use in Texas history.

Now, at least here in Texas, this is reason enough to write a story on the topic. But I need to localize it. Conduct my own survey, perhaps. Interview relevant school officials. Talk to kids who smoke. Hang out with them long enough to get an idea of what's up but not so long that I develop a hole in my lung because of the second-hand smoke. Since the fact that a fourth of all sixth graders use tobacco is shocking, I might use that as an angle, might go talk to a few sixth

graders and to a few high school students who began smoking as sixth graders.

Since under-age smoking is illegal in Texas, sources may not want their names faces attached to a story about tobacco use in the student newspaper, so I'll consider using unnamed sources.

Scott S. Greenberger's lead in his Dec. 1 story in the *Austin American-Statesman* began like this:

PUFFING ON A CIGARETTE as he leaned against a downtown drug store, 17-year-old Rick Short offered a terse explanation for his unhealthy habit, which he began when he was 10.

"Got to have something in my mouth," he said simply.

A study released Monday by the Texas Department of Health suggests that when it comes to tobacco, many Texas teen-agers share Short's philosophy.

It then provides the results of the TDH survey as well as quotes from several authoritative sources. It's a solid example of daily journalism. But a high school newspaper is published once a week at the most, once a month in most cases. So play down the statistics and play up the human interest angle. I might build my story around an adult who began smoking as a teen, then later quit. For example:

AS A YOUNG COACH, Bill Smith would puff down three or four packs of Winstons a day.

"It's how I dealt with stress," he said. "Some days, the pressure of the job was so much that I'd have two cigarettes going at the same time."

But all that ended three days after his 45th birthday. He had a heart attack and underwent open-heart surgery to repair arteries, constricted after years of smoking.

"I laid in the hospital bed and thought about my family, that I'd never watch my daughter graduate from high school or kiss my grandchildren, and I cried and vowed never to touch another cigarette," Smith said. "And I haven't."

That was five years ago. Not only has he kicked

the habit, Smith is encouraging others to do the same. He said he finds recent surveys showing that almost half of Texas teens occasionally use tobacco distressing.

"I started smoking when I was 15," Smith said. "I thought it was cool. Pretty soon, I realized how disgusting a habit smoking is, but I was hooked. I was a young coach, under a lot of stress, and I couldn't quit."

In 1998, Smith underwent triple bypass surgery. Doctors took five lengths of artery from his legs to replace the clogged blood vessels near his heart.

"I remember thinking as they wheeled me into surgery, 'I'm too young to be doing this.'" Smith said. He added that doctors told him the vessels were constricted because of all his years of smoking.

Smith said he hopes it won't take surgery to convince others to quit. He added, "If anyone needs a little additional incentive to quit, I can show them a pretty nasty scar on my chest."

And all those statistics and other cyber bric-a-brac about reduced oxygen supply and high blood pressure? I'm going to pull the most relevant data into a sidebar fact box, and I'll cite the source. But they don't belong in this story.

For this story, I'm going to find the local angle and build a narrative around local sources, their experiences, their motivations, their anecdotes. I'm not going to simply copy and paste data from Web site A into formula story B.

■ GET THE BIG PICTURE

Say a student chooses to write about cheating: I'd allow him to do some traditional research — a review of periodicals, Internet, etc. Get the big picture. See if there's a news peg. For example, the American Federation of Teachers recently announced results of a survey showing that four in five students say they've cheated.

Next, I'd go to the adult authorities at the school: academic dean, director of curriculum, key teachers. What's their take on the situation? I'd also interview beginning teachers as well. Is it a problem here? In what way? Tests?

Plagiarism? Projects? What's being done to combat it, if anything? Do parents think it is a problem?

Much of this will be deep background. Some of it will show up as direct quotes. But the purpose is to provide the reporter with a clear view of the situation at your school. And this is critical. The story must be localized to your school. Don't go into an Internet chat room and elicit four of five comments from faceless strangers who may or may not be high school students. And even if they are, they're not students *in your high school.*

And make certain your facts come from reliable sources. The problem with using the Internet is it's so difficult to know whether the information on any given Web site is factual, accurate and reliable or merely plagiarized from some other unreliable source. If you have any doubt, don't use it.

Now that you have the big picture established, collect stories. To make the story interesting, you need to wrap the facts around human drama. If you can't find an interesting source at your school, then either you're not looking hard enough or cheating isn't a problem at your school. In that case, cover something else.

But if your school is like almost every school, cheating is a reality, even if it isn't an epidemic. Consider the story of the beginning teacher who caught the valedictorian cheating. Or the story of the bright kid who is pressured to cheat in order to help another kid pass. Or maybe the story of the student who cheats now and then, out of sheer laziness or boredom.

From all of this information, you should be able to develop an excellent story, sidebar, infographic package.

■ IN SUMMARY

Computers have made our lives easier, albeit more frustrating at times. The Internet has given us immediate access to a glut of information. And this is not to suggest that students should not use reliable sources from the Internet. There's nothing wrong with using a quote from an authoritative source on a legitimate Web site. In a story about

LOCALIZE THE FOLLOWING STORIES

■ Outbreaks of food-borne illness are on the rise in U.S. schools, according to an U.S. General Accounting Office report.

■ A national poll suggests that teachers value their unions, and almost half of them rated the unions as "absolutely essential."

■ Earning a master's degrees entirely online is becoming more common among educators, studies show.

■ More teachers nationwide are including bioterrorism as part of their biology curriculum.

■ The national unemployment rate for 16- to 19-year-olds continues to rise, according to the U.S. Bureau of Labor Statistics.

increased student tobacco use, I'd have no problem with including a quote from the U.S. Surgeon General.

However, I would have a problem with a student who visits the U.S. Surgeon General's web site, copies 25 inches of data and pastes it directly into something that he's calling a local story.

The heart and soul of journalism — newspaper and yearbook — remains the persistent reporter who attaches a name and a face to a situation and shows readers what all the facts and numbers mean. For example:

SHOWCASE ■

By **PATRICK HEALY**
Grosse Pointe South High School,
Grosse Pointe, MI

FOR SHIANNE MADAR, Columbine High School is more than a name in the news that echoes with stories of gunshots and grenades. The school that witnessed America's deadliest school shooting was a bike ride away from her house for 15 years.

Last Monday, Madar sat in her living room and watched an American tragedy unfold in her old neighborhood

Exhausted and sick, Madar had dragged herself home after taking the morning MEAP tests and flopped onto the couch to sleep for the rest of the day. Around 1 p.m. her aunt came downstairs, looking like she had stared death in the face. She had.

"Turn on the TV, something has happened in Colorado," she said. "There's been a shooting."

Dressed in the same black trench coats they wore every day to school, two students of the affluent Littleton, Colo. high school walked into the parking lot and started shooting. The high school juniors laughed as they shot their way into the cafeteria, through the hallways and into the library, witnesses told reporters.

The students, Eric Harris and Dylan Klebold, killed 13 people and wounded dozens more before they took their own lives, police told the Associated Press.

"That could have been me," Madar said, remembering images of students fleeing the school. "I could have gone to Columbine High School."

At South, Principal Arthur Miller discussed the shootings on the morning announcements. Up until then, Madar had controlled herself by shutting out the conversations of flocks of students discussing the killings. But Madar said she couldn't block out the voice on the PA, and as Miller's announcement carried on, she started crying.

Madar ducked out of her math class to dry her eyes with bathroom paper towels, then she walked down the hall into one of the counseling sessions the school offered. There, with red eyes and clenched hands, she started talking about her hometown.

She lived a few miles away from Columbine High School in Lakewood, a town that lies in the shadow of the Rocky Mountains. It is a place where the neighbors throw regular block parties and everyone knows everyone else, or at least acts like it, Madar said.

Lakewood and Littleton are two neighboring cities different only in name, she said. Two Grosse Pointes nestled in the mountains.

"It's a school just like South. If it (the shooting) could happen there, it could happen here," she said.

Some of her best friends had either lived in Littleton forever or moved there from Lakewood. At marching band competitions the rival squads from the two schools would hang out together, sometimes go for pizza. Madar said she doesn't remember the names of most of the kids she met on those trips. Only faces and voices. She has no idea whether they are dead or alive.

"The people that I've known were there," she said. "It was a good community. The people were good. How is life going to go on at that school?"

Columbine High School was named for Colorado's state flower, the columbine. Madar's mother grows the bright blue and yellow flowers in her garden, and Madar has a picture of one taped to the door of her locker. She said she put up the picture because seeing columbines made her smile, reminded her of home.

After last Monday, she said she'll never look at the flowers the same way.

COMPARE & CONTRAST

LOCALIZE & FOCUS STORIES ABOUT...

WHICH WOULD YOU RATHER READ?

A bare-bones article about Students Against Drunk Driving (SADD) —

S tudents again participated in the SADD Wake-Up Rallies, which were part of a collaboration between the Office of National Drug Control Policy's National Youth Anti-Drug Media Campaign and SADD. SADD conducted five Wake-Up Rallies in cities throughout the country this fall.

The main messages of the Wake Up rallies were:
■ Marijuana is addictive.
■ Marijuana endangers teen drivers.
■ Youth who smoke marijuana take more risks that can hurt their futures.
■ Youth who smoke marijuana don't do as well in school.
■ Parents need to know that they have the power to keep kids drug-free.

. . .or this feature, written by Kristin Pitts of Shawnee Mission (Kansas) Northwest HS?

A lcohol? That's what my mom puts on my cuts!" said a chubby boy, pointing to a few scrapes on his pale arms.

"Not that kind of alcohol, stupid," yelled two boys in unison.

"O.K. guys, let's try to calm down a bit," senior Adam Fitzwater said in a perfect, let's-get-down-to-business tone. As he shuffled through anti-drug papers and "ways to say no" worksheets, one of the boys took a long, imaginary sword out of his Jansport back pack and stabbed a boy in a yellow Pokemon-shirt, who immediately fell to the gym floor with dramatic flair.

To the fifth graders at Christa MacAuliffe Elementary School, drugs and alcohol aren't an issue. They live in a world filled with Goosebumps books, Nicklodeon, Electric Lime crayons and bright red Spiderman lunch boxes. But today,

members of SADD and STAND have brought up an issue that will affect the children in the future.

"Put yourself in this situation. You are at a friend's house and he offers you some alcohol. What do you do?"

Fitzwater read just loudly enough to be heard over a group of girls who were running away screaming from a little boy who had just finished picking his nose.

"I would take the alcohol and throw it in the oven so that it would melt," said the boy who had just recovered from the stab wound.

"No, no, no!" said a boy in gray sweatpants, in a voice that could only have been learned from an exasperated parent. "If you put it in the oven, it will explode into a bazillion pieces."

Fitzwater held back a laugh. Just as a group of girls was lining up to do a skit about how to say no to marijuana, a little girl asked what seemed to be on everyone's mind.

"We're only in fifth grade. Why would a fifth grader do drugs?"

There was something about the way she asked it, with a mix of logic and curiosity that seemed to catch everyone's attention. They paused, dumbfounded.

"That's a good question," senior Nick Adams answered. "I don't know why a high schooler would either."

Her question had posed a good point. Why would they do drugs?

"At first, it feels weird to talk to little kids about what to do if they are offered alcohol or tobacco at a party," senior Angie Bramlett said, "but we have to talk to kids when they are younger so they can get the idea of saying no into their heads."

As the kids went home in their parents' mini-vans, they were prepared—prepared to say no to anything that might interfere with a life of Nicklodeon, Goosebumps and Electric Lime Crayons.

■ Drugs/Alcohol
■ Sex/Gender issues
■ Issues of race
■ Environment
■ Local/National
■ Politics
■ Animal rights
■ Military
■ College/ university issues
■ Teaching/ Education
■ Freedom of Expression
■ Social Issues
■ Economic Issues
■ Crime
■ Technology
■ Internet
■ Health issues

Photo by **JASON KINDIG**
Duncanville High School, Duncanville, TX

MAKE YOUR STORY FLOW

A unified story expresses a single idea or theme. It doesn't bounce from one topic to another. It blends angle, focus, order, interpretation, description and other elements into a coherent and satisfying narrative.

11

Attempts to reduce reporting or writing to a series of steps are futile because the process isn't step-by-step. It's a lot more complicated than that. Building a story is not like building an automobile engine. The thousand or so engine parts are separate and replaceable but certainly not interchangeable. You can't replace a spark plug with a radiator cap.

In the successful story, the parts flow into one another. It's difficult to tell when theme ends and angle begins. Unlike an automobile engine, which is built one piece at a time, a story evolves from a blend of theme, angle, focus, organization, interpretation and description. Unity is the sum of the story's individual parts.

A unified story expresses one main point, and all information in the story develops or drives that point. More importantly, the writing flows in a logical order, with each sentence and each paragraph building upon the one before it and setting up the one to come. At least, that's the idea. You can tell pretty quickly when the reporter doesn't get there.

For example, consider the following story:

THERE IS AN ODD fellow in our town. His name is Clarence Chapman, and he owns a junk business. He used to be a farmer and also worked in a foundry but had to quit for health reasons.

Clarence is a graduate of Tamaroa High School. He served in Germany during World War II, then moved back here to set up business. His wife of 30 years, Marilyn, died in 1973. "I miss her a lot," Clarence said.

His hobbies include reading and gardening. He also spends a lot of time in front of his house, waving at people. Clarence does it because he said he is afraid people had forgotten to be friendly.

Another person who waves with Clarence is his 36-year-old son. Sam is a college graduate in philosophy and has been working with his father for 10 years. Sam said his favorite philosopher is Eugene Levy-Strauss. "I don't know why," Sam said. "He just made a lot of sense to me."

■ STACKING DATA ON TOP OF DATA

Now, what is this story really about? Well, it's not about anything in particular. It's a collection of unrelated facts. It lacks unity because the writer never selected a specific theme, never explored interesting angles, did no or very little research, failed to describe either the persons or the scenes, and never placed the action into a context. Instead, the writer stacked one piece of disjointed data on top of another, rendering all of it irrelevant.

So what that this guy likes to wave at

HOW TO USE A PARTIAL SENTENCE

English teachers may ban them, call them incomplete sentences. But good writers know when and how to use partial sentences. Here are three excellent leads that employ partial sentences to establish pace and tone.

EXAMPLE A

They had never flown in a plane. Never worn eye black. Never seen so many football fans.

The run to the state semifinals by the 1952 North Dallas football team — the Cinderella Bulldogs" — was all about milestones. It was the school's first playoff appearance in 16 years. And today, 50 years later, it is still the school's most recent post-season trip.

EXAMPLE B

After Jean Wheeler gave birth at age 17, she didn't know what to do when her son cried. Or how to change his diaper. Or when to switch from milk to cereal.

She learned quickly, though, through the school's Pregnancy Education and Parenting Program.

Without the program, "I wouldn't have graduated, said Wheeler. Now 19, she works two jobs, including part-time work at the school district day-care center.

EXAMPLE C

Rachel Ferguson never thought her dad, a telecommunications engineer with two advanced degrees, would be out of work. Ever.

Her father, Richard, worked for a company that put him in charge of a large NATO communications project in Brussels, Belgium. He earned more than $100,000 a year and sent Rhian to an expensive private school. Life for the Fergusons was good.

"He is so smart, and he worked so hard," Rachel said.

Then everything changed. Her dad's company downsized and cut his job. He has been out of work ever since.

---

people. Who cares?

So what that he has a son. Who cares?

So what that the son majored in philosophy. What does that have to do with anything?

Well, read the following story, and you can see how successful writers—in this case, Andrew H. Malcolm of *The New York Times* — take what otherwise may look like irrelevant data and turn it into a wonderful story.

TAMAROA, ILL.—FOR ALL but 900 people in the world, this sleepy southern Illinois community is little more than a 40-mile-an-hour speed zone on the way to somewhere else.

But back about 1970, something unusual began to happen here, something so weird drivers would slow down and turn their heads to stare as they passed on Route 51. Some people would even drive by again or stop their cars and demand to know what was wrong.

What was happening up there on the north end of Walnut Street was that someone was waving. Just standing or sitting there in front of his place waving, like the old days.

He would wave at people in cars and trucks, on tractors and bikes—even pedestrians would get a wave.

For 12 hours every day in rain and snow and summer sun, this guy would sit in front of his shed and wave at everyone, as if he was friendly and cared about them.

Then in 1976, the unusual man was joined by his son. So there were two people waving at everyone, whether they knew them or not.

"We just decided," said Clarence Chapman, Tamaroa's first unofficial waver, "that the world had maybe forgotten how to be friendly-like, locked up in their air-conditioned cars and basements and all. So Sam and I wave. We're just saying, 'Hi. Howdy. How are you? Nice day.' That sort of thing."

The trouble is that waving friendly-like is catching.

Many passersby now actually wave back. Some honk their horns. A few shout to the men they've never seen before: "Hello!" Many stop to chat or swap tall tales.

There are unconfirmed sightings of people waving in other parts of this depressed town. And if the Chapmans are a little late getting out some morning, the regulars will still toot their horns and wave back as if both men were there waving away.

At least some of them do. "Kids always wave," says Clarence Chapman. "But by the time they grow up, it seems like some of them stop waving. Oh, I guess they think it's too strange or something."

Of course, this kind of irrepressible friendliness is annoying to some motorists. Some even yell an obscenity. "We smile real big and wave back," said Sam Chapman, "and think to ourselves it's real good that some folks are just passing through."

Clarence Chapman is a 64-year-old former farmer forced out of that business by economics and out of a foundry job by asthma that still starts him coughing if he laughs too hard. He walks on a cane now, wears a thin mustache, a straw cowboy hat, a Rin-Tin-Tin string tie and whatever slacks and shirt he can find at home, across the road from his junk shop.

"We call it junk," he says. "But after you buy it, you can call it anything you want."

Sam Chapman is 36 and has been waving for 10 years, since he graduated from college with a major in philosophy. "The demand for philosophers was somewhat soft then, as now," Mr. Chapman says. So he joined his father's junk business.

The junk business in rural southern Illinois is not a high-pressure occupation. It provides ample time, year-round, for at least one of the Chapmans to wave at every passing person.

At mealtimes, Sam and Clarence take turns going indoors so they do not miss an auto. In between, they listen a lot to the birds in the sassafras trees.

Some passersby require comment: "There goes the Knight boy home from Bible school to mow the lawn." "Old Harold must be hitting the suds already today. He's got his missus driving." "Don't know those folks. Hi. How are ya?"

The two men might even break into song, which tells neighbors that life is progressing normally. "You can hear them clear up to my house," said Phyllis Ferguson. "They're not stuck-up or anything, just old-fashioned friendly."

They don't have a phone. "Somebody wants us," says Sam, "they can come see us."

And they're too busy to watch television. "In the old shows," says Clarence, "crime didn't pay. Now, you look at TV and wonder if maybe it might."

They are not bothered by non-wavers. "It just ain't some people's way to wave," says Clarence Chapman. "But you can tell the city folks right off. They're the ones that think waving is strange."

■ PERFECT BALANCE AND COORDINATION

So what that this guy likes to wave at people? So what that he has a son? So what that the son majored in philosophy?

Are these important considerations? Of course they are. We see a man who is conducting his own crusade against the isolation of today's world, who is clinging to an old ideal we should love our neighbors, whether we know them or not, and who is making some progress.

We can picture him—a cane at his side, a thin mustache, a straw cowboy hat, a Rin-Tin-Tin string tie and "whatever slacks and shirt he can find at home, across the road from his junk shop" as he and his son sit on the front porch, talking about people driving by and waving at each passing car.

It is particularly important to remember this story was published in *The New York Times*—the house organ of snooty city folks who probably think waving is strange. The story begins with an interpretation: "For all but 900 people in the world, this sleepy southern Illinois community is little more than a 40-mile-an-hour speed zone on the way to somewhere else."

It isn't an editorial comment. It's the reporter's assessment of the situation, and he's probably right. We feel comfortable with the reporter's assessment because the lead immediately presents two facts: the town population and the speed zone, simple but good reporting of pertinent details.

In a non-too-subtle dig, Mr. Malcolm rubs the

THINK LIKE A STORYTELLER

Ask the kinds of questions that Lisa Pollak, the Pulitzer Prize-winning feature writer for the *Baltimore Sun*, poses to herself:

■ Who in this story has something at stake?
■ Who is most affected?
■ Who is nobody paying attention to?
■ What about this story moves me?

QUICK TIP

How to meet deadlines:

■ Set mini-deadlines. Allow time for several drafts to be read, edited, proofed and corrected.

■ Give yourself plenty of time for major stories.

■ Make sure you understand the assignment.

■ Work on the story every day.

■ Don't repeat tasks.

■ Finish the task that must be done first. Then, move on.

■ If you bog down, seek help.

■ Cut your losses. If the story isn't going to pan out, dump it and move on.

readers' noses in their silly conceptions of rural folk, their condescending attitudes and their fear of strangers. "You can tell the city folks right off. They're the ones that think waving is strange."

What a perfect ending. This story embodies all of the elements. It appeals to our better instincts. It touches our hearts and funnybones. It takes us somewhere and brings us back home.

It is this type of unity—a beginning, a middle and an end, working in perfect balance and coordination—that make this story so successful.

■ **PULLING THE FACTS TOGETHER**

Consider the following situation. Texas public school students participating in a series of journalism contests were required to write a feature story, based on the following facts:

■ **SITUATION:**

JANELLE KLEIN is the drama teacher at the high school and is a member of a local comedy troupe. She has been employed at the school for 11 years. She has guided the school's one-act play to seven district championships, six regional titles and two state championships. She is married to Frank Klein, an engineer for the Texas Highway Department. She and her husband have three children.

In addition to her job at the high school, Janelle is a member of the Laff Staff, a group of improvisational comedians who work at a local comedy theatre. She also founded the Clown Care Unit (CCU), a group of comedians who visit ailing children and their parents at the city's four hospitals. The clowns' purpose is to alleviate the fear and confusion of hospital stays and to provide moments of humorous routines for sick children.

St. Michael's Hospital recently opened a new Children's Hospital for youngsters with life-threatening and catastrophic illnesses. Two or three days a week, the clowns, dressed in mock hospital garb and bearing such names as Dr. Comfort, Dr. Stubs and Dr. Funnybone, make the rounds at local hospitals to visit sick children. Usually, the clowns perform a 20-minute parody of hospital personnel, food and procedures and then make the rounds on the floors to visit children too sick to leave their rooms. You are writing for the issue of the student newspaper to be distributed Friday, April 3.

■ **DIRECT QUOTES:**
JANELLE KLEIN

I have enjoyed my 11 years at Leaguetown High School, and I'm going to miss the students. I can't overstate how important I think it is to continue to support the fine arts in high school. Basic curriculum in high schools is very much overemphasized. Students need a well-rounded education of core classes as well as enrichment classes. I joined Laff Staff because I enjoy performing, and I think it is good for students to know that their teachers can do as well as teach. However, this project has grown more important for me each year, and with the opening of the new Children's Hospital at St. Michael's, the need for this service is especially dire.

Clown Care got its start in 1991 when an official at St. Michael's Hospital asked if the Laff Staff would entertain at a gathering for patients and their families. A fellow member of the Laff Staff, Jeff Gordon, and I obliged. We put together a 20-minute parody of doctors and hospitals, and it was the most fulfilling 20 minutes of my professional career. It was from that experience that the CCU plan took root.

This project came out of an unconscious place in myself. After going through a lot of feelings of loss and grief when my best friend's son died a few years ago, this gave me a feeling of celebration and joy, of healing after his loss. Call it a love and caring, God, a higher consciousness—whatever—I want to give my life to this project.

The nurses and doctors have been extremely supportive of our efforts. They accepted that we were there as part of their world. I had one ugly encounter when we first started. A hospital staff member said, "Clowns don't belong in the Intensive Care Unit." So I said, "Neither do children." I won that one.

I've encountered so many extraordinary young people that it's hard to single one out, but I do think a lot about one young man named Christian, who had a chronic heart ailment and was very angry and very lonely. For more than a year, we spent time with him, trying to reach him. One day, I taught him a "mind-

DON'T REPEAT YOURSELF

The transition sentence provides the fact. The direct quote provides opinion or elaboration on the fact. Do not repeat the same information from the transition sentence or paragraph to the direct quote. Note how the transition sentences (in bold) repeat the same information as the direct quotes. This isn't good.

The wrestling team and the school in general are in for a real treat this winter. With the start of the new school year comes a new teacher as well as a new coach, and he is coach Dean Shelton.

For 14 years, Shelton has coached at Madison High where his teams have won nine district, five regional and three state wrestling titles.

■ **Many wrestlers say they look forward to Shelton's arrival.**

"I'm really looking forward to his arrival," Miles Ryan, senior, said.

■ **Others say they can't wait for the season to start.**

"I can't wait for the season to start," sophomore Mitch Wilson said. "Coach Shelton is sure to build a winning tradition here, and I'm excited and honored to be a part of it."

■ **Other players say they expect to learn new techniques.**

"I hope to learn new techniques," Mike Wiggins, senior, said. "Coach Shelton knows what it takes to win."

■ **Of course, wrestlers said they would miss coach David Cippelle, who retired.**

"I like my fellow wrestlers will most certainly miss Coach Cippelle," Javier Cruz said. "Absolutely. He was a good man and will remember him fondly."

reading" card game, and he began to open up. He took great pride in fooling one of his real doctors with the card trick.

I later told him he was good enough to join CCU, but he said, "I'd love to, but I can't walk." I told him, "Oh, you can walk." Of course, he hadn't taken a step in eight months.

Within two weeks, he had found a pair of tennis shoes and was on his feet as a $2-a-day CCU performer. After that he blossomed, and I think it gave him the strength to battle against his mounting medical problems. He died two months after open-heart surgery, but those last few years of his life were full of joy. He didn't die a lonely and angry young man.

I've had a few rejections, but I don't let them bother me. My responsibility is not to save the children but to love them and give joy and celebration, not to make them accept it. That's their choice.

DR. ALFRED NASH, director of the Children's Hospital of St. Michael's

Most of us thought it was a wonderful idea, but we were not sure how it would work and if it would be accepted by the parents of sick children. But the clowns' techniques were so disarming, they captivated everybody immediately.

As hard as it is for children to be sick, it is equally difficult for parents to have sick children, and a lot of us at the hospital sometimes forget this. Indeed, we—the doctors, nurses and staff members—thoroughly enjoy the shows even when the clowns are poking fun at us.

MELINDA MATTHEWS, mother of Carrie, age 5, a sick child

The clowns are wonderful. One day, we were all in the room when Dr. Stubs (Janelle) stuck her head in the room and asked, "I hope I'm not bothering you." Then, she pulled up beside the bed, pulled out several crumpled sheets of paper, a huge pencil, and began asking her, "Are you married? Any children? Does your nose ever turn red?" Then, she plopped a big red nose on Carrie. Finally, she asked, "Have you ever had a how-long-can-you-go-without-laughing test?"

EDITING IS THE FIRST THING YOU DO, AND THE LAST

Don't confuse editing with proofreading. Editing begins with the identification of a specific theme, the development of a creative angle and the selection of the best quotes, the most interesting anecdotes and the most relevant and important details.

It ends with a careful examination of each word, sentence and paragraph for clarity, conciseness and cohesiveness.

> All good writing begins with think time. Think time includes researching, interviewing, brainstorming, and clustering thoughts on paper. If I have done a good job of thinking, a story almost writes itself. If my thinking is thin, the story will never be good.
>
> — Nancy Ruth Patterson Roanoke, VA

Carrie answered "no" to all of the questions. Stubs then took out a large wind-up clock from her bag and let it drop to the floor. Of course, Carrie giggled, and Stubs said, "You only lasted four seconds. Want to try again?" So he planted a red nose on me, and Carrie just erupted with laughter. For a few moments, at least, her mind was off the pain and trauma of being ill.

■ **EXTRA INFORMATION**

The Clown Care Unit recently received a $25,000 grant from the Charles Altman Foundation, to be used mostly for props, salaries and administrative overhead. On Monday, March 23, Klein announced she would leave the school at the end of the school year to devote her full attention to improving and expanding the Clown Care Unit project.

■ **GO THROUGH THE PROCESS**

What is this story really about? What lead will capture the reader's attention? Can you tell the story in a logical order without losing the reader? Which information do you use? Which do you omit? Which quotes are used as direct quotes, which as in-direct quotes? What are your transitions? And finally, how do you end this story so that the reader is left with a sense of resolution and satisfaction?

If you can do these things, then the story will have unity. Let's see if it's possible:

THE DOCTOR DRAGGED a chair to the side of the bed, pulled out several crumpled sheets of paper and a huge pencil, and began the interrogation.

"Are you married?"

"Any children?"

"Does your nose ever turn red?"

"Have you ever had a how-long-can-you-go-without-laughing test?"

The patient, 5-year-old Carrie Matthews, answered "no" to each question. The doctor—Dr. Stubs—then took out a large wind-up clock from her bag and let it drop to the floor.

Carrie giggled.

"You only lasted four seconds. Want to try again?"

She did. But to no avail. Doctor Stubs planted a red nose on Carrie's mom, and with that, the patient erupted into laughter.

For a few moments, Carrie's mind was off the pain and the trauma of being ill.

Since 1986, the Clown Care Unit, a group of comedians who visit ailing children and their parents at the city's four hospitals, has worked to alleviate the fear and confusion of hospital stays and provide moments of humorous routines for sick children. It recently received a $25,000 grant from the Charles Altman Foundation.

The CCU was founded by drama teacher Janelle Klein, who announced March 23 that she was leaving the school after 11 years to devote her full attention to improving and expanding the project.

"Clown Care got its start in 1991 when an official at St. Michael's Hospital asked if the Laff Staff would entertain at a gathering for patients and their families," Klein said. "A fellow member of the Laff Staff, Jeff Gordon, and I obliged. We put together a 20-minute parody of doctors and hospitals, and it was the most fulfilling 20 minutes of my professional career. It was from that experience that the CCU plan took root."

Although apprehensive at first, doctors and nurses have been extremely supportive of the troupe, Klein said.

"I had one ugly encounter when we first started," she said. "A hospital staff member said, 'Clowns don't belong in the Intensive Care Unit.' So I said, 'Neither do children.' I won that one."

Klein said she has had a few rejections.

"But I don't let them bother me," she said. "My responsibility is not to save the children but to love them and give joy and celebration, not to make them accept it. That's their choice."

Among her success stories was a young man named Christian, who had a chronic heart ailment and was very angry and very lonely.

"For more than a year, we spent time with him, trying to reach him," Klein said. "One day, I taught him a 'mind-reading' card game, and he began to open up.

"He took great pride in fooling one of his real doctors with the card trick. I later told him he was good enough to join CCU, but he said, 'I'd love to, but I can't walk.' I told him, 'Oh, you can walk.' Of course, he hadn't taken a step in eight months. Within two weeks, he had found a pair of tennis shoes and was on his feet as a $2-a-day CCU performer.

"After that he blossomed, and I think it gave him the strength to battle against his mounting medical problems," Klein said. "He died two months after open-heart surgery, but those last few years of his life were full of joy. He didn't die a lonely and angry young man."

Klein said she would miss teaching. She's proud that she proved the "those who can, do; those who can't, teach" myth wrong. But with the opening of the new Children's Hospital at St. Michael's for youngsters with life-threatening and catastrophic illnesses, the need for this service is especially dire.

"After going through a lot of feelings of loss and grief when my best friend's son died a few years ago, this gave me a feeling of celebration and joy, of healing after his loss," Klein said. "Call it a love and caring, God, a higher consciousness—whatever—I want to give my life to this project."

■ MISSION ACCOMPLISHED

This story is unified, coherent and stylized. It begins with a descriptive scene that doesn't just tell us the purpose of the CCU. It shows us.

It is as though we've walked into a hospital room and are witnessing a doctor's finest bedside manner. This anecdote sets up the statement, "For a few minutes, her mind was off the pain and trauma of being ill."

The scenario also prepares us to meet Janelle Klein, who founded the organization.

The writer knows the story of the organization is more important than Klein's announcement she will leave the school at the end of the term.

However, because this story is being written for a student publication, Klein's resignation is an important news fact and must be mentioned early in the article. But we should not mistake this additional piece of information for the theme of the story. The theme should remain focused on the program and the children it serves.

The services are outlined in specific detail. We learn of the successes and failures. Abstract statements are followed by concrete examples. The story of Christian provides a perfect example of the lengths Janelle and her companions went to reach these children.

Again, this anecdote connects a name and face to the program. Remember "60 Minutes" producer Don Hewitt's comment about the difference between subjects and stories? The clown care unit is a subject. A young man named Christian, whose life was made richer by the clown care unit, is a story.

The story then returns to the present, with Janelle saying she'd miss the kids but that pursuing this dream is her destiny. Note the addition of the interpretive, "Those who can, do; those who can't, teach" statement.

Finally, the writer searches for and finds a statement that provides the reader with a sense of resolution.

We are left with a statement—"I want to give my life to this project"—that resolves the situation. This is what Janelle is doing, this is why, here are the results, and this is where she goes from here. The last paragraph leaves us with a sense of satisfaction.

■ BE YOUR OWN EDITOR

Sure, you have an editor or two who'll proof and polish your story before it lands on the page, but you should edit your own copy before popping into the pipeline. Here are a few questions to ask yourself before submitting any story:

1. What is the theme of the story? Write it in a single sentence.
2. Why did I choose this angle?
3. Who are my primary sources?
4. Why did I select them? Why should I care about them?
5. Who are my secondary sources?
6. Why did I select them?
7. What is the story nutgraph?
8. Are all news questions answered?
9. Does the story flow? Is information provided logically and orderly?
10. Do a variety of sentence lengths provide pace?
11. Have I eliminated all unnecessary words, particularly passive verbs or redundant adverbs

TRANSITIONS ARE THE STRING THAT TIES THE STORY TOGETHER

Your story needs to flow seamlessly, almost effortlessly. To do so, you must master transitions: words, sentences, paragraphs. They're used to:

■ show time. Then, meanwhile, now, later.
■ cite examples: for instance, thus, for example.
■ emphasize a point: indeed, moreover, in particular.
■ change point of view: however, but, of course, also.

They move the story from subject to subject, character to character, time to time.

and adjectives?

12. Is all information accurate?

13. Are spelling, stylebook rules, grammar correct?

14. Does the tone match the content?

15. Have I provided description, dialogue, anecdote and/or drama?

16. Does the ending provide reader satisfaction and/or resolution?

17. Have I written for my intended audience?

18. Have I submitted information for your sidebar infographic or secondary story?

If you can answer "yes" to each of these questions, your editors will worship you.

■ WORKING TOGETHER

Keep in mind that your story will, in all likelihood, be published in a student publication and thus read by hundreds if not thousands of your peers as well as two or three English teachers whose day isn't made until they find a comma splice or subject-verb disagreement.

You want the copy to be flawless, but the process must go beyond a search for correct punctuation and proper attribution. Perfectly edited copy is of no consequence unless each story has substance and is unified. Achieving this demands that reporters and editors form a special relationship that goes beyond boss-employee or veteran-novice. Editors and reporters must be equal partners in the pursuit of excellence.

The former editor of the Westlake High School (Austin, Texas) *Featherduster* offers an example of a strong editor-reporter relationship.

SHOWCASE ■

By **LAURA MATTHEWS**
Westlake High School, Austin, TX

THE ONE THING that I tried most to establish as editor was a working relationship with every staffer. This did not mean being the most popular person on staff; people generally do not appreciate being reminded about deadlines even in the sweetest manner ("Bill, if you don't get that story in, I will have to hang you by two toenails instead of three").

Since on the *Featherduster* I edited the majority of the copy before it ever got to the adviser, I was the one who told the reporter that his lead was nonexistent or that he was going to have to interview someone outside the journalism staff for his in-depth story on the student drinking problem.

Obviously, this task demanded patience and courtesy, and the realization that each staffer had a different personality and had to be dealt with accordingly.

I also had to constantly remind myself, however, that the story I was editing was someone else's story, not my own. The writer might not have written the lead I would have written, but he or she had spent time and energy on the story, and deserved to be able to recognize it when it appeared in the paper.

I made a concerted effort, therefore, to edit copy with each writer rather than for them. I found that staffers responded better to someone discussing their paper on a one-to-one basis rather than to getting it back with ambiguous remarks all over it.

Working with staffers in person forced me to listen to their ideas. The staffers appreciated my taking extra time to sit down with them rather than my rewriting their stories and making editorial decisions without their knowledge or consent.

When I did have to write comments on papers, I tried to illustrate what I was saying in the margins with (hopefully) funny comments and exaggerated examples. The staff as a whole also brainstormed together at the beginning of each issue to come up with story ideas and voted as a group on its stance for the editorial each issue.

Making the effort to involve every member of the staff took more time than any other aspect of my work as editor—many times it would have been easier just to do the job myself, and sometimes I did. That effort to take everyone's ideas seriously, however, gave me some credibility as an editor who cared about something other than her monthly column, and I believe it helped the staff work together as a whole so that no one can ever accuse the *Featherduster* of being an editor-adviser product.

COMPARE & CONTRAST

AVOID THE 'BIG PICTURE'

To most people, the holiday season is a time when their family gathers together for a holiday meal, sings holiday songs and opens one another's presents while surrounded by an atmosphere of love.

Unfortunately, this isn't always the case. And the holiday season is particularly difficult for children of divorced parents.

In a few cases, the family will still celebrate together, but many teens will divide their time between the parents.

"I plan to spend half of Christmas day with my mom and the the other half with my dad," junior Jason Kyser said.

FOCUS ON THE INDIVIDUAL

Like most Americans, Jason Kyser will celebrate Christmas day with his family. Both of them.

Like many students who have divorced parents, Jason finds special celebrations such as birthdays and holidays a balancing act.

"My mom and dad get along real well so it's not a big deal," he said. "But I have friends whose parents hate each other, and that really creates a lot of tension. The parents even get into fights over who spent the most on gifts. It gets pretty vicious."

The holiday season is stressful enough on its own, psychologists say. However, dealing with divorced parents and step-parents makes it more difficult.

"I'll spend Christmas at my mom's house," said a senior, who asked not to be identified. "I went to my dad's last year, and I was treated like I wasn't even there. I got the feeling that his new wife thought I was intruding or something. I swore I'd never go back, and I won't."

THIS LEAD IS TOO GENERAL

The 26th amendment gave all eligible 18-year-olds the right to vote, but many do not exercise this right. According to Project Vote, a Washington, D.C.-based organization, fewer than 35 percent of 18-year-old eligible voters will cast a ballot in the 1992 election. Overall, 59 percent of eligible voters are expected to exercise their rights in this election.

Students say they don't plan to vote because of apathy. Others say they don't understand the issues.

REPORT IN TERMS OF PEOPLE

Sandra Tate rolled her eyes. She'd heard this line before, and she wasn't swallowing it.

"I'd vote if I thought it'd do any good, but these three guys don't impress me one bit," she said. "I don't believe any of them really understand my problems."

Sandra is like a lot of 18-year-olds: old enough to vote but not interested. In fact, only 35 percent of the 18-year-old eligible voters are expected to cast a ballot this year.

"The issues are so complex, it's hard to know what to do," senior Kelly Brennan said. "I listen to the commercials and read the paper, and all it does is confuse me. I don't think any of them are telling the truth. And no matter who wins, I'm still living where I live today, and I'm still paying taxes."

But not all teenagers are so apathetic.

"This country needs a major change, and that's why I'm supporting Vermont Gov. Howard Dean," senior Jon Richmond said. "I think the country has tilted too far to the right. It scares me that our government wants us to trade our liberty for security. Without liberty, what's worth protecting anyway?"

■ Repeat key words. For example:

Because of last week's fire, the administration has introduced a new policy on storing dangerous chemicals.

The policy includes…

Key word: policy.

■ Use a synonym, abbreviation or pronoun. For example:

Because of last week's explosion, Supt. Harold Sudds said the chemistry department can no longer store TNT in soup cans next to open flames.

"Seems to me, we were just looking for trouble," Sudds said. "Any more explosions, and someone is going to have to answer to me."

Photo by **COURTNEY MCKEOWN**
Bryant High School, Bryant, AR

MAKE IT ERROR-FREE

Proofreading is one thing. Sure, it's important to catch all those misspelled words and misplaced commas. But editing is more than that. It's making sure the story's lead, pace, tone and flow are just right.

12

Editing is a matter of balancing standards and personal whim. It's difficult. It's frustrating. It has to be done. Great writing is great rewriting. Too often, students get the wrong impression that reporters dash into the office, rip off 10 or 12 pages, zip it past a copy editor and wait for the Pulitzers to roll in. It doesn't work that way. Reporters labor over their leads. They juggle parts of the story, cutting and pasting on the computer to create a piece that balances message, tone, pace, clarity and all those other considerations – at least as perfectly as their skills permit. Consider the following story:

THE CHS MIGHTY Marching Bulldog Band raised over seven hundred dollars selling Christmas trees last month. The money is part of their fundraising effort to go to the Orange Bowl Parade of Bands next January.

"We have wanted to go to this festival for several years but could not afford it," according to Band Director Jerry Downs. "If we stay on target, we will have sufficient funds to afford this trip."

Brad Nichols, Band President, said hauling the trees was very hard work, but also said, "It will be worth it because everyone is looking forward to going to Miami. It'll be great to be on the beach.

I am proud to be a member of the band."

Let's proof the story.

AS PART OF ITS fund-raising effort to go to the Orange Bowl Parade of Bands next January, the band raised more than $700 selling Christmas trees last month.

"We have wanted to go to this festival for several years but could not afford it," band director Jerry Downs said. "If we stay on target, we will have sufficient funds to afford this trip."

Band president Brad Nichols said hauling the trees was hard work but added, "It will be worth it because everyone is looking forward to going to Miami. It'll be great to be on the beach and away from this cold weather."

We've dropped all the adjectives (the CHS Mighty Marching Bulldog . . . .)

The band is an it—not a "they," so we've changed "their" to "its." We used "more than" rather than "over," which is used when referring to crossing a barrier or intervening space, as in "The cow jumped over the moon."

Some might argue that "band director" preceding Jerry Downs should be capitalized.

> About the best you can do with a bad piece of writing is to knock off the rough edges, so a reader can choke it down with as little effort as possible. The proper way to improve wretched material is to rewrite it, but time too often precludes that. Consequently, all you can do is ease the reader's burden as much as possible, making sure everything is understandable on one reading."
>
> — Martin L. Gibson
> *Editing in the Electronic Era*

USE A COMMA WHEN...

USE A COMMA...

▪ you have a phrase or nonrestrictive clause at the beginning of a sentence with a comma. Example:

As the guru of South Carolina scholastic journalism, David Knight is often asked whether grits are better served boiled or fried.

▪ you have a compound sentence. Example:

The apple pie was delicious, but the cherry pie was even better.

DON'T USE A COMMA...

▪ when you have a compound verb. Example:

Joe has been principal at the school for 10 years and has driven a bus all of those years

▪ after the final entry in a series. Example:

When Bubba grows up, he wants to own a monster truck, a bass boat and the biggest television on the market.

However, band director is a position—not a title. The same goes for "head football coach" and "cheerleader sponsor."

When in doubt, consult the *Associated Press Stylebook and Libel Manual*.

Delete "very."

Now that the story's proofed, we can see that we still have a bland albeit clean story. It's time to take the editing to another level. First, let's determine what part of this story our readers will most likely care about.

Do readers care Brad Nichols is proud to be a member of the band? Doubtful. A bunch of young people risking frostbite is more interesting than the fact that they raised $700 to go to Miami. So let's develop that angle by asking a few questions.

"While you were freezing, what did you say to each other?"

"Did people get into arguments?"

"How did you feel?"

"What did they look like?"

"What was the best part of the day?"

"What was the worst part of the day?"

With this information and more, you can create a compelling story. For example:

HUDDLED AROUND A SMALL heater, four band members waited for the next customer and argued.

"I'm not going out there again. I wait

the last guy," junior Roger Wharmund said. "It's your turn."

"No way. I'm freezing," senior Angel Walker answered. "Let Ann go. She hasn't been out in an hour."

"I can't go. Look at this blister," sophomore Ann Hughes said. "My hands will never recover."

"You should have worn gloves," senior Brad Nichols answered. "What did you expect? That unloading Christmas trees would be fun?"

These students and others spent Friday hauling Christmas trees from a refrigerated truck to an outside lot, where the fog and snow gave the event a festive holiday atmosphere that lasted only until the students started shivering.

Why all this? For two years, band members have raised money to pay for next January's trip to the Orange Bowl Festival of Bands in Miami, Florida. Still, the thoughts of sunny beaches did little to warm the band members as they braved the bone-chilling weather.

"It was fun at first, but after a while we all got tired and cold," Hughes said. "We tried to break up the boredom with a little snowball fight, but even that didn't help."

The story of a group of band students, earning money for a trip to Miami, now has concrete meaning. We can appreciate their dedication. Before, it was an abstraction. Here's another example: the first game of the season. In this case, it's football, but it could be any sport. Too often, sports is even more carelessly edited than news or features.

THIS YEAR'S FOOTBALL TEAM will open their season on the home field here Friday night against the state's top-ranked team and defending state football champion, the Lakewood Panthers.

"I know their the top-ranked team in the state, but if they're not ready to play, we could surprise them," Jim Wandell, coach, said. "We have had good workouts. If the ball bounces our way a few times, we have a chance to be in the game with them. We are starting 11 new players, including eight juniors and two sophomores. I hope our inexperience doesn't hurt us too much."

"Lakewood has a great tradition, but if we play our game and give 100 percent, we stay with them," Kevin Brooks, a 6-2, 185-pound junior, said. "Our only JV loss last year came against Lakewood so we have a score to settle."

As a sophomore, Brooks quarterbacked the junior varsity to a 9-1 mark. The Panthers defeated us last year, 48-21, on their way to a perfect 15-0 season and state championship.

Let's clean up the blaring errors. In the following story, note the use of transition sentences between paragraphs and the deletion of the first person reference in the final sentence. We also changed "their" in the second paragraph for "they're."

THE TIGERS WILL OPEN the football season here Friday night by hosting the state's top-ranked team and defending state champion, the Lakewood Panthers, a 48-21 winner over Taft last year.

"I know they're the top-ranked team in the state, but if they're not ready to play, we could surprise them," coach Jim Wandell said. "We have had good workouts. If the ball bounces our way a few times, we have a chance to be in the game with them."

EDITING CHECKLIST

■ Use specific nouns and active verbs.

■ Avoid "to be" verbs. Rather than " Jones will be leading. . . .," write "Jones will lead . . . ."

■ Avoid sentences that begin with A, An, The and There.

■ Avoid wobble words, such as very, many and really.

■ Keep sentences short (25 words or fewer).

■ Keep paragraphs short.

■ Keep nouns close to their verbs.

■ Limit the number of dependent clauses and prepositional phrases in each sentence.

■ Be consistent in style on punctuation and on abbreviations. For example: NHS or N.H.S.?

■ Avoid clutter, such as "order up," "go and attend," "smile happily," or "tall skyscraper."

■ Avoid misuse of the apostrophe, especially in its/it's.

■ Use anecdotes and examples frequently and effectively.

■ Use direct quotes that provide meaningful information rather than clichés or predictable data.

■ Say as much as possible in as few words as necessary.

■ Never let personal opinion slip into a news or feature story, especially in transitions and conclusions.

■ Maintain a consistent and appropriate tone.

■ Answer all news questions, and never raise questions without answering them.

■ Avoid legal, ethical, taste or fairness problems.

DON'T BE AFRAID TO ASK FOR HELP

A story is a living organism. It comes to life as soon as the fingers touch the keypad and exists as long as a reader remembers it. It cannnot be treated as though it's another school assignment to be completed, submitted and forgotten.

Making a story unforgettable required talent, skill and diligence.

SIDE NOTE

This article by a young journalist with whom I work was written from the same fact sheet that is provided on pages 146-148. I've edited the story by striking out unnecessary or inappropriate words and sentences and placing changes in italics. Note that it required little proofing.

At the same time, compare the angle and tone of this story to the story on pages 148-149.

In all fairness, I did not direct the writer in any way so the story takes more of a news than a feature angle. This is the angle that most beginning student journalists would take, but not necessarily the one that I would recommend.

Right — but not well written

Being "correct" isn't enough to satisfy readers

Janelle Klein, Leaguetown's drama teacher for the past 11 years, announced March 23 that she would leave the school in May ~~in order~~ to devote her full attention to improving and expanding the Clown Care Unit project.

The Clown Care Unit, founded by Klein in 1986, consists of a group of comedians who visit ailing children and their parents at the city's four hospitals. The project began when an official at St. Michael's Hospital asked ~~if~~ the Laff Staff, a group of improvisational comedians who work at a local comedy theater, ~~would~~ *to* entertain at a gathering for patients and their families.

"A fellow member of the Laff Staff, Jeff Gordon, and I obliged," Klein said. "We put together a 20-minute parody of doctors and hospitals, and it was the most fulfilling 20 minutes of my professional career. It was from that experience that the CCU plant took root."

St. Michael's recently opened a new Children's Hospital for youngsters with life-threatening and catastrophic illness. The clowns' purpose is to alleviate the fear and confusion of hospital stays and provide moments of humorous routines for sick children. Alfred Nash, director of the Children's Hospital at St. Michael's, *said he* wondered how parents of sick children would react. After watching one of the shows, *he said* he knew the project would work.

"Janelle's and other clowns' techniques were so disarming, they captivated everybody immediately," Nash ~~stated~~ *said*. "We—the doctors, nurses and staff members—thoroughly enjoy the shows even when the clowns are poking fun at us."

Although Klein *said she* receives much support from doctors and nurses, she has ~~had to face~~ *faced* ~~some~~ rejections as well.

~~Klein comments,~~ "I don't let them bother me," *she said*. "My responsibility is not to save the children but to love them and give joy and celebration, not to make them accept it. That's their choice."

During her 11 years at Leaguetown, Klein guided the one-act play to seven district championships, six regional titles and two state UIL championships. She *said she* hopes that strong support will continue for fine arts in high school.

"I have enjoyed my 11 years at Leaguetown High School, and I'm going to miss the students," Klein said. "Basic curriculum in high schools is very much overemphasized. Students need a well-rounded education of core classes as well as enrichment classes."

It is not easy for Klein to leave, but she admits she is ready to move on.

"This project has grown more important for me each year, and with the opening of the new Children's Hospital at St. Michael's, the need for this service is especially dire," Klein said. "Call it a love and caring, God, a higher consciousness—whatever—I want to give my life to this project."

The Clown Care Unit recently received a $25,000 grant from the Charles Altman Foundation, to be used mostly for props, salaries and administrative overhead.

Klein is married to Frank Klein, an engineer for the Texas Highway Department. She and her husband have three children.

Wandell said the team is young but talented. "We are starting 11 new players, including eight juniors and two sophomores," he said. "I hope our inexperience doesn't hurt us too much."

Among the new starters is quarterback Kevin Brooks, a 6-2, 185-pound junior who quarterbacked the junior varsity last year to a 9-1 mark.

"Lakewood has a great tradition, but if we play our game and give 100 percent, we stay with them," he said. "Our only JV loss last year came against Lakewood, so we have a score to settle."

The edited version is clean and informative, but it doesn't capture the drama of the moment. So let's look for a new angle: Taft's youth going against Lakewood's tradition and talent? Anchor the story on one or two of the first-time Taft starters. Capture their anxiety and excitement. That's the real story.

FOR AS LONG AS HE can remember, junior Kevin Brooks has wanted to play varsity football for the Taft Tigers. Tonight, he'll get his chance, although he wishes it came against slightly less formidable competition: the Lakewood Panthers, the state's top-ranked team and defending state champions.

Like 11 of his teammates, Kevin is starting his first game.

"We've had good workouts, so I think we'll be ready," he said. "But we're all very aware of how good Lakewood is, year in and year out. We're not intimidated by them, but we respect them a whole lot."

That respect is based on a 48-21 varsity loss to them last year. Even the junior varsity, which Brooks quarterbacked to a 9-1 mark, fell to the Tigers, although by a 24-21 score on a hotly-contested pass interference call.

"We beat them, and the officials beat us," Brooks said. "Two of our touchdowns were called back, and they got a touchdown on a very questionable call late in the game to pull ahead.

THERE MUST BE A BOOK OR WEB SITE ON THAT

There probably is.
    A well-stocked journalism classroom should contain one or all of the following reference books:

■ A good dictionary is absolutely essential. It should be the most used book in your publications lab.

■ A thesaurus comes in handy, especially for headline writers. Roget's is the most popular, but the *Webster Book of Synonyms* is quite handy.

■ The *Associated Press Stylebook and Libel Manual*. Most students are shocked to discover the wonderful sections on sports, libel and caption writing.

■ Don't hesitate to call upon the reference librarians at your school or public libraries. They are willing and trained to check a specific fact. Get to know them.

■ Also, invaluable information is available on-line.

AMERICAN ASSOCIATION OF NEWSPAPER EDITORS (ASNE):
www.asne.org

POYNTER INSTITUTE FOR MEDIA STUDIES
www.poynter.org

AMERICAN PRESS INSTITUTE
www.journaliststoolbox.com

AMERICAN COPY EDITORS SOCIETY
www.copydesk.org

THE SLOT
www.theslot.com

THE ELEMENTS OF STYLE
www.bartleby.com

NO TRAIN, NO GAIN
www.notrain-nogain.org

AVOID BABY PUPPIES

And other words that repeat information. Here are a few examples:

■ absolutely sure
■ advance on
■ annual birthday
■ auction sale
■ brief moment
■ canine dog
■ close proximity
■ co-conspirator
■ crazy maniac
■ dead corpse
■ enter in
■ female cow
■ forward progress
■ filled to capacity
■ foot pedal
■ free gift
■ free of charge
■ gale of wind
■ Jewish synagogue
■ kneel down
■ maximum limit
■ mutual agreement
■ new recruit
■ next subsequent
■ past history
■ past precedent
■ peaceful tranquility
■ real experience
■ reason why
■ refer back
■ same identical
■ share together
■ sum total
■ totally abolished
■ tuna fish
■ verbal discussion
■ written down

❝ However, the reporter who thinks both verbally and visually would look for a descriptive anecdote to hammer home the point that violence happens to individuals and has little to do with statistics and surveys. ❞

▨▨▨▨▨▨▨▨▨▨

GET A REAL QUOTE

Editing weak content is an exercise in futility. Every story must have a theme thoughtfully conceived and an angle developed through observation and interviewing.

Take, for example, the following story about Jello wrestling, in which the principal participated and, as expected, was pretty much ganged up on. Everyone, it seemed, wanted to bury him.

But here's the quote:

"I felt like the event promoted school spirit. I wanted to see a positive image from everyone and for students to have fun with the other schools."

I doubt this quote reflects his thoughts as he was wiping Jello out of his eyes, hair and ears. I'd like to know what was really going through his mind.

I've thought about that game every day since, and I can't wait to get on the field against them Friday night."

■ EDIT FOR STYLE AND SUBSTANCE

On June 11, 1993, Texas newspapers reported that 83 percent of teachers responding to a survey by the Texas Federation of Teachers say they see a significant problem with student discipline and misbehavior. Summarized the *Dallas Morning News*: "More than 1,400 teachers from 200 school districts across the state painted a picture of schools rife with profanity, threats and disrespect of school rules."

Now, you want to update and localize this story for your school paper. A non-thinking student reporter would rehash the story from the daily newspaper, going so far as to attribute information to the newspaper itself. The lead to this story would have been, "Violence, particularly against teachers, is a growing problem in schools, according to a survey conducted by the Texas Federation of Teachers."

A more ambitious reporter might talk to school officials, but the story would still focus on the results of the survey. This lead might be "Students are relying on their fists and, in some cases, knives and, frighteningly enough, even guns to solve their disagreements with teachers, said school officials, who added that campus violence is reaching epidemic stages."

However, the reporter who thinks both verbally and visually would look for a descriptive anecdote to hammer home the point that violence happens to individuals and has little to do with statistics and surveys. The lead to this story might be:

JAMES MILLER WAS CALLING roll in his first-period history class last month when one of his 14-year-old students started shouting, throwing paper and walking around the room. The Stockard Middle School teacher's cue to send him to the office came when the boy pulled a marijuana cigarette out of his pocket.

But before Mr. Miller could fill out the principal's referral form, witnesses said, the youth punched him repeatedly in the face, slammed him against a chalkboard and knocked him out.

A classroom full of stunned eighth-graders looked on as the boy kicked the unconscious teacher in the chest and fled.

Mr. Miller was left with a broken nose, loose teeth, eye damage and bruises. He has been on medical leave since the attack Jan. 7 at the Oak Cliff school.

In Dallas and other urban school districts across the nation, the safety of teachers and principals is a growing concern.

In the 1991 fall semester alone, there were 47 assaults against Dallas Independent School District staff members, district security reports show. In each of the two previous school years, the total for both semesters was about 60 assaults.

– Anna Macias, *Dallas Morning News*

GRAMMATICAL LEADS

Because they often emphasize the news questions "why, how and so what," grammatical leads are excellent ways to open interpretive or analytical stories. They also provide a welcome relief from leads emphasizing who, what, when or where. Here are a few we recommend:

PARTICIPIAL PHRASE—A participial phrase begins with a present tense verb or past participle (a verb working as an adjective) and features action. It answers "why" or "how."

■ As a present participle:
Cashing in on his dreamy pout, droopy blue eyes and cute tush, Billy Cacophony pursued his dream of rock 'n roll stardom, despite his inability to sing or play a musical instrument. "Just look how far good looks and little else took Britney Spears and NSync," he reasoned.

■ As a past participle:
Stunned by the desecration of his beloved 1968 Mustang convertible, Principal Melvin Adams formed vigilante groups to track down and kill seniors responsible for the outrage.

GERUND PHRASE—Begins with a gerund (the "ing" form of a verb working as a noun) and features action or an interesting detail. For example: Jogging is boring.

Typing 30 words a minute with a minimum of three mistakes and without breaking a finger nail is the requirement for passing Mrs. Joyce Bigby's business class.

INFINITIVE PHRASE—Begins with "to" plus the simplist form of the verb and features purpose or dramatic action. As an adverb:
To maintain his last thread of sanity, Latin teacher John Vector dismissed class.
"The kids think they speak Latin in Latin America and that 'pro-bono' is a U2 groupie," he muttered in disgust.

As a noun:
To piggy-back on her brother's fame, looks and dance steps is Janet Jackson's recipe for success in the rough and tumble world of entertaining a crowd of ditzy girls.

PREPOSITIONAL PHRASE—Begins with a preposition and features one aspect of the story which the reporter feels deserves special attention.

After reading the staff editorial denouncing the administration's dress code, the principal tossed the student newspaper to the floor, stamped his feet and screamed, "Heads will roll."

NOUN CLAUSE—Features the substance of announcements, decisions or beliefs, and begins with that, how, why, whether, what or when.

That vocational education and all electives except foreign language be eliminated from the secondary curriculum was the proposal of a group led by Mortimer Huxley.

How the state plans to finance public secondary education in the next four years was the focus of a weeklong confrontation between the Governor and the Legislature.

TEMPORAL CLAUSE—Features the time element and begins with when, while, before, since or as soon as.

When students return to school next fall, they will encounter new discipline, parking and attendance codes.

While Principal Melvin Adams talked to freshmen about the evils of vandalism, six seniors were painting pink and green happy faces as well as creative graffiti on his prized new Dodge pickup.

WE WANT MORE LEADS LIKE THESE

CONCESSIVE CLAUSE
Begins with though or although and expresses difficulties to overcome or unusual circumstances.

Although he had failed to turn in a single assignment or pass a test, super jock Biff Stanley was genuinely shocked that he failed to pass World History. "But I'm the quarterback," he argued.

CONDITIONAL CLAUSE
Begins with if or unless and expresses speculative interest or condition.

If the prom were held tonight, students would have nothing to eat and would dance to whatever music could be generated from a boom box.

'Carefulyl editing ensures less erorrs'

1. There will be a meeting of the Albert Einstein High School Student Council on Monday afternoon at 2:30 P.M. during which they will discuss next month's elections.

The Student Council will discuss next month's elections at 2:30 p.m. Monday.

■ Lead with the subject. Get rid of the "to be" verb and padding.

2. Competing on November 24th in the Rotary Club's first annual speech contest will be Jim Daniels and Gloria Bailey.

Jim Daniels and Gloria Bailey will compete Nov. 24 in the Rotary Club speech contest.

■ Lead with the subjects, Jim and Gloria. Get rid of "to be" verb. Abbreviate November.

3. On Monday, Bill Thomas, who is a senior right here at Albert Einstein High School, took top honors in the Student Journalist of the Year Contest, that was sponsored by the Journalism Education Association.

Senior Bill Thomas won the Journalism Education Association's Student Journalist of the Year Contest, Monday.

■ Lead with Bill and follow with verb. Take out name of high school. Tighten up. Remember: give as much information in as few words as possible.

4. Our Fighting Nerds won the game that they played last Saturday against the hated Enrico Fermi Atoms by the final score of 3-0.

The Fighting Nerds drilled the Enrico Fermi Atoms, 3-0, Saturday.

■ Get rid of "our" and other editorial comments. If they won the game, they must have played it, and the score is the "final score."

5. When asked about the big game next week, Coach Gary Morgan exclaimed that he feels our

Varsity boys basketball team will be ready to battle their opponents, the Enrico Fermi Atoms.

Coach Gary Morgan said the boys basketball team will be ready for Fermi High.

Or: The boys basketball team are ready for the Fermi Atoms, coach Gary Morgan said.

■ Avoid "when asked." It's unnecessary padding. Use the verb "said." If he said something, then he probably believes it. Don't use "feels" as a synonym for believes or said. Remove the first person plural pronoun (our). On the matter of boys, boy's or boys': pick one and be consistent.

6. At the present time, the Albert Einstein High School American Studies class is studying the past history of World War II.

American Studies is reviewing the Great Depression and World War II.

■ If American Studies is studying, then they are studying at the present time. Again, get rid of school name. All history is past.

7. Last Saturday, the French club held a fund-raiser, the Club raised over $400.00. The money will be used to cover costs of a trip to Quebec over spring break. The fund-raiser is part of a two-year effort. The Club raised money by selling Krispy Kreme donuts.

To help pay for its spring trip to Quebec, the French Club raised more than $400 by selling Krispy Kreme doughnuts last week.

■ Use an infinitive phrase to answer the news question "how." Follow with noun (French Club) and verb (raised). Note: $400, not four hundred.

8. To end world hunger and paying its delinquent printing bills are the 2 main goals of this year's Newspaper Staff, according to Editor Luanne Jenkins.

he exclamated.

Ending world hunger and paying its printing bills are the newspaper staff's main goals, editor Luanne Jenkins said.

■ Use a gerund ("ending" and "paying") to answer "what." Newspaper staff need not be capitalized. Use "said." Another option: The newspaper staff's goals are ending world hunger and paying its printing bills, editor Luanne Jenkins said.

9. The Albert Einstein debate club competed in the Garden City Debate Tournament and placed fourth overall in the competition. The tournament was held Friday in Garden City. Joe Smith was named the tournament's top debater.

Joe Smith was named top debater, and the Debate Club placed fourth at the Garden City tournament, Friday.

■ Finishing first is bigger news than fourth. So lead with Joe. Note the comma after "debater." It separates parts of a compound sentence. Get rid of all the padding.

10. Jones said thirty one percent of his students are members of the democratic party, twenty two per cent were born in Oct., and another 6% were born in the northeast. "But they all love God, country, and apple pie," exclaimed he.

Jones said 31 percent of his students are members of the Democratic Party, 22 percent were born in October, and 6 percent were born in the Northeast. "But they all love God, country and apple pie," he added.

■ Write numbers 10 and above as numerals unless they're the first word in a sentence. "Percent" is one word, and don't use the % sign. Spell out months and capitalize names of political parties. You don't need a comma before the last item in a sequence, so remove the comma after "country." Nouns precede verbs: he said, not "said he."

11. The Albert Einstein High School Student Council held their first meeting at 2:00 p.m. Wednesday afternoon in the library. At the meeting, the members of the council voted to cancel the homecoming dance. They voted to do this because of low attendance at the dance the last 2 years. The dance was originally scheduled for the first of November.

Due to low attendance the last two years, the Student Council cancelled the Nov. 1 homecoming dance.

■ Get to the heart of the news. Open with a causal clause that answers "why" and follow with who (Student Council), what (cancelled), when (Nov. 1) and what (homecoming dance).

12. The twenty one year old English teacher that won $2,300,000 in last week's state lottery commented incredibly that she would not quit her job. "This won't effect my life at all," she said.

The 21-year-old English teacher who won $2.3 million in last week's state lottery said she would not quit her job, despite her new-found wealth. "This won't affect my life at all," she said.

■ Style: 21-year-old, $2.3 million. Use the verb said. Remove editorial comments (incredibly). Also, a person is a "who," not a "that." A fire hydrant is a "that." Affect is a verb. Effect is a noun.

13. The Albert Einstein High School Band will be hosting their annual Spaghetti Dinner Tuesday. The dinner will be held Tuesday evening in the school cafeteria from 6:00 p.m. to 9:00 p.m.

The band will host its annual spaghetti dinner from 6-9 p.m. Tuesday in the cafeteria.

■ Lead with band, then verb. Singular subject (band) gets a singular antecedent (it). Put time elements together. Note: time precedes date, and it's 6 p.m., not 6:00 p.m.

BOB'S 10 TOP PET PEEVES

If you want to get on my bad side, just do one of these:

■ Abuse AP Style rules dealing with numbers.

■ Place verbs before nouns for no good reason.

■ Separate nouns from verbs for no good reason.

■ Misspell separate, believe or surprise, or confuse its for it's or who's for whose.

■ Use a synonym for the verb "said" for no good reason.

■ Use passive tense for no good reason.

■ Use "that" as a personal pronoun for a person. People are "who" — not "that." Lawn chairs are "that."

■ Put the school name or school initials in a story or headline for no good reason.

■ Refer to a band, squad or team as a "they."

■ Use first or second person in news or feature story.

■ **FIND THE HEART OF THE STORY**

So again, editing is more than searching for errors in facts, style, grammar and punctuation. It's searching for the heart and soul of the story, and a good editor often sends the reporter back into the field for better quotes, an interesting anecdote or descriptive details.

Journalists must become familiar with the many good books on editing. Both students and teachers should have at arm's length a copy of *The Elements of Style* by Strunk and White and an Associated Press stylebook. Traditional textbooks contain a chapter on editing and all of the horrors of using "which" when you meant "that," so we won't rehash every danger here, except to note a few essential guidelines:

■ Make certain the reporter has answered all news questions. All news questions may not be equal, but all must be answered somewhere in the story, better sooner than later, especially if the time element is in the future. If your opening sentence is "The annual choir concert will be in Hogg Auditorium Monday," make sure you tack on the time. "...in Hogg Auditorium at 7 p.m. Monday."

"When" news leads are rarely appropriate, but readers should expect the reporter to tell them the time and date of an event. Note: AP style requires time to precede date: 7 p.m. Monday rather than Monday at 7 p.m.

■ Look carefully at verb tenses. Many students mix present and past tense freely. For example, one attribution may state, "John says." and the next, "Mary said." Be consistent.

■ Don't trust the computer's spell check program. Keystroke errors can turn a sentence such as "Mothers use doctor" into "Mothers sue doctor." Big difference. One of my favorite slips: a headline that announced that two students had spent the summer working as "Candystrippers" at a local hospital. I think they meant "Candystripers."

■ Read critically. In an article about a student suspended for perpetrating some prank on the school, the reporter wrote, "The student was suspended infinitely."

That's a long time. The reporter probably meant "indefinitely."

In another case, a reporter interviewed a student about a censorship issue. The student was a cheerleader, but that had no relevance to the free press issue. Still, the story contained the following line: "Being a cheerleader, press rights are important to me," Suzy said.

First, it's a dumb quote and should have been taken out of the story. Then, you have to wonder how being a cheerleader makes Suzy especially sensitive to freedom of expression issues.

Finally, one reporter wrote, "Michael Jordan was his boy hood idol."

Was Jordan a child hoodlum?

■ Double check the spelling of every name. You can't imagine how many times a simple name like my own has been butchered. The worst was when I received a letter—no joke— from my own dear mother, addressed to "Bobbie" Hawthorne.

It just goes to show: anyone can make a mistake. Don't take chances. All factual errors are not equal. Misspelled names are the gravest of all mistakes.

■ Make sure your verbs support your sentences. The verb is the most important word in the sentence, and no amount of padding sentences with adjectives and adverbs can replace the imaginative verb.

Rather than, "He *slowly drank* his cola," consider "He *sipped* his Diet Coke." Better still, "He *nursed* his Diet Coke."

■ Make certain the antecedent agrees with its pronoun. Too often, students write, "The team began their season."

Team is an it—not a they. A squad is an it. So is a band, a club, a council and any other collective body of persons. The cheerleaders are a they. The National Honor Society is an it.

■ Watch for misplaced modifiers. "The administration has been working on developing a humane method of penalizing ineligible players for approximately eight years."

Penalizing players for eight years sounds anything but humane. A good editor will make this correction: "The administration has worked for approximately eight years to

WHAT CAUSES WORDINESS

PASSIVE VERBS
Joan is a clarinet player.
Joan plays clarinet.

There were two small dogs barking at the mailman.
Two Chihuahuas barked at the mailman.

Junior Joan Milbrett will be competing in the National Spelling Bee.
Junior Joan Milbrett will compete in the National Spelling Bee.

FANCY WORDS
Benny matriculated to Austin.
Benny moved to Austin.

EMPTY WORDS (REALLY, VERY, SEVERAL, MANY, ETC.)
Several students on the newspaper staff worked really, really hard for a couple of days to build the web site for the *Crier*, the school's student newspaper.

Four sophomores worked three days to build the student newspaper's Web site.

STATEMENTS OF THE OBVIOUS
It's football season again. This year's WHS football team will open season play next Friday against our hate rivals, the Seaweed High Sandfleas.

The football team expects to avenge last year's 21-0 loss to arch-rival Seaweed Friday in the season opener.

ADJECTIVES & ADVERBS
The Japanese car rolled slowly down the street.
The Lexus inched down the street.

PREPOSITIONAL PHRASES
Milton went down to the store on the corner.
Milton visited the corner store.

UNNECESSARY PRONOUNS
State Rep. Pat Robinson said that she would not seek reelection.
State Rep. Pat Robinson said she would not seek reelection.

SYNONYMS FOR "SAID"
"I hate oatmeal," Dudley exclaimed.
"I hate oatmeal," Dudley said.

"WHEN ASKED..."
When asked about the loss to arch-rival Seaweed High in the opening game, coach Joe Studmaker said, "I'm still sick about the loss."

"I'm still sick about the loss," Studmaker said.

REPETITION
Mr. Lundgren's pet tarantula was able to make his escape.
Mr. Lundgren's pet tarantula escaped.

SOFT TRANSITIONS
Supt. Jeff Archer announced that he has suspended 31 seniors for involvement in a widely reported off-campus hazing incident.
"I am announcing the suspension of 31 seniors," he said. "Given the egregious nature of the conduct depicted in the videotapes, I'm not sure mere suspension is punishment enough."

Supt. Jeff Archer suspended 31 seniors for involvement in a widely reported off-campus hazing incident.
"Given the egregious nature of the conduct depicted in the videotapes," Archer said. "I'm not sure mere suspension is punishment enough."

CLOSE ISN'T CLOSE ENOUGH

Phonics is nice, but there's no excuse for misspelling these words:

- absence
- accommodate
- analysis
- cemetery
- congratulations
- decathlon
- eligible
- embarrassing
- exaggerate
- familiar
- gauge
- harassment
- inoculate
- judgment
- license
- mathematics
- millennium
- minuscule
- misspell
- noticeable
- occurred
- occurrence
- pastime
- perseverance
- personnel
- persuade
- privilege
- questionnaire
- receive
- relieve
- separate
- sophomore
- supersede
- surprise
- unanimous
- weird
- yield

❝ Rather than simply "editing" stories, coach your reporters in a one-on-one fashion. Talk to them. Be available throughout the reporting process. Before the first draft, let the reporter tell you what the story's about. After the first draft, let the reporter suggest how it can be tighter, better organized, more descriptive. After publication, discuss strengths and weaknesses. ❞

AVOID BEING THE WORLD'S WORST EDITOR

Live by the following rules, and you'll find journalism to be a lonely experience.

GOING IT ALONE. Working with people is as important as working with copy.

REVISING IT YOURSELF. It may be faster, but you're better off letting reporters rewrite it themselves.

EDITING WITHOUT READING. Read it all the way through first.

CHANGING WITHOUT CONSULTING. Writers organize stories for a reason. Editing without asking can destroy a story.

EDITING IN WORDS THAT ARE INCONSISTENT with the style, tone, rhythm or mood of the story.

PLAYING BULLY. Work with reporters. Be a leader, not a boss.

BOGGING DOWN IN THE STYLEBOOK. Don't edit only for mechanical precision. Edit also for theme, focus, organization, readability, thoroughness and accuracy. Ask: What's missing? What's wasted? What's confusing?

OVERPLAYING YOUR HUNCHES. Avoid making too many changes for which you cannot cite a specific rule or offer a succinct explanation.

"It just doesn't sound good" is a weak explanation. There should be a reason. This is a subjective business so realize that you don't have to win every time.

develop a humane method of penalizing ineligible players."

■ Use your own words. I can still recall an article announcing the separation of Princess Diana and Prince Charles, in which a reporter for a Texas newspaper wrote:

CHARLES WILL LIVE during the week at Clarence House . . . . On weekends, he will continue to repair to Highrove, the country mansion and estate in the Gloucestershire Hills outside London.

To repair? Texans repair their pickup trucks, not themselves. Drop the pretensions. If you mean begin, don't say commence. If you mean use, don't say utilize. If you mean hurry, don't say expedite. Don't be a snob.

■ Make certain the tone matches the content of the story. A serious topic demands a serious, sober lead. A story about a fund drive for African famine victims began, "Catching on to the latest trend is something everyone seems to know how to do, and journalism students are no exception. They started a two-week money drive with the hope of raising a substantial sum of money for Ethiopia and other poverty-stricken African nations."

Famine isn't a trend so to classify it as something like wearing your jeans backward shows the writer is trivializing famine.

■ Say what you mean, and mean what you say. Syndicated columnist Molly Ivins wrote about the time her newspaper published the following line: "State Sen. Roy Goodman, R-Manhattan, heir to the Ex-Lax fortune and a usually regular Republican, voted with Democrats Tuesday night . . . "

■ IT'S A TEAM THING

Editing is not solely the responsibility of the editors. Reporters must make every effort to see that their stories are factually, grammatically and stylistically correct.

Good editing starts with the assignment. Too often, a reporter has no idea what the editor wanted—because the editor never said and the reporter never asked. It should be no surprise when the reporter fails to give the editor what he or she wanted.

If editor and reporter agree from the outset on the purpose of the story, the selection of sources and how the story will be used, the final editing becomes a process of picking nits—with the understanding, of course, that any nit can make or break a story.

COMPARE & CONTRAST

FIRST DRAFT

The summer after my sophomore year, a group of fellow students and myself planned a vacation to travel through several countries in Europe for two weeks. Our parents left us in the radical and enlightened hands of my History teacher Bob Kuhl.

His name suits him perfectly. He had always caused a little controversy at my school. He had long hair, he was anti-Republican (and anti-Democrat for that matter), he sometimes wore tribal garb from some of the many places he'd visited (these customary ensembles sometimes resembled dresses), he never taught us straight from the book, and frankly, he was smarter than any of our other teachers or parents. Coming from a school where the president's daughters attended and everyone drove an SUV, his political views and insightfulness were misunderstood, and at the same time, he frowned upon our shallow behavior.

Quite honestly, I don't know what was going through his mind when he decided to escort 16 kids between the ages of 16 and 18 to Europe when some of what I believed to be the most immature and ignorant kids from my school would be accompanying us.

SECOND DRAFT

The summer after my sophomore year, I signed up to travel across Europe for two weeks as part of one of those "Summer in Europe" programs that are a rite of passage for suburban kids like myself. I wanted to go in large part because the chaperone would be my history teacher, Bob Kuhl, and his girlfriend.

Mr. Kulh's name suits him perfectly — cool. He's a rebel. He has long hair. He's virulently anti-Republican (and mildly anti-Democrat for that matter). He occasionally wears native garb from Nigeria or Patagonia or Catalonia or one of the other places he'd visited, even if it more closely resembles a dress than a shirt and pants. He teaches from the heart and the mind, never from the state-adopted textbook, and frankly, he is smarter than any of our other teachers or parents.

As a teacher at the school the Bush twins attended, where students were just as likely as not to drive a SUV or new Ford 150, Mr. Kulh's political and social observations and opinions were often misunderstood. Some people — especially the Rush Limbaugh dittoheads — think he is a commie. Trying to teach a class of 16-year-olds who believe Tarrytown is reality must have been torture.

So I can't imagine what was going through his mind when he volunteered to escort to Europe 16 kids between the ages of 16 and 18, several of whom were without a doubt among the most immature and shallow from Austin High, who would be far more interested in Lansome than the Lourve.

◄ Here are the first three paragraphs of a piece written by Sarah Hawthorne, my daughter, during her senior year at Austin High School. While she rarely asked me to edit her writing, on this occasion and for whatever reason, she asked me to read this essay. I enjoyed the first draft very much, but (she'll tell you, there's always a "but...") we worked together to simplify the opening sentence, add more visual details and observations, a touch of alliteration and create a more natural flow.

Photo by **CHRIS FALLON**
Richmond High School, Richmond, IN

FEATURE STORIES

13

PUT IT IN THE YEARBOOK

Photographs alone cannot tell the story of the year. Nor can infographics and alternative copy. The yearbook can only capture the sights and sounds of the year if it contains vivid, detailed reporting and writing.

Several years ago, I presented a writing lecture to yearbook editors on the next to the last day of a summer workshop. The three days prior to my lecture had been devoted to developing theme packets, building ladders and learning design. I began with a basic editing exercise, assuming that editors edit and could use some polish doing so. Apparently not. The editors acted as if I had asked them to clean a chicken coop.

"We really don't edit copy," a young lady told me.

"Well, what does a yearbook editor do?" I asked.

"I — we — organize information," she replied.

"And what do you organize?" I answered. "Socks? Clothes hangers? Paper clips?"

No response.

"You organize words and pictures," I said. "Words and pictures. Facts and images about this year, this school, this group of people at this special moment in their lives. And because you organize these facts, you must think journalistically. You're not creating a work of fiction here."

I then panned the class and asked, "You do think of yourself as journalists, don't you?"

Again, no response.

"Well, don't you?," I repeated in my best I'm-about-to-get-cheesed-off voice. "How many of you think of yourself as a journalist?"

Not one of the 45 students in the yearbook editors' class on the next to the final day of a summer workshop raised a hand.

■ TELL THE STORY OF THE YEAR

Why do I mention this? Because too many yearbooks have released themselves from the obligation to report and write on the flimsy excuse that they're not really producing journalism but rather a picture or a memory book. And no one reads all that copy anyway. People who buy yearbooks — I guess we can't call them "readers" — just want flashy graphics and 20 snapshots per spread of classmates gawking at the camera.

I disagree.

Whether the yearbook is a social activity at your school, purely extracurricular, or five full-credit courses in the language arts curriculum, the yearbook should be journalistic. And yes, a lot yearbooks are producing outstanding coverage and writing. Still, it must be stressed: it's impossible to tell the story of the year unless the book is journalistic, and it's impossible to be journalistic by running spread after spread of lists, quote blocks, fill-in-the-blanks, Dewer's profiles and endless lists containing thoroughly predictable data.

STYLE TIP

Spell out percent as one word. Don't write, "The stock market fell by 20 per cent." Or "The stock market fell by 20%."

Write, "The stock market fell by 20 percent."

■ What did you do over spring break?

Slept. Caught up on homework. Went skiing. Went to the beach.

■ What did you do at the beach?

Swam. Got sunburned. Got attacked by a shark. Tried to pick up girls. Couldn't. Had blood all over me from the shark bite.

Oh my.

■ YEARBOOK IS JOURNALISM

Having a journalistic publication — newspaper or yearbook — means you cover news. Reporters choose the best way to tell the story. It may be a list. It may be a quote block. It may be a story that analyzes how Fact A produced Result B and Unintended Consequence C. It may be a combination of all three.

As for the charge that students don't read yearbook copy, who can blame them? I find it interesting that some experts consistently justify the latest graphics *ESPN Magazine* can offer on the contention that students demand the most sophisticated design, and yet dumb down the book verbally because the same students are too lazy or dim or both to read a five-paragraph block of copy.

Well, the problem isn't with the reader. It's the five-paragraph block of copy that boils down all the excitement, anxiety, bravado, stupidity, charm, grace, dopiness, innocence, hilarity, boredom, anger and joy of the high school experience into inspiring statements such as:

TRYING TO MAKE THE WORLD a better place to live was the goal of the Key Club. Members made the local community a better place to live by conducting food drives, cleaning up vacant lots, helping needy children and visiting elderly citizens."

Or:

"EACH OCTOBER, students swarm the halls and neighborhoods ringing doorbells, raffling tickets and washing cars in an effort to raise funds for club activities, and this year was no different!"

Sound familiar?

Or:

"COMMUNITY SERVICE unites people together. I take great pride in giving back a little to those less fortunate than myself. I feel good about helping people. It's amazing how giving up just a little bit of my time and effort can make someone else's life a whole lot better."

Or:

"WE HAD A LOT OF FUN washing cars, except on that Saturday when the cold front came through. Unfortunately, I lost two fingers to frostbite. But it was worth it because we raised enough money to go to the National Milk Museum in Winnebago, Wisconsin!"

Who's going to read this? No one, not even the writer. It isn't written to be read. It's written to fill a hole on a spread. It's written to fulfill a design requirement.

It doesn't have to be this way. Like student newspapers, yearbooks don't have to pretend they're dishing up a constant stream of late-breaking news. Their content should be features — narratives that engage the reader's senses and emotions. And the best way to do that is to attach a face to the copy. Personalize the story. Make it about someone in particular.

If you're writing about the Key Club, don't dwell on the purpose of the club and rehash its list of goals and achievements. It's not a big secret that the purpose of Key Club is to serve the community. Ten, 20, 30 years from now, your classmates won't crawl up in bed with their yearbooks, flip through the club section and ask, "Honey, what was the purpose of the Key Club?"

"Wasn't it all them do-gooders? Seems I recall them always running around, trying to make things better. Whatever happened to those people?"

"They all went to law school. Ironic, huh?"

The point is this: readers know the purpose of the Key Club, the student council and the rest of the clubs. They know that the choir sang songs, the French Club studied French, the swimmers swam and the debaters debated. They know pep rallies and proms were held, that Shakespeare was taught in English, that kids worked after school, and that journalists faced deadlines. They know the surface-level data. So, there's no point in

LEAD WRITING POINTERS

- Open with a clear statement that gives the reader new information. Don't state the obvious.
- The opening statement should focus on the most interesting aspect of the story.
- Keep your sentences short and simple. Nouns precede verbs.
- Use colorful, precise, visual nouns.
- Use active, sensory verbs that describe specific action. "Trudged" rather than "walked." "Jabbered" rather than "talked quickly."
- Avoid beginning with "a," "an" or "the."
- Avoid "this year," the name, initials and/or mascot of the school.
- Write in third person generally. Avoid first person plural (we, us, our). Don't editorialize.
- The lead should introduce a theme,and the remainer of the story should develop it. Go for depth, not width.

publishing a story like this:

TRYING TO MAKE THE WORLD a better place to live was the goal of the Key Club. Members made the local community a better place to live by conducting food drives, cleaning up vacant lots, helping needy children and visiting elderly citizens.

"I am glad that I was a member of the Key Club," senior Cindy Thomas said. "We learned a lot about caring for our community, and we had a lot of fun doing it."

■ CAPTURE THE DETAILS

Such superficial coverage trivializes the real contributions made to the community by Key Club members. Now, it is possible that your school's Key Club contributed little or nothing to the community. Fine. Don't write about them.

But if the Key Club had a positive impact on the school and community, then show this in human terms. Find out what it was really like to be a member of the group. Attend at least one Key Club function that doesn't include the reading of the minutes. If the club visited elderly citizens at a local retirement center, tag along. Go the first time just to watch and listen. Pay attention to little details. Which student was merely going through the motions, patted a couple of hands, endured one or two stories, then bolted for the exit?

Which students really cared, took the time to listen, even if the story-teller lost his place from time to time or seems to have trouble remembering entire decades? Whose body language said "This is neat!" and whose said "Get me outta here!"

If possible, just sit and watch. Take a few notes, but for the most part, let the experience sink in.

Then, focus on one or two subjects and move in close. Listen to conversations. Pay attention to sights and sounds: The old woman, what was she wearing? What were the color of her eyes? How smooth were her hands? How sharp was her memory? How precise were her words? What did she talk about?

Take it all in. What did the place smell like? Then, ask yourself, "What is this story really about?" Figure that out.

"Ultimately, kids join the Key Club not to pad their resumes but to really bring a little joy to someone else's day."

Now, illustrate this in human terms. Attach a face and a personality to the story. And find a way to show rather than tell. For example:

ALONE IN THE SHREDDED back seat of the old yellow school bus, senior Nicole Moore cries, her tears trickling down her cheeks, dripping onto her brick red Jansport backpack. She holds a white lace hankerchief. It had belonged to her grandmother, who died two years ago.

"Visiting the nursing home is always so difficult because it reminds me of my grandmother," Nicole says.

She and 12 other Key Club members spend at least one afternoon per month at the Hillsdale Retirement Center, where for two or three hours they serve refreshments, chat, sometimes play checkers or dominos. Nicole works the room like a pro,

STRONG COPY REKINDLES FADING MEMORIES

Basically, a yearbook is a picture book though it serves other functions. The visual appeal does not mean that writing can be ignored. Much to the contrary.

It puts an even greater onus on the reporter to write with clarity, precision and conciseness. Over time, readers will forget names and dates. The details of the photos will soften, and the writing will fill in the blanks. So the precious space dedicated to copy must be packed with details: sights, sounds, emotions.

QUICK TIP

In telling a story, consider:

◼ Framing. Is it the aim of the writer to tell the story through the old woman's point of view or the Key Club member's?

◼ Voice. As a writer, do you sound sarcastic, cynical, melancholy, melodramatic or pompous? Your writing will reveal a voice that tells the reader, "This is so sad" or "This is too dumb for words."

◼ Tone. What is the mood of the story? What are the atmospheric details: somber or giggly? How formal are your words? Is he a dunce or a chowderhead? Did he pry open the door, or jimmy it open?

pouring tea, serving cookies and making small talk with the old folks.

But she reserves most of her time for one special friend.

"I met Mrs. (Anna) Segretti on my first visit to the center, and we had an immediate connection," Nicole says. "Her husband died in World War II and she raised six children alone, working as a nurse. She put every one of her children through college and then went to college herself. She's lived the most amazing life."

Nicole often brushes her friend's hair, which is mostly gray but retains enough hint of red to suggest that years ago, she must have been stunningly beautiful. Even today, she resembles a very old Holly Hunter.

"She likes to tell me about her children, how proud she is of them," Nicole says. "And she listens to me, lets me tell her about my problems. I talk to her about my parents, about boys. I tell her things I can't tell anyone else. She reminds me so much of my grandmother."

With that, her eyes swelled and glisten, and she turns away.

This story shows what it means to be a member of the Key Club. In 25 years, Nicole is going to read it and she is going to cry. People who don't know Nicole, don't know Anna Segretti, who weren't members of the Key Club might feel a little lump in their throats, too.

So, what's the difference between the story above and most copy, yearbook or newspaper? It attempts to inform and entertain, which should be the goal of all journalistic writing. It tells readers something they didn't already know. Like all good writing, it incorporates literary devices such as plot, character development, setting and drama, yet it's a piece of non-fiction. It's accurate in tone, detail and context. Most importantly, it uses a narrative to drive home its theme.

This approach can work for almost any story. Say, for example, you want to write about students and their jobs. The typical feature will sound something like this:

JOBS ARE AN important part of many students lives. They work after school and on weekends to earn money for cars, college or just pocket change. Whatever the reason, students claim that jobs are important.

"My parents don't have a lot of money, so I work three days a week and one day each weekend," senior Randy Dortsch said.

Other students say it is hard to juggle jobs with after-school activities such as cheerleading, band and sports. "Because I am a cheerleader, I have to work hard to keep up with my grades and work on top of that," sophomore Cathleen Fulham said.

Regardless of the situation, students sacked groceries, pumped gas, delivered pizza and flipped hamburgers to raise much needed cash.

I can't imagine anyone reading it. A few people might scan it. Randy and Cathleen will be pleased to see their names in print, but that's about the extent of it, which is sad because Randy and Cathleen probably have a couple of interesting stories to tell. If I were writing this story, I'd focus on Randy, get to know him. I might visit him one night at work. Get a feel for the place.

Later, I'd talk to him about his job. What does he like about it? What does he hate? I'd ask him to describe the worst day on the job. What is your boss like? How do you juggle working 20-25 hours a week and maintain a 4.0 grade point average? Why do you work so hard? Is there a reason?

Finally, I might ask Randy if he's a little bitter that he is missing much of his senior year.

I'm sure each answer will prompt another question or two. So let's assume he answers all my questions, and that I've done a reasonable amount of reporting, that is, visiting him at work and home, observing and listening. My story might go like this:

IT'S 3 A.M., and senior Randy Dortsch is slumped over the oak desk in his room, surrounded by posters of Tim Duncan and Shakira, cramming for a physics final the next day. He's been studying since 11, first Huxley's *Brave New World*, then

AVOID COMPOSITES.

SHE INHALED deeply and tried to relax her muscles. She uncurled her sweaty palms and warmed up the scales mentally. The curtain opened and the lights shined brightly on her face. The accompanying music began. She counted the measures, took one more deep breath and belted out her solo.

He clutched his instrument in his shaking hands. His eyes scanned over the sheet music one more time. The tempo to the song ran through his mind, and he could almost feel the beat before it started. He raised his trumpet to his lips, took a deep breath and played on the downbeat.

This is a nice lead. It perfectly describes the butterfies that students experience just moments prior to taking the stage.

The problem? This lead isn't about real people. It's a composite, a fancy generalization.

The next paragraph of the story states, "Whether singing or playing an instrument, fine arts performance classes that included choir, band and orchestra, allowed students to express themselves."

The story continues with the traditional quote/transition formula. It flows in a logical order. It's well edited. It's a nice piece of writing. But I never learn anything about the girl with the sweaty palms or the boy with the shaking hands. I believe you can do a better job of explaining the purpose of art in school by showing how it has affected one or two students' lives, by going deeper, getting inside their heads, discovering their motivations, their fears and their triumphs.

Write about real people — not composites.

Spanish and now physics. He had hoped to put in at least an hour on an essay he needs to write for his application to Iowa State, but it'll have to wait until tomorrow — after work. It's due next Thursday, so he has the weekend.

Like many seniors, Randy leaves straight from school, three days a week, for work, in this case, at Tarrytown Pharmacy, where he stocks shelves and runs the cash register until 9, then helps with clean-up. He rarely leaves until 9:30, then rushes home for a quick bite — his mom often brings his favorite microwave pepperoni pizza to his room. He catches a few minutes of Sports Center and then, around 10:20, hits the books.

"I'm a little driven," he said. "I have to work, and I have to make good grades. I've pretty much pushed everything else aside. I have no social life to speak of. I would have liked to be on the debate team this year, but it takes up too much time. I know that I'll need good grades and a lot of money to get into ISU. I'm hoping for a scholarship of some kind, but if I don't get one, I plan to make enough money this year to pay most of my first year."

Randy's parents are divorced. His mother is a personnel director at a downtown bank. He hasn't seen his dad in years. He has two siblings: a 15-year-old sister, Hanna, and an 11-year-old brother, James.

"I don't see the family as often as I'd like to," Randy said. "Next year, I'll be out of here and my brother and sister will remember me as just the guy who stayed up too late.

"I work hard, but not as hard as my mom," Randy added. "Hanna and James will need her help more than I do. I'm a little jealous of those kids whose parents have a lot of money, who don't have to worry about paying for college or a car. I wish I didn't have to work this hard, but I do. I'm cool with that."

I know a lot of kids like Randy. They deserve to have a similar story written about them. They'll read it, and everyone else will, too. You just did. Why? Because the story deals with human spirit, determination and grit. It isn't

ESTA LETRA ES TERRIBLE

Does this lead tell you anything you didn't already know or could figure out?

The purpose of the Spanish Club is to provide an opportunity and a forum for students who speak Spanish or are learning to speak Spanish to get together and speak Spanish.

How can you avoid such trite copy? By knowing about the subject fully before you begin writing, by searching for the most interesting and important information to pack into the lead and by empathizing with your readers so that you can provide them with the information they need and in the form and tone that they will value.

about an abstraction: students with jobs. It's about something concrete: one extraordinary young man whose situation is not unlike that of thousands of high school seniors across America. By telling the story of one, we tell the story of them all.

This style of writing is demanding. It requires a considerable investment in time — interviewing sources, gathering details, writing, editing, rewriting and proofing.

The payoff is a piece of writing that will be enjoyed forever. It's a source of pleasure for the reader and pride for the reporter. Twenty five years from now, I doubt anyone will care whether the design of the book is six columns or 212 grids. But no one ever forgets a well-written story. It possesses a timeless quality all of its own.

■ A PERSONAL STORY

In high school, I was a starting defensive back and wide receiver for the White Oak Roughnecks, a 13-1 state semifinalist from Northeast Texas.

I hadn't thought much about this until my local newspaper, the *Austin American-Statesman*, published a story about the Pflugerville Panthers, one in a series of articles about championship teams from Central Texas. Pflugerville, then a small farming community north of Austin but now a suburb, is the reason we weren't state finalists. They beat us, 7-6, on a bitterly cold December night at Wildcat Stadium in Temple, a city of 70,000 located half-way between Austin and Waco.

It broke our hearts. I can still remember how we sat in our uniforms and cried—even Danny Denton, Mr. Cool—as our coaches treaded their way through the crowded dressing room after the game to try to console us. I'm certain two or three of them were as broken up as we were.

But time and life go on, and, as I said, I only think about that game when I'm forced to drive by Wildcat Stadium—it's right on Interstate 35—en route to Dallas or to visit my family back in East Texas. Seeing that stadium is like looking at a tomb.

The story in the *American-Statesman*

CAPTURE THE BIG MOMENTS

Yearbook coverage should focus on highs and lows. Show the connection between extremes:

- School/non-school
- Work/play
- Friends/enemies
- Sanctioned/non-sanctioned
- Organized/disorganized
- Formal/informal
- Alone/in the mob
- What we wanted/what we got
- What we loved/what we hated
- What we deserved/what we received
- What we felt/what we showed

brought back a lot of memories. The reporter, George Brazeale, interviewed Pflugerville players and coaches, who gave the game a sense of historical perspective. It was as cold to them as it was to us. They were as thrilled in victory as we were devastated in defeat. Strangely enough, they said they more vividly remembered their win over us than their 45-7 loss to Sonora the following week in the state finals—just as I have over these years preferred to remember our come-from-behind win over Barbers Hill the week before we lost to Pflugerville.

So what?

The reporter's article reminded me of the power of writing to rekindle emotions, and it made me wonder why yearbook reporting—particularly sports reporting—doesn't attempt to concentrate on the emotion-packed moments of teenage life. Certainly sports embodies and magnifies all of the trials of adolescence, but coverage too often consists of a collection of data: scores, season records and obligatory, as well as largely meaningless, quotes that never capture the essence of either a game or season.

For example:

THE FRESHMAN BASEBALL TEAM ended its

season with a 3-16 record. The district record was 1-11. Thirteen boys comprised this team with four managers, two bat girls and two coaches.

"We had a rough season, but we played hard and never gave up," said coach Bill Thibodeaux.

The highlight of the year was a season-ending 3-2 win over Clear Creek, and the low point was the 22-0 loss to Madison.

"Even though we didn't win a lot of games, we had fun," catcher Orlando Abieta said. "I'm looking forward to next season."

Didn't exactly raise the hair on my neck. How about you? Probably not. Successful copy should give meaning to the facts, the data. It should do more than tell the reader what happened. It should show why and how the events happened. It should capture what it was about the game or the season that the players and spectators will most likely remember.

How is this done? Stop me if you've heard this before: through observation, interviewing and interpretation. Compare the above story to this one:

CATCHER ORLANDO ABIETA figured he had nothing to lose, so in his final appearance at the plate, he decided to switch from batting right-handed to left. With his freshman teammates down 2-0 in the bottom of the last inning to Clear Creek but with runners on the corners, Abieta took a first strike call, then swung wildly at a high, outside pitch.

"Time out!" coach Bill Thibodeux called and called Abieta to his side.

"Orlando, we can tie this thing up with a single," Thibodeux said. "You sure you want to stay on that side of the plate?"

"Yes sir," Abieta answered. "I can hit this guy."

"All right," Thibodeaux said and gave him a soft tap with a closed fist on his right shoulder. "Go get 'em."

Abieta took the next pitch low and outside, another just inside. Then, with a 2-and-2 count, he lined a fastball down the first base line that rolled to the fence, scoring Sergio Cardenas from third

and Adam Tyler from first. As the right fielder relayed the ball to the second baseman, Abieta rounded third and headed toward home.

"We'd blown so many games this year, I figured this was a chance to win one," he said. The pitch from second rolled left of homeplate, and Abieta slid under the catcher's mitt, scoring the winning run that ended a 12-game losing streak and gave his teammates, coaches and the 15 or 20 hardcore fans a reason to celebrate the end of what had otherwise been a difficult season.

How does a reporter get a story like this? First, he or she goes to games, pays attention to the players and the drama, of rising action, peak moments and reflection, not just the numbers. You can crunch the details — scores, win/loss record and statistics —into a sidebar. The copy should tell the story of the season — in this case, of how championship moments are gleaned from a losing season.

The same is true for the winning team. It is not enough to write, "The team surpassed its wildest dreams." You must provide specific examples and poignant anecdotes that make an abstract statement such as "They surpassed their wildest dreams" real and meaningful.

For example, which of the two stories more successfully captures the essence of victory?

PLAYING IN NEAR-FREEZING weather, the Vikings stopped a late fourth quarter drive to preserve a 17-14 victory over Jefferson in the state championship game. The Vikings finished the season with a 14-0-1 record, the best mark in the school's history.

"The kids surpassed all of our expectations," coach Ernest Buckner said. "More than a few times, they could have given up, but each time, they reached down deep and found the character to win."

The season opened with a 20-17 win over Roosevelt, followed by consecutive wins over Glenview, 14-10; Kennedy, 28-24; and Taft, 17-7, with the lone blotch on an otherwise perfect record being a 24-24 tie with Parkcrest.

BRING US AN ORDER OF POWERFUL WRITING ON THE SIDE

While a main copy block may deal with homecoming or prom, the sidebar may deal with one person's perspective of the event. Or it may deal with an unusual element of the story.

For example, in addition to the major copy block about the championship basketball game, the sidebar may explain how the top scorer played in great pain with a strained knee.

As in all writing, the reporter must isolate a specific theme for the story, develop an interesting angle, gather information, organize the information, write, proof, edit and rewrite.

That's a lot of work for a three- or five-paragraph story. But there's no other way.

The remainder of the story lists scores, statistics and highlights without attempting to humanize the story other than attaching a name to a number. All data is mulched into a single story, as though it were all equally important. Meanwhile, we get no sense of who these young men were or of what they experienced. We know only that they won a bunch of games.

Chances are, the typical yearbook reader already knows that.

Now, consider the following story:

TWENTY MINUTES after the game had ended, they remained on the frozen turf of Remington field, players and their girlfriends, coaches and parents, hugging one another, slapping backs and strutting up and down the field. They pinpointed where Jeff Reymer scored on a crucial third-down fingertip catch, and where Ron Vaught planted his helmet in the ribs of Jefferson's all-state quarterback Patrick Whaley, knocking the football loose to stop a late fourth-quarter drive and preserve the 17-14 win.

Long after most of the fans had escaped to their cars, they braved the 25-mile-per-hour winds and near-zero wind chill, refusing to surrender the moment and thumbing their noses at Mother Nature as only state champions can do.

"I wanted the moment to last forever," Viking senior offensive guard Billy Gammon said. "I doubt that I'll ever have as big a thrill as winning the state football championship."

The victory was a most unlikely one. Unbeaten Jefferson entered the game as the state's top-ranked team and had been touted as one of the best teams ever. In 14 games, the Lions outscored opponents 497-98. In the semifinals, they routed defending champion Clearwater, 42-0, with Whaley throwing six touchdown passes.

The Vikings, on the other hand, won ugly, struggling in game after game, getting the big break that kept the season going. In the semifinals, Randy Kane blocked an extra point to save a 21-20 win over Madison.

"Whatever it took, that's what these kids did,"

coach Ernest Buckner said. "This is not even close to the most talented team I've coached, but these kids have character and tenacity. We were a little lucky, but we made our own luck."

What makes this story successful? It focuses on human emotions—"I doubt that I'll ever have as big a thrill as winning the state football championship"—rather than on scores or statistics. It embraces meaningful interviewing with specific details—*"they remained on the frozen turf of Remington field, players and their girlfriends, coaches and parents, hugging one another, slapping backs and strutting up and down the field. They pinpointed where Jeff Reymer scored on a crucial third-down fingertip catch, and where Ron Vaught planted his helmet in the ribs of Jefferson's all-state quarterback Patrick Whaley."*

Notice that the story doesn't replace data with emotion. Instead, it uses emotion to give meaning to data.

Notice too these great quotes. These aren't meaningless statements of the obvious as so many quotes in yearbooks often are. A statement such as "We are glad that we won and proud of this team. The boys played hard and gave 110 percent all the way" can be used for almost any team, any year. Instead, the coach's quote is candid and specific, more conversational than stilted, as though he were talking to the friend rather than being stopped in the hall by a reporter.

As important as anything, the story possesses a meaningful degree of interpretation:

The Vikings, on the other hand, won ugly, struggling in game after game, getting the big break that kept the season going.

It then supports this interpretive statement with an example: In the semifinals, Randy Kane blocked an extra point to save a 21-20 win over Madison.

Look at the big picture—pre-season expectations, injuries, weather, freak accidents, luck, team attitude, fan support and strategy changes—and then come to a conclusion as to

ALTERNATIVE COPY

Alternative copy works occasionally. For example, rather than stodgy and wordy club briefs, consider something like this:

FUTURE TEACHERS OF AMERICA
President — Jim Jones
Vice President — Sally Smith
Treasurer — Bobby Horton
Secretary — Casey Crawford
Activities: FTA Teaching Day, Sept. 25; Secret Pal Teacher Program, Oct. 10.
More information: Susan Riggins, Room A3-210

Rather than cliché "New Teacher" feature, try this:

DAN JONES, HISTORY
Book — Cider House Rules
Movie — Saving Private Ryan
Singer — The Beatles
Hero — My dad
Pet peeve: Kids who don't care

If you're writing a personality profile about the new principal, pull the biographical or statistical data out of the story and place it in a fever chart, table or *USA Today*-like fact box. Alternative copy is perfect for today's attention-deficient readers. Readership studies show that people like microwave journalism: factoids, maps, time-lines, step-by-step directions, top 10 lists, question/answer, pull quotes and *Harper's* Index.

I am anti-dumb alternative copy, all those brainless surveys, lists and pull quotes that state the obvious and exist only to fill up space.

For example:

WHAT DID YOU DO OVER SPRING BREAK?

■ Nothing — 41%
■ Went skiing— 13%
■ Went to the beach— 15%

■ Caught up on homework — 20%
■ Responded to endless stupid yearbook surveys — 11%

WHAT DID YOU LIKE BEST ABOUT HOMECOMING?

"The dance" — Sarah Jones, junior
"I liked it when they named me Homecoming Queen" — Rachel Green, senior
"Winning the football game" — Josh Wester, sophomore
"When the water tower fell over" — freshman James Merrell

WHAT IS YOUR FAVORITE THING ABOUT THANKSGIVING?

"Eating turkey and dressing"
"Shopping for Christmas presents"
"Watching Texas beat A&M again"
"Dressing up like a pilgrim and scaring little children"

I'm not real big on those "fill in the blanks" stories that have been popping up in yearbooks, coast to coast.

My favorite thing about _____ was _____. And I'll never forget how _____ made me so happy while _____ made me so sad. Yes, it was a _____ year, full of _____ and _____ and _____. Just thinking about it makes me want to _____.

The bottom line on alternative copy: it's no substitute for substantive reporting and rich writing. Rather than a random pull quote that states, "Losing to Seaweed High was a real disappointment. They are our biggest rival, and we really wanted to win that game," get the real story. What happened? How? Why? Capture the drama of this game. You can always further develop it with pull quotes or a list, but write the story first.

TIRED OF TRADITIONAL COPY? GO ALTERNATIVE

One of the more interesting developments in yearbook is alternative copy.

Rather than traditional lead/quote/transition formulized writing, alternative copy comes from such diverse inspirations as David Letterman's Top Ten List, Nickelodeon magazine and the typical fill-in-the-blank multiple choice test.

Use open-ended statements, poetry, lists, how-to advice, and fill-in-the-blank sentences.

The objective is to produce copy that is highly personal, that in fact forces the yearbook readers to become copywriters themselves.

the team's degree of success or failure. A 5-6 mark isn't always a losing season, and a 7-4 record isn't necessarily a winning record either. If Vanderbilt University finishes with a 5-6 record in football, they'd probably declare a holiday. However, if Nebraska finishes 7-4, they circulate petitions to fire the head coach and all of his assistants. It's all a matter of perspective and context.

This recipe of observation, interviewing, interpretation, will work for any sport—individual or team, varsity or JV, male or female. The bottom line is not so much to record the historical data—a scoreboard can do that just as easily—but to build the story around a prevailing emotion, the one thing people are most likely to remember.

Successful sports copy should do for the yearbook readers what George Brazeale's story about the Pflugerville Panthers did for me: it should remind them, as in my case, of how much it hurt to lose that football game or how great it was to win.

■ OTHER TRADITIONAL COVERAGE

Take chances with section copy also. Consider the following club coverage:

CLUB INDUCTIONS and initiations came in all forms, ranging from formal to informal, but each held a special meaning for the participants.

The Future Teachers of America held its induction at Mr. Gatti's. "Having the ceremony at Mr. Gatti's was nice because it let us go out and eat pizza," sophomore David Dixon said.

Some inductions were more formal, however. The Spanish Club held its ceremony at the Glenview Country Club.

"Being inducted into Spanish Club was special because it was the beginning for me to get involved in more school activities," junior Marc Schwartz said.

Other clubs were more outlandish. Big Sisters dressed up their Little Sisters for the day in outlandish costumes.

"My sister put me through the ultimate embarrassment. I looked really bad and had to do some crazy stuff," sophomore Tammy Tamblin said.

What is the main idea of this piece of copy? That clubs conduct inductions? That inductions are different? Either way, the writing is boring, and the content rehashes the obvious. What have non-club members learned that they didn't know or couldn't figure out? What emotions have been captured? Will club members want to read this copy block in five or 10 years?

Probably not. So how do we salvage this? First, ask yourself, "What is the point of this story?" Inductions are times for excitement, nervousness and, in a few cases, outlandishness.

Then, find specific examples to support this main idea. Tammy Tamblin said she was put through the ultimate embarrassment. What was it? Describe it. Re-create the scene. Put it in a context. Show us what inductions mean, but make certain you do not glamorize or condone hazing.

"YOU! DOG-BREATH. Come here. My shoe's untied."

Sophomore Jason Whaley cringed. He knew the voice. It had been ringing in his ears, in his face, for days. And he knew he'd been caught again. For a moment, he considered acting as though he hadn't heard—and trying to disappear into the hallway crowd. But failure to hear the calls of senior musicians was one of the primary sins of aspiring band members—kind of a "what you don't know can hurt you." So he accepted his fate, walked over, bent down and tied—for the third time that day—Tyrone Bigg's Air Jordans.

"Thanks, Cat Barf. Now evaporate," Biggs said as his friends looked on and laughed.

Although hazing is illegal, for Jason and other students like him, joining clubs involved being subjected to one or two humiliations.

"Most of it is in good humor, but a few seniors go a little overboard," Jason said. "One of my friends had his clothes stolen while he was in gym class. And girls are pushed into boys' bathrooms all the time. It can get a little cruel."

Of course, not all inductions are so harrowing. The National Honor Society inductions are extremely formal. Held at the Glenview Country Club, the ceremonies involve tuxedos, formals and candles.

"We want members to appreciate the gravity of the situation," NHS president Barbara Richmond said. "While we don't take ourselves too seriously, we do have this one time of the year when we act with dignity and reflection."

Jason wasn't so lucky. Still, he survived the experience. And his message to next year's freshmen? "Get ready. I'm going to put them through hell," he said.

■ **ACADEMIC COVERAGE**

The typical academic coverage goes like this:

"THE PURPOSE OF BIOLOGY is to teach students about living organisms and the world around us. Teachers did this in a variety of ways, including a trip to the Smithsonian Museums in Washington, D.C.

Asked why students need to learn biology, Mrs. Sharon Cutworth said, "So that they will have an appreciation for all life, including their own."

Classes are not important. What students learn in classes is. Occasionally, a reporter will focus on what students do in class. For example:

TAKING VITAL SIGNS, admitting patients, assisting doctors in the emergency rooms, helping maintain hospital equipment and facilities. All were experiences students in Health Occupation Students of America (HOSA) had through their health occupation classes.

HOSA is a leadership club for students in Vocational Health Occupation Education (VHOE). Through class experience and work with the club, students interested in medical careers could find out more about that career.

"The program is developed mostly for students wanting to pursue a career in the medical field," Emily Sparks, health occupation teacher, said. "The VHOE class and corresponding work responsibilities

were designed to give the students some hands-on training on what a medical career is like."

Informative? Yes.

Interesting? Not very, which is a shame, given the powerful nature of the content. Medicine is a life-and-death career. Let's capture some of that drama in the copy. What were students' most frightening experiences? Describe the hustle and bustle of the emergency room. Tell us about the relationship between a student and a patient. Capture the sensory details and the emotions of the moment.

IT WAS 3:30 IN THE MORNING, and most of the staff on duty in the emergency room of North Hills Medical Center figured the big action for this Thursday night was over. A few had taken time to sit back, put their feet up and pull out a paperback novel. Senior Ioana Pavel was sterilizing a gurney when a 1982 blue Mustang squealed into the driveway, barely missing a concrete walkway. The driver then sat down on the horn.

Racing outside, doctors found a 16-year-old boy, almost paralyzed in fear, his jeans soaked in blood. He had been playing with his dad's 38-caliber gun and had accidentally shot himself.

"The kid said his parents were out of town, and he was too embarrassed to call 911 so he drove himself to the hospital," Pavel said. "He wanted to know if there was any way doctors could sew him up and let him go so that he wouldn't have to tell his father. He was more afraid his dad was going to kill him than he was of bleeding to death."

While brushes with life and death were rare, students in the Vocational Health Occupation Education classes got an inside look at America's health care system.

"At first, I thought we'd be doing a lot of menial labor, but that wasn't the case at all," senior Rita Martinez said. "We were in the rooms with the doctors and nurses. I helped restrain a man who had had a drug overdose. It was fascinating, and it certainly reinforced my plans to become a doctor."

UNIFY IDEAS. ENGAGE READERS. GO PARALLEL

The purpose of parallel structure is to unify ideas and to engage readers in an easy-to-follow thought process.

Parallel sentences create pace and set the tone for a story. For example:

Junior Sharon Hess has seen it all. The taunting, the teasing, the bullying. Students teased about their clothes. Teased about how they speak, what they say. Teased for being "stupid," teased for being who they are.

"I think it's horrible," Hess said. "For some people, going to school is torture."

QUICK TIP

Any time you have a choice between words, always choose the one with the narrower meaning. For example:

WEAK: "The new principal wore an expensive watch and a colorful shirt."

BETTER: "The new principal wore a Rolex and a Tommy Bahama shirt."

■ PEOPLE COVERAGE

Without interesting copy, the people section turns into row after row of mug shots. If you attend one of those mega-mall high schools, searching for the few dozen portraits among the thousands of faces can become tedious in a hurry.

More than any other section of the book, the people section is the perfect place for the personality profiles and student life activity coverage. For instance, the junior section may profile an accomplished musician or actress. The feature section might look at the stress of taking driver training classes. Another section might include a feature on spring break vacations or participation in scavenger hunts. Show how this freshman is typical of all freshmen, how that junior is different from any of his classmates.

The bottom line is this: Features must be timely, built on interesting direct quotes, descriptive and unique. This is hardly the case with the following copy block, found on the social studies page of the faculty section:

THE STUDY of man, his past, present and future, is dealt with in the social studies department. History, government, humanities and economics are presented to the classes. A working knowledge of these subjects is vital to a student's education.

"Those who do not know history are doomed to repeat it," social studies department chairman Ron Poling said. "Each course presents a little of all the rest as much of the information is entwined."

That's it. Everything you want or need to remember about the social studies department. This copy satisfies none of the purposes of the yearbook. It serves no historic purpose. It doesn't record the facts, dates or figures of the year. It cannot be used in years to come as reference material. Nor can the school show it off as a public relations tool because it fails to show that writing or thinking skills are taking place in the classroom. It's not strong copy.

This is. From the 1999 Duncanville (TX) *Panther Tale*, it's a touching tribute to a beloved teacher who died mid-way through the fall semester.

HE WAS A MAN with thousands of kids and dozens of wives.

George Spraberry was never married. Maybe that is how he got away with buying roses on Valentine's Day for all the female faculty at the PACE school, where he served as a counselor.

Maybe that's how he was able to take kids into his home, offer them rides where they needed to go, buy them clothes and help them pay for college.

"He really loved the underdog kid," PACE principal Dr. Ruth Richey said.

"But on the night of Nov. 20, the heart that had no end for those who knew him fell asleep, weakened from a heart attack earlier that afternoon.

"We cried at school We cried at the funeral home. We went home and cried some more," Dr. Richey said. "He was an irreplaceable working partner."

Mr. Spraberry's career in education spanned almost 40 years, with the majority spent in Duncanville. He was the only band directors here for many years and was the counselor at Reed Junior High School for 15 years prior to his 1989 retirement.

Mr. Spraberry came out of retirement when Dr. Richey asked him to join her at PACE.

When PACE opened, Mr. Spraberry became a devoted volunteer. For the past five and a half years, he has been a part-time employee with full-time commitment to the PACE students and staff.

Although the district couldn't afford to pay him to work full-time, he stayed at the school to help the students, whom he considered to be his family.

Here's another superb feature. Titled "The Heart of the Matter," by Heather Daniel, it's one of my all-time favorite features and comes from the Casa Robles High School yearbook. (Orangevale, CA)

I'M PICKING MY WAY through the muddy grassless Senior Square during a chilly, windy afternoon following yearbook when I see them, her arms circling his waist, her hands stroking his back while she gives him a notorious "under the jacket" hug (reserved only for the romantically involved). I'm trying not to stare, trying not to invade their privacy, but then I realize they won't notice me anyway.

My steps slow to a shuffle and then I stop. How can they do that, just stand next to the picnic table and ignore everything: the conversation of their friends standing three feet away, the argument taking place across senior square, their test in geometry next period? I guess when they are together everything else stops.

His hands are joined tightly at the base of her back, returning her hug and letting her lean into his arms ever so slightly. Her face is upturned toward his, a cleat invitation for a hasty kiss when no one's looking. She smiles and murmurs something near his ear. A secret smile. I guess it's kind of like an under the jacket hug. It's a smile that comes when you have somebody, and at that moment that's all that's important. She smiles back...the same secret smile.

This is the third day that I have watched them, and everyday it's the same thing: exchanging under the jacket hugs and secret smiles. I look at them and think to myself, do they really think that they're in love?

Love? More like hormones and tight clothes that cloud teenagers' judgment. They can't possibly think that they are going to stay together and get married-can they? What would happen if they broke up? Will she suffer from a secret smile withdrawal? Will he die if she doesn't warm him with an "under the jacket" hug? The average relationship in high school, it seems to me, lasts for about one school dance and fours dates. It's foolish for anyone to believe that's enough time to fall in love, or for that matter, out of love.

Yet look around campus, what do you see? Endless tiny soap operas. Some teenagers constantly whine about finding a date to homecoming. Yet as the dance ends they complain about trying to dump their date. Do high school teenagers even know what love is? I know I don't.

I watch them caught up in their own little couple world, whispering couple things, and exchanging couple glances. And I notice something-something different...something that isn't quite an "under the jacket" hug or a secret smile. It's not an action, or a look, or the way they hold hands. It's something special, between just the two of them, and no one else.

I think then that if I asked them, about this something that they have, they wouldn't know what I was talking about. Maybe it's respect, or maybe it's friendship or love. I don't know, but they have it. And it makes me think then that maybe it isn't so silly to have a relationship in high school. I think that it must be nice to be together with someone. She doesn't have to think about getting a date to homecoming, she already has one. He doesn't have to worry about anyone not being there to cheer him on at his football game, she is his biggest fan.

Well, I wonder, why shouldn't they be together? No matter how bad their days are they know that there is someone who likes them even if they fail their geometry test, or forget to do their Spanish homework. I wonder to myself, is high school such a bad place to learn what love is? To fall for that gorgeous blond who sits across from you in economics and flashes you that perfect smile. To learn how to care and be cared for.

The bell rings, and it's time for me to go to physics. The couple quickly kiss and hurry in different directions, one toward the B-wing, the other toward the F-wing. I finish picking my way through the muddy, grassless Senior Square and smile when I realize that tomorrow they will be there, underneath the tree, leaning against the picnic table, exchanging secret smiles and under the jacket hugs.

I know what you're thinking. It uses first person. That's fine. Straight news and feature writing should remain third person, but when the reporter is a part of the story, as is the case above, then it's permissible to use first person to show the relationship between the action,

THE TRUTH RESTS IN THE DETAILS

Pay attention to the little details that tell the real story, that create scenes in your readers' minds.

Don't write, "John was an angry boy."
Instead, write, "John strummed his fingers, three of which contained the initials 'F-T-W.'"

Don't write, "Angie was nervous."
Write, "Angie plucks her eyebrows when she's nervous. By the time of the interview, she had none."

> **Good profiles have anecdotes that reveal how the person became who they are. The subjects of profiles could be people who are on the brink of chance, unusual people, people in the community others may have wondered about but never bothered to notice, such as someone who styles the hair of dead people."**
>
> — Susan Ager
> Detroit Free Press

setting and reporter. This doesn't happen often.

■ **STUDENT LIFE COVERAGE**

Typically, students spend four years in high school, and most of it isn't spent sitting in class, participating in clubs or playing on teams. It's spent hanging out.

Student life stories should preserve the day-to-day activities, the moments that occur before, between and after the regimented activities of the school. The difficulty here is the tendency to ignore, minimize or dismiss these routine activities as legitimate copy possibilities. Students too often judge copy in the traditional news value structure—news must be about unusual or important events or prominent persons—which isn't always true. Certainly, pep rallies, homecoming, class elections, drama productions, mid-term tests, prom, graduation—the benchmark events—must be covered.

But that coverage should be balanced against the reality that more time in high school is spent hanging out, working at minimum-wage jobs, wandering the malls, partying on weekends, driving up and down the road, and—above all—trying to woo the opposite sex. Not all students are beauty queens and National Honor Society officers, but 99.9 percent of high school students know what it's like to try to fit in, to find a niche and a gang, even if the gang consists of five geeky freshmen girls who occupy the seventh through eleventh chairs in the flute section of the concert band.

The trick to successful copy in general—and student life copy in particular—is to capture those emotions shared by all students. You can't list every name of every person who went to the prom, even though I've heard students complain, "Well, if we don't list everyone, they'll get mad."

Let them. You pick your sources because they're a part of the group, or they're apart from the group. .

And you don't want to publish a lot of predictable data—the prom was held at the Four Seasons Hotel, the theme was "Midnight in Havana," the band was "The Runny Noses"

WRITING TRICKS

KEEP YOUR NOUNS CLOSE TO YOUR VERBS

WEAK: Junior Bobby Harris, the star quarterback of the undefeated Bronco team that will play in the state championship game Saturday in Portland against a 9-4 Seaweed High outfit, broke his leg.

GET TO THE NOUN QUICKLY

WEAK: The star quarterback of the undefeated Bronco team that will play in the state championship game Saturday in Portland against the 9-4 Seaweed High outfit, Bobby Harris broke his leg.

AVOID PASSIVE VERBS

WEAK: Matt Jones is planning to attend the University of Chicago.

BETTER: Matt Jones plans to attend the University of Chicago.

AVOID POMPOUS DICTION. AVOID FOREIGN PHRASES TOO.

Unbeknownst, amongst, amidst, Leitmotiv, Gestalt, Sine qua non, Cognoscenti, etc.

and everyone had a great time. Duh!

But with a little empathy and creativity, you can capture the anxiety, the excitement, the weirdness that the prom generates. For example:

SENIOR CHRISTOPHER SANCHEZ waited until the last minute to find a date for the prom.

"I knew all along who I wanted to ask," he said. "It just took me a long time to work up the courage to call her. I called her on the Monday before."

In the end, his date — junior Amanda Maldonado — agreed to accompany him to the prom, held at Riverside Center. But other procrastinators were not so lucky.

"I had a date, then she backed out on me, and by the time I got around to asking someone else, I was too late," said senior David Wesolowski. "I went with a group of guys and frankly, we all felt like losers. We bailed about halfway through and hit it for the lake. It won't go down as one of my better high school memories."

Of course, prom is one of those "big moments" of high school. Any competent school journalist should be capable of cranking out a story that at least reports the who, what, when, where, why and how—even though that's not the real story.

But how does one report the not-so-major events—those Friday nights without dates, the five minutes between classes, the evenings at home with the family? I once attended an academic awards banquet during which the tennis coach announced, "And for the best dressed tennis doubles team in the district, Elaine and Judy."

The tennis players erupted in laughter.

What was that about?

Later, the director of the school's one-act play did a little dance, then high-fived the air. Members of the troupe jolted to their feet in applause.

What's going on there?

Open your eyes. Seek out those stories that capture the heartbeat of the year. For every student who rented a helicopter and whisked his date to the prom, there's another kid whose dreams of romance didn't come true, or at least fell far short of expectations.

For every kid whose name was on the A-list at the popular parties, there's half a dozen who spend their Friday nights flipping hamburgers or taking tickets at the local cineplex. Their stories need to be told, too. And the news is not that they're holding down part-time jobs. The news is that they have dreams, ambitions, frustrations, anxieties of every nature and occasionally great triumphs. I believe that's what readers want to remember.

Your job is to help them.

SHOWCASE

By **HANNA CHALMERS**
Angleton High School, Angleton, TX

KEEPING A 4-YEAR VOW to La Vigen de San Juan, Rosa Riones sat on a stool in San Juan, Mexico and had her long black curls cut for the first time since she was in the seventh grade.

The same promise was one that had worked for her in the past.

When Rosa was born on Aug. 20, 1977, she weighed only three pounds. The doctors told her parents that the baby's chances of living were slim, but if she survived, she would likely be handicapped.

"My mother didn't have faith or hope in me because she had already lost two children," Rosa said. "But my father had faith that I would be strong enough to make it and live. My mom didn't even name me. It was my father who named me after my mother, Rosa Marie Briones."

Her father kept his faith alive and swore to the Virgin that if Rosa lived, they would let her hair grow for five years and then take her to San Juan to have it cut and given to the Virgin's statue.

Little Rosa beat the odds and grew healthy. When time came, she traveled to San Juan to uphold the promise. She sat on a stool for a moment of prayer, then the nuns blessed her long braid with Holy Water and cut it.

As time passed, Rosa faced another challenge. At 15, she began to hang out with the "bad crowd" and got into several fights at school.

However, she realized if she did not change her ways, her school career would be wasted, so she vowed that if she got on-task and graduated in 1996, she would make the long trip to Mexico again to cut her hair as a gift to the Virgin.

For the past four years, she not only made her grades but became a key leader in several clubs and campus activities.

"My parents respected what I had done and were willing to take me to keep my promise," Rosa said. "I miss my long hair because when I dance and turned, it swirled a neat way, but I made the promise so I could finish school, and I kept it."

ARE YOU LOOKING THROUGH A TELESCOPE OR A MICROSCOPE?

In her influential short book, *Yearbook Copy*, Judie Gustafson wrote, "Basically, all the yearbook is either telescopic, giving a broad overview and a total picture, or microscopic, looking at all the little pieces and details."

The purpose of high-quality copy:

■ to record facts
■ to preserve the flavor of the year
■ to recall the emotion or mood of the year
■ to focus on the consequence, importance or success of an event or activity.
■ to discover the unknown, unusual or unique.

Photo by **LINDSAY BENEDICK**
Oakville Senior High School, St. Louis, MO

STUDENT PRESS

Shana Kendrick

EXPRESS YOURSELF

Sometimes, it's just as well to cover an event from a subjective rather than objective position. Columns, staff editorials and entertainment reviews offer a creative way to mix news with informed opinion.

14

CHAPTER HIGHLIGHTS:

■ Match content and purpose to type of column.

■ Make column as personal as possible.

■ Find and develop your voice.

■ Write to express, not impress.

Do you enjoy meeting new and interesting people? Ridiculing them? Telling people what's wrong with the world and what ought to be done to make it right? Getting your name and picture in print for something other than public intoxication or petty vandalism? If so, you could have what it takes to become a successful opinion columnist.

Heavens knows we need them. Most high school columns resemble high school feature stories: bland, abstract, superficial, right-off-the-top-of-the-head on deadline musings about little or nothing. And I'm being kind here.

High quality columnists are reporters first, writers second, propagandists third or fourth or fifth. Of course, the landscape is crawling with successful columnists who are hacks, lackeys and political junkies. It's good to know the difference.

If you scan the typical daily newspaper editorial pages, you'll see pictures of writers smoking pipes, holding their hands on their chins, looking stern and serious. Other than being unbelievably unphotogenic, what do columnists have in common?

■ They are intrigued by people. Basically, they like them.

■ They see ordinary events in new and unusual ways.

■ They are willing to take chances. They are willing to put themselves on the line, sometimes to reveal something about themselves that is personal and sensitive.

■ They consider themselves independent.

■ They feel strongly about issues and want—no, need—to share their opinions with others.

Many columnists are intrigued by people, see ordinary events in unusual ways, take chances and consider themselves independent.

So why do some columnists become stars who appear on David Letterman while others are sent back to covering school board meetings after one or two attempts? Because they have cultivated a clear and unique voice. For some columnists, the voice exploits a God-given talent or skill. Others discover their voice through a lucky break. But a lot of it is work. They have polished their craft to the stage where the average reader can identify the writer merely by reading the lead of the story.

Maureen Dowd of *The New York Times* comes to mind. So does Leonard Pitts of the *Miami Herald*. I can pick out a Dave Barry column from a stack of 1,000 imitators. No one writes about exploding cows and ear hair like Dave. And no one writes about politics with

QUICK TIP

Know what you're talking about. Your opinion is only as good as your facts. And remember: the smallest fact error obliterates the credibility of the rest of the column.

the same sense of sarcasm and bewilderment as Molly Ivins.

But that shouldn't stop you from trying. As a beginner, you should read a lot of columnists, find a few you like and learn from them. I didn't say plagiarize them. Instead, find a writer whose style and voice most appeal to you as a reader and who comes closest to representing your own writing style and voice. In other words, don't try to come off like George Will if you have the vocabulary of Gomer Pyle.

Most of the national columnists write either editorial topic, analysis, mood or humor columns. Let's look at each briefly:

■ **EDITORIAL TOPIC COMMENT**—This column presents opinions or ideas about topics that are currently of special interest and have strong personal impact upon the readers. The form has been called the "news-behind-the-news" column.

Often, editorial topic columns mirror the staff editorial in structure: lead that introduces the situation and presents clue to stance; body that explains; conclusion that recaps stance and includes call to action.

However, that need not always be the case. Consider the tongue-in-cheek approach to a serious topic. Also, notice how the writer uses two principles of effective news writing: tell a dramatic story and focus on an individual.

SHOWCASE ■

By **MARK HORVIT**
Sharpstown High School, Houston, TX

JOE SAT IN his fourth period class staring at the teacher while his mind slipped further and further into oblivion. The droning voice over the P.A. had interrupted his classes so many times it only sent him deeper on his journey.

Suddenly the lunch bell rang, snapping him out of his trance. He collected his books and walked out into the hall. Though he didn't look like the type, Joe was the worst kind of criminal—

he left the campus for lunch. Joe was a smart guy, but he couldn't understand what the problem was. He was 18, old enough to be drafted, but he couldn't go to McDonalds for lunch.

He made his way to the parking lot. He walked past the restrooms. Since he didn't smoke cigarettes or take drugs, he had no reason to go in. As he walked past a row of lockers, several of them exploded, and smoke filled the hallway. Joe continued, oblivious to the commotion. He was used to this kind of thing. After all, he had been going to public schools for 12 years.

He passed by a classroom where an English teacher attempted to read Shakespeare while students in the back of the class were dipping Skoal and misusing pharmaceutical products. This didn't faze him, either.

Walking through the patio, he watched a group of kickers ramming a freshman against a tree. Finally, he reached his car, turned the key in the ignition and headed for the exit. Right before he got there, a white car with flashing red lights blocked his way. The security man got out and walked to Joe's car.

"I hate to do this," he said as a smile crossed his face, "but kid, you're busted."

He paused for a moment, then added, "You know, it's students like you who give public education a bad name."

■ **PERSONAL REFLECTION**—These columns can be humorous, sentimental, melancholic or any combination thereof. Among the devices good columnists use in writing personal reflection columns are anecdote, exaggeration, puns, narrative, scene development and fictional dialogue.

While columnists may write about themselves or their experiences, the messages these columns carry are universal. When Anna Quindlen of *The New York Times* writes about her mother, she also reminds us of our relationships with our parents. When Bob Greene, formerly of the *Chicago Tribune*, writes about what it was like to be a geeky high school kid, he reminds his readers, many of whom are well into middle age, what they were like at 15, too.

The goal of each personal reflection column is to appeal to the reader's emotions. The reader should feel the writer's rage, sadness, joy or excitement. Consequently, the reader should also feel rage, sadness, joy or excitement.

The next column fulfills that lofty goal even though you do not know Frank. It was part of a newspaper staff's coverage of the death of a young man.

SHOWCASE

By **DEBORAH GEMBARA**
West Springfield High School, VA

FRANK ABRUZZESE did not walk, he sauntered. He didn't talk, he mumbled. And Frank never just made eye contact, he initiated a stare down.

With Frank, the expression "what you see is what you get" held little meaning because what you saw was a wiry 16-year-old whose 6-1 frame enjoyed reclining back in its seat and allowing his long arms and legs to spill over into the aisles. Frank was a self-described "trifling hoodlum" who wore little expression but a smirk and sported a flat top which emphasized his unusually pale ears and his piercing black-brown eyes.

To understand Frank was to understand that Frank was a casework in contradictions. Understated and often reluctant to even read his own writing, Frank never turned in a column or story without a proud "check out my lead" or "my end is kickin'." One of his dreams included shocking his entire class by being named valedictorian. Nothing Frank ever turned in was less than 100 percent, which often left this editor in awe.

When it came to something he believed, he would not take no for an answer. This was evidenced in his vision for a story on basketball fashions. Although countless editors had rejected Frank's idea, he produced a list of 23 reasons why this would make a great story. Frank wrote that

story, and it appears in this issue.

What Frank could not express verbally, he could express on paper. Frank was a mumbler whose closest friends often requested translations. Despite this, his writing was clear, compelling and without trepidation. It was indicative of his own straightforward manner, a manner that on occasion got him into trouble. This disconcerting honesty for his writing allowed people to feel closer to Frank.

This was particularly true of Frank's final column, a tribute to Magic Johnson. In reading and hearing Frank's worship of a hero who appeared larger than life to him, one does not see Frank's lightly mustached upper lip or his dark, close shaven head. One sees the boyish heart that did not want to stop believing in his childhood hero even when it appeared as if the hero had fallen. One sees Frank Abruzzese turning his head and brushing roughly at the tears that threatened to spill onto his cheek as he listens as the last line of his tribute is read in class. "Call me a dreamer. Call me a fool. But I believe in Magic."

Although few outside the newspaper staff had a chance to witness Frank's amazing ability to pour images and reality into anything he wrote, all who knew Frank will not forget his ability to make people laugh. Frank Abruzzese possessed an arsenal of one liners that could take the wind out of anyone's sails. His victims usually received a characteristically mumbled "sorry" following a Frank attack.

Frank would come over to my house, and I would ask him to take off his shoes before coming into my house. Frank would invariably be dressed in his Bulls jacket, a T-shirt depicting Michael Jordan, baggy jeans and black hightops. "Come on Frank," I'd say, "take off your shoes," only to hear, "No way man, someone's gonna steal them." My retort would always be, "Yeah Frank, my dad's in the closet waiting to make off with your shoes."

The shoes did come off but not without some warnings from Frank that I was "gonna need oxygen" once I smelled his feet. On the last time

SUREFIRE COLUMN IDEAS

- Weird things you find in lockers.
- Driver's education war stories.
- Cheapest things to do on a date.
- The date from Hell.
- Creative ways to turn down a date.
- Family car trips.
- Allowances: how much and for what?
- Things teachers/adults hate to hear from students.
- Things students hate to hear from teachers/adults.
- Useless items people pack for camps/trips.
- White lies teens tell their parents.
- Stupid graduation gifts and what to do with them.
- One really horrible day at work.
- Things Dads do to embarrass their daughters.

❝ Before writing a column, select a subject. This complex process should begin first thing in the morning. Simply stare into the bathroom mirror and say, "Mirror, mirror on the wall, can you give me any column idea at all?" It won't.

— Russell Baker
The New York Times

Frank came over though, he took off his shoes, flashed me a cheesy grin and proudly stated "I came prepared. I got me some new socks."

As hard as I try, I think it will be a long time before I enjoy another Thanksgiving. For many years to come, Thanksgiving will remind me of the wake and funeral of a 16-year-old boy, one who would never see his high school graduation, his senior prom or his next birthday.

I find only one thing more horrifying than the fact that Frank Abruzzese's life would know only 16 years. That is that Frank Abruzzese would become a part of my past, a memory. Never again would he anger me to the point of violence and slip in a quiet "sorry." Never again would we talk about the direction of his love life, and never again would I watch him, like a little boy, dissolve into laughter.

▪ **VARIETY**—And then there's everything else, which out of convenience, I've lumped into one category called "variety." These columns appear in the form of a list, a letter to my parents, the lyrics of a song . . . whatever.

The following column was written by a 13-year-old at a Houston-area junior high school. I have long since misplaced her name or even the name of the school. But I still love this column.

I HAVE OFTEN thought how boring life would be if I didn't have an older sister. In addition to having twice as many clothes as I normally would, I also get to bug her.

Bugging an older sister isn't simple. It takes skill, creativity, talent and the ability to look innocent when you get caught in the act. You must be cunning, devious and, above all, unmerciful. If you are just a beginner, here are a few tips to get you started:

1. When a boy calls and you answer the phone, tell him she's using the bathroom.

2. Put soap on her toothbrush.

3. Tell her dates when they come to pick her up that she even gargled for him.

INVITE READER INPUT

Encourage readers to write you. Print in every issue of the newspaper the policy for accepting letters. The policy should deal with length, deadlines and what may and may not be printed.

At the same time, take equal pains to make certain that any letter published is authentic and legally protected. Every letter must be signed. Check personally with individuals to guarantee that signatures are not fakes.

Finally, letters must be free of content that might be libelous, obscene, slanderous or potentially disruptive of the educational process.

Remember: If it's printed in your newspaper, you're responsible for it.

AND IF NO ONE WRITES?

If the readers won't come to you, then go to them by conducting surveys and printing the student comments.

▪ Ask intelligent questions about an important issue or event. "What is your favorite color?" doesn't qualify.

▪ Connect the survey to the lead editorial.

▪ Carefully word the question so that students can understand it and respond to it.

▪ Avoid asking more than three questions per survey. The first should be a warm-up question to help readers begin thinking about the real questions you expect to use.

▪ If you want 10 or 12 usable responses to print, you need to survey at least 100-200 persons.

▪ Print only those comments that lend insight and information to the issue at hand.

4. Call her boyfriend by her previous boyfriend's name. Say "oops" and look innocent.

5. When she is on the phone, ask her if she knows she has a pimple on her cheek. Dodge the pillow she throws at you.

6. Ask her boyfriend how much he's going to spend on her at Christmas. Tell him your family thought her last boyfriend was cheap.

7. Tell your sister her boyfriend has hairy fingers.

8. Offer her peanut butter and bologna sandwiches when she's sick.

9. Tell her scientists have made an amazing new discovery that kissing guys will make hair grow out of your ears.

10. Show everyone the baby picture of her naked on a rug.

11. Ask her if her jeans are supposed to be that tight.

12. Tell her she has panty bulge when she doesn't.

These are just a few things to get you started. Once you practice, you'll find it's easy to get the hang of it. Just remember to look innocent and deny everything. When you grow up, you'll have many funny times to look back on and laugh at. It's not bad having an older sister at all—it's fun if you just go about it the right way.

■ WRITING THE OPINION COLUMN
■ REPORT FIRST

Write second. Interviewing and observing are the most important elements of column writing. Get people to talk and use their anecdotes in your columns.

■ MAKE IT PERSONAL

Make your column as personal as possible.

■ Weak

Do you smoke? If you can read this, then you're old enough to know that smoking cigarettes can kill you. Cancer is the leading cause of premature death in this country, and most cancer is caused by smoking cigarettes. So why are you smoking? Just to look older? Don't be a loser. Stop smoking now. Remember: butt out and be a winner.

■ Better

I used to listen to Dad from my bedroom down the hall every morning, hacking in the bathroom, choking for a breath of air. Every morning. Every day. Monday. Sunday. His face puffed out, his eyes teary and bloodshot. Coughing and choking and spitting and puffing on a Marlboro, deep, desperate drags that burned like a kitchen match. Every morning, before his shower, before his first cup of Maxwell House, the first thing every day. Tuesday. Saturday. Coughing and choking and draggin' on a Marlboro, waking me and my brothers to the sound of his lungs exploding. Every friggin' day.

Until last week.

■ MAKE PEOPLE THINK

Express an opinion that will generate discussion. Take a stance on something of importance. Don't be so vague that you merely state the obvious. Make certain the column is of consequence, which means you must pay attention both to the substance of the subject and to the treatment of the subject. This one isn't.

MAJOR YUK

TEENAGERS HAVE always been interested in clothes, and as the years go by, fashions have changed. No one wears Nehru jackets any more. So far this year, the most popular colors are mustard and purple. Floral and hyper-color shirts are very popular, as are AG, Paper Denim & Cloth, Marc, Frankie B, Earl and Seven jeans.

Teenagers are also picky about how they wear their hair. Layers are hot this season. Long or short, layers work great with any face shape and hair type. Choppy ends are a popular alternative to the classic styles. Shattered ends create maximum movement and versatility.

As one walks the halls throughout the year,

A COLUMN IS LESS FORMAL THAN AN EDITORIAL

Whereas the opinion column can take any number of forms, the staff editorial usually consists of a lead that introduces a situation and tells the reader how the staff feels about it, followed by the body explaining the staff position.

Editorials also offer solutions and then introduce and rebut other viewpoints. It may close by restating the staff stance and advising readers to take a specific action.

The staff editorial is generally written in third person.

QUICK TIP

Take a stand. Don't fret, hem and haw. If you're not willing to state your opinion about a topic, then don't write about it.

one will see guys and girls wearing different brands of clothes and wearing their hair in different styles, but in the end, everyone wears his or her own style. That's what makes us individuals! So just be yourself and you'll be cool.

■ TAKE A STAND

The point of an opinion column is to state an opinion, not merely regurgitate the sentiments of those on the extremes of any issue.

MAJOR YUK

ABORTION IS a very complex issue that the United States Supreme Court may decide this fall. Many people think abortion is murder and are willing to protest in front of clinics and even be arrested.

Meanwhile, others believe that it is the right of the woman to control her own body and that if abortion is outlawed, it will force women to rely on back-alley doctors in unsanitary conditions.

Both sides seem to have a valid point. No one really wants to see a baby aborted, but should we make abortion illegal?

It doesn't look like either side is listening to the other, and this is a battle that may be fought in the courts and legislative chambers for years as well as on the daytime talk shows.

Maybe it's time you gave this some attention. Abortion: murder or freedom? Think about it.

■ DON'T CHEERLEAD

It's not your job to crank up school spirit or excite students into doing somersaults in the hallways before the big game.

MAJOR YUK

WHAT IS SCHOOL spirit? Webster has 15 definitions of spirit, but none of them seem to apply to our school. School spirit is important for a school. If a school has spirit, it can back its team on to victory. A school with students ready to yell can help a team win.

But such was not the case last week. The Tigers lost because of the lack of school spirit. And some students have the nerve to ask, "What's wrong with the team?"

There's nothing wrong with the team that a little support couldn't cure. We have an explosive group of running backs, a punishing defense and a great coach.

So you may ask, "Why have we lost our first six games if they're so good?" Before we can totally blame the team, other questions must be asked: How many fans helped or hurt the team? How many games have you attended? Do you stay for the entire pep rally? How many times have you given a word of encouragement instead of a negative word after a loss?

Blaming the players doesn't help anything. If a team is to do well, it's going to need more than great athletes. It's time students pulled together to support the team. Maybe this way, we won't lose our last four games.

And maybe Webster will include a 16th definition of spirit: Lincoln High School!

■ DON'T CHAT WITH THE READER

People chit chat when they have nothing meaingful to discuss. Space in your publication is too valuable. Don't waste it on idle banter.

HELLO ONE and all, and welcome back to Huskyland. It's time to get back to the busy schedule of attending school at 8 o'clock and working your way through the day. No more lying around the pool to get a suntan. Instead, it's sitting in a desk, taking notes, listening to lectures and cracking the books.

School is a lot of work, but it can be a blast, too. School is what you make it. It's all up to you.

As your monthly columnist, I hope to be discussing many items of importance this year. This month, let's begin by discussing extracurricular activities. Many people don't get involved because everything is reserved for the so-called popular people. NOT! Maybe these popular people are the ones who are involved, but how do you think they got to be popular in the first place?

All of the extracurricular activities are for you, so don't think it's always the popular people who get selected. You are only letting yourself down and maybe others if you don't try out.

Well, that's it for this month. See you next time. And remember, get involved and you will be the one who gets the praise and the glory. You may even become popular, too! Like me!

■ DON'T RAMBLE

Have a point, get to it and keep the column focused on it.

MAJOR YUK

THE TEENAGE YEARS are supposed to be the best of our lives, and in many cases, they are. No adult responsibilities. No full-time job. No kids. No bills to pay, except perhaps for a car or clothes. Yes, being a teenager has its advantages.

Still, there are many pressures that teenagers face. Most adults think that teenagers have nothing to worry about. They think, "Oh, you're just a kid." But what do they know? The truth is, we have so many decisions to make such as "Should I have sex?" or "Should I do drugs?"

And then, there's the whole issue of belonging.

Not all young adults can play sports, be a cheerleader or be newspaper editor. So where do these teenagers turn to? All too often, they turn to gangs.

Does beating up people make you feel good? Do you enjoy participating in drive-by shootings? If so, maybe being in a gang is the best choice for you. We're not saying being in a gang is right or wrong. That's your decision to make. Just remember, there are safe and rewarding alternatives such as school clubs and other community organizations. The point is, the choice is up to you. Beating up people may make you feel good. But do you really want to be the next victim of a drive-by shooting?

■ LOOK FOR AN INTERESTING ANGLE

What facts might have been overlooked? New Yorker Jimmy Breslin won the Pulitzer Prize in the 1960s for political commentary. One of his finest efforts dealt with the assassination of President John F. Kennedy. But he approached the story from a different angle. While the world's media assembled outside the rotunda of the Capitol in preparation for the burial, Breslin stood in the cold, talking to the man who dug the grave. While others covered the global implications, Breslin reported what Kennedy's death meant to one man—a man not much different from all of us.

■ LOOK FOR IRONY OR SYMBLOISM

In one of her short stories, novelist Joan Didion wrote about the 1968 riots in Berkeley, CA. She found irony in the fact that several members of the Black Panthers—a radical, anarchist group—were also enrolled in a local hospital health plan.

■ TARGET AN AUDIENCE

For example, Erma Bombeck had a long and successful career writing for and about middle-class suburban housewives.

At the same time, remember that columnists best succeed when they reach beyond members of their own clubs or cliques. The best columns speak to all students—not only athletes, honors students or musicians—and deal with universal themes and subjects. A column about the "date from hell" will be enjoyed by the National Merit scholars as well as the so-called "at risk" students if it is clever, insightful and realistic.

Traditionally, these columns would appear on the editorial or op-ed page. But that's not written in stone. The Glenbard East (Illinois) staff covered the debate surrounding the release of Spike Lee's movie *Malcolm X*. In addition to a review of the movie, one editor wrote an article about how the film reflects a trend of movies that transcend the barriers

> ❝ No editorial writer ought to be permitted to sit in an editorial room for month after month and year after year, contemplating his umbilicus. He ought to go out and meet people. ❞
>
> — H. L. Mencken

of cinema and become social statements. This alone was a provocative issue for a student journalist.

Accompanying the article was a sidebar column examining the commercialization of Malcolm X's legacy. This style employs news and opinion elements.

SHOWCASE ◼

By **JEFF SARMIENTO**
Glenbard East High School, IL

X. NEVER IN history has the 24th letter in the alphabet stirred up as much of a following as it has in today's pop culture.

From the seemingly ubiquitous X-cap to the "By any means necessary" portrait T-shirts, a fashion statement has emerged from a 1960s social statement.

Before the filming of the much-hyped Spike Lee movie, Lee and other celebrities such as Michael Jordan began sporting the X-cap to popularize a fad that had already festered in Chicago. The X pays tribute to Malcolm X, a black civil rights activist of Martin Luther King's day. Malcolm led a militaristic black Muslim movement and became a martyr for his people.

This symbol of black pride caught on and gained popularity among urban youth. X jackets, T-shirts and boxer shorts find a place in sportswear and fashion wear stores.

The average shopper is likely to see as many different styles of X-caps as Sox caps. The colors of the apparel usually include black and white, shades easily matched with nearly everything in urban fashion.

Street wear trends drift out of the city and eventually land in affluent suburbia, where teens exploit it.

"The X fashion started when Cross Colours got popular over the summer," senior Waleep Burrell said. "You can find X stuff at stores such as Journeys."

Students understand that there is more to X wear than black and white stitching, and they maintain the image of their hero.

"I think they show pride in their heritage," freshman Reyes Moreno said.

"People who don't know about Malcolm should quit perpetrating," said junior Ty Cockrell, who owns a pair of X earrings as well as several T-shirts.

However, the "statement" has lost some of its meaning because a tribute to the activist has faded into another way to make a buck.

"I think that the T-shirt designers make them half for the message and half for the profit," freshman Jon Woodall said.

"The designers should put the profits into helping the homeless and not just put it in their pockets," Burrell said. "I know that's what Malcolm would do with the money."

Junior Fred Hall, who refrains from wearing X paraphernalia, claims that people do not understand Malcolm X enough to pay tribute.

"People disrespect him when I see them tipping their caps left or right and banging with them," he said. Hall suggested that students should spend their time finding leaders in their own generation instead of wearing out the leaders of another time.

"Malcolm was a bold leader and he did what he did, but it's over," Hall said.

Burrell thinks differently. "We do have good black leaders who serve as role models, such as Michael Jordan and Jesse Jackson," he said.

Others think that the X phenomenon is simply a passing fad.

"It's the same as the African necklaces people wore two years ago," sophomore Fawne Hall said.

However, the X-wear symbolizes a newly found black pride. Burrell sports a thick X medallion around his neck. "I'm proud to wear it because kids can look to see what I stand for," he said.

The statement also extends across color lines as non-black students have also caught on to X-fashion.

"It bothered me at first," Burrell said, "but it's their choice to wear what they want."

Woodall suggests it is not a racial issue. "It's just a letter on a piece of clothing."

Relating the X craze to the yearly demand for the latest Air Jordan shoes, freshman Ivin Dionte said, "It's more of a fashion statement. Once something new comes in, X will play out."

■ FIND THE PERFECT VOICE

No one sang like Frank Sinatra. Old Blue Eyes had a voice and a style all his own. The same may be true for a few of the more contemporary singers, although I haven't heard enough of the current crop of teen heart-throbs to name names.

Like Sinatra, successful columnists have a voice and a style all their own. It is important to note the difference between voice and style. Voice is the tone of your writing. In one article, your voice can be angry or sarcastic; in another, nostalgic or sentimental.

Style is the composite of content, diction, structure and mechanics. It is not something you can teach apart from the other elements. It is based on individual choices in terms of words, rhythms, constructions and forms of expression characteristic to the writer. It gives the writing energy, emotion and individuality.

How can you develop your own voice? First, by realizing that when it comes to writing columns, there are no etched-in-stone rules.

Voice allows the reader to hear an individual human speak from the page—to establish confidentiality between the writer and the reader. It sets the illusion of a private conversation with the writer.

As mentioned previously, each writer has a number of voices. Consider how you speak differently to your parents when you're trying to explain why you're 30 minutes past curfew and when you're insisting that you cannot babysit your younger sister.

The way writers use voice tells the reader

how they feel about a topic. This succeeds so long as the writer is honest, neither too cute, too sophisticated or too sentimental. Honesty alone—not superficiality and not artificiality—convinces. Your column should reflect your personality. This one certainly does.

SHOWCASE ■

By **HANNA RICKETSON**
Bryant High School, Bryant, AR

"OKAY," THE SHORT, redheaded, freckled-all-over salesgirl smiles, "What size are you, honey?"

"I don't actually know," I mumble. "I keep getting bigger."

I stand there knowing that no bra will fit today. Because no bra has ever fit.

My mother intervenes.

"This is Hanna, and what she needs is a bra with some support. You can see she's pretty big in the chest area and she's getting a lot of neck and back pain. What she has now just isn't working."

"Well what are you wearing now?" Sherry asks.

"Forty-four double D," I answer slowly, hoping no one else in the store is paying attention. Sherry lets out a belly laugh. "You are NOT a double D!"

No kidding. Why does she think I'm here?

We walk past crayon-colored bras made with lace and embroidery and polka dots. We end up in the back of the store near some wide, shallow metal drawers labeled with letters deep into the alphabet.

Sherry pulls out ugly bra after ugly bra and I begin to wonder if they store them in drawers to keep from scaring small-breasted women and little kids.

She leads me back to a dressing room stall while my mother finds a chair. The walls are lined with magazine pages from the '40s and '50s

MAJOR SINS OF COLUMN WRITING, PART 1

■ Gossip. Go ahead. Try to slip something past the adviser. There are lots of unemployed lawyers out there looking for an easy bundle.
■ Slang, jargon and lingo. Go ahead. Use it. It lasts forever. NOT!
■ Play on words that border on profanity such as "bull sheet" and "jock shorts." Grow up.
■ References to bodily functions. We don't want to hear about them.
■ Religious comments, especially those that belittle religion or preach. It's not the newspaper's job to save souls.

Don't write about Man," E. B. White wrote. "Write about a man." Roughly translated, that means don't write about the student body, write about the sophomore who is thinking of moving to a private school because his classes are too large, the hallways too crowded and the curriculum too unfocused."

featuring tall, skinny women in knee-length slips.

"You try one on and then I'll come in, okay?" It isn't really a question, so I can't help but agree.

For an hour, I try on boring beige bra after boring beige bra, and Sherry comes in to look at every one.

"I guess we'll have to go up a size," she keeps saying.

At one point she asks me if I'm in the bra. "Huh?"

"Well what you have to do is bend over and push the breast up into the cup. Don't be afraid to jiggle it a little."

Oh, my God.

Sensing that I'm uncomfortable, she picks up a huge bra and holds it out in front of her eyes.

"I used to have this friend," Sherry says, "and she would always put her bras over her eyes like this and stick out her tongue like a bug."

Oh, my God.

"Honey, I just can't seem to figure out what size you are. Let me bring in some expertise."

She walks off. I wait and wait, watching under the stall door for her black sandals to return.

Finally she opens the door and comes in with a short Hispanic woman in a pink sweater.

"This is Else," Sherry tells me. "She's been working here for 16 years, so she really knows her bras. Tell Else what size you came in in."

Reluctantly, I answer.

"Oh no, mamacita, no no," Else chuckles.

Am I missing the funny part?

We go through the trying on process again until we find a bra that both Sherry and Else are pleased with.

"Yes, this is going to leave her enough room so that she's not uncomfortable," Else explains to Sherry. On the job training. "You seem to be sagging a bit, chica. Let's pull up the straps."

She and Sherry get one on each side of me and take to the straps. They're tugging rather aggressively and at this point I can't help but bust out laughing.

"Do you want me to bring your mom in?"

Sherry asks.

"Oh sure," I answer. Let's all look at me in my new bra.

Mom enters with Sherry. Four people in this tiny stall.

"What size is this?" she asks.

"This is a 40 F," Sherry informs her.

"Well! Okay, baby...." Mom seems at a loss for words at the moment. We all stand awkwardly until she remembers our purpose. "Now is this going to give her enough support?"

Sherry and Else take turns reassuring her, gesturing to the straps, the shape of the cups, the four snaps in the back.

Finally I leave, much embarrassed, carrying a new beige bra that could easily serve as a hat, and dreading the day I'll have to come back and go through the whole process again.

■ WRITING TIPS

Though hard-and-fast rules on writing don't exist, you can learn from time-tested advice:

■ BE CORRECT

Get the story right both in terms of detail and context. Look for and capture the significant detail, the revealing anecdote and the prevailing mood. Make certain the tone and style of the story match the mood. Finally, edit closely so that the story is structurally, mechanically and stylistically correct.

In particular, pay attention to verb tense and parallel structures. For example:

WEAK: After leading cheers at the homecoming pep rally, senior Pearly White met her boyfriend in the parking lot, kisses him on the lips and then blushed while her friends squeal and swooned.

Note the tense inconsistency (see changes in italics).

BETTER: After leading cheers at the homecoming pep rally, senior Pearly White *met* her boyfriend in the parking lot, *kissed* him on the lips and then *blushed* while her friends *squealed* and *swooned*.

Another common problem is consistent

point of view. For example:

WEAK: Swimming instructors must be patient if they work with children. You must acknowledge that some children have never swum before, and you must acclimate children to the water.

BETTER: Swimming instructors must be patient if they work with children. *Instructors* must acknowledge that some children have never swum before, and *they* must acclimate children to the water.

■ KEEP IT SIMPLE

A forceful sentence relies on a subject, a verb and an object. But additional phrases and clauses often add helpful details. The length is unimportant as long as each sentence is straightforward and clear. If you're describing Mortal Kombat, don't write: *Imbued with a veritable plethora of emotion, Joe depressed the button, thereby eliminating his video adversary.*

Remember: you're writing for an audience of readers, not a group of AP English teachers. Don't try to impress readers with your command of the thesaurus and the *Handbook to Literature.* Avoid this:

MAJOR YUK

THE SCENE IS that of a Guatemalan prison, a cold, dank, cement-block edifice as foreboding as the Bastille or the Black Hole of Calcutta. Screams reverberate up and down the corridors, an undulating procession of horror, a nightmare worthy of Dante. At one end of the passageway is a tenebrous room, illuminated by a solitary bulb that swings softly, back and forth, to and fro, back and forth, like a hangman's noose.

A surfeit of blood cakes the walls. In the middle of the room sits an oak stool, and on the stool slumps a man of advancing years, pummeled into submission, his hollow eyes entreating his captors for mercy.

"I implore you in the name of God to cease this torment," the supplicant timeworn agrarian pleads, not unlike Polonius of Shakespeare's *Hamlet* or perhaps the tragic Antigone. "Open your eyes and hearts! Let us stand together as members of the working class and struggle against our common enemy, the bourgeoisie."

Like Procrustes, the sadist jailers chortle and recommence their evil deeds on our tragic hero who is but a wretched farmer. Ignoring his pleas, they extricate his fingernails and decimate his proletarian digits.

"Alas, the injustice of it all. My catharsis. Grant me my catharsis!" the tiller of the soil declaims before slipping into a blissful and tranquil unconsciousness as his wife and children huddle in the mid-day drizzle outside the prison gates, waiting to reclaim his scarred and bruised body.

This, my friends, is our challenge, our duty, if you will. Liberty or tyranny! No man is truly free until all men are free. To the ramparts, I say. Contribute to Amnesty International. Adieu!

■ BE CONCISE

WEAK: The vehicle we were looking for was a van that we planned to use on our vacation.

BETTER: For our vacation, we wanted a van.

WEAK: The 6-11 center on the basketball team lowered down his head and walked into the journalism classroom.

BETTER: The 6-11 center ducked into the journalism lab.

■ BE PRECISE

Say what you mean, and mean what you say. In one column, a young woman was writing about her experience as a teen mother. In what was otherwise a thoughtful and poignant column, she wrote, "I got pregnant in December *while I was playing basketball.*"

Picture that.

Use only relevant information and in a logical sequence.

WEAK: Coach Linda Sullivan, who is a deaconess at the First Baptist Church, said the team is not in the same class as the top-ranked

MAJOR SINS OF COLUMN WRITING, PART 2

■ Comments that poke fun at an individual's disabilities, infirmities or physical conditions.

■ Columns that call attention to themselves, such as the "Letters to me" when columnists answer letters so that they'll have the last word on the subject.

■ Rip-offs, such as imitations of Ann Landers or Dr. Ruth.

■ Horoscopes unless you can provide specific information such as winning lottery numbers.

■ Comments that are intended to offend. One student, in what was supposed to be an analysis of the U. S. policy in Somalia, described starving Africans as looking like "chocolate-covered skeletons." Thankfully, the obnoxious statement never appeared in print.

Tigers, whom they play Thursday night.

Now, what does the fact that she is a deaconess at the church have to do with her predictions about the Thursday night game?

It might be possible to use the fact that she is a deaconess as part of a play on words.

BETTER: Coach Linda Sullivan, who is a deaconess at the First Baptist Church, said the team doesn't have a prayer against the top-ranked Tigers Thursday night.

■ USE DYNAMIC NOUNS AND VERBS

Any time you have a choice of words, choose the one with the narrowest meaning. The power of your writing will come from the ability of your words to evoke images and emotions.

WEAK: I could tell by the funny look on her face that she was mad.

BETTER: I could tell she was mad by the way her face turned blood red and the veins in her forehead stretched like a cheap pair of double-knit slacks. The meat cleaver that she clutched as she shrieked, "Prepare to meet thy doom!" was a dead giveaway, too.

■ MATCH TONE TO PURPOSE

If you're writing about a serious topic, take a serious approach. If you're writing about something odd or funny, take a witty or satirical approach.

Master the use of words. Find new and more precise words with which you're comfortable. But if you want to say "help," don't say "succor." If you want to say "agree," don't say "concur." If you mean "clear," don't write "lucid."

In addition, avoid colloquialisms, slang, jargon and clichés. Down South, we like to say "I'm fixing" when we mean "I am about to." For example: "I'm *fixing* to watch the Longhorns beat the Aggies like a step-child."

The cliché "beat 'em like a step-child" always sends the politically correct crowd through the roof, but that's not reason enough to use it. Avoid clichés. Like the plague.

■ KEEP IT SHORT

Focus on a narrow topic. Write about people, not subjects. If you write about an issue, do so in terms of people. Rather than a column that preaches on the evils of cigarette smoking, write one that analyzes or interprets the actions of a person who is trying to help teens kick the habit.

It bears repeating: Be true to yourself. Stretch your talents. Explore. Take risks. But don't try to be someone you're not.

■ BREAK THE RULES

Occasionally. And know why you're breaking them. Good writers break rules to achieve a stylistic or rhetorical effect.

To vary your rhythm, use a sentence fragment occasionally. I'm not suggesting that you should omit a noun or a verb arbitrarily. But there are times when a sentence fragment works quite well. Like right now.

And don't get too hung up on mechanics. Too many teachers worry about mechanics to the exclusion of the more important content. Concentrate first on what you have to say. Worry second about whether you dotted all the I's and crossed all the T's. Your editors and adviser will help you with this.

■ USE FICTIONAL DIALOGUE

Several years ago, I came across a column written about a Texas law that purportedly allows newborn babies to be legally abandoned within 30 days of birth. The columnist made lots of serious, legal points and asked several rhetorical questions, such as "Is this the proper way to invoke a sense of responsibility amongst the youth of our country?" Overall, the piece was stuffy, bombastic and way too serious. I wanted to say to the kid, "Lighten up." Exaggerate the point with a little fictional dialogue. For example:

"HONEY, CAN WE TAKE THIS baby back?" Vicki Bob said. "All he does is eat, cry and poop, and he's keeping the dogs awake at night and creating such a fuss that I can't even hardly hear Jerry Springer on TV. We got to do something!"

"Okay by me," Bubba replied. "Heck, we got nine others anyway. We can take this one back on our way to Jimbo's Gun and Bait Shop cause I'm dang near out of shotgun shells. And maybe you and I can celebrate our second wedding anniversary by picking up a six pack of Big Red and a pickled egg or two."

■ SPICE IT UP

The writing must have rhythm. Sometimes it should gallop. Other times it should trot. The pace varies according to the subject and the mood. Political differences aside, from whom would you rather hear a speech: Jesse Jackson or George W. Bush?

Let's face it, Bush is to oratory what Keanu Reeves is to acting. And regardless whether you like Mr. Jackson, you have to admit that knows how to give a speech. He peppers his speeches with anecdotes. He knows how to use colorful touches such as hyperbole, alliteration, allusion and personification. His "Keep hope alive" speech sent shivers down my spine. Consider this excerpt from one of Jackson's speech:

WE HAVE A president who has traveled the world but has never been to Hamlet, North Carolina. Yet we must not overlook Hamlet.

It was there that 25 workers died in a fire at Imperial Foods, more women than men, more white than black. They worked making chicken parts in vats heated to 400 degrees, with few windows and no fans. The owners locked the doors on the outside. The workers died trapped by economic desperation and oppressive work laws.

One woman came up to me after the fire. She said, "I want to work. I don't want to go on welfare. I have three children and no husband. We pluck 90 wings a minute. Now I can't bend my wrist, I got the carpel thing. Then when we're hurt, they fire us—and we have no health insurance and no union to help us. We can't get another job because we're crippled so they put us on welfare and call us lazy."

I said you are not lazy, and you are not alone. Her friend, a white woman came up and said:

"I'm seven months pregnant. We stand in two inches of water with two five-minute bathroom breaks. Sometimes we can't hold our water, and then our bowels, and we faint."

We wept together.

If we keep Hamlet in our hearts and before our eyes, we will act to empower working people. We will protect the right to organize and to strike. We will empower workers to enforce health and safety laws. We will provide a national health care system, a minimum wage sufficient to bring workers out of poverty, paid parental leave. We must build a movement for economic justice across the land."

No doubt, the power of this statement comes not only from the writing but from Mr. Jackson's delivery. Still, I believe its ultimate power stems from the fact that it focuses on specific people rather than political rhetoric and speaks to the heart as much as the mind.

■ READ

I'll be blunt: you can never expect to become a competent writer unless you read a lot. Extensively. Voraciously. Your development of diction and understanding of rhythm can come only from reading widely and deeply. Read not just for content but for voice, tone and rhythm. Occasionally, compare a piece of excellent writing against something you've written. The following column is a good place to begin.

SHOWCASE

By **CLARE BUNDY**
Duncanville High School, Duncanville, TX

"CLARE!"

Her voice filters through two insulated walls, three doors and a mirror.

And it's still loud enough to abuse my ears above the running shower water which, five seconds ago, was blissfully peaceful.

I turn off the water.

ELEMENTS OF A REVIEW

■ A strong lead that lets the reader know immediately whether you liked it— whether the "it" is a movie, restaurant, book, play, video game or CD.
■ Background information. Major stars. Brief plot description. Sequel? Prequel? Update of an earlier review? Whatever. Bring the reader up to date.
■ Strengths of the piece, if any, but don't gush over it.
■ Weaknesses, if any, but don't savage the piece.
■ Ending that leaves no doubt as to the critic's opinion. This may include a recommendation but it's generally unnecessary.
■ Remember: the shorter, the better.

> ❝ A review is an odd hybrid combining elements of news writing, editorial writing and feature writing. It should be timely, informal, local and opinionated. If all goes right, it might even be fascinating.❞

"What?" I scream back.

"Come HERE!"

I trudge into the hall from the bathroom, dripping all over our 'universal rust' carpet.

Entering my room, I sight the source of the formidable voice. Lillian.

Lillian is half harpee, half vulture. Lillian is angry. Lillian is my 18-year-old sister.

I peer over her shoulder to see what the reason for her wrath is.

An eyeshadow applicator.

She fingers the spongy end, whips around and wipes her hand on my white terry cloth robe.

"That's BLACK, Clare!"

"Thank you. You're very observant, Lil."

"I get out a *special applicator* every morning so you won't use it for that black crap you put on your eyes, and what do you do? You *use* it, and now it's black, too! You *know* I only use brown!"

And she storms out of the room, leaving me with ringing ears and a severe case of the "So what's!"

I return to the bathroom to blow-dry my hair. Lil's leaning over the sink, using a new applicator on her eyes. I roll mine, and they automatically stop at a light pink scar on her tanned back; an arc starting up near her left shoulder and trailing off at her right shoulder blade.

My brief anger at being verbally abused disappears, and I flash her my brief "Good-morning-to-you" smile.

I don't know what the scar means to her. I've never asked. Not that we don't talk; many a night she's crept into my room at 1 a.m., pushed under the covers, and whispered, "Clare . . . .you up?" And we launch into a one to two-hour discussion on guys, our parents, our feelings. Life.

But we don't talk about the scar, or its origin: a tumor, the size of a grapefruit, that was on her lung when she was only 7 years old. We don't talk about the specialists flown in, the risky operation performed or the roll of film our father dedicated to taking final pictures of the little blond girl he expected to lose.

We don't talk about it, but I haven't forgotten. Every time Lil turns her back, I remember when she came back home to us. Changed by the pain of 52 stitches and blood tests twice a day, doctors shaking their heads and a morbid hospital atmosphere, my sister returned a different person.

She came back an angry child I didn't much care for because my 6-year-old mentality couldn't possibly understand. My 17-year-old mind can. And does.

Yet my brain is often distracted by her 15-minute oratories on "Why Clare shouldn't borrow a shirt without asking" or "The advantages of good housekeeping." She is a neat nut. And she has a temper. These two traits do not mix so well.

She once got so mad at my little sister, Terese, for leaving an uneaten plate of spaghetti in the spotless kitchen that she chunked that plate, along with its cold, congealed contents, right into my younger sister's room. Terese yelled upon finding it, huffed and puffed while she cleaned it up, and rolled her eyes at me as we passed in the hall.

"I can't wait until she goes to college," Terese said.

"Yeah," I agreed with a grin.

But it's not exactly true. Lil's yelling, but she's alive. Really alive. And now that her bed's empty, my sleep's not being interrupted at night, and I'm not being hollered at for a lost earring, I kind of miss it. But she won't be gone for good. She was almost gone forever.

I'll keep in mind the scar: a symbol for me of good fortune and a "Gee, it's great to be alive!" outlook. And I'll keep in mind the talks about guys, our parents, our feelings.

Life.

Ain't it grand!

■ WRITING REVIEWS

My 10-year-old daughter and I had an agreement. If I'd shell out $6 for her to see a movie, she'd say it was awesome. *Jurassic Park* and *Ernest Saves Christmas* were equally awesome in her opinion. This says a lot more about 10-year-olds than it does about either movie.

High school students are a little like this. After shelling out a week's pay for a dinner date or concert ticket, students expect the experience to be awesome, and, at least in terms of concerts, as long as the band lays on the requisite amount of smoke and lasers and cranks out the maximum level of sound, it usually is, at least by teenage standards.

At least, that's the impression I get from reading the concert reviews in student newspapers. Students have limited funds, so they carefully spend their money on the events they really want to see. Given that they can afford to see only so many concerts, teens are likely to select the ones they expect to most enjoy. The concert reviews reflect this reality, and I don't have a problem with their verdicts.

But I do have a problem with the tendency to rehash the program rather critique the concert. Instead of reviewing the performance, young critics too often recite the order in which the songs were played and what the performers were wearing. How often do we need to hear that rock and roll musicians wear ripped blue jeans and spandex? How surprised can we be that the show included lasers and smoke? Or three encores?

Evaluate the performance in context to the entertainer's career and hype. A U2 concert will generate phenomenal publicity. Was the performance equal to the hype? If so, why? If not, why? Don't just rehash the play list.

The same is true for movie reviews. Too many provide little more information than is available in the final credits. For example:

IN *CROSSROADS*, Lucy (Britney Spears) is an innocent high school valedictorian who is debating what to do with her life. When she was 10, she made a pact with her two best friends to stay together forever. They put their wishes for the world in a box and then buried it with the intention of digging it up on the night of their high school graduation.

By the time that night finally rolls around eight years later, they have gone their separate ways but decide to dig up the box anyway. The moments spent reminiscing draw them together again, and they decide to take a road trip. Mimi (Taryn Manning) is pregnant and needs money to support her child. She wants to travel to Los Angeles to pursue a singing career, so Lucy and Kit (Zoe Saldana) sign on as her backup singers and off they go. Their hunky driver, Ben (Anson Mount), is one of Mimi's friends who has a shaky past. The four travel across the country in search of their dreams but run into some roadblocks along the way.

This is a sort of good movie. It was funny at times

THE GREATEST TIP ON REVIEW WRITING OF ALL TIME

Watch the hyperbole. High school students tend to describe movies, albums and books in exaggerated terms: the best album since Sgt. Pepper, the worst movie of all time or at least 1989, the most awesome concert experience since the Middle Ages, and so on.

Take a chill pill and just tell the reader in simple and reasonable terms what you thought about it.

but just plain stupid at others. If you're a Britney Spears fan, you won't want to miss it. But if you don't like Britney, then you might want to skip it.

So what has the reader learned here? Not much. The general plot, but not a lot more. Is it a good movie? Don't know. It's okay if you're a Britney Spears fan. That doesn't say much. Compare it to this excellent review.

SHOWCASE ■

By **ERIC LEFENFELD**
McCallum High School, Austin, TX

I DON'T UNDERSTAND why people critize Britney Spears' acting ability. Considering her career thus far has been a gigantic charade engineered by various record executives, it really is no surprise that the pop star is taking the leap from shallow, cliched songs to a shallow, cliched movie. Ironically, one of the aforementioned songs is seemingly played constantly throughout the last third of the film.

The only satisfaction I got out of this movie was looking around the theater and seeing it half empty. Don't get me wrong. I went into *Crossroads* with an unbiased attitude. I do not hate this movie because it is a star vehicle for Britney Spears. I hate it, simply put, because it is a bad movie. The generically-titled *Crossroads* is the story of three friends who have drifted apart over high school. You have your three basic stereotypes: the naive virgin who just wants to be independent, the popular diva who must overcome her self-centered personality and the pregnant trailer trash. Unfortunately, Britney is not the trailer trash. That would have made an interesting movie.

Over the course of a wild and wacky road trip, the girls find each other, and themselves, as they reach the crossroads of life. If that sounds like nothing more than sugary fluff, imagine these characters towering over you for an hour and a

half, spouting out dialogue that would make Ed Wood shriek in disgust. Multiply that dreadful feeling by 10 or 20. Think about rotten meat. You now have a partial understanding of the experience that is *Crossroads*.

Since this movie is fictional, I guess Britney's character, Lucy, is tired from singing since everything she says comes out in a quiet, mousy, whisper. She enunciates and slowly pronounces every word to an unbearable point. The good thing about the requisite love interest, played by Anson Mount, is that we have a new Keanu Reeves on our hands. This guy's blank stares could put a rabid dog to sleep. Dan Aykroyd is in this for the paycheck, and it shows. The man is phoning in his performance, and every time he was onscreen, all I could think was, "This guy was in *Ghostbusters*? How the mighty have fallen."

No Britney Spears venture is complete without exploiting the young singer's body, and *Crossroads* is no different. Here we get two extended scenes of Britney cavorting in her skivvies. Last time I checked, Britney's target audience was the pre-teen set. Apparently, the movie's producers, wise beyond belief, didn't want to alienate another frighteningly large fan-base: perverted old men. You have to love Hollywood; they make movies everyone can appreciate.

I, of course, cannot truly judge the merits of a Britney Spears film. I am neither a 10-year-old girl nor a perverted old man. I guess all the perverts snuck out back, leaving me with the opinions of Erin, a 10-year-old girl, who was quick to say that she wasn't a fan of Britney before she saw the movie.

"She's funny," said Erin, in reference to Britney's performance.

I think this ambiguous statement speaks for itself. *Crossroads* may not be a good movie, but if the kiddies like it, what's the harm? Fortunately, there are hundreds of better movies for children to watch, so that is not even an excuse. *Crossroads* should be avoided like the plague. I didn't even have to pay for my ticket, and I still stand by my convictions. With any luck, this movie will bomb, Britney Spears will fall into obscurity, and we will all sleep a little better at night.

Why does this review succeed where the other failed? First, it is obvious Eric knows a lot about the genre, and this knowledge allows him to compare and contrast the movie to others of that ilk. Bluntly speaking, he is a credible authority on the subject.

Second, the review is written with great style and confidence. He doesn't rely on catchy one-liners or clichés. It's authoritative and legitimate without being pedantic or preachy.

A review—whether of a book, film, album or restaurant—should attempt to convey an honest and fair criticism, pro or con. This criticism is gained through accurate observation and appropriate reporting. In almost all cases, this reporting involves listening, reading or viewing the performer's full body of work. It isn't fair to either reader or performer to judge the performance in a vacuum. So if you're reviewing the latest John Grisham novel, tell the reader how it compares to his earlier books as well as to suspense novels of other writers.

As for reviewing music, it makes no sense to go down the playlist and say the same thing about every song. Review the CD as a single piece of art. How does it stack up to its contemporary competition? If it's an established band, how does it stand up to previous work? I'll show my age here, but it would make little sense to review *Sgt. Pepper* without mentioning *A Hard Day's Night, Help, Rubber Soul* and *Revolver*. How did the Beatles get here from there? Where do they go from here? Consider this review, written by Michael Hardy of Austin Westlake High School.

THE NEWS OF BEN FOLDS FIVE's breakup, with the inevitable announcement of a solo release by front-man Folds, was a great disappointment. The cliché is, of course, that the fragmented parts don't add up to the whole. However, as was the case with Roger Waters'

departure from Pink Floyd, Ben Folds leaves behind very little. On their final album, *The Unauthorized Biography of Reinhold Messner*, the Five was little more than a backup band for his personal musical ideas (much like *The Wall* was for Waters).

So it comes as no surprise that his 2001 solo record, *Rockin' the Suburbs*, is the natural progression from that point. True, he's slimmed down a little: there is less orchestration and less distortion. This time, he seems more interested in character portrait and melodic flow than witty couplets and strong beats, which is, of course, the irony of the single and MTV hit "Rockin' the Suburbs." It doesn't fit on the album at all and, in fact, is concerned only with clever lyrics and rockin' riffs. Sadly, it doesn't amount to much, and worse, paints a poor picture of the rest of the record.

To become a critic rather than simply a writer, heed these additional tips on writing reviews:

■ Avoid the first person singular. Keep yourself out of the article. Rather than "I enjoyed the concert," write "The concert was superb." And explain why.

■ Do your research. If you're writing about the latest Martin Scorcese film, go back and watch *Mean Streets, Raging Bull* and *Goodfellas*. Read as much about Scorcese and his films as possible. Become an expert.

■ But remember, you're not writing a research paper. The point is to critique the film. What did you like about it? What didn't you like? It's your opinion. Don't steal direct quotes or critical comments from *Rolling Stone* or *Entertainment Weekly*.

■ Make certain the review carries a byline and is clearly labeled as opinion.

■ Don't try to impress the reader with your knowledge of jargon. Write for the average reader, not the studio president or movie director. And don't freak out in a spasm of new-age pseudo-babble. *The film takes it agitprop story about the wonders of Soviet collectivization and turns it into a poetic —*

DON'T ATTACK YOUR READERS

Okay, so you didn't like the movie. That's fine. Explain your reasons. But don't turn on your readers.

"Overall, I give this CD a minus 2 out of five. The only reason I didn't give it a minus 5 was because of the cool photo of the nude girl in chains on the cover. Other than that, I would recommend this only to the dregs of society. In other words, freshmen. Ha!"

Grow up.

almost Jungian — visual mediation on the organic cycles of life and death. What the heck does that mean?

■ Pay attention to the audience reaction. It might be worth noting that every member of the packed house walked out halfway through Sylvester Stallone's latest film after throwing their drinks and popcorn at the screen.

■ Don't show off your knowledge of cultural esoterica. In other words, don't compare Vin Diesel's latest romper-stomper to Japanese director Kon Ichikawa's 1959 classic *Fire on the Plain*, which maybe 100 people in the world, none of whom attend your school, have seen.

■ Avoid clichés, such as "I laughed. I cried. I experienced the full range of human emotion. I was completely carried away . . . "

■ Work to convince the reader. Make the reader feel, "Hey, that's how I felt." Even if readers disagree with you, they should respect your point of view and opinions.

■ Bring the review to a satisfying conclusion. For example: *The Bourne Identify is essentially one long chase sequence, and it's constructed almost entirely from suspense tropes we've seen before, but (director Doug) Liman infuses it with such chilly European flair that it's impossible not to enjoy the ride.*

■ Keep it short. Make your points as concisely as possible and move on. The hamburger was greasy and the french fries cold. What else is there to say? Take your cue from Time magazine's "Short Takes."

■ Give it a grade. Thumbs up or thumbs down? One star or four? An A, B or F?

Note how the following column incorporates all of these suggestions to create a convincing argument.

SHOWCASE ■

By **LAUREN JAGNOW**
Glenbard East High School, IL

GENGHIS KHAN, notorious conqueror of Asia, has gone into the restaurant business.

Well, not really. However, the Mongolian restaurant at 2942 S. Finley Road in Downers Grove has chosen to name its establishment after the most famous Mongolian who ever lived.

Though you may not expect hospitality from a restaurant named after a barbarian, Genghis Khan offers exotic, inexpensive food and quality service as well as a unique atmosphere.

The food is served buffet style with a variety of meats, noodles and vegetables that are stir-fried before your eyes by two skilled chefs using long wooden sticks to flip and stir the food on a sizzling grill.

Mongolian cuisine differs from Chinese food in that it is considerably spicier. A seemingly innocent plate of noodles and beef should be eaten with a glass of water close at hand.

Not all the food is spicy, though. Combinations such as pork with pineapple chunks and peanuts taste sweet and juicy.

There is enough variety on the buffet table that you can create mild entrees or those that will generate tears. The choice makes it possible for all diners to please their palates.

There is also a prepared food buffet that offers spicy Sesame beef and fresh seafood such as Alaskan crab legs and jumbo shrimp as well as rice, stir-fried vegetables and slightly sour but tasty Mongolian bread.

The atmosphere at Genghis Khan is relaxing and pleasant.

Careful, though, you could become hypnotized if you stare for too long at the two panes of water filled with moving bubbles.

With a pot of tea in front of you and a plate of appetizers ranging from pickled cucumbers to egg rolls, your meal at Genghis Khan is like eating with Genghis Khan himself.

Only you won't have to worry about getting clubbed during dessert.

■ STAFF VS. PERSONAL OPINION

It is important to distinguish between the staff editorial and the personal opinion column. The staff editorial stands as the statement of the newspaper as an institution—not that of the individual writer.

While the purpose of the staff editorial may be the same as the personal opinion column — that is, to praise, criticize, defend, endorse, etc.—the style is different. In most cases, the staff editorial is written in formal English. Conjunctions and sentence fragments (a.k.a. "minor sentences" when used for stylistic or rhetorical effect) are avoided.

In many cases, the staff editorial follows a specific formula:

- introduction of problem
- statement of staff stance
- supporting evidence for staff stance
- introduction of alternate point of view
- rebuttal of alternate point of view
- summary remarks
- call to action

Note how it's used in the following newspaper staff editorial:

MAYBE SOME STUDENTS sacrifice studies to work. Perhaps they spend the money they earn frivolously. And it's possible they suffer socially by packing in the hours on the job.

But if they do, so be it. This is a matter for students and their parents to resolve. The last thing students need is the federal government keeping track of how many hours they work, how many hours they study, and how many hours they spent debating or playing football.

Recently, a committee of child-labor experts recommended that Congress should give the Department of Labor the authority to limit the number of hours children under 18 can work during the school year. The Fair Labor Standards Act of 1938 gives the Labor Department the authority to limit work hours only for children under 16. The committee's report says Congress should expand that authority to include 16- and 17-year-olds. According to the report, *Protecting Youth at Work: Health, Safety, and Development of Working Children and Adolescents in the United States*, young people who work long hours during the school year are more likely to let their grades slide and get involved in alcohol and drug abuse. The recommendation does not cover work-study programs such as DECA.

We concede that it is difficult to juggle studies, work, extracurricular activities and social obligations. In a perfect world, students would go to school full-time, participate in some activity after school, then hang out with their friends that evening. But this isn't a perfect world. Many juniors and seniors need the money they earn working for college. Some students are the primary wage-earners in their families. Their jobs put bread on the table.

And it is wrong to assume that all jobs are detrimental. Many jobs teach responsibility, promptness and teamwork as well as specific, marketable skills. It's simplistic to think that all teens are stuck in dead-end jobs delivering pizza or grilling hamburgers.

The merits of balancing studies and work should be debated and decided by students and their families, not the government. Federal child labor laws protect children under the age of 16. Young adults don't need federal bureaucrats enforcing a one-size-fits-all policy that tells them when they can work and when they need to study.

A powerful editorial, no doubt, and in the old days, the newspaper model would have called for a page 1 straight news story and a page 8 staff editorial about the proposed federal regulations. No longer. Reporters are free to cover such stories as news-analysis, news-feature or opinion column.

Of course, this isn't for beginners. More personal, analytical and interpretive writing styles allow trained journalists to tell stories in dramatic, insightful ways. And while this style allows the reporter to break a few of the traditional rules, it does not allow the reporter to do a lazy or flippant job of gathering information. Quite the contrary. The personal approach requires an even greater attention to accuracy, detail and context. Anything short of a concentrated effort can lead to charges that the coverage is unfair, biased or irresponsible.

THE PURPOSE OF AN EDITORIAL IS TO LEAD

Editorials can:

- praise or criticize
- attack or defend
- propose or oppose
- entertain or warn
- instigate or advocate or take a stand on any issue that your editorial board believes to be important to your readers.

The bottom line: editorials lead. They should appeal to the student body's better angels: knowledge, logic and morality.

Photo by **CYNTHIA SOTO**
Riverside High School, El Paso, TX

PUT YOUR HEART INTO IT

15

You are on the verge of a great adventure. As a journalist, you will have a chance to grow as an individual and to change your school, community and world for the better. It takes a lot of work, but it's worth it.

CHAPTER HIGHLIGHTS:

■ Good writing is rewriting.

■ Good writing takes time and effort.

■ But the payoff is well worth it.

I hate to write, but I love to have written. That line by legendary writing instructor Nancy Patterson of Virginia pretty much sums up the philosophy of many journalists. Writing is hard work. It's time-consuming, frustrating and sometimes tedious. And this comes on the heels of the hours and hours we've spent reporting—gathering facts, interviewing sources, watching and listening, thumbing through magazines or newspaper clippings for background information.

The great majority of time spent on a story involves collecting information, not writing. But as time-consuming as reporting is, it's the actual writing that most often drives us nuts. We cram all of this information into our brains and expect it to simmer until done. And when it doesn't pour out in flawless prose, we pull our hair out.

When the words won't come, when we can't remember what we want to say or how we want to say it, we question our sanity. Why did I sign up to be a reporter? Or an editor? Why put myself through this?

The thought of blowing it off zips through our minds. "Who reads this stuff anyway?" we ask ourselves. For the moment, we entertain the thought of turning in a story that isn't our best effort. But then we realize that doing so would not so much betray the subject and our readers as it would ourselves.

Ultimately, writing is a personal experience, an act of self-love. We have something to say. We want people to listen, so we put ourselves on the line. We reveal our insecurities, our dreams, our passions. It takes courage and effort.

I believe it is this unwillingness to compromise our own sense of self-worth that frustrates so many young writers. It manifests itself in different ways. For example, a few former students attempted to convince me that they suffered from writer's block. I would have believed them had they written anything, which, of course, they had not. Rather than writer's block, they were stifled because their stories weren't writing themselves. They wanted the words simply to fly out the ends of their magic fingers.

It would have been nice, but that's not how it works. So get used to it. If you want to be a journalist, expect some pain. Buy aspirin. Find a shoulder to cry on. Be prepared to miss a few hours of sleep. I can think of nothing more torturous than searching for the perfect angle, the perfect lead.

So if someone tells you they love to write, don't buy it. If they truly love to write, then they're not working at it hard enough.

> ❝ While writing isn't easy, it brings great personal satisfaction to have written something that you're proud of, a story on which you gladly place your name. ❞

■ LEARN TO LOVE TO WRITE

I don't say this to scare you off. Quite the contrary. I want you to fall in love with the sweet agony of reporting and writing. It can be fun, even thrilling. Too many students are turned off by teachers who think writing is nothing more than an exercise in punctuation. I once heard an English teacher say, "I warned my students that if they used a passive verb, it was an automatic D."

I thought, "You're the kind of teacher who'd flunk John Irving."

That teacher probably used writing as a form of torture. "Write 500 times, 'I will not use a passive verb.'"

While writing isn't easy, it brings great personal satisfaction to have written something that you're proud of, a story on which you gladly place your name. When the adviser is prodding the reporter to just get it done, it takes a special steel to respond, "Yeah, but it's my name on the story. I can't just give my readers junk."

The desire to do well comes not so much from others—the adviser, the staff, the school or the state press association—but rather from within. The standards of others may help tap that self-realization and pride in a productive way, but the desire to want to produce as perfect a product as possible must exist. Otherwise, no amount of external pressure will pry it out.

This desire to produce also arises from a need to serve. The joy of writing leads to a special result: the joy of reading. As staff members produce carefully crafted words and reflect emotions as well as ideas, readers respond. Even students who rarely read assignments will read the writing of their peers if those writers put energy and imagination into their work. At those schools, readers complain when they haven't received their paper for two weeks. "Why do we have to wait so long for another issue?" Or, "Why didn't the staff work during vacation so there would be an issue sooner?"

And though educators may not believe it, many of those demanding "their rights as readers" are the non-scholars in the school. But even students who fail courses or cause trouble in school are people, too. You can speak to them in ways that show that somebody cares and that life can be interesting.

Quite simply, it's a genuine thrill to have someone you don't know—a person out of your social and educational orbit—tell you that they enjoyed reading an article you wrote. You realize that your writing has legs. It travels beyond the limits of your imagination, and you realize that you are contributing to a literacy of your world. Even better, you have helped others to be informed, to be vital, to enjoy life on a new dimension—and to feel the joy of fulfilling dreams and the sadness of others' hardships.

I work with men and women who have graduate degrees but who are not writers. They are expected to compose at least one column each month, September through May. It's my job to edit their columns.

■ GOOD WRITING TAKES TIME

Only one or two of these people are naturally gifted writers, but they all have a basic understanding of the written word. The difference in the quality of the columns boils down to the amount of time each spends on his or her column. A few whip them out in an hour, columns that rehash one of two or three themes, all of which are perfunctory to the point of cliché. Participation is good. Sportsmanship is important. Rules are necessary. Blah, blah, blah.

For them, writing is an exercise no different than filling out a form.

Others spend time with the columns. They don't especially look forward to writing them. It takes time and work. It takes concentration. But they put forth the effort so that their columns are an extension of their personality and character. They know they will be judged by their written comments. The publication is circulated to 33,000 teachers and school administrators in Texas alone, as well as to a few hundred others throughout the nation. The widespread circulation sufficiently scares them to do as good a job as possible.

■ THE BEST YOU CAN DO

I want you to share their fright. I want you to remember that your story will be distributed to every student in the high school, that every reader may take the publication home, that every parent may take the publication to work the next day. I want you to realize that every person in your community may have a chance to see your story. I want this to scare you so badly that you'd never dare turn in a story that didn't receive your maximum effort and was worth reading.

Perhaps it won't be perfect. But it should be the best story you can produce in the time you're given to write it. John Lennon once said that he never finished writing a song—he simply recorded the latest version in time to include it on the latest Beatles album. You should feel the same way about your stories. You will always find a better way to write it, but when the deadline rolls around, you should have produced the best draft possible.

I also want to share the exhilaration, the sheer fun of working hard on a story or column. Because you deliberately strive to provide something for everyone—from the lowly freshman to the all-powerful school board—you record as many scenes of life as possible. You record the energy of Friday night parties and the acrid smell of the locker rooms and the din of the band hall. You record the moments that made the school and community proud—when the National Merit scholars are named—as well as the facts that the powers-that-be might wish were left brushed under the rug.

With so many possibilities to unleash your creativity and spirit, you and your fellow staffers will experience the rush of going from blank pages to pages bearing thousands of words and art and photos. Quite frankly, I'm a little jealous of you. You are about to have some of the most important, the most thrilling, the most painful experiences of your life. Some of this can be attributed to the fact that you're a high school student. But much of it stems from the fact that you're part of a very special collection of teenagers.

Finally, remember that you're a beginner, no matter how many years you've served on the staff. You're going to make mistakes. Even though your adviser and editors are there to cover for you, mistakes will slip through. It

happens to everyone. You have to learn to forgive yourself and press on.

■ WE ALL MAKE MISTAKES

Over the years, I've written hundreds of articles and columns. Now and then, I thumb through them. While reading these clips brings me some satisfaction, I always second-guess myself. Why did I use that lead? What did I mean by that? Who was I trying to impress when I used that word?

Occasionally, I'm embarrassed by something I've written. As a young reporter, I wrote what has to be one of the worst leads in the history of American journalism. The story involved the rewriting of Texas bank regulations, and I had interviewed at length the president of a local bank. To my eternal shame, I wrote: "In this fruit salad called life, the banker is the top banana."

It had little or nothing to do with changes in bank regulations. At the time, though, I thought it was clever. Now, it makes me cringe. I blame my editors. I was young and stupid. They should have been watching out for me. Why didn't they save me from myself?

In high school, I wrote a pre-game football story that our opponents found fit to duplicate and plaster throughout their school. They thought I had dissed them. I didn't mean to. It just came out that way. Of course, this unexpected motivation didn't please the head football coach. If we had lost the game, I'm sure he would have blamed me.

These lapses aside, I'm proud of my writing. I want you to feel the same way about yours. I hope you can pick up your newspaper or yearbook 25 years from now and read one of your stories with pride. I hope the stories entertain you, rekindle a few emotions, take you to back when.

They will if you'll put some heart and soul into them, if you'll strive for something greater than mere correctness. They will if you'll abandon the strangulating traditional writing styles in favor of more narrative, descriptive approaches. It requires more work. It takes great dedication. But the effort is well worth it. And when you're finished, you may admit that you may not have loved writing it, but you'll love having written it.

OTHER THAN WRITER'S CRAMP, WHAT'S IN IT FOR YOU?

Few of you will enter journalism as a career. You'll go on to live productive lives.

Hey, that was a joke.

But seriously, only one or two of a hundred kids who participate on a student publication go on to make a career out of journalism. But all students who report, write, edit, design, sell ads, shoot photographs, and hang around the school pub benefit. Why?

■ They're better writers.

■ They learn to think more clearly and critically.

■ They're more aware of the world around them.

■ They learn to more intelligently consume the media.

■ They learn to meet deadlines.

■ They learn teamwork.

■ They learn to solve problems.

■ They learn to cope.

■ They get a chance to read really cool books like this one.

Photo by **CHRIS HANEWINCKEL**
Downey High School, Downey, CA

THANKS

I couldn't have done it without the guidance, advice, inspiration, examples, emotional support, technical abilities, nagging, browbeating and otherwise hands-on help of the following people and staffs;

CHAPTER HIGHLIGHTS:

■ A lot of people gave me a lot of help. And I owe them, big time.

I OWE a great debt of gratitude to the following people, who helped define, shape, organize, clarify, proof and edit this book:

■ Howard Spanogle, who edited the first edition of this book. Lori Oglesbee of McKinney, TX, who edited the second edition of this book.

■ Gary Lundgren and John Dalke, Jostens, Inc., for their design and graphic contributions as well as overall support and guidance.

I am grateful to the following people for their contributions, suggestions and support: Dan Austin, Orangevale, CA; John Bowen, Lakewood, OH; Bob Button, Charlottesville, VA; Nan Cayton, Fairmont, WV; Hope Carroll, York, PA.; Pat Graff, Albuquerque, NM; H. L. Hall, Nashville, TN; Rick Hill, Dallas, TX.

Also, David Knight, Lancaster, SC; Jack Kennedy, Littleton, CO; Deanne Kunz, Austin, TX; Pete LeBlanc, Antelope, CA; Terry Nelson, Muncie, IN; Sandy Hall-Chiles, Dallas, TX; Rhonda Moore, Austin, TX; Jeff Nardone, Grosse Pointe, MI; Mitzi Neely, Longview, TX; Kyla Perry, Devine, TX; Candace Perkins, Kent, OH; and Julie Price, Lansing, MI.

Also, Mary Pulliam, Duncanville, TX; Rob Melton, Portland, OR; Carol Richtsmeier, DeSoto, TX; Betsy Rau, Midland, MI; Laura Schaub, Norman, OK; Earl Straight, Morgantown, WV; George Taylor, Tamaqua, PA; Randy Vonderheid, Austin, TX; Tony Willis, Carmel, IN; Wayne Brasler, Chicago, IL; Tim Ellsworth, Jackson, TN; and Scott Winters, Bismark, ND.

I also am indebted to my colleagues and friends at the University Interscholastic League.

I APPRECIATE the many newspapers that granted permission to reprint stories or portions of stories: the *Austin American-Statesman*, the *San Antonio Light*, *The New York Times*, the Associated Press and the *Boston Globe*. In particular, I appreciate the *Dallas Morning News* for its many contributions to this text.

I also am grateful to the following student publications (listed in no particular order):

■ *Panther Prints and Panther Tale*, Duncanville (TX) High School.

■ *The Tiger Rag*, Irving (TX) High School.

■ *Jackets Journal*, Arlington Heights (TX) High School, Fort Worth.

■ *The Rambler*, Temple (TX) High School.

■ *The Lion*, Lyons Township High School, LaGrange, IL.

■ *The Tower*, Grosse Point South High School, Grosse Point, MI.

■ *The Talon*, Eisenhower High School, Lawton, OK.

■ *The Echo*, Glenbard East High School,

JOHN DALKE
Cover/interior
design, art

MIKE McLEAN
Photography

HOWARD
SPANOGLE
Editing

LORI OGLESBEE
Proofreading

SARA
AGOSTINELLI
Index production

GARY LUNDGREN
Project manager

Lombard, IL.
- *The Little Hawk*, City High School, Iowa City, IA.
- *U-High Midway*, University High School, Chicago, IL.
- *Serif*, Tarpon Springs (FL) High School.
- *The Arrow*, Utica (MI) High School.
- *The Torch*, Sharpstown High School, Houston, TX.
- *The Regit*, Spring Woods High School, Houston, TX.
- *Lone Star Dispatch*, James Bowie High School, Austin, TX.
- *Cat's Tale*, Sulphur Springs (TX) High School.
- *Featherduster*, Westlake High School, Austin, TX.
- *Excelsior*, Stillwater (OK) High School.
- *The Regit*, Spring Woods High School, Houston, TX.
- *The Lion's Tale*, R. L. Turner High School, Carrollton, TX.
- *The Angle*, Angleton (TX) High School.
- *Mohigan*, Morgantown (WV) High School.
- *Episode*, Yorktown (IN) High School.
- *Maple Leaves*, Fairmont Sr. (WV) High School.
- *The Eagle*, Labay Jr. High School, Houston, TX.
- *The Searchlight*, Eastlake North (OH) High School
- *Lyncean*, Winona (TX) High School.
- *Campus Corral*, Central High School, San Angelo TX.
- *The Lance,* West Springfield (VA) High School.
- *North Winds*, Northside High School, Roanoke, VA.
- *Prospective*, Bryant (AR) High School.
- *The Blue & Gold*, Center High School, Antelope, CA.
- *HiLight*, Carmel (IN) High School, Carmel.
- *The Bagpipe*, Highland Park High School, Dallas, TX.
- *Northwest Passage*, Shawnee Mission Northwest High School, Shawnee, KS
- *The Update*, Dow High School, Midland, MI.
- *Rampages,* Casa Roble High School, Orangevale, CA.

COLOPHON

The Radical Write, was printed and bound by Jostens, Inc. of Minneapolis, MN, in its Topeka, KS, plant. The book was designed using Adobe PageMaker® 7.0 and Jostens YearTech.®

Inside pages are printed on 70# matte stock with black ink and a blue green spot color accent [Jostens Tempo 320].

Two font families are used throughout. The serif text copy is displayed in Worldwide™ 1, designed by the Shinn Type Foundry, www.shinntype.com, specifically for contemporary newspaper design. A slightly condensed, subtle finish gives Worldwide a contemporary style while reducing distortion on newspaper web presses. Avenir, a modern sans serif font, appears in several weights including Book, Medium and Black for sidebar text, labels and headlines.

The cover is lithographed in process color and gloss laminated. The red background is selected from the Shocking Colors palette of the Jostens Process Color Library. Endsheets are printed in blue green [Jostens Tempo 320] on Jostens Transicolor 280 stock.

- *Magician*, Muncie Central High School, Muncie, IN.
- *Maroon Messenger*, Devine (TX) High School.
- *The Shield*, McCallum High School, Austin, TX.
- *Wingspan*, Cypress Falls High School, Houston, TX.
- *Bagpipe*, Highland Park High School, Dallas, TX.

MANY OF the examples are from Texas publications. While countless others may have been used from publications throughout the nation, I opted to use the examples with which I was most familiar and comfortable.

And of most importance, I am indebted to the hundreds of students and advisers at workshops and conventions, whose enthusiasm for this style of reporting and writing convinced me that young readers want more from their publications than data.

INDEX

ABOUT THE AUTHOR

BOBBY HAWTHORNE is the former director of academics for the University Interscholastic League, where he directed the nation's largest program for academic extracurricular activities from its headquarters at The University of Texas at Austin. For 20 years, he directed the Interscholastic League Press Conference, Texas' student press association.

Hawthorne teaches at journalism workshops, conventions and seminars across the U.S. In 1998 and 1999, he taught in Romania and Hungary for the Center for Independent Journalism, based in New York City and affiliated with *The New York Times*.

He is author of numerous books and manuals including *The Coverage of Interscholastic Sports* and *The Journalism Teacher's Writing Manual*. He's an avid fan of the Beatles, Frank Sinatra and the Texas Longhorns.

ABOUT THE DESIGNER

JOHN DALKE designed and formatted the cover and interior pages of this edition of *The Radical Write*. Currently a junior at Montana State University, he is working toward a degree in graphic arts. In addition to his studies, Dalke teaches design and technology workshops across the U.S. and served as editor of the university's weekly student newspaper, *The Exponent*. Dalke, like thousands of other students during the last decade, developed his journalistic writing skills by studying *The Radical Write* and working on his high school publications. Dalke has earned many honors while working on the national award-winning student publications advised by Linda Ballew at Great Falls (MT) High School. He served as editor of the 2001 *Roundup* yearbook, an NSPA Pacemaker winner, and as design editor of the nationally recognized student newspaper, The *Iniwa*.

ABOUT THE PHOTOGRAPHER

MIKE McLEAN captured the photographs on the cover and chapter introductions. A Dallas-based freelance photojournalist, his clients include corporations such as American Airlines and Motorola. As a student at Irving (TX) High School, McLean first developed an eye for photojournalism in courses taught by Sherri Taylor. Before graduating, he served as photo editor of the nationally acclaimed student newspaper, the *Tiger Rag* and the CSPA Crown winning yearbook, the *Lair*. Two decades later, McLean is still involved in scholastic journalism as he mentors photojournalists at workshops across the country. McLean's contributions were recently recognized with his induction into the National Scholastic Journalism Hall of Fame. As a staff photographer for the *Dallas Times Herald*, McLean served on a reporting team nominated for a Pulitzer Prize for its coverage of the crash of Delta flight 191 at the DFW Airport.

Printed in USA. © 2003 by Jostens, Inc. (Item #2000)